# BUILDING THE EDUCATIONAL STATE:
## CANADA WEST, 1836-1871

# *Studies in Curriculum History Series*

General Editor: Professor Ivor F. Goodson
　　　　　　　University of Western Ontario, Canada

1. Social Histories of the Secondary Curriculum: Subjects for Study
   *Edited by Ivor F. Goodson, University of Sussex*

2. Technological Revolution? A Politics of School Science and Technology in England and Wales since 1945
   *G. McCulloch, E. Jenkins and D. Layton, University of Leeds*

3. Renegotiating Secondary School Mathematics: A Study of Curriculum Change and Stability
   *Barry Cooper, University of Sussex*

4. Building the American Community: Social Control and Curriculum
   *Barry Franklin, Kennesaw College, Georgia*

5. The 'New Maths' Curriculum Controversy: An International Story
   *Bob Moon*

6. School Subjects and Curriculum Change
   *Ivor F. Goodson, University of Western Ontario*

7. The Formation of the School Subjects: The Struggle for Creating an American Institution
   *Edited by Thomas S. Popkewitz, University of Madison–Wisconsin*

8. Physics Teaching in Schools 1960-85: Of People, Policy and Power
   *Brian E. Woolnough, University of Oxford*

# BUILDING THE EDUCATIONAL STATE: CANADA WEST, 1836-1871

**Bruce Curtis**

 The Falmer Press

THE ALTHOUSE PRESS
London, Ontario, Canada

| | |
|---|---|
| UK | The Falmer Press, Falmer House, Barcombe, Lewes, East Sussex, BN8 5DL |
| USA | The Falmer Press, Taylor & Francis Inc., 242 Cherry Street, Philadelphia, PA 19106-1906 |
| CANADA | The Althouse Press, Faculty of Education, The University of Western Ontario, London, Ontario, Canada, N6G 1G7 |

© B. Curtis 1988

*All rights reserved. No part of this publication may be reproduced, stored in a retrieval system, or transmitted in any form or by any means, electronic, mechanical, photocopying, recording or otherwise, without permission in writing from the Publisher.*

First published 1988

**Library of Congress Cataloging in Publication Data available on request**

ISBN 1-85000-275-4

**Canadian Cataloguing in Publication Data**

Curtis, Bruce
    Building the educational state, Canada West, 1836-1871

Bibliography: p.
Includes index.
ISBN 0-920354-20-3

1. Education and state – Ontario – History.
2. Education, Elementary – Political aspects – Ontario – History. I. Title.
LA418.05C86 1987   379.713   C87-094664-1

Jacket design by Caroline Archer

# Contents

*Preface* by Philip Corrigan     9

Introduction     12

**Part One: 'A dangerous Foe in the Bosom of the Community': Educational Reform in Canada West, 1836-1850.**

Chapter One: Educational Reform in Canada West, 1836-1839     22

Chapter Two: Responsible Government and Educational Reform, 1840-1846     51

Chapter Three: Public Construction and Educational Reform, 1846-1850     97

**Part Two: 'The conscience is an infinitely better disciplinarian than the rod.' Educational Administration, 1850-1871.**

Chapter Four: Contestation of Pedagogical Space     140

Chapter Five: Struggles Over School Attendance     183

Chapter Six: Training the 'Good' Teacher     217

Chapter Seven: Building School Knowledge     267

Chapter Eight: Pedagogy, Punishment and Popular Resistance     312

Conclusion     366

*Bibliography*     383

*Illustrations*     416

*Index*     433

# List of Illustrations

| | | |
|---|---|---|
| 1 | 'The march of the intellect' | 416 |
| 2 | Pine Grove School, Denham Township, 1870s | 417 |
| 3 | The Elementary School, Actinolite, Ontario | 418 |
| 4 | Schoolhouse, Blenheim Township, School Section 10 | 419 |
| 5 | The Old Schoolhouse, Picton, Ontario | 420 |
| 6 | The Schoolhouse, Glenwood, Ontario | 421 |
| 7 | First known school, Williamston, Ontario | 422 |
| 8 | The Schoolhouse, School Section 6, Whitchurch, York County | 423 |
| 9 | Schoolhouse, York County | 524 |
| 10 | 'Improved' schools of the late 1860s and 1870s | 425 |
| 11 | 'Improved' schools of the late 1860s and 1870s | 426 |
| 12 | Egerton Ryerson, Superintendent of Education | 427 |
| 13 | John George Hodgins | 428 |
| 14 | Archibald Macallum | 429 |
| 15 | The Toronto Normal School, circa 1860 | 430 |
| 16 | A lesson at Uno Park School | 431 |
| 17 | The burning of the Parliament buildings, Montreal 1849 | 432 |

# Preface

Bruce Curtis takes us on a journey in this book, an original journey, to a place which, insofar as we know it at all, we know too well and too easily. In his journey through this past he travelled without maps--- for they are part of misleading mythologies and disguising discourses. This pioneering book is a report, or better, a series of reports. Curtis makes us *see differently*. He also offers implicit connections--- and this may turn out to be one of the more significant features of his writing--- from that defamiliarised past to some of the very peculiar features of our current situation. The voices of the present are resonant with the historical voices Curtis records: 'In all free governments [sic] the welfare and safety of the government depend upon the national character of the inhabitants, and that national character depends upon their national education.' 'Education should be directed in reference to ... the good of the world.' Dr. Charles Duncombe wrote these remarks in 1836, but the propositions they contain echo those found in the recent unprecedented proliferation of investigations, commissions, reports and pronouncements on 'education' *and* 'governance.'

This is, then, a timely book. It does more than report back from long journeys. The writing releases voices where there had been silences, reveals contradictions where there had been assumptions of smooth singular authority, points to politics where there had been dull administration, and to complex differences where there had been assumptions of simple dichotomy or even uniformity. All of this is accomplished by methodological innovations sustained by the clarity of the account. What we have in this book is a genealogy of the *embodied* educational state. Tracing the detailed filiations and lineages from the 'civilizing project' of (particularly) the Scottish Enlightenment, Curtis shows how the *forms* of schooling in Canada West partake of a double formation. That which was primary--- and intentional--- focuses upon the forming of schooled subjectivities. Here, where schooling was intimately connected with governance and 'habitude' as organised moral regulation, was the explicit curriculum and pedagogy, teaching and evaluation. This later--- much later--- becomes so sedimented, so obvious, that it took the 1960s' 'new sociology of education' to rediscover it as the 'hidden curriculum.' That which was secondary focused upon the learning of social and life skills, oriented to far wider features of the division of labour than 'occupations.' Although the latter--- those other 'subjects' that schools constructed and transmitted— have come to be seen to be what schooling was 'really about', they only continue (today as then) to operate through the more diffuse media of instruction and information which are intensely moral, that is to say, political.

This book marks its distance from all the prevailing and contending versions which claim to tell their stories of schooling: education as a Good Thing (and there should be more of 'it'); schooling as imposed coercively on a totally resisting population; schooling as consensually imbibed by a totally accepting population. Instead what is shown here entails the pre-occupation of given social relations by practical, administered forms of 'The Educational Idea.' Such a pre-occupation is accompanied by complementary features of the same state formation, albeit not yet in their accomplished (and neutralised) obvious forms, as statistics, cartography and all the other sciences and techniques of social classification. The productivity of *this* schooling, in the context of *that* state education, when we learn to see it, is entirely operative to produce --- that is, *construct* --- truths about persons. It is in this nexus of fluid, flexible but coherent formations, that we can trace an archeology of subjectivities---- gendered, sexualised, classed, raced and ethnicised, *and* aged. That is: located, graded, documented, *and* accounted for.

From this side of that long, contradictory, violent cultural revolution it was difficult— at least until, metaphorically, the day before yesterday— to see in those most natural of institutional arrangements which we call schools any of the marks of this making. 'Problems' (and to be sure, 'problem children') are discovered in schools through different lexical and semiotic disciplines. But like the continual (re)discovery of 'Poverty,' 'Educational Problems' remain among the mysteries of modernity. This is because our vision has been obscured by the seemingly tedious obviousness of the routines and rituals of state schooling. However 'problems,' the axiom runs, are made, not simply taken. In this fine, exemplary study we witness the contested process of educational making. We are taken on a journey here with a variable lens camera. We read (hear) the voice of a reforming theorist concerned with the possibility of schooling as pleasure. We are made to notice the situation of the schooled, the size of the room, the arrangement of the desks, the dress of the teacher. We travel with teachers too, themselves on a journey, and we see them placed— again, then as now— in a labour process that has at its centre the resolution of the unresolvable: Treat Each Child As An Individual, and, Keep Order In Your Classroom.

In the Irish University Press' 1000 volume reprint of 'British' (largely English) Parliamentary Papers for the years 1801 to 1899, there are 95 volumes on Slavery, 55 volumes on Education, 44 volumes on Industrial Relations, and 36 volumes on Canada. Bruce Curtis, theoretically, methodologically, historically, offers a critique of both the contents of such official documentary systems (within the focus of his study) and of the boundaries that such neat subject-headings pretend to convey. Schooling in Canada West offered the enticement to embody the social subordination of a slavery (of obligation and sustained deference, of character) in the name of desires and pleasures of knowing and doing. In making that profound and deeply disturbing question visible, Bruce Curtis offers a way of seeing that goes beyond the limits of the Canadas. It is a tracing of how part of the media of modernity were made, and with what consequences for all of us, differently, now.

Philip Corrigan
Toronto
January 1987.

# Introduction

This book is about the organization and implementation of a system of public elementary schooling in Canada West (called Upper Canada until 1840 and Ontario after 1867) from the late 1830s to 1871. It situates educational organization in the bitter, protracted and complex political struggles over the *form* of the colonial state which dominated Canadian society from the Rebellions of 1837-8 to the resurgence of agrarian radicalism in the late 1840s. It analyses the educational settlement of 1850, under which most sections of the governing classes accepted a largely centralized system of public instruction for Canada West. I then detail the practical construction of an educational state in the two decades after the School Act of 1850. Particular attention is paid to the experience of the first generation to be publicly schooled, and to the forming of schooled subjectivities.

This study concentrates on three things: on the translation of a specific class and gendered understanding of the nature, purposes and occasions of education into a system of state schooling; on the emergence, stabilization and normalization of techniques, practices and devices of mass schooling; and on the management of the persistent popular opposition which public schooling provoked.

The Educational State in Canada West was constructed out of a multi-faceted process of political struggle. Educational organization was directly implicated in ongoing political conflicts in the 1830s and 1840s over the nature of the colonial state itself, and over the existence of the colonial connection between Canada and England. Educational organization was directly implicated in political struggles between town and country, where the main issue was local autonomy as opposed to centralized rule. Educational organization was directly implicated in periodic movements of agrarian radicalism, in which republican farmers, often in alliance with artisans and some members of the professional classes, looked towards the construction of a democratic republic in the Canadas. Educational organization was directly implicated in struggles between the 'respectable classes' and those beneath them for political consciousness. Educational organization was directly implicated in persistent conflicts between men and women over access to the means of employment and over the respective social capacities of members of different genders.

The educational state was constructed out of these conflicts, but it also mediated them. While political conflict propelled the process of educational state formation, educational structures and practices in turn aimed at the reconstruction of political conflicts. For the governing classes, the educational state was 'the social', a domain organized spatially, temporally and discursively, where political conflicts were to be remade. In this Educational State, social peace and harmony were to prevail. Here members of different social classes, genders, religious sects, and (to a much lesser extent) ethnic groups were to encounter one another on conditions of a specific 'social equality'. At the same time, participants in the educational state--- students, teachers, trustees, electors and parents---- were to internalize and embody principles of social tolerance, respect for legitimate authority, and for standards of a 'collective' morality. Political conflicts were to be remade in the educational state through the remaking of political subjectivities. What is at work here is the making of (modern) social identities.

The equality of participants in the educational state was not intended to destroy the inequality which characterized Canadian social organization. Educational reformers in the governing classes consistently stressed both the necessity and the beauty of class differences and of the social subordination of women. Lessons taught in state schools reinforced this message, and educational administration in practice was a form of political domination. Still, those active in pursuit of state education imagined a kind of educational equality, and this vision, limited as it was, nonetheless gave rise to its own peculiar forms of social conflict. These in turn propelled the further development of relations in the educational state. Once the initial interventions were made to establish a *state* educational structure, attempts by different groups and classes in Canada West to realize the promise of educational equality and self-determination conflicted with the concern of governing classes to preserve and reproduce inequality in society. Out of this process of conflict grew many of the institutions, devices, practices and techniques of power which solidified the educational domain. Many of these forms of power and empowerment persist.

Conflict assumes the existence of antagonistic or competing interests. In educational reform, the interests of the governing classes in Canada West predominated. This is not to say that one class in society made the educational state, nor that subordinate classes made no impact upon the course of educational development. Quite the contrary: educational reform did not end political conflict. Rather, it framed political conflict, it set conflict on a new terrain and changed some of its terms. The analysis presented here is not a 'social control' analysis in which attention is paid only to the concerns and fears of ruling groups--- in which history is seen as the unfolding of the will of one social class. Persistent and durable social conflict surrounded both educational construction and educational administration. These conflicts are at the centre of the processes investigated here, precisely because they contribute, differentially, to the social texture of schooling and because they reveal how the context of a kind of schooling became absorbed as its content.

Yet it must be stressed that the construction of an educational state took place through conscious human activity. Members of the governing classes conceived, planned, struggled for and set out to build an educational state. This is not to say that all members of the governing classes did so, that educational organization was equally important to all of them, nor that active educational reformers were entirely successful. Nor is it to argue that the construction of The Educational State was always, only or unambiguously in the interests of governing classes. But educational reform was certainly neither spontaneous nor universally popular. It was a *project,* a set of conscious initiatives guided by clearly articulated goals. On the whole, educational state builders had an explicit conception of their own class interests, and defined the good of 'society' in keeping with them.

As I document and detail in what follows, the central concern of governing classes in *state* education was the reconstruction of popular character and culture. Members of the governing classes were particularly concerned that the conditions of social independence which characterized political-economic organization in the Canadas might lead to the destruction of political authority, property relations and Christian religion. Education was seen as a means for the remaking of popular culture and character, for the transformation of tastes, for the solidification of genial *habits,* for the creation of a popular intelligence capable of appreciating the 'rational merits' of bourgeois society. Educational practice was centrally concerned with political self-making, subjectification and subordination; with anchoring the conditions of political governance in the selves of the governed; with the transformation of rule into a popular psychology. By the same token, educational provision, as state formation, was about *rule,* about what Philip Abrams called 'politically organized subjection.'[1] Political conflicts about what should be taught, how, to and by whom, on what conditions, and so forth, were at once conflicts about who should rule and be ruled, and of what rule should consist.

State schooling was not *primarily* about transmitting skills of literacy and numeracy. It did not fill an educational void. State school reformers routinely argued that it would be far better to leave the masses completely *ignorant* than to teach them to read and write without forming their moral character.[2] But they[3] also confronted a population which was already largely literate. The network of local elementary or common schools which grew up in the 1820s and 1830s provided a basic literacy for most people in Upper Canada. State school reformers sought not simply to create a literate population, but rather to reorganize and regulate both the acquisition and the exercise of the skills of literacy.

Again, public education was not in any simple sense the result of a humanitarian concern on the part of the governing classes to increase the numbers of colonial schools. Locally controlled elementary schools predated the state educational project, and while the numbers of schools certainly increased under the educational settlement of 1850, control over local schooling was also wrested away from local school supporters, teachers and students. The construction of this Educational State was accomplished only through the destruction of a prior educational organization and the marginalization of the structure of educational possibilities it presented. *Education* was certainly not synonymous with *state schooling* in the 1830s and 1840s. That we often equate the two today is another accomplishment of this Educational State.

This study is also concerned with the development and solidification of practices, devices, techniques, and instruments of educational governance. The examination, classification, promotions, report cards, the training of teachers, pedagogical technique in reading and writing, seating arrangements, the design of schools, attendance records, expulsions, suspension and exclusions---- I could continue--- were all products of the social and educational conflicts studied here. For most of those of us who experienced state schooling, the contours of the educational map were drawn when we arrived. School practices preceded us and neither we, nor those we knew, had experienced an alternative educational reality. The material existence of schooling was solid, and most of us were, and had no choice but to be, children, pupils, students--- the objects of the educational gaze. But this educational reality did not greet students in Canada West in the period from the mid-1830s to the 1870s (and later) in the same way. On the one hand, none of the commonplaces of school 'administration' existed. On the other hand, many students *had* lived an alternative reality and were not in household or community 'children.'

Before state educational administration in Canada West, and throughout the formative period, people of very different ages attended school and learned some combination of what interested them and what teachers were able to teach. In the households of most classes, young people contributed to domestic economic well-being as soon as they were physically able, and this was by the age of six in most cases. Boys and girls nine years old were regularly engaged in agricultural labour. State schooling, in conjunction with more general political economic transformations, was influential in the remaking of young people into 'children'. State schooling became a place for the systematic administration and reproduction of 'childhood,' and of the social institutions needed to sustain it, like the 'family.'

The process of compressing a part of the population into the social category 'schoolchild' went forward through the saturation of educational space with devices and techniques of administration. Many of the common practices of public schooling arose out of attempts by state administrators to discipline a recalcitrant population.

I am particularly concerned here with the resistance and opposition which surrounded the construction and, more especially, the administration of the educational state. I take very seriously the practical reactions of those subjected to state schooling. It has been customary for critical historians of education to seek opposition to state schooling in the public realm. Opposition has been sought in the activities of organized public groups: trade unions, voluntary associations, parents' groups, educational reform associations. But after the educational settlement of 1850 in Canada West there is little evidence of the existence or activities of such groups. The accomplished settlement of 1850 transformed the nature of educational conflict by establishing state schooling as the dominant form of educational provision *in principle.* This has enabled many educational historians to argue that state schooling was desired by the population as a whole. My way of seeing is quite different. I argue that state schooling did not eliminate educational conflict or resistance. Rather, it changed the form of conflict and resistance. Explicit political struggle over the social form of education became practical struggle over involvement in and management of the dominant form. Arguing as I do that state schooling was intended as a process of self-making, of subjectification, I pay particular attention to the immediate reactions of those subjected to and informed by it. Educational practice exerted its force upon and built its consensus within the population especially at those points where it found students' senses of themselves. It is here that it seems one should seek educational opposition.

Of course, in some ways, this is a difficult notion. The reality of the Educational State is sufficiently solid that many may regard the reactions of the student as suspect in principle. The 'schoolchild' is, by definition, a flawed entity in need of discipline and training, an incomplete social subject which must submit to the process of schooling for its 'own' good. This, I argue repeatedly, is an accomplishment of the Educational State and not a fact of nature. Again, this conception of resistance and opposition is difficult given the small resources most students possessed for the articulation of systematic alternatives to state schooling. The possibility of romanticization is ever present in such a conception of resistance.

However, I do wish to stress at the outset that the governing classes and central educational administrators agitated for state schooling on the grounds that it would be intrinsically pleasurable to those experiencing it. As I detail in what follows, bourgeois pedagogy claimed to have unlocked the secrets of human psychology once and for all. Pedagogical practice was claimed to be in perfect accord with a general human nature and psychological constitution. State reformers claimed that schooling would proceed by attracting the interests of students, by strengthening their capacities for independence and reflection, by broadening and deepening many of their senses. Students, they promised, would love schooling. That students did not in fact love or enjoy schooling will be made quite clear in what follows. Faced with popular opposition to the practices of state schooling, educational administrators did not seek to reform these practices to make schooling really pleasurable. Rather, they sought to construct administrative devices to suppress opposition. The reactions of educational administrators to opposition provide a measure of state schooling in its own terms.

This book is divided roughly into two parts. The first part, which includes chapters one through three, details the political debates over educational construction and discusses the educational experiments which took place in Canada West from 1836 to 1850. The circumstances and content of the educational settlement of 1850 are detailed in this part of the book. In the second part, which includes chapters four through eight, a detailed examination of the processes involved in the practical construction of an educational state is made. Here such questions as the boundaries of the educational sphere, the recruitment of the student population, the training of teachers, the definition of official knowledge and the management of educational violence are discussed.

A word about sources, method and some acknowledgements. The material on which this study is based comes from the massive record collection of the Education Office for Canada West housed in the Public Archives of Ontario. The Education Office undertook a massive correspondence with its field officers and with almost anyone else who cared to consult it about educational matters. By the early 1860s, the Office was receiving about 650 letters a month and responded in some way to a large majority of these. This massive body of correspondence has been preserved, and this study derives primarily from a careful scrutiny of it for the period 1842-1871. This involved the staff of the Public Archives in a considerable amount of labour, for which I am grateful. I have supplemented the correspondence files with an investigation of related primary sources. The massive 28 volume *Documentary History of Education in Upper Canada* and the related collections compiled by the Education Office Deputy, John George Hodgins, have also served me well. The methods and models of educational organization adopted in Canada West were a distillation of a wider

European and American experience. As far as possible, I have consulted the main works of educational theory and practice readily available to Canadian reformers in the first half of the nineteenth century.

Documents speak through the voices we can hear and in response to the questions we can ask. My thinking about educational state formation is grounded in a Marxism sensitive to cultural forms and informed by Foucault's analysis of power and subjectivity. Many other writers have shaped my concerns here, and their work is presented in the accompanying bibliography.

My interest in the education archives was first stimulated by debates with Bob Gidney and Wyn Millar. Geoff Kay made me understand the importance of state administration. My research was supported financially by a post-doctoral fellowship from the Social Sciences and Humanities Research Council of Canada. Without that support this study would never have been made. Wilfrid Laurier University underwrote some of the book's pre-publication expenses. Peter Erb provided an essential computer programme, and Laurier's computing staff aided in the production of the final copy. I had the good fortune to hold my post-doctoral fellowship at the Ontario Institute for Studies in Education, where a close working relationship with Alison Prentice allowed me to try out many of the ideas expressed here. My writing of this book was sustained by the tireless and constant encouragement of Philip Corrigan and Graham Knight. My exposure to Philip Corrigan's brilliant attempts to connect moral regulation, cultural forms and state-building has profoundly shaped this work. His circulation of the work to others, his comments on parts of the manuscript and his comradeship I deeply appreciate. The project of this writing will be extended in research forthcoming from the SSHRCC-funded 'State Formation Project' which Philip Corrigan and I co-direct, and from which, with the associated work of Bob Lanning and Shmuel Shamai, this book has greatly benefitted. Graham Knight read and commented at length on parts of the manuscript and my understanding of the work was very much influenced by his insight, irreverance and comradeship. Michele Martin's patience, affection and encouragement sustained the production of this book in all its phases, from conception to execution.

## Notes

1. Philip Abrams, 'Notes on the difficulty of studying the state,' cited in Philip Corrigan and Derek Sayer, *The Great Arch: English State Formation as Cultural Revolution.* (Oxford: Blackwell, 1985).
2. For instance, in Robert Sullivan's *Letters and Lectures on Popular Education.* (Dublin: William Curry, 1842), we read,

> ...if children be not taught the duties of love and obedience to parents, respect and subordination to superiors, the principles of truth and honesty, and, in a word, the precepts and practice of morality, it is better for themselves, and safer for society to leave them enitrely uneducated; for bad as ignorance is, education without <u>morality</u> is a thousand times worse. (32)

Sullivan, a former inspector of the Irish National Commissioners, was headmaster of the Dublin Normal school when John George Hodgins, the deputy superintendent of education for Canada West, attended that institution in the late 1840s. OISE library contains a copy of Sullivan's work presented by the author to Hodgins. The copy contains Hodgins' editorial marking of passages suitable for reproduction in the *Journal of Education.*

3. See in this regard, R.D. Gidney, 'Elementary Education in Upper Canada: A Reassessment,' in M.B. Katz and P.H. Mattingly eds. *Education and Social Change: Themes from Ontario's Past.* (New York: New York University Press, 1975.) and H.J. Graff, *The Literacy Myth: Literacy and social structure in the nineteenth century city.* (New York: Academic Press, 1979.)

# Part One

## 'A dangerous foe in the Bosom of the Community': Educational Reform in Canada West, 1836-1850

# Chapter One:
# Educational Reform in Canada West, 1836-1839

In the 1830s in Upper Canada (as Canada West was known from 1791-1840) state involvement in the elementary education of the population generally was limited to the enabling legislation passed initially in 1816. Under the School Act of that year, any group of resident proprietors capable of providing a school of a certain size was empowered to assemble for educational purposes, to select from amongst its members three school trustees, and to hire a teacher. These teachers were to be examined before District Boards of Education appointed by the executive branch of government, and the conduct of their activities in the schoolroom was subject to the approval of those Boards. Qualified teachers were eligible to receive a portion of a state school grant-in-aid.

The Act was designed by members of the colonial executive as a measure of centralized regulation of popular elementary education, but from this point of view it was never seen to be satisfactory. A great many elementary schools never came within the purview of the Act. Few teachers were ever examined by District Boards of Education, which tended to be situated in District towns at some remove from most schools. Schoolmeetings permitted under the Act became one of the few local organs of democratic self-government in this period where local government was largely in the hands of appointed justices.[1]

During the 1820s, the executive government attempted to extend its influence over popular education through the creation of a colony-wide General Board of Education under the direction of the Bishop of York (Toronto), John Strachan. The General Board received legal recognition under a School Act of 1824, which placed District Boards of Education under its tutelage and which gave it control over the large body of lands (the 'School Lands') set aside by the legislature in 1797 for the support of elementary education. The General Board attempted to influence the books used in schools, and sought the organization of monitorial schools in the colonial towns. One such, the York Central School, was established, and the Board supported a second school in Kingston through the Midland District School Society.

However, struggles between branches of the colonial state over the question of the powers of elective bodies led to serious attacks upon the General Board of Education and its president. The Board was criticized in the House of Assembly for sectarian educational activities, and for mismanaging the lands at its disposal. Its administration of the Central School at York was attacked in the late 1820s, and in 1833 the General Board was disbanded and the relative autonomy of District Boards of Education restored.

Throughout the decade of the 1830s, parliamentary parties in Upper Canada addressed the question of educational organization. Members of the Reform party, whose interests ranged from religious disestablishment, to heightened powers for elective bodies, and at the extreme, to republican rule for the colony, more or less consistently sought to create the possibility of an extended elementary education for the population under the control of local property. The Tory party, in contrast, sometimes spoke directly for the executive branch of government, and sought to use existing structures of appointive government in the locality to extend an elementary educational system which would be controlled from the centre. At other times, the party took a more independent stance and sought local property taxation in a centrally administered educational system. Both Tory and Reform parties agreed on the necessity of some system of educational reform in the closing years of the 1830s.

Throughout the decade, however, the coterie of merchants, lawyers and professionals who composed the colonial Legislative and Executive Councils exercised veto powers over the efforts of parties in the elective branch of government to reform educational organization. Contemptuous of the capacities of local property, alarmed by the possibility of local democracy and religious disestablishment, the 'Family Compact' as it was known, blocked efforts by the colonial Assembly to reconstruct popular education.

In part what was at issue in these debates over educational organization and management was precisely the larger question of the nature of the state itself. This was a debate amongst the representatives of propertyholders. All assumed the state would defend the interests of property in general, but how precisely these interests were best organized through state forms was very much in dispute. Tories, generally speaking, sought a highly centralized state structure, in which the efforts of local property would be closely guided by a social elite, loyal more or less to the state church and supportive of the colonial connection. Reformers tended to champion local property and local electoral democracy (of and for male proprietors), but at the margin of the party a political space existed for much more radical views. Many Reformers adopted a Smithian liberalism in which social order and stability were seen to be products of small-scale capitalist development. The maintenance of class distinctions figured less centrally in Reform than in Tory policy, and a measure of social mobility was explicitly urged. At the margins, Reform policy tended towards radical democracy and republicanism, but the Party as a whole had a hodgepodge character, uniting political tendencies which proved quite contradictory during the Rebellion of 1837 and in the later 1840s as well.

In the views of the English Radicals who surveyed Upper Canadian educational organization in the late 1830s, local property was also encouraged to develop and manage educational institutions, but such institutions were to be subordinated to a central authority. Indeed, English Radical writers on the Canadas also regarded local electoral democracy as essential for economic growth and cultural development. They regarded local democratic institutions as educational in themselves: as providing outlets for talent, as disciplining the population in sound techniques of self-government. At the same time, however, central state bodies and officials should exert a strong regulatory function over local organs of government. By both privilege and prestige, central authorities should be strong enough to check the possible 'excesses' of local proprietors.

The issues in educational organization over which these differing positions were articulated included the place of elected versus appointed officials in the system; the location of taxation powers; determination of curriculum and school rules; and the question of coordination and supervision or inspection. Yet, debates over educational organization were not narrowly 'educational'. The modes of social regulation— the state forms— which should prevail in Upper Canadian society were at the centre of these debates. Tories clung more or less firmly to a position in which regulation of the population as a whole would be exerted by strategically situated local elites: clergy, justices and magistrates, large proprietors, with school teachers as their agents. Reformers, especially radical Reformers, looked to the reconstruction of individual character as the key means of social regulation. They maintained that social order should be implanted in the selves of individuals. If such orderly selves obtained, the social barriers to class mobility could be sharply relaxed. These adequately constructed characters would then be competent to manage their own political affairs, and capitalist development would be accompanied by social order.

The position of the English Radicals was also one in which governance was to be located in character structure. Sound character would be encouraged by definite kinds of political activity, but regulatory institutions such as inspection would guarantee that sound character was in fact formed. Inspectors were to be members of social elites, and the sphere of local governmental autonomy, while real, was to be quite restricted. Radicals sought local institutions of government in part for the contribution these would make to producing an 'intelligent' population: a population capable of 'correctly' appreciating its political privileges. This formal/formative aspect of local government was of equal importance with any concrete operations local government might perform. Educational reform was inextricably state formation, both in terms of institution-building and in terms of the political characterization of the population. Educational politics demanded the formation of new institutions for the making of disciplined selves. At the same time, the local administration of these institutions was an activity which would shape the selves of *administrators*--- especially male electors, trustees, propertyholders and others--- in desirable ways. The domestic subordination of women, which state school reformers supported and sought to extend, would ensure that the disciplining of male selves would have disciplinary consequences for women as well. The reform of education was the creation both of new state institutions and political subjects.

The position of the Reform party in the Assembly was well illustrated by the report on Education delivered by Dr. Charles Duncombe in 1836.

## The Duncombe Report: Radical Reform Views of Education

In 1835 the Upper Canadian House of Assembly appointed Charles Duncombe, Thomas Morrison and William Bruce to a Commission of enquiry into the organization and management of systems of college and elementary education. The appointment was made while the School Act of 1835, passed by the House, was about to be vetoed by the Legislative Council. Charles Duncombe, a medical doctor, a member of the left wing of the Reform party, and the leader of the rebels in the Western District in 1837, was sent on a tour of the United States to investigate and report upon the organization of various educational institutions, including prisons, asylums, penetentiaries and public schools. His report of 1836 and the legislation based upon it contained a wide-ranging analysis of the social necessity of education and of the means to reconstruct it.

Insofar as it was representative of Reform policy generally, Duncombe's Report situated the educational concerns of Reformers clearly in the mainstream of British and American radical liberalism. Duncombe read and cited with approval such leading liberal educational reformers as Lord Brougham, the Edgeworths, Emma Willard, Dr. Spurzheim, J.Orville Taylor, and the Boston School Committee. He investigated and subsequently advocated educational institutions and practices supported by these writers. Canadian Reformers were also more directly connected to the English Radicals. Duncombe's colleague, William Lyon Mackenzie, corresponded with Joseph Hume, served as a Canadian agent for the Society for the Diffusion of Useful Knowledge in the 1820s, and communicated directly with Lord Brougham in the 1830s.[2]

The educational policy of the Reform party--even of its radical wing--was far from a populist policy. Reform policy called for the reconstruction of popular educational practices and prevailing educational organization. This reconstruction contained very definite disciplinary elements, and while it championed the interests of small property, it sought to reconstruct popular culture and morality in the interests of property in general.

For Duncombe, as for most other nineteenth century educational writers, education was a tripartite process, whose components were physical, intellectual and moral. While these components were inextricably connected, moral education was by far the most important amongst them. Physical education was the necessary basis of the student's moral and intellectual development. Without regard to the health of the student, the educational process would be unable to generate and sustain that physical energy necessary to the development and operation of good moral habits. But without good moral habits, the student would engage in practices and activities that would eventually undermine his [3] physical health. Intellectual education was necessary both as a source of pleasure for the individual, and because mature individual will was essentially rational. But without sound moral training, intelligence would be engaged in activities dangerous for the state, religion, and social order.

Education was first and foremost a moral discipline for Duncombe. The generalization of sound moral discipline was necessary to enable Upper Canadians to meet the challenges to the structure of society provoked by what Duncombe called the 'interests of commerce'. In his view, the growth of commodity production and exchange brought people into contact with different societies and modes of life, and contributed to a general and irresistible progress of political liberty. Commerce generated popular intelligence (both knowledge and the capacity to receive it) and if not regulated by sound moral discipline, this increased popular intelligence would lead to the destruction of civilization. 'Man is bursting the chains of slavery, and the bonds of intellectual subserviency; and is learning to think, and reason, and act for himself', wrote Duncombe. [4] The moment was rapidly approaching in which Upper Canadians would have to decide 'whether disenthralled intellect and liberty shall voluntarily submit to the laws of virtue and of Heaven, or run wild to insubordination, anarchy and crime.' In a 'free' state like that of the colony, 'the welfare and safety of the Government depend upon the national character of the inhabitants.' This national character in turn 'depends upon their National Education.' In states like Upper Canada, the necessity of 'virtuous intelligence in the mass of the community' was particularly great because the masses were 'not held in restraint by physical force.' Because the state did not rule despotically, the people must either 'voluntarily submit to the restraints of virtue and religion,' or else 'inevitably run loose to wild misrule, anarchy, and crime.'

Moral self-regulation was the product of a general system of education. Indeed, Duncombe emphasized the imperative necessity of generalizing education. Rising political liberty required the preparation of 'the rising generation for the regulation and enjoyment of Free, Civil, and Religious Institutions.' Political- economic changes invalidated the traditional assumption that education should be closely limited to those filling a small number of positions in the governing hierarchy. The growth of bourgeois social relations demanded that 'an army of faithful, intelligent, enterprising, benevolent men' be 'trained up, and sent forth to be leaders in the great enterprises of the day.' Far from education restricted to a few, 'Teachers and Statesmen, Farmers and Mechanics, Authors and Artists, all are wanted in this work, and wanted in greater abundance than can be supplied.'

Duncombe accepted the liberal critique of 'classical' education. Given the changed political-economic conditions of the world, it had become 'criminal to acquire knowledge merely for the sake of knowledge.' Education was to be 'practical', directed towards this world and its conditions. 'The man must be disciplined and furnished according to the duties that lie before him.' Education was also to encourage social mobility. 'Men' were to be encouraged to develop the 'habit of self-dependence.' They were to be impressed with the fact that social position came not from birth or inheritance. Rather, if a person were to be 'ever anything he must make himself.' Education should produce a general flexibility of mind and a capacity for manoeuvre within the boundaries of a firm moral discipline. The mind was to be 'so trained that like a ship in good trim it would answer to its helm, and adjust itself to its circumstances however variable the winds and the currents in the stormy sea of life.' Education should ennervate and activate the powers of the individual for social ends. It should work to 'give energy and enterprise to the mind, and activity to the whole man.' This Reformer, charged with a vision of a harmonious and liberal bourgeois order, sought 'men who will take the field, and whose souls are fired with a zeal for active duties in the service of the world.' These 'men' were to be schooled to a spirit of benevolence and to an active orientation to the welfare of others.

As a bit of 'verbal opinion', Duncombe argued, these were facts any person could see. However, the 'practical opinion' of Upper Canadian society 'as exhibited in systems of education, particularly in Schools,' was quite different. Granted there were teachers and schools in almost all communities, but these were charged only with the intellectual education of children. Students were certainly learning, for 'however dull the child, or incompetent the Teacher, at the end of each year it will be found ...that the memory at least if no other faculty, is to some extent cultivated.' This encouraged parents and school visitors to believe that 'the money employed' in education was 'not entirely spent in vain.'

However, Duncombe maintained, if one asked how many of those taught in the course of a year had been 'improved in the government of their temper,' or how many had been made 'more docile and obedient' and 'more mindful of their highest obligation to God,' the question would be deemed both impertinent and irrelevant. Education was popularly misconceived as an intellectual exercise. Yet any observer could see that the school as an institution was productive in a much larger sense than this. Students spent as much as 'six hours every day' in that institution and they associated with 'companions of all varieties of temper, character and habit.' Children were 'proverbially creatures of imitation and accessible to powerful influences.' The school, whether intended to be so or not, was inevitably a moral force. Schooling produced character and thus its organizational principles were of great importance to social order.

> If the government of Schools be so administered as to induce habits of cheerfulness and implicit obedience; if punctuality, neatness, and order in all School employments are preserved for a course of years it must have some influence in forming useful habits. On the contrary, if a child is tolerated in disobedience and neglect, if School duties are performed in a careless or, irregular and deficient manner, pernicious habits may be formed that will operate disastrously through life.[5]

The failure of the existing system of schools to place moral education directly in the centre of the educational process was not due to the incapacity of teachers to improve their students. Nor was it because religion in schools was not effective in improving children, nor even because children could not be convinced of this fact. Like optimistic liberals generally, Duncombe believed moral training was marginal to educational practices because its importance was simply underestimated. People did not generally understand what competent teachers might do in this regard, and the teachers generally employed in Upper Canada were not trained in effective moral practices. Finally, schools were so crowded that 'it is utterly impossible for Teachers to attempt properly to discharge their most important duty, without so neglecting what parents consider the only business of a Teacher [i.e., teaching to read and write] as to occasion dissatisfaction and removal either of Teacher or pupils.'

Duncombe argued that the reconstruction of popular education in Upper Canada demanded two major social changes. First, 'public sentiment' had to be changed to allow for the training of teachers. Second, the parents of students had to be convinced 'to pay the price for such a division of labour as will give' to trained teachers 'time and opportunity for the discharge of their most sacred duties.'

## Female Teachers

The large numbers of teachers required in a reconstructed educational system were unlikely to come from the male population. Existing political economic circumstances made this unlikely, as did 'natural' gender differences. Men had open to them 'the excitement and profits of commerce, manufactures, agriculture, and the arts.' They held a natural aversion to 'the sedentary, confining, and toilsome duties of teaching and governing young children.' When one regarded the 'scanty pittance' paid most teachers and noticed that 'few men will enter a business that will not support a family,' it became obvious that women must be trained as teachers.

Here necessity and nature were happily in harmony. Women, according to Duncombe, were 'fitted by disposition and habits, and circumstances, for such duties.' Women were necessarily 'the guardian[s] of the nursery, the companion[s] of childhood, and the constant model[s] of imitation.' However, the education of women in Upper Canadian society had yet to receive the serious attention it deserved. Females were 'sent first to one school and then to another; they attend a short time to one set of studies and then to another; while everything is desultory, unsystematic, and superficial.' Their education was prey to 'the notions of parents, or the whims of children, or the convenience of Teachers.' If women were to be adequately prepared for the important social position they might occupy in a liberal bourgeois society, their education must be reconstructed. Duncombe suggested that the leading 'Female Schools in the Province' should establish a common course of instruction parallel to that offered by colleges for young men. It was perhaps not necessary to give women 'titles of honour' after their completion of such a course, a practice which might 'provoke needless ridicule and painful notoriety,' besides being in 'very bad taste'. Still, a uniform course of instruction for women would overcome many of the flaws in the prevailing organization of their education.

As with the education of men, women's education was to become practical, an education directed to the world of experience. 'The taste of the age' had changed with respect to women, 'and instead of the fainting, weeping, vapid, pretty plaything, once the model of female loveliness, those qualities of the head and heart that best qualify a woman for her duties, are demanded and admired.' These duties centred upon 'all those thousand minutinae of domestic business' with which women were naturally charged. Education, to fit woman for her domestic roles, should encourage what Duncombe took to be her strongest and most natural traits of character: 'her warm sympathies, her lively imaginations, her ready invention, her quick perceptions.' At the same time, 'those more foreign habits of patient attention, calm judgment, steady efficiency, and habitual self-control, must be induced and sustained.' Women's education should include the sciences taught to young men, Duncombe argued. Women should not be restricted to one teacher, but should be exposed to subject specialists. They should be taught by teachers who used the requisite apparatus for scientific instruction, even if 'their progress in many of the sciences never needs to be so extensive' as that of men.

In short, the reconstruction of education as a means of moral regulation demanded the training of female teachers. Even if educated women did not become teachers, Duncombe argued their importance to the moral well-being of society was central, for it was woman whose 'hand stamps impressions on the immortal spirit which must remain for ever'. A female Normal School was a necessary part of Reform plans for educational reorganization.

Duncombe's analysis of the role of education in society was that of radical liberalism. Education was necessary to ensure that the possibilities for wealth and freedom generated by the growth of commodity production and exchange could in fact be realised. This necessity involved the generalization of education, its re-orientation towards matters of conduct, and the broadening of educational roles and opportunities for women.

## Method

With respect to pedagogical method, Duncombe wrote relatively little. For the sake of brevity, he 'omitted all those principles which are the most commonly insisted on in training the young student.' He signalled his support for the 'inductive' pedagogy promoted in liberal circles (and to certain extent in the English socialist movement as well),[6] and pointed to a school run by 'The Rev. Mr. Peers, of Louisville, Kentucky,' as a model.

The Rev. Mr. Peers was 'teaching his students the art of self government and self instruction.' He governed in the schoolroom 'not at all by fear', to which he objected 'as a governing principle,' whose tendency was to debase and lessen 'the dignity of man', but rather by 'cultivating and strengthening the social virtues, and increasing intellectual enjoyment.' Duncombe supported this attempt to anchor character formation in the capacity of the student for pleasure, and found it particularly enjoyable to observe on the faces of Mr. Peers' twenty boys 'a strong wish to be correct in all their answers to his questions, and [a] desire to please.' These students found the process of learning so pleasurable that they heard daily scripture lessons with interest, and understood so well the world about them that their lessons were 'not a parrot-like noisy or showy imitation of some eminent literary man, but the knowledge of mind, of thought and of reflection.' The Rev. Peers' instruction served 'to store the minds of his pupils with facts and ideas that may serve as a basis for the supert structure of the most useful kind.' He exposed his students to a wide array of innovative educational apparatus, including glass laboratory furniture, an 'electrifying machine' and an 'air pump'. Duncombe also signalled his support for specialist teachers in several subject areas and for the gymnastic exercises of 'some kind of useful labour.'

In light of our later investigation of the actual translation of educational policy into local practices, it is important to note Duncombe's optimism about the social possibilities of education, and his expectation that students would experience educational pleasure.

Education was seen to have the force to transform the world, and, crucially, the old 'despotic' forms of social regulation were no longer sustainable. In a changing world, regulation must be anchored in the characters of individuals. However, since this form of regulation involved extending, expanding and selectively developing the capacities of individuals, they would enjoy their experience of it. Like many liberal bourgeois intellectuals, Duncombe looked to the growing capitalist order to make people free and contented. Freedom was defined as a particular form of self-regulation, and individual freedom formed the basis of social order. In this regard, Duncombe had much in common with Egerton Ryerson, author of the School Act of 1850. By the standards of an hereditary aristocracy, these conceptions are quite radical. They contained a progressive dimension in their focus on social mobility, a limited liberation for women, and upon 'pleasure' in pedagogical matters. Of course, education was intended to produce a due subordination among the educated to God, the state, and the structure of worldly authority. The moral practices of education were congenial to the existing distribution of property and to women's subordination. These practices were consciously opposed to the prevailing conditions of popular culture and morality. But the radical dimension of the social reforms of the rising bourgeoisie should be stressed.

## Organization

Still, questions remained about educational management. Duncombe put the issues clearly:

> The proper organization of a board of instruction is a matter of of great moment, and of difficult attainment. All agree that they should be united among themselves; that they should be men of learning, apt to teach, unimpeachable in their life, gentlemanly and winning in their manners, industrious in their habits, energetic and enterprising in their character, interested in their work, and faithful in the performance of their duties. But how to obtain

such, how to keep them such after they are put in place, and how to get rid of them rapidly if they prove not to be such, are questions that have never been satisfactorily settled.⁷

However, while there were debates over staffing, selecting and policing boards of instruction, Duncombe took it for granted that there would and should be boards of instruction: i.e., that educational organization would be systematized, and supervised by respectable *men*.

The draft legislation which accompanied Duncombe's report sought to reconstruct education, as its preamble put it, in order to produce 'peace, welfare and good government,' 'benefits so much desired by the thinking portion' of the population of Upper Canada. In Duncombe's plan, the representatives of male propertyholders and taxpayers were to organize the educational affairs of society. In contemporary terms, a large portion of the social product was to be directed to this end, and a corps of administrative officers was to manage these resources.

The draft legislation doubled the provincial school fund derived from general revenues and school lands, and introduced the principle of local property taxation to an annual maximum of 100 pounds for the construction and furnishing of schools. The schools were to be systematized and coordinated through the office of an appointed provincial Superintendent of Common Schools. This officer was to distribute monies, to gather information and to report to the legislature annually on the conduct of schooling. He was also empowered to publish plans for the improvement and management of school finance and government. He was accorded the right to intervene in all educational disputes which could not be settled locally.

Effective school management was entrusted to six officials annually elected by propertyholders in each township. These officials were to be three commissioners of schools, and three educational inspectors. Commissioners were to determine the boundaries of school districts and to apportion school monies. They were to gather school statistics from particular schools and to transmit these to the provincial Superintendent. They were to be a corporation for the purpose of holding school property. With the three school inspectors, the commissioners were to hold annual examinations of candidates for teaching and to grant certificates of qualifications to such teachers. Only schools kept by lisenced teachers for at least three months a year were to be subsidized from the state school fund.

Commissioners and inspectors together were empowered to visit all schools at least once annually and to 'give their advice and direction to the Trustees and Teachers of such Schools, as to the government thereof, and the course of studies to be pursued therein.' They could annul the certificates of teachers they thought unfit.

Each school was to be routinely managed by three trustees elected annually in each school district (again by propertyholders & ratepayers). These trustees could call school meetings at any time, and these meetings could determine the level of local school taxation, choose a site for a school house, and appoint a district tax collector and clerk. Trustees were to contract with teachers, to furnish and keep the schoolhouse in repair, to pay teachers and organize the collection of school taxes, and to move to distrain the property of tax defaulters.

Finally, the legislation envisaged the establishment of four provincial normal schools, one of them for women, when the permanent school fund reached a certain level, and allowed districts at local option to tax themselves for the construction of schools of agriculture, horticulture, and manufacturing or industry.

The legislation was silent on the question of pedagogical method and curriculum content. Presumably these were matters left entirely to local option, although with normal schools in operation, one might have anticipated a tendency towards standardization in these matters.

In short, Reform educational policy contemplated the construction of a substantial educational administration. With the election of township officers, collectors, clerks, and with the appointment of a provincial superintendent, the legislation anticipated the addition of several thousand officials to the administration of education. Yet educational management would be relatively decentralized. Reformers did not contemplate leaving education entirely to the local community, but nonetheless allowed property at the township level more or less complete autonomy in educational matters. Local proprietors were to assemble more or less at will and to tax themselves as they saw fit for educational purposes. The state subsidy was to match local effort, embodying the Reform principle that central government should mainly support the efforts of property in the locality. Duncombe seems to have regarded the property qualification in the educational franchise, in combination with the character of local residents prepared to stand as commissioners and inspectors, as sufficient guarantees that the system would produce those benefits sought by the 'thinking portion' of the population.[8] The legislation also anticipated substantial organs of local electoral self-government in Upper Canada at a time when local government was almost entirely in the hands of appointed justices. Educational reform implied institution building.

Duncombe's draft legislation died on the order paper with the elections of 1836. Shortly thereafter, the Rebellions of 1837-8 provided Upper Canadians with a much more practical education. An attempt by an armed force of radical farmers, artisans and professionals to seize the parliament at Toronto was turned back by the local militia. A similar rising in the West of the colony was less successful. Leaders of the Rebellion fled to the United States, where some of them undertook a series of armed incursions along the border which lasted until 1841. In Lower Canada, a much more extensive and bloody *patriote* uprising was suppressed in 1837 and again in 1838 by regular army troops. In both provinces, rebel leaders were hung or transported.

## After the Rebellion: Tory Views of Education

The left wing of the Reform party was devastated by the Rebellion and the events which followed it. The leaders of the left either fled the country or remained to face imprisonment, transportation, or execution for their activities. The Executive and Legislative Councils used the large Tory majority in the House of Assembly to vindicate the educational activities so sharply criticized by Reformers during the early 1830s. At the same time, the colonial oligarchy, through the Legislative Council, blocked even Tory attempts in the House to reconstruct popular education.

Mahlon Burwell's Common School Act of 1838 passed the House of Assembly by a large majority. The bill was a close transcript of the educational views of the Bishop of Toronto, John Strachan, as expressed before an educational committee of the House in 1832. It included an important rider which allowed District Treasurers to pay local school teachers their shares of the government money in the usual fashion. The financial upheaval associated with the Rebellion meant that for 1837 most teachers were paid their shares in the state school fund in the form of promissory notes which they could cash only at considerable discounts.

Burwell later claimed that his general educational plans were inspired largely by those of the Scottish cleric and philanthropic activist Thomas Chalmers, as expressed in the latter's *Essay on the Parochial Schools of Scotland*. Burwell proposed to support local elementary schools from three sources: an annual legislative school grant; a matching grant raised by local taxation organized through the Quarter Sessions, and monies received from the sale of school lands. The lieutenant-governor was to appoint a central General Board of Education which would govern elementary education. The General Board, which was also to function as a District Board of Education for the Home District, was to distribute school monies for the province as a whole, to collect school statistics, and to formulate general rules for school management and government. Appointed District Boards of Education were to distribute school monies locally, to examine teachers, and were empowered to settle all local educational disputes in a binding fashion.

In the Tory plan, local administrative duties were to be carried out by commissioners of schools elected in each township. These commissioners were to establish the school districts and to hold regular school examinations. In each school district, property holders were to elect three school trustees who were to hire teachers, manage and furnish the schoolhouse, and, most importantly, who were empowered to levy a local rate for school building and maintenance. The trustees were also empowered to fire teachers 'for any misdemeanor, or impropriety of conduct.'[9] With the possible exception of teachers, all these officials were to be male.

But while Burwell's School Act placed educational organization more directly under the control of officials appointed by central government and retained the leading powers of school taxation in the hands of the Quarter Sessions, the bill was nonetheless vetoed by the Legislative Council. Ostensibly this was because the rate proposed--- 1 1/2 pence on the pound---was seen by the Council to be excessive in a period of economic depression.[10] However, the Legislative Council and the colonial oligarchy contemplated a rather different use for the colony's educational resources, which had been under the control of the Assembly since 1833.

The Grammar School Act of 1839 vindicated the secondary educational policy of the executive branch. A new body of lands was appropriated for the support of elite grammar schools. This new appropriation brought the lands fund back up to the 500,000 acres granted originally in 1797, by replacing lands diverted earlier by the executive for the support of the Central National School, Upper Canada College and King's College. The district schools established under the Grammar School Acts of 1807/8 were declared to be public schools within the definition of the original land grant of 1797. The revenue from the sale of school lands in the hands of the Receiver General, which had been placed at the disposal of the Assembly in 1833, was invested in provincial debentures, the proceeds of which were to be directed towards needy grammar schools. The Council of King's College was given control over this money and over the conduct of grammar schooling generally.[11]

Immediately after the Rebellion, then, and despite the lessons it might have taken from the struggles for local control over elementary education in the early to mid-1830s, the colonial executive was most concerned with reasserting its interest in control by a state church over secondary education funded out of public resources. As the Bishop of Toronto put it in a letter to Lieutenant-Governor Arthur in May of 1838, during the Rebellion 'Church people were almost to a man loyal.' 'It is a grave question,' he emphasized, to remove the official status of the Church of England. Such a 'religious Level' was certain to make the colony 'a moral waste and a hotbed of sedition and discontent.'[12]

Yet this position was becoming increasingly untenable. Politicians and important proprietors were increasingly convinced of the necessity of systematic instruction of the population, and most observers were coming to see a state church as incapable of organizing this. Religious diversity could not be overcome through a church establishment, and moderate Tories and Reformers alike were arguing that *property*, not religion, was the best educator. While debates raged over whether property could act most effectively through local electoral self-management or through the construction of central educational bureaucracies, most participants in the public debates over educational organization increasingly looked to *property* as the basis of educational management and administration.

## Sullivan's Report

This broad agreement did not end the struggles among political parties over the question of educational organization: far from it. Key issues remained to be resolved, and plans for educational reorganization were numerous.

In a 'Report on the State of the Province' delivered to the Lieutenant-Governor, Sir George Arthur, in 1838, Robert Baldwin Sullivan, himself later President of the Legislative Council, stressed the necessity of effective political socialization in the colony. The colonial government had unwisely encouraged the settlement of Americans. The result was that 'in the bosom of this community there exists a treacherous foe.' The presence of this population and the colony's proximity to the democratic republic--- 'that arena for the discussion of extreme political fantasies'--- meant that even natural subjects of the Crown were 'carried away by the plausibility of republican doctrines.' The spirit of democracy which prevailed, and which made 'every man' into 'not merely a speculative but a practical statesman' meant that every minor personal dissatisfaction became a 'ground for organic change in Government,' and 'a reason for revolution.'

For Sullivan, the solution to this dangerous Canadian political problem was certainly not 'responsible government'. Elective councils, he argued, would merely subject the governor to incessant changes of opinion, which would ultimately issue in civil war. The successful governance of the Canadas demanded a firm imperial control over foreign affairs and financial matters, coupled with a prudent control over internal matters. Certainly no elective body should have the power over finance which would enable it to interfere with the conduct of Her Majesty's government. Sullivan maintained that the colonial executive must always have the power to oppose itself successfully to the 'people's' representatives on certain occasions. 'While the possession of the means of carrying on the Government for a time in opposition to the popular voice' was 'essential to the preservation of colonial relations,' this power nonetheless did not present the same 'danger to the civil & political liberties of the subject' that it might in the imperial state. This was because the colonial population was under the 'Guardianship of the Imperial Legislature', whose only interest was 'in preserving the inhabitants of the dependencies of the crown in peace contentment & tranquillity.'

But, if such a form of government were to be constructed, and 'were the Crown revenues of sufficient amount,' Sullivan argued that 'there is no object in which they could be better expended than in the promotion of Education or in the direction of Education in a proper Channel.' 'Incalculable' evils had resulted from the 'want of Government superintendence' of popular education. True, the parliament had spent money on education, but parliamentary monies were 'frittered away in insignificant sums through the country and no general or uniform system has been attempted.'

American teachers were common in many parts of the colony, teachers who 'for the sake of obtaining employment' had 'swallowed the oath of allegiance which disagrees so ill with them that the rest of their lives is spent in attempts to disgorge it.' These teachers subjected the youth of the colony to republican propaganda. They were 'utterly ignorant of every thing English' and could not instruct Upper Canadians in their political obligations to the British Crown. They used American books and glorified the heroes of the American War of Independence and the War of 1812. Upper Canadians learned from American geography books that the state of Rhode Island was as important as the eastern hemisphere, and England appeared as 'a pitiful little island filled with tyrannical Landlords and very fat clergymen, and a great number of squalid tenants and labourers.' Ireland was presented as a 'joyless land of bogs, pigs and catholics, and Scotland an out of the way place in which the mountains and the men had a national and barbarious prejudice against decent covering.'

Upper Canadians educated in this manner came to see the 'british soldier as a person whom it would be honorable and glorious to oppose with the rifle.' A person so educated could not 'become a good subject of the Crown of great Britain', nor be brought to think 'colonial connection with England either an honor or an advantage'. The 'noble and good sentiments' of the person educated by an

American adventurer were all 'enlisted on the side of revolution and independence.' This meant that an important part of the colonial population was 'accessible to motives of adherence to the Government by means of terror and coercion, or through the equally base channel of personal & pecuniary advantage.'[13]

Sullivan argued that governmental forms congenial to the colonial connection could be sustained in the Canadas only if the character structures necessary for their sustenance were implanted in the body politic through education. The problem for Sullivan, as for bourgeois educational reformers generally, and whatever their particular position with respect to the question of elections, was to fix the 'noble and good sentiments' of the population on the proper object. Education was in large part about the making of political selves; about the construction of forms of character and types of moral regulation where loyalty would be firmly anchored in feeling and belief. In Sullivan's account of the Rebellion of 1837, no fundamental reforms in the nature of the colonial administration were necessary. Rather, the population had to be instructed in its political duties and encouraged to both love and internalize them.

However, other observers, sharing Sullivan's belief in the efficacy of education, nonetheless sought political reorganization as a means to achieve it.

## The Durham Report: English Radical Views of Canadian Education

This aspect of the debate over educational organization was focused around Lord Durham's critical *Report on the Affairs of British North America,* published in 1839. Durham criticized existing political rule in both the Canadas, and made specific reference to the power exerted in the upper province by the small group known as the 'family compact'. 'The bench, the magistracy, the high offices of the Episcopal Church, and a great part of the legal profession, are filled by the adherents of this party,' Durham wrote. 'By grant or purchase, they have acquired nearly the whole of the waste lands of the Province; they are all-powerful in the chartered banks, and, till lately, shared among themselves almost exclusively all offices of trust and profit.'[14] Durham argued that such concentrated power necessarily produced opposition. The House of Assembly necessarily criticized the ruling group for jobbery and corruption, although Assembly members were themselves often equally guilty in this regard. However, Durham did explicitly approve of the tactics of colonial Reformers, and, implicitly then, of their objectives as well.

Durham particularly criticized the absence of effective local governmental organs in Upper Canada, both as means of resolving political disputes, and as necessary means to industrial progress. Roads, post-offices, mills, schools and churches were largely absent, he maintained, due to the absence of powers of local government. This meant that people 'may have a rude and comfortless plenty, but they can seldom acquire wealth.' Even the few wealthy land-owners were unable to 'prevent their children from growing up ignorant and boorish.' Durham suggested that the absence of the means of instruction in the colony was due in part to the fact that the 'lands which were originally appropriated for the support of schools throughout the country' had for the most part been 'diverted to the endowment of the University, from which those only derive any benefit who reside in Toronto.'[15]

Durham did not present a plan for the strictly educational reconstruction of Upper Canada, but such a plan was articulated for Lower Canada. Arthur Buller headed a commission investigating the educational condition of the lower province and surveyed respectable opinion extensively. His plan for Lower Canadian educational reorganization closely approximated that eventually adopted in Canada West.

Buller was sharply critical of Lower Canadian educational organization. The broad powers of management exerted by locally elected trustees, and the direct appointment of schoolmasters by the parliament produced an inefficient system riddled with corruption. Schoolmasters were often the most virulent opponents of the colonial connection and Buller claimed to 'have been assured by many witnesses that the 'Minerve', an exciting and seditious paper, was in frequent use in the schools as a class-book.' Parental indifference to education was said to be general, the schools were poorly supplied with books and apparatus, and the result was that the 'peasantry' as a whole was almost completely ignorant. Lawyers assured Buller that prisoners, witnesses and petty jurymen were generally illiterate. Existing schools could simply not contribute to sound political governance.

A main cause of social unrest in the colony in Buller's view was the antagonism existing between what he called the 'races'. French and English were schooled apart and this ensured 'racial' intolerance. Since the Radicals generally argued that the continued existence of Lower Canada as a British colony demanded its anglification, Buller insisted on common schooling of French and English, whatever the protests of the Catholic clergy. Buller argued that Catholic control of education was impracticable and unjust and proposed a religious education based upon principles common to both Protestants and Catholics.

In the matter of school funding, Buller wrote that 'the principle adopted in the American systems would perhaps be the best,' with local taxation raising funds to match central educational grants in the countryside, and to double them in the towns.[16] Buller cited approvingly the suggestion of Dr. Meilleur to the House Education Committee in 1836,

> d'obliger tous les enfans à aller à l'école de leur arrondissement respectif, depuis l'âge de 6 ans jusqu'à celui de 12 inclusivement, excepté dans le cas d'absence en assistant à une autre école, et ce sous peine d'une amende.[17]

The elementary school system was to be supported by local model schools and by three normal schools for the efficient training of teachers. At the outset, Buller proposed to oblige all teachers to attend model schools for part of the year in order to assure their qualification. With these training institutions in place, with a guaranteed annual salary of thirty pounds, a house, and fuel, and with 'the further prospect of promotion to a model school,' the system should be able to 'hold out sufficient inducement to men of character and talent.' Buller suggested that schoolmasters be placed in other offices, such as the administration of the Registry Act. Hence 'there would be a safety-valve for all that waste talent,' which existed in Lower Canada, which found 'no outlet under the present system' and which was in consequence 'endangering society by its irregular outbreaks.'[18]

Whatever concessions Buller was prepared to make to the 'American' practice of local taxation for education, he insisted that the 'vitality of every system of education must essentially reside' in 'the provisions for inspection and supervision.'[19] Paper educational schemes were very well, but 'all is of no avail unless that scheme is watched,' and its principles guarded by 'an honest and active inspection.'

This inspection was not to be carried out by the Catholic clergy, although Buller was prepared to allow resident clergy to co-manage local district schools with elected trustees. Nor were locally elected officials to be trusted to inspect their own schools: the past history of Lower Canada showed that local elections bred corruption and inefficiency. Locally elected officials could manage the details of school operation, but a strong measure of central control was essential.

Buller's plan for regulating the educational system presumed organs of elected local government. In each unit of municipal government, school commissioners were to be elected to hold school properties, distribute school monies and make annual reports. Commissioners should divide the municipality into districts, and three trustees should be elected in each district to manage the schoolhouse. Each municipality should also establish a board of school visitors who should visit the schools at least three times (irregularly) a year. The province as a whole should be divided into three inspectorships, and the Governor should appoint three full time school inspectors. These officials were to be paid the comparatively enormous sum of 400 pounds per annum, with a further 100 pounds for travelling expenses, and were to hold office at pleasure.

The inspectors were to deal with all educational questions arising in their administrative districts. Their efforts were to be overseen by a 'superintendent or chief officer of instruction' whose office was to be 'one of the highest dignity in the province.' This officer was to refrain from party politics. He was to manage the school fund, to specify books to be used, hours of attendance, and so forth in all funded schools. 'His decisions' should be 'binding in all matters relating to school discipline,' and with his office and secretary at the seat of government, he was to have 800 pounds per annum as salary. Buller concluded his proposals with the remark that he had

> made no attempt at originality, but [had] constantly kept in view as models, the systems in force in Prussia and the United States, particularly the latter,

as being more adapted to the circumstances of the colony. The office of inspector is somewhat new to that system, and provides against its most serious defects.[20]

The English Radical vision of the well-governed Canadas included systematic educational organization under firm central direction. Buller, with his desire to create 'room for talent', anticipated that participation in administrative activity, and the possibility of an educational career line, would channel the political energies of men of talent from the middle ranks in safe directions. Concessions to local democracy were clearly seen to be necessary, but these concessions did not accord real educational power to the locality. Inspection by officials whose salary placed them at least economically amongst the ruling groups was seen to be essential. The power to specify what would be read and done in the schools remained with the central authority.[21] Education was to to be systematized and made part of conscious central state policy. Good governance was held to involve the political socialization of the population by the state.

## The Education Commission of 1839

The publication of the Durham Report in the Canadas provoked serious popular demonstrations in favor of political reform and colonial autonomy. 'Durham' marches and meetings proliferated, featuring red flags, the burning in effigy of Sir Francis Bond Head, and violent clashes between 'Durham' men and Orangemen.[22]

Shortly after the publication of the Report, the Upper Canadian Assembly learned that the funds of King's College were being maladministered. The bursar and registrar were unable to account for about 6000 pounds, and a demand arose from the Assembly for an investigation of all government departments. Lieutenant-governor Arthur established a general Commission of Government Departments, including an Education Commission charged with investigating elementary educational organization. The Commission's Report of 1839 is the last clear statement of Tory educational policy before the Union of the Canadas in 1840.

The Commission was composed of H.J. Grasset, dean of Toronto,

S.B. Harrison, judge of the Home District, and J. McCaul, vice-president of King's College. Two of these officials were appointed to the (second) General Board of Education in 1846, and all three later sat on the Council of Public Instruction.[23] The Commission's terms of reference called for it to investigate the past and present state of colonial elementary education, to investigate school funds, to produce an account of the constitution and revenues of King's College, and to articulate a plan for the 'diffusion of Education in Upper Canada.' The Commission proceeded for the most part by addressing circular letters to Legislative Councillors and Tory M.P.P.s known to be interested in education, and to several well-known and moderate educators. The latter included Dr. Craigie of the Ancaster Academy, and the Rev. Robert Murray of Oakville. Murray was appointed first Assistant Superintendent of Education for Upper Canada in 1842 and Craigie was one of his regular correspondents while he was in office.

The Commission reported that elementary education was in a sorry state in the colony. Ten of the thirteen colonial districts reported a total of only 651 grant-aided schools in existence, with enrollment totalling only 14,776---a small fraction of the juvenile population. Many of the teachers receiving the state grant were 'found unfit for this responsible station, from their want, either of literary or moral qualifications.' This was held to be a result of their low pay. The Commission recommended raising teachers' salaries and the establishment of Township Model Schools, to be supplemented by a Provincial Normal School for teacher training.

Next to low salaries, the Commission attributed the sorry state of the schools to the absence of effective central control over the content of education. The schools were said to be using American books whose political content, 'however fit for dissemination under the form of Government which exists there, cannot be inculcated here without evil results.' The Commission recommended that all schools use one set of text books.

The plan for educational reorganization proposed by the Commission urged the creation of an 'Inspector General of Education' and of a 'Provincial Board of Commissioners' to exert 'general control of Common Schools.' The Inspector General was to be a salaried official, and was to supervise the conduct of common and grammar schooling generally. This officer was also to be chairman of the

Board of School Commissioners. The latter body was to frame rules and regulations for all schools, to specify the texts to be used in the schools, to prepare and publish such books, and to determine 'the location of the School Houses'. The Inspector General was annually to collect and report 'accurate information of the System of Education, and its practical working.'

At the next level of government, appointed District (county) Boards of Trustees were to administer the schools. Each of these Boards was to have a salaried secretary who was to inspect the schools 'as often as circumstances may require, but all, at least, once annually.' Local school units were to be managed by those paying for the conduct of the school. These were to be either 'Shareholders' or others 'who had become eligible by making a donation of a fixed amount, or value, to the advancement of education in the Township.' The Commission allowed that these local district managers might be elected by propertyholders, although this was clearly not necessarily to be the case. School funds were to be raised by a 'direct tax of three farthings in the pound,' and as no organs of local elective government were mentioned by the Commission, it seems that this tax was to be levied by the Quarter Sessions.

The 'respectable' opinion sampled by the Education Commission of 1839 was unanimous in its condemnation of local control over educational organization. Many correspondents concerned themselves with the question of obtaining 'qualified' teachers to replace those hired by local school managers. The Rev. Robert McGill of Niagara argued that teachers should be trained in normal schools to follow a curriculum specified by a General Board of Education. Once appointed to a school, teachers should be removed from office only at the instigation of this Board. McGill argued that the course of instruction given in the elementary schools 'must be a very plain matter.' Dr. Craigie of Ancaster argued that a District Board of Education should have the power of determining the location of schoolhouses, and should be capable of 'appointing, promoting, or removing Teachers; of investigating any complaints by, or against them.' A paid secretary appointed by the Board should inspect all schools.

Implicit in most of the remarks made to the Commission is the conventional Tory contempt for the capacity of local property to manage its own educational affairs. Robert Murray, later first

Assistant Superintendent of Common Schools for Canada West, was more explicit than many. In his view, the central educational defect in Upper Canada was the power local trustees exerted over the selection of teachers, a power he described as 'an insult to common sense'. He claimed that trustees were 'appointed without any regard to their education,' and were thus altogether 'unfit to judge, either of the qualifications of a School Master, or of the progress of the pupils.' The power of trustees subjected teachers to 'the whim and caprice of every child attending the school'. Teachers were entirely 'at the mercy of the public, who, proverbially, have no conscience,' and direct public control over teachers made their position 'more precarious and degraded than that of a shoeblack.' An efficient system of education in Murray's view would be one in which 'Teachers would be protected from the interference of the public, and encouraged in the discharge of their arduous duties, and the Government would be put in early possession of the whole, even in its most minute movements.' Murray was quite emphatic that 'to leave the supervision' of education 'in the hands of the electors of each district [i.e.,school section]' would 'disappoint the reasonable expectations of the Government' with respect to the efficacy of education.[24]

Just before the Union of the Canadas in 1840, then, representatives of property in the colonial parliament and 'respectable' opinion generally agreed on the necessity of educational reconstruction in Upper Canada. Education on a systematic basis had come to be seen as an essential means of governance for the colony. Yet debates raged over the exact form this educational governance should take. Implicit in these debates were opposing conceptions of the capacities of small proprietors, and opposing visions of the form of the state in Canada. It was in the decade of the 1840s that these debates were ultimately resolved.

## Notes

1. R.D. Gidney, 'Elementary Education in Upper Canada: a Reassessment,' in M.B. Katz and Paul Mattingly (eds) *Education and Social Change: Themes from Ontario's Past* (New York: University Press,1975):3-26. See also in this regard, Bruce Curtis, 'Schoolbooks

and the Myth of Curricular Republicanism: The State and the Curriculum in Canada West,1820-1850' *histoire sociale/Social History* 16(32):305-29.
2. M. Fairley, *William Lyon Mackenzie* (Toronto: University of Toronto Press,1965):92-3;45-6.
3. In much of the discourse of educational reform with which I am concerned in this study, the masculine pronoun is used to refer to both genders, except in rare instances where women's education is explicitly addressed. When reformers spoke of school management, and the political dimensions of educational organization directly, they operated on a patriarchal terrain whose landscape most of them viewed with pleasure. I will use the masculine pronoun in the text in places where it is clear that reformers intended it. I will use the neutral pronoun 'it' to refer to 'the scholar', the 'parent' the 'teacher', in all cases where 'he' is not clearly demanded. If the reader experiences a certain dissonance in reading 'it' in these instances, it might reflect on the import of gendered pronouns in those instances.
4. Duncombe signals his intense awareness of that phenomenon described by E.P. Thompson, *The Making of the English Working Class* (Harmondsworth:Penguin,1965) as the 'crisis of moral economy' of the late eighteenth and early nineteenth centuries. A reading of the enlightenment writers who see/anticipate the consequences of the generalization of commodity production and exchange for political order contributes to a better understanding of the discourse of educational reform. See, for instance, John Millar, 'The Origin of the Distinction of Ranks'[1779] reprinted in W.C. Lehmann, *John Millar of Glasgow,1735-1801*, (Cambridge:Cambridge University Press,1960); Adam Smith, *Lectures on Jurisprudence* (Indianapolis:Liberty Classics,1982).
5. J.G. Hodgins, ed *The Documentary History of Education in Upper Canada* (Toronto: L.K. Cameron,1894-1910), II:294
6.In this regard see Brian Simon (ed) *The Radical Tradition in Education in Britain* (London: Lawrence & Wishart,1972).
7.Hodgins, *Documentary History*, II:295.
8. The entire text of Duncombe's Report and legislation is found in Hodgins, *Documentary Education,* II:289-322. For the Rebellion of 1837 see S. Ryerson, *Unequal Union.* (New York: International Publishers, 1968.); Colin Read, *The Rising in Western Canada.* (Toronto: University of Toronto Press, 1982.)

9. Hodgins, *Documentary History*, III:280-3.
10. Hodgins, *Documentary History*, III:128-9.
11. Hodgins, *Documentary History*, III:170-5.
12. C.R. Sanderson, (ed) *The Arthur Papers* (Toronto: University of Toronto Press and Toronto Public Library,1942) I:103-4.
13. The complete text of 'Mr Sullivans Report on the State of the Province 1838' is in Sanderson, *The Arthur Papers*, I:132-54.
14. Sir C.P. Lucas (ed) *Lord Durham's Report on the Affairs of British North America*, (Oxford:Clarendon Press,1912),II:148.
15. Lucas, *Lord Durham*, II:184.
16. Lucas, *Lord Durham*, II:184
17. Lucas, *Lord Durham*, III:280.
18. Lucas, *Lord Durham*, III:283.
19. Lucas, *Lord Durham*, III:283.
20. Lucas, *Lord Durham*, III:287-8. It is remarkable to note that the English Radicals were treating inspection as a standard and essential element of the provision and regulation of state institutions and policies at local sites, and, that at the same time, they described this practice as 'somewhat new' to the Americas. Modern state practices considered quite ordinary in England--although in fact they were even there merely being constructed--are seen as lacking in the Canadas.
21. Philip Corrigan makes this point forcefully in his very useful essay, 'On Moral Regulation: Some Preliminary Remarks,' *Sociological Review*, 29(2),1981:313-337.
22. For example, Sanderson *Arthur Papers* III:118.
23. Hodgins, *Documentary History*, III:240-1.
24. Hodgins, *Documentary History*, III:252-64.
25. For all correspondents to the Commission of 1839 including those cited, see Hodgins, *Documentary History*, III:265-83.

# Chapter Two:
# 'Responsible Government' and Educational Reform, 1840-1846

In keeping with the assimilationist views of the imperial state and its Governor-General, Lord Sydenham, the first parliament of the United Canadas passed a School Act in 1841 which applied to both parts of the colony. The political struggles of the 1830s were muted in the first parliamentary session after the Union. The Reform party had been devastated by the Rebellion and its aftermath, and was firmly in the hands of what had been its right wing, a group of moderates who sought political reform within the confines of the colonial connection. The property qualification for both sitting in parliament and voting for candidates was substantially raised under the Union, and Sydenham's 'law of the bludgeons' secured the election of a parliament supportive of the Union itself.[1]

Sydenham sought a 'reign of harmony' with government by 'able men' selected by the Crown regardless of party affiliation. Political confusion and the absence of firm party lines in the first session enabled him to create a coalition of the centre. Led in parliament by Samuel Bealy Harrison and Henry Draper, supported actively outside the house by Egerton Ryerson and others, the governing party was opposed in the main by French Canadian members and by the liberal Reformers led by Robert Baldwin.[2] However, despite the best efforts of the Governor-General, by the end of 1841 a majority in the Assembly had come to support 'responsible government' for the Canadas.

The concept 'responsible government' was notoriously vague. It meant quite different things to different interests both in and outside the Assembly. Given the absence of a republican interest in parliament after the suppression of the Rebellion, the most radical interpretation of responsible government came from the 'ultra-Reformers' associated with Robert Baldwin. The latter sought the modelling of colonial administration on English parliamentary practice, with ministries selected by the majority party in the house holding office only with the confidence of that majority. The colonial state was to be self-governing in all internal matters, although foreign policy was to be largely beyond its purview. To the 'high' or 'compact' Tories this was a dangerously republican conception. To more moderate Tories, 'responsible government' meant government by men possessed of 'responsibility': technical competence and high moral worth. 'Responsibility' in the last sense was something which some of its proponents thought might be produced or at least sustained by educational efforts upon the population at large.[3]

In public, Lord Sydenham took a very equivocal position with respect to the question of parliamentary autonomy, although his private opposition was clearly expressed.[4] The issue came before the Assembly in the debate on the throne speech in the first session of 1841, and liberal Reformers demanded some explicit statement from the Sydenham ministry on the question. After a considerable amount of waffling from William Henry Draper, who attempted to divert attention from the central issue--- that the Governor should be subordinate to the Executive Council, which in turn should be subordinate to the parliamentary majority--- the Assembly adopted the 'Harrison Resolutions'. Draper reluctantly acceded to the proposition that a ministry which did not have the support of the majority of the Assembly should resign or call new elections. To Reformers, this clearly seemed to establish the *principle* of parliamentary autonomy.[5] However, parliamentary conflicts over ministerial responsibility, conflicts indeed over the *form* of the Canadian state, continued to shape educational organization in the 1840s.

The Sydenham ministry acted early in the session to present an educational bill, drafted by the Solicitor-General East, Charles Day. This bill was remarkable for its signalling of the demise of the old oligarchic interests in educational policy. The Act based upon it was remarkable for the extent to which it confused educational practice in Canada West.

In debate over the bill in the House of Assembly, some members insisted that educational organization must be free of religious sectarianism, and moderate Reformers argued that social education would ensure good government. James Price, the member for York, for instance, argued that both the popularity of the ministry and the progress of the colony depended upon 'the moral instruction of the people.' Such instruction would give to the government 'materials to work on' and would give 'power to the people---a power which will be a formidable check upon bad government and a strong support to a good one.' However, to be effective, such instruction had to be 'free from sectarianism.'[6] Criticism of the disposal of the School Lands of Upper Canada by the colonial oligarchy was loud, and members debated a variety of schemes for the generation of educational revenues. Some members cited the example of the state of Connecticut, where schools were successfully supported out of land sales and rentals. Other members--- among them the influential Francis Hincks, who later authored the School Act of 1843--- argued that granted lands had consistently operated as barriers to settlement in Canada West. Hincks sought the extension of local powers of taxation to support educational expenditure.[7] Debates over sources of school revenue continued into the 1850s.

In draft, Day's bill provided for a centralized and appointive educational administration. The schools were to be managed by a Chief Superintendent of Education, appointed by the Governor-General and holding office at pleasure. The Chief Superintendent was accorded broad powers to frame 'such regulations and instructions as he shall deem necessary' for educational administration, and he was also to apportion school monies and to collect information. The Chief Superintendent was to appoint five people ---two of them resident clergy--- to be a District Board of Examiners. Boards of Examiners were to specify the course of study, the books to be used, and the rules and regulations for school administration in each District. The Boards were empowered to examine and qualify or disqualify school teachers, and their members were also to operate as paid school inspectors. Each Board was to report annually to the Chief Superintendent on the conduct of education.

The draft bill also vested District Councils created under the District Councils Act of 1841 with powers as District Boards of Education. The District Boards were to define school units according to the distribution of the juvenile population. They were empowered to levy a property tax for educational purposes, including the construction of school houses and the purchase of books. District Boards were also to report annually to the Chief Superintendent.

In a further centralizing initiative, the bill abolished the office of local or section school trustee. Trustees were to be replaced by five school commissioners elected in each township. Township school commissioners were to be responsible directly to appointed District

Boards of Examiners. The commissioners were to choose and acquire school sites, to hold school property as a corporation, and severally to manage township schools. Commissioners were to inspect schools to ensure that the rules and regulations specified by Boards of Examiners were followed. They were empowered to hire and fire teachers lisenced by Boards of Examiners, and to exempt indigent residents from school taxes. In the towns and cities, the town or city councils were to have the same educational powers as District Councils, and here the Governor-General was to appoint Boards of Examiners directly. Urban councils were to act as commissioners of schools.[8]

The bill was attacked by Reformers in committee and radically altered. The key appointive office of Board of Examiner was abolished, although the School Act of 1841 also eliminated the local school trustees who had been at the centre of educational organization in Upper Canada from 1816. While the question of colonial political autonomy remained unresolved, Reformers generally opposed any radical educational centralization.

The School Act of 1841 created the office of Superintendent of Education for the Canadas with an annual salary of 750 pounds. This official was to manage the provincial school fund, taken from general revenues, which initially amounted to fifty thousand pounds per annum, twenty thousand of which were directed towards Canada West. Part of the inspectoral duties attributed to Boards of Examiners in the draft bill now devolved upon the Superintendent, who was to visit each municipal district annually to 'ascertain the State of Common Schools therein.' Technically, this could not have resulted in inspectoral practice at the level envisaged by the draft bill. The Superintendent was also to distribute educational monies amongst District Councils, and to collect educational information. He was to draw up and publicize plans for improving colonial educational organization, but was granted no power to enforce or implement these plans.

District Councils were to function as Boards of Education. The Act allowed them to designate as a school section any part of their District in which at least fifteen people between the ages of five and sixteen were resident. District Boards were given the power to tax local property to the amount of fifty pounds in each school section for a schoolhouse, and to an additional ten pounds annually for books and supplies. The granting of each District's portion of the school fund was conditional upon the District Council raising at least an equal amount by local taxation. Taxes were also to be assessed on the parents or guardians of students.

The management of local educational matters was to be in the hands of five elected Township Commissioners of Common Schools. Each township school was to be supervised directly by at least one Commissioner, and collectively the Commissioners were to specify the course of study and school rules and regulations for all township schools. Commissioners were empowered to hire and fire teachers and 'to hear and determine all disputes which may arise...in respect to Common Schools within their Township or Parish.' In addition, they were to appoint two of their number inspectors and these were to visit all township schools at least once a month. No payment was provided for these officials.

No school was to receive a subsidy from the common school fund unless it had at least fifteen students in attendance for at least nine months of the year. In towns and cities, the act preserved the appointed Boards of Examiners contained in the draft bill.[9]

The School Act of 1841 was a serious but confused attempt to discipline the educational market through the construction of public administrative structures. The ambiguities produced by the Act can be traced to the political situation out of which it emerged. The centralized organization proposed in the draft bill was subverted by Reformers in committee, but no clearly articulated plan for local autonomy took its place. Reformers opposed imperial control over internal colonial affairs, but were internally divided on the exact form of the colonial self-government they sought. Again, debates over elective versus appointive organs of local government divided the Assembly and delayed passage of the District Councils Act of 1841, upon which the School Act depended. The same debates were echoed in the opposition of many teachers and local proprietors to the elective office of Commissioner of Common Schools.

As Gidney and Lawr have pointed out,[10] it soon became apparent that one superintendent of education could not oversee the Act in both parts of the colony, yet the Act was in effect for three months before Robert Murray was appointed Assistant Superintendent of Education for Canada West. No funds were provided for printing the Act, and officials charged with administering it frequently knew neither the Act's provisions, nor where to find out about them. More importantly, the Act was entirely dependent upon the operation of the District Councils Act for all of its financial provisions, yet the District Councils Act was stalled in the legislature until after the School Act came into effect.

Some District Councils then refused to follow the provisions of the School Act for educational taxation at all. Others collected a school tax but refused to distribute it according to the provisions of the School Act. In these cases the financial provisions of the Act could not be followed directly, yet teachers were keeping schools in the expectation of public funding. Where District Councils refused to act, Township Commissioners were directly liable for teachers' salaries, and this made them reluctant to sign contracts with teachers. Eventually the government decided to distribute the grant to all districts anyway, but this took nine months---until April of 1843. In addition, the Assistant Superintendent had no power to resolve local educational disputes, even where these had general policy implications. Bitter conflicts arose in many localities over such questions as the right of female teachers to share in the school fund.

## Schooling under the Act of 1841

Nonetheless, the School Act of 1841 did create a state educational bureau which was increasingly active in the accumulation of knowledge concerning local educational organization and which was increasingly in a position to agitate and propagandize in favor of public educational construction. The central office in Canada West printed standardized forms for educational reporting which were sent to District Councils, and even for 1842 District Boards of Education generated a considerable body of information about such things as school populations and teachers' salaries and qualifications.[11] The Assistant Superintendent of Schools undertook an educational tour in 1842, and collected hundreds of written reports from individual teachers concerning their schools.[12] While the Assistant Superintendent had no statutory powers to intervene in disputes over general school policy, he did urge and propagandize local school authorities on policy questions. The central bureau began that voluminous correspondence with local school participants which eventually enabled it to closely monitor local educational activity. The forms of knowledge/power on which the educational state relies and through which the educational state was constructed were generated in part by the School Act of 1841.

The information collected under the Act of 1841 allows a more comprehensive view of educational organization in Canada West than that possible for the 1830s. The invitation issued by the Assistant Superintendent during his tour of inspection of 1842 to all teachers and others to write to him on the means to improve educational organization also produced a wide variety of plans and projects.

Township Commissioners were elected in 245 of the 315 townships in Canada West for 1842. The Education Office preserved detailed reports of the rules for township school management articulated by about fifty of these bodies of Commissioners. In many instances, the Commissioners were content simply to specify the hours of attendance, the dates of school holidays, and the books to be used in schools. The regulations specified were various, and no uniformity existed from one township to another in such areas as the length of the school day or the precise course of instruction to be followed.

Some Township School Commissions published detailed rules and regulations for the organization and conduct of local schools. Among the most elaborate were those published by the Commissioners for Charlotteville in the form of a list of 'Rules and Regulations.' They specified the school terms, both winter and summer, with hours of attendance and lunch breaks. The teachers were to teach 'as may be required, Spelling, Reading, Writing, Arithmetic, Geography, English Grammar and Book-keeping.' The books they were to use 'as far as practicable' were named. Teachers were to bar 'small children not attending as scholars' from the schools, to turn out 'large scholars refusing to comply with the Rules,' and to exclude 'scholars having contagious diseases, such as Measles, Mumps, Whooping cough or Itch.' Teachers were commanded to do nothing other than teach during school hours, and to supervise the scholars on their way to and from the school. 'Silence and good order' were to be promoted during school hours, all diversions from studies were prohibited, and teachers were to encourage 'a spirit of emulation' amongst the scholars. Teachers were to prevent the scholars from injuring the schoolhouse or its contents, to prevent 'profane or indecorous language' as well as 'teasing, hectoring' and other forms of ill-treatment. They were encouraged to investigate the behaviour of students regularly.

With respect to the conduct of study, the Charlotteville Commissioners instructed teachers to classify scholars according to branches of study and capacity, and to hear daily spelling lessons. Attendance was to be recorded on a form prescribed by the Commissioners and all the above rules were to be posted in the schoolroom and read to the scholars. Schools with an average attendance of at least fifteen were to receive forty pounds a year, those with twenty, fifty pounds, and those with twenty-five were to receive sixty pounds a year.[13]

Two questions which interested many Commissions concerned the character of religious instruction in the schools and the use of corporal punishment in school government. While many Commissions recommended the daily reading of the scriptures, many at the same time instructed teachers to avoid religious discrimination. 'The teacher is not to make any doctrinal comments to his classes on the scriptures,' wrote the School Commissioners in Fredericksburgh Township.[14] 'No teacher shall be a partisan in religion or politics, neither in the School nor out of it,' ordered the Fitzroy Commissioners, 'nor shall anything Sectarian be taught in said Schools.' All scholars here were 'to be treated with the same kindness and attention' regardless of any 'differences in religion.'[15] The teachers in Smith Township were to 'carefully avoid every kind of annoyance to the children on account of their particular creed.'[16] 'Each Teacher shall be free to prefer what communion he pleases, but no Teacher shall be allowed to make himself a partisan in either religion or politics,' wrote the Commissioners for Pakenham Township.[17]

Many Commissioners attempted to specify the offences for which corporal punishment might be administered, and in some cases as well to minimize or eliminate its use. The visiting Commissioners in the village of Queenston were unusual for their remark that 'the Rod & Reproof give wisdom, but a child left to himself bringeth his parents to Shame,' and for the range of offences for which they recommended the application of physical punishment. These included 'fighting swearing lying...stealing backbiting talebearing tattling... idletalking... calling of nicknames twilling [twitting?]' and 'ridiculing.'[18] Most School Commissions limited the application of physical force to the 'moral offences': 'telling lies maltreating other children or using bad language' in Ekfrid Township; 'lying, swearing, stealing violence, obstinacy, and other serious offences,' in Burgess Township, and 'Disobedience, Lying, Swearing, and ill using one another' in North Sherbrooke Township.[19]

In addition to specifying the occasions for corporal punishment, many Commissions were also concerned to specify the instruments and targets of punishment. In Dumfries, punishment was to be applied in such a manner 'as that no permanent injury can possibly happen to the offender.'[20] In North Sherbrooke Township, only a 'leathern strap or Taws on the open hand' was to be used, and in Fitzroy, only a 'Slender Switch' was permitted.[21] The School Commissioners for Gainsborough Township ordered that 'all corporal punishment shall be inflicted by the rod, to the exclusion of cuffing, pinching, pulling by the ears, or any other barbarous mode.'[22] 'No Schoolar' was to be 'Struck on the head with the hand or whip' in Wellington Township.[23]

Several Township Commissions were concerned to replace physical by moral force as the primary means of school government. These attempts anticipated in a different organizational form part of the progressive thrust of the pedagogy put in place by later School Acts.[24] Corporal punishment was to be severely limited, and the target of pedagogical power was increasingly seen as the 'heart' or 'character' rather than the flesh and the outward forms of behaviour. In Dumfries Township, for instance, the Commissioners wrote that 'no scholar shall be subjected to corporal chastisement but as a matter of last resort.' This was to happen only 'after the case has been investigated and openly declared in School.' Corporal punishment was to be eliminated as a casual means of school government, 'disgrace and not lasting pain or injury being the object sought as a means of amendment.'[25] James Fowler, a teacher in Burgess Township, was urged by his Commissioners to 'stimulate his Scholars to diligence and progressive improvement rather by moral suasion than by corporal punishment.'[26] The teachers in Gosfield Township were instructed to 'govern by persuasion and gentle measures, so far as may be practicable.'[27] Punishments in the Township of Smith were to be 'devoid of cruelty' and on 'no account injurious to modesty or health.' The teachers were not 'on any pretence' to inflict that 'kind of punishment which has a tendency to weaken the sentiment of honor.'[28] This concern was probably addressed to the common practice of beating young students on their bare buttocks, although it may have applied as well to various forms of humilation—such as compelling students to cross-dress—which were also employed.

Some Commissions anticipated many of the regulatory devices with respect to punishment later adopted by the Council of Public Instruction under the School Act of 1850. For instance, punishment registers, generalized under the Act of 1850, were adopted by the Pakenham Commissioners of Common Schools. A teacher named And. Dickson reported that the Commissioners allowed him to punish scholars upon their hands with a piece of leather, but he was required to 'make a note of the punishment, the number of blows given, and the cause of their infliction.' This note was 'to be given to the Commissioners, it being their intention to substitute as soon as possible moral discipline only, for physical correction.'[29] The regulations specified by the Commissioners of Yarmouth Township were particularly detailed. The Commissioners insisted that 'a Person who is a Religious or Political brawler' should not be hired as a school teacher, and also that 'Males and Females' were 'to be taught in the same class.' If the teacher 'sees fit', however, 'the Males and Females shall sit on Separate Benches.' The Commissioners' eighth rule read,

> The punishment to be inflicted by the Teacher should be, First, Reading aloud the rule violated, Secondly, Insertion of the offenders name under the head of Bad Conduct, in a book to be kept for that purpuse, and to be laid before the visiting Commissioner. Thirdly, private and public admonition. Fourthly, detention after School hours. Fifthly, special complaints to be made to the Parents, Guardians or Commissioners. Sixthly, If the rod be necessary, it should only be used in extreme cases, and when inflicted, it should be done with certainty and effect, But all passion, or cruelty in its application ought to be avoided.[30]

Although the School Act of 1841 moved direct control over education away from the local school section in principle, in practice many of the features of local markets in education remained. The school reports for 1842 reveal a considerable local variation in all aspects of educational provision— itself a feature of the market determination of schooling. Teachers, for instance, varied considerably in capacity and experience, in what they were prepared to teach and in what they were able to teach. While there were many teachers relatively incompetent at transmitting the skills of literacy, there were at the same time many others who had been professionally trained, or who were highly educated.[31]

The records for 1842 contain no information about particularly sophisticated female teachers, and District Boards of Education, which were required to categorize teachers according to capacity, uniformly placed women teachers in the lowest administrative category.[32] Few women teachers wrote to the education office directly, while a great many males did do so. This is one reflection of the social subordination of women, especially their absence from the public realm itself. It is also probably related to ongoing debates about the proper gender of teachers, which I shall discuss below. In the patterns of community schooling which prevailed before 1841, women were generally hired in summer to teach young children, while men taught the popular winter schools. Relatively fewer opportunities existed for sophisticated female teachers in the colony as a whole, although urban female academies did exist.

Amongst the male teachers, several were trained in such institutions as the Kildare Place Society, the Royal Observatory and Glasgow Normal School.[33] Itinerance was common. Donald Mac Dermid, for instance, was born in Perthshire, Scotland in 1780 and emigrated to Canada soon after 1800. He taught at Perth, Upper Canada, for three years after his arrival, and then was a school master in Glengarry County for a further four and a half years. He went into the lumber business, but was soon bankrupt, and during the war of 1812 served as Lieutenant of the Glengarry militia. He was wounded at Ogdensburgh and then served with the military commissariat at Coteau du Lac. After the war Mac Dermid secured the position of schoolmaster and postmaster at Coteau du Lac, before returning to Upper Canada in the 1820s with a military pension. When his pension was withdrawn (for unknown reasons) Mac Dermid took a school in Martintown. He taught there for about ten years before moving to another school in Cornwall Township where he remained at least until 1843. In September of that year, Mac Dermid criticized the School Act of 1841.

> A number of Teachers in this District, frequently correspond with me, and complain bitterly, of their situation, asking how, or when, are they to be bettered in pecuniary matters, and in Books for their Schools.[34]

While Mac Dermid moved frequently during the course of his teaching life, other teachers remained for much longer periods in one place. William M. Edward wrote in 1842 that he had taught the village school in Lancaster 'during the last 18 years, without intermission.'[35]

Several teachers provided detailed accounts both of method and of curriculum content in their schools. Among the more sophisticated was a teacher named George Elmslie, who in 1842 was teaching at Bon Accord in Nichol Township. Elmslie (1803-1869) was born in Aberdeen, Scotland and received a college education, after which he worked as a dry goods merchant. In Canada, he found pioneer farming overly laborious and turned to teaching, holding his first school in his house, and later in a school house he built on his farm. In addition to the school at Bon Accord, Elmslie also taught in Elora, Ancaster, Guelph, Hamilton and Alma, where he died of a stroke.

In November 1842, Elmslie wrote at length to the education office, describing both his school and the method whereby he conducted it. He claimed to have taught at Bon Accord for four years, and to have thirty-five scholars in four classes. Elmslie wrote,

> It will be seen that the System of Education followed in the School is that which was first practised & brought to perfection in the great Sessional School Edinburgh, usually termed 'Intellectual' ---the fundamental principles of which are, that the scholar from the moment he begins to learn the simplest lesson shall be made to understand it--- the employment of Monitors--- and free scope allowed to emulation. Its advantages are manifold--- the scholar is at once deeply interested in his tasks--- he daily amasses a store of useful knowledge--- the reasoning faculty, by hourly exercise is strengthened & enlarged--- lessons of religion and morality are

more deeply impressed on his mind, & his progress is vastly more rapid than under the old system....In the more recently settled Townships it is often exceedingly difficult if not impossible, to obtain a supply of Books sufficient to instruct a class by the ordinary method--- in the Sessional School, in teaching these branches [English Grammar and Geography] no Books are used.[36]

Walter Thomson of Raleigh Township gave a much more ordinary account, and one which probably approximates what most teachers were doing in Canada West as a whole. He used Mavor's *English Spelling Book,* Murray's *English Reader,* Walkingame's *Arithmetic,* and Walker's *Pronouncing Dictionary* along with the New Testament as class books. He described the school day in this way:

1st Class--read in the Testament twice each day
' ' ' ' English Reader ' ' '
Exercises in Spelling ' ' '
On Saturdays---revise the Tables which they have committed to memory from the Spelling book & Arithmetick---
2nd Class---read in the English reader four times each day
Exercises in Spelling twice each day
On Monday repeat the tables from Spelling Book
3d Class--read in the Spelling book four times each day
Exercises in spelling twice each day
4 Class ---Spelling on the book four times each day
Exercises in spelling once each day
5 Class--learning the alphabet

Thomson added, 'the first class consists of six which I mean to form into a grammar class as soon as books can be procured--- I presume Murray's Grammar will meet your wishes. I do not think I shall have any class for Geography this year.'[37] Like most active teachers, Thomson actually engaged his students directly for only a small portion of the time they were in school. For state school reformers, this was seen as 'inefficiency.'

The town of Picton was said by Luke Wallis, the President of its Board of Police, to contain 288 people between the ages of 5 and 16 in 1842. Wallis claimed that the Board of Police had not divided the town into school districts, because it was too small, and parents in consequence sent their children to whatever school they chose. Five different schools from Picton sent reports to the Assistant Superintendent for 1842, and these reveal that schooling here was sharply divided along lines of gender, and perhaps of class as well. Louisa Ingersoll's trustees testified that she had 'faithfully and punctually demeaned herself as a Teacher' during the period January 1842 to January 1843. Ingersoll had 45 girls on her class list, 25 of whom were under sixteen. Sarah Mitchell taught elementary subjects to 28 girls, and Eliza Bradford taught elementary subjects and 'needlework' to 25 girls and 3 boys. Ahira H. Blake, Secretary to the Prince Edward District Common School Teachers' Association, wrote two contradictory accounts of his Picton school in 1842. In the first, he claimed to have had 104 different scholars on his class list, with an average attendance of 56 from January to October. In a second account, certified by his trustees, Blake reported a total of 148 students on the roll, with an average attendance of 90. Of these 148, there were 37 females and 111 males. The fifth school held in Picton in 1842 was John O'Donnele's classical school, where sixty students--forty of them male--- learned elementary subjects and Latin and Greek.[38]

## Poverty and the Debate over Female Teachers

Most teachers claimed that the Act of 1841 led to a direct decline in their average incomes. Thomas Smyth wrote that teachers in his neighbourhood were generally paid 'a miserable and uncertain issue of agricultural produce.' His own share of the provincial school fund for a year's effort was nine pounds ten shillings and threepence, less than he regularly earned under the Act of 1816.[39] 'Under the old system,' wrote Edward Lane of Brockville, 'the Teachers were engaged by the public at a certain monthly rate of wages, averaging about 12 dollars per month...say 36 pounds per annum--- Board Lodging & Washing found them worth 20 pounds---- Government allowance averaging 10 pounds--- making a total of 66 pounds.' However, under the Act of 1841, the grant and fees together would give only 43 pounds a year for a school with 25 students, and a day labourer was making 2/6 to 4/ a day, or on average 50 pounds a year.[40] A teacher in Vaughan Township claimed he taught for six months without being paid, and then earned a total of eight pounds, seven shillings and eight pence after paying his board and lodging, for nine months' work. This was less than under the Act of 1816.[41]

When some local school administrators discovered how small their share of the school grant was to be, they renegotiated the agreements they had made with teachers. Samuel Goshe, who taught in Drummond Township, claimed that he had initially been hired for 28 pounds, with 'Board and every other accomodation.' The local school supporters then decided to pay him the school grant and a matching grant raised by taxation, which produced a total of fifteen pounds. 'And then,' Goshe continued, I would have to 'pay my Board out of that pecuniary Trifle, which would leave me with seven pounds ten.'[42] 'Language was inadequate, to lay before you the distressful condition of many of the Teachers families,' wrote Thomas Graffe, on behalf of the Brockville School Teachers' Society. 'Many of them have not the necessary means of procuring Bread for the present year.' The teachers were unable to 'get employment from farmers as labourers' because they were not 'accustomed to labour' and because 'the farmer can employ ablebodied men who are adequate to perform any labour they may wish to set them about.' In consequence, the position of teachers was one in which 'to abandon School keeping they see poverty before them, and to continue it they have poverty staring them in the face.'[43] The Assistant Superintendent wrote that 'in one case which came under my own personal observation the Teacher actually died from the effects of starvation.'[44]

Town and country teachers respectively attempted to claim unequal shares of the state school fund in this situation. When Wm. H. McGuire heard that the town teachers in Brockville were agitating for a larger share in the school fund, he wrote to defend the claims of the country teacher. 'The schools in Towns, in point of numbers,' he wrote, 'are twice, or thrice as large as Country Schools; and in the next place, Teachers in Towns receive half as much more for tuition. Furthermore, 'when it is considered, how much more comfortable a Town Teachers can be, than one in the Country; —the latter having to tramp thro' mud and mire in the spring and fall —ploughing kneedeep thro' Snow in Winter, often two miles & upwards —sleeping here tonight; there tomorrow night— sometimes warm, sometimes cold, and oftimes hungry—— and all for eight, or ten dollars p month —I think it is pretty plain, who has the best of the bargain.' The town teacher could regularly get 40 to 50 scholars, according to McGuire, 'and in most cases his wife has 20 more.'[45]

However, a teacher from Cobourg urged the Assistant Superintendent to 'take into consideration that the Teachers of Cobourg labour under great disadvantages, such as paying House Rent and Taxes, and providing Fuel and provisions.' 'Country Teachers,' on the other hand had 'no House Rent to pay, no Taxes to pay, no Fuel to provide that costs them more than a mere trifle; and indeed they may procure provisions by raising Potatoes Wheat and Pork etc.' As a town teacher, this correspondent noted that he had 'the mortification of seeing exposed to my view and offered for Sale here in our Streets, good and cheap Provisions and Clothing; without being able to procure either a Barrel of Flour or an article of Clothing.' 'Now pray Rev. Sir,' he concluded, 'is not this a most distressing Situation for a respectable Schoolmaster to be in.'[46]

In this situation, a common reaction of male teachers was to form associations with other male teachers to attempt to exclude women from public funding. School masters' associations sprung up in various parts of the colony, particularly where District Councils were hesitant about carrying the provisions of the Act of 1841 into operation. These associations aimed at mutual improvement and self-education for their members. Ahira H. Blake, the Secretary of the Prince Edward District Common School Teachers' Association, claimed that his Association's members joined together in 1842 in a serious effort at self-improvement. They worked hard during the winter of 1842-3 to raise their educational qualifications and were making good progress. However, since 'the same amount of money was paid last winter to female schools as to males the number of female teachers has more than doubled.' This meant that an increasing number of male teachers were unemployed either entirely or during the summer months, and if 'employed again for the winter their task will be rendered doubly laborious in having to erase the false instruction imparted through the summer.' Not only were female teachers incompetent, in Blake's view, but the Commissioners never bothered to examine them. If the employment of women teachers continued, Blake feared that male 'Teachers will not be obtained for Winter Schools our Association designed and highly calculated to promote the best interests of Schools will become extinct, and we will see our prospects more deplorable than before.'[47]

W.H. McGuire, whom we have seen above defending the country teacher, complained in 1843 that the 'manner in which the sum for 1842 was distributed, was anything but satisfactory, to a great portion of the Teachers' in his district. 'To the detriment of old & capable Teachers,' he claimed, the grant had been shared with 'Great numbers of Females (mostly American) and boys.' 'The truth is,' he continued, 'if a Dog had sent in a Certificate, I believe he would have received a share.'[48] John Brown of Binbrook village wrote to the education office demanding to know if School Commissioners could 'appoint a female to be teacher in a School District which is nothing like being qualified; who according to her own confession can go [no] further in figures than the Simple Rule of Three; in all probability not proficient in that Rule, who possesses no qualification only that of a Seamstress.' He demanded 'is it not contrary to the School act to recognize Female Teachers: —and should not this Female be paid by her employers alone.'[49] R.R. Mackie expressed the sentiments of many male teachers in claiming that 'it cannot be expected that competent [read male] Teachers can, or will be obtained since for a very trifling consideration Females, having no pretensions to Education have the chearge of Schools.'[50]

Women did not often respond directly to these charges, at least not in correspondence with public educational officials. As men spoke against women teachers' educational interests, other men spoke for them. John Flood of Richmond claimed that there were two female schools in the Township of Goulbourn and in them the 'scholars were taught as well as any others in the Township, and if they had not been appointed by Commissioners to these schools, the schools would not have been in operation, for no other teachers could be obtained.' Flood added that these female teachers had received 'very little indeed for their time & labour.' They were 'in distress' and a 'share of the Government money would be to them a great relief.'[51] The official charged with distributing the state school fund in the town of Hamilton wondered if he should 'consider female teachers as entitled to a proportion----It so happens that more than half of the children of the Town are under the tuition of female teachers. It appears to me in justice they are entitled to it.'[52] Agnes Kirkland confronted the Assistant Superintendent of Education directly and presented him with a letter from the Rev. J. Flanagan of Binbrook, attesting to her high moral character. Flanagan wrote that he was 'not aware that the act recognizes Female Teachers at all, but in case it does, and that any distribution of money be made to such, I respectfully suggest that she be entitled to her share.'[53]

This debate is interesting in several respects. It is perhaps the first instance in Canada West of the public participation of women being addressed at length by a state agency, and the debate over women teachers raised the issue of women's legal status as well, since as several people pointed out, the School Act of 1841 employed the masculine pronoun throughout. Administratively, the debate pointed out the limitations of the office of Assistant Superintendent of Education since that officer could not intervene here to formulate policy. Robert Murray, the officer in question, was compelled to appeal to the Secretary General, and to 'justice' in the abstract until that official ruled on the question.

Initially, Murray took an ambiguous position on the issue. He pointed out to his urban correspondents that since no town in Canada West had appointed teachers according to the regulations of the School Act in the year 1842, all teachers who had kept a common school were equally eligible to share in the school fund. However, Murray argued that it was town Boards of Police and City Councils which could determine precisely what a 'common school' in fact was. If the Board of Police in Picton, for example, decided that the women teachers of the town were not in fact keeping common schools, it was not necessary for the Board to pay them.[54] In February of 1843, Murray added to a member of the Hamilton Board of Police that 'the School Bill does not expressly exclude female Teachers.'[55] However, by June of 1843, Murray wrote to the Rev. William Reid of Grafton that 'the School Commissioners have in very many cases all over Canada West appointed female Teachers whenever they judged it prudent to do so....The Executive have recognised this interpretation by admitting female Teachers to receive their proportion of the School fund.'[56] His opinion with respect to the legitimacy of supporting female teachers, he said, was strengthened 'by finding that it is in accordance with the views of nearly all the members of the Legislature.' 'I believe the Corporation in Kingston have divided the Town into four School Districts and intend to appoint a male and a female Teacher in each School District, of which I very much approve.'[57]

In the countryside, where the practice of hiring female teachers for summer schools and male teachers for winter schools remained general, Murray's position generated substantial resistance. The School Act of 1841 challenged this practice by making no mention of different kinds of elementary schools, and by allowing women to be paid under the same conditions (if not at the same rate) as men. Murray argued that female teachers could share in the school fund, but that to do so they must come under the authority of School Commissioners. Nothing in the School Act deprived female teachers 'of any privilege which they previously possessed.' However, 'Commissioners are at liberty to judge of their qualifications, and appoint them the same as males.' Since the Act gave 'no discretionary power to the Commissioners regarding' female teachers, they must be hired 'on the same terms, and with the same rights and privileges as Male teachers.'[58] This position called into question the popular and common rural practice of hiring male teachers to teach older and more advanced students in winter schools, and female teachers to teach beginning students in summer schools. The female teachers were expected to be less qualified in formal terms than the male, and were paid considerably less as well. Of course, this practice made the formation of a professional teaching corps impossible. Few teachers either male or female could earn enough thereby to live entirely by teaching, and teaching could not exist as an entirely distinct branch of the social division of labour. The imposition by the educational Commissioners of a common standard of qualifications tended to undermine this organization of teaching, and it also tended to define school teaching as a separate occupation. This in turn provoke a conflict over which of the two prevailing kinds of schools, and which of the two genders of teachers, would be supported by government monies.

## Disciplining the Educational Market

As I shall argue at more length below, Assistant Superintendent Murray was particularly interested in 'elevating the station' of the school teacher in Canada West. The School Act of 1841 worked a major transformation on the social organization of teaching, or at least attempted to do so. For the first time, the more or less free market in schooling was disciplined by a logic of public administration. One of the consequences of this was a change in the conditions for the distribution of schools in town and country. The Act specified that either District Councils or urban councils were to divide their respective jurisdictions into school districts, and that only one school in each of these districts would be supported as the public school. In the towns, this led to a sharp reduction in the numbers of schools which could be funded, and in the countryside, it led to a rapid multiplication of such schools with a subsequent decline in teachers' salaries.

Administratively, the Act of 1841 situated the office of teacher in a public bureau. The Act envisaged the superimposition of an educational administrative grid upon the colony as a whole, and only one teacher was to exist as the official state teacher in any cell of the administrative grid. While 'the people are at perfect liberty to appoint as many Teachers in a School District as they may see cause, they cannot claim any of the public monies for their Support.'[59] The central education office in Canada West repeatedly reaffirmed the public character of the teacher's office and the right of tenure of teachers except for bureaucratically specified misdemeanours. Murray insisted that Commissioners of Common Schools could remove teachers from their position only 'for immorality or inattention.' Where these reasons for dismissal did not exist, 'the School with its emoluments constitute the Teachers legal inheritance.'[60] The Assistant Superintendent repeatedly compared the teacher's office to the landholder's land. 'Your school was your estate,' he wrote to William Poole of Carleton Place, 'your title was the sanction of the Commissioners.'[61] Similarly, the share a teacher had in the school fund was regarded by the education office as that teacher's alienable property.[62] As we shall see, this strategic disposition of 'official' teachers provoked persistent conflict over the question of teachers' practical loyalties.

The official historian of education in Canada West claimed that the demise of the School Act of 1841 was largely due to the criticism directed against it by the Education Commitee of the Home District Council. The Committee, chaired by J.W. Gamble, a Tory lawyer and lumber manufacturer, criticized the Act as 'objectionable in principle, complicated in detail, and altogether inefficient for the desired object.' The Committee complained that the existence of waste land in most townships made it technically impossible to site schools according to any uniform geographic model, and the Act outlawed the union schools which crossed township limits. To finance the schools, the District treasurer would be compelled to maintain at least four hundred separate school accounts, which was difficult and laborious. The Committee also opposed the office of Commissioner of Common Schools. 'The giving of the whole control of these Schools to the Commissioners, without laying down any uniform system of proceeding for their guidance is open to serious objections.' The Act was said to be incapable of producing any educational improvement because 'it neither provides a supply of educated men for teachers, a uniform system of education, nor adequate means for the support of the Schools.' The Act led to a multiplication of schools to the point where the total funds available for each teacher would average only twenty-two pounds and ten shillings a year. The Committee suggested that at most the Act would have allowed for the support of twenty schools in a Township. There were often twenty-six. All of this was exacerbated for teachers by the fact that the government money for 1842 was paid only in 1843.[63]

Few participants in elementary educational organization were content with the operation of the School Act of 1841, yet criticism of the Act and suggestions for its reform varied. While many correspondents to the education office urged some measure of 'public' education, there was certainly no consensus even amongst these correspondents. In addition, little record exists of what the majority of local school supporters sought in the way of educational reorganization.

However, we do know what many male teachers thought about the Act. Henry Lively, a teacher from Simcoe, wrote to Robert Murray twice with detailed criticism of existing educational organization and with suggestions for educational reconstruction.

Lively was especially critical of the elected School Commissioners, who he claimed were incompetent because of their illiteracy and corruption. 'The teachers stand on slippery ground,' he wrote, 'their situation is very precarious.' Good teachers were turned out of their schools by Commissioners who sought to hire their own friends and relatives, and the Commissioners were prepared to pay women as much as men. Lively claimed the best school in his district had been given to the brother of one of the Commissioners, the second best to the daughter of a Commissioner, and the school in Port Dover to the wife of one of the Commissioners. 'She sat for months with only 3 or 4 children in the school, boasted of making a shirt a day for hire during school hours, her number did not average more than ten, yet she made her Time account of attendances to 25, and so was paid the highest premium.' Another school in the neighbourhood was 'taught during the whole of last year by one of the Com'rs. He attended about ten oclock in the morning, and dismissed about half past two or three o'clock in the evening. His farm was near and his wife occasionally taught whilst he was at work in the fields.'

Lively complained that the common practice of making the teacher collect the fees or 'rate bill' levied on parents was obnoxious, 'for the teacher has to dun the farmer two, three, or four times a month, every month in the year.' Farmers only had money in the period from November to February, and this system of collection generated bad feeling. The existing system was so uncertain, that teachers were 'changing places oftener than a turnpike-gate-keeper.' A teacher 'dare not take a house or buy a cow, for he knows not but he may be dismissed before the end of the week.' Lively suggested that all people under the age of 21 and all women be excluded from teaching. Teachers should be made permanent after a qualifying examination before a competent board. The office of School Commissioner should be abolished, with the placement of 'their duties in respectable hands.'[64]

Male teachers' organizations agitated for teachers' control over key aspects of educational administration. Robert Spence, editor of the Reform Dundas *Warder*, wrote that teachers in the vicinity of Hamilton had been collectively managing their own affairs since 1838. Half a dozen schools had been regularly inspected and lectured to by Mr. [Patrick?] Thornton on a voluntary basis, and these schools were 'far from being the least in character of their teachers.' The teachers suggested that this system should be extended. They were not opposed to Commissioners exerting most of the powers accorded them by the Act of 1841, and they had no desire to be 'mixed up in fiscal arrangements,' which they thought best managed by District Councils. However, 'as teachers alone can give effect, to any system of education, they and they alone, should regulate the course of study to be adopted, the books to be used, and the various means to be applied, in order to promote the advancement of common school training on a uniform and efficient plan.' Teachers, in this scheme, would control curriculum and pedagogy within a system organized around Boards of Education composed of experienced teachers elected annually by property holders. Each Board of Education would establish a District Model School and appoint a master to it, who in turn would also serve as District School Inspector. Elected School Commissioners would arrange school finance, choose locations for schools, and so forth.[65]

A very similar plan was urged by the teachers of the Brock District. These teachers sought to have the taxation clauses in the School Act made mandatory, rather than optional. They suggested the establishment of a District Model or Normal School, or, failing that, the obligatory attendance of all teachers at some training school for one month of the year. They were especially insistent that teachers and not School Commissioners control the 'internal organization of schools.' They saw the 'formation of District Boards of Education' as an 'indispensable step towards' educational uniformity. These Boards should 'be composed in whole or at least in part, of practical teachers who shall have the privilege of composing rules...and also of examining and certifying teachers found qualified.' Among their other concerns were the exclusion of female teachers from equal pay in order to relieve school*masters* of 'a mortified feeling of degradation, very injurious to the beneficial exercise of their calling.' Americans were to be excluded from teaching, each school should provide a dwelling for the teacher, a fund for schoolbooks should be established, and finally, 'the Scriptures be required to be used as a class book in every school situated amongst a Protestant community.'[66]

A group of teachers in Sidney Township argued for the creation of a career line in the occupation.

In all other occupations in this Country a great

> probability exists by common prudence and industry of rising in it---the Clerk may become the Merchant, the journeyman the Master--- the farm servant the landed proprietor but the School Master remains always the same....The well trained disciplined School Master regarding the pursuit as his regular dependence is almost unknown and will continue so until some adequate provision is made for his support and the standard of qualifications is so regulated as to ensure him respect from the possession of the requisite talents.

This was to be done through the creation of pay categories for teachers and the creation of a Board of Appeal for fired teachers.[67]

Teachers were particularly critical of the office of Commissioner of Common Schools. D.R. Macleod wrote that 'the C.S. commissioners elected are not qualified to examine teachers,' and urged that teachers be 'examined by the Superintendent or by a board of examiners appointed by him.'[68] Johnston Neilson of Carleton Place claimed that annual elections produced illiterate School Commissioners and encouraged educational discontinuity. Nielson suggested that District wardens should assemble all resident doctors, lawyers and clergymen and make them a District Board of Education.[69] Patrick Wood, who had been trained by the Irish Kildare Place Society, urged central control and supervision of the educational system, and the direct payment of teachers by the state.[70] Robert Mowbray of Aldborough Township proposed that school teachers be made parish officers on the Scottish model, and be paid to keep records, register marriages, and so forth. He proposed a regular teacher's salary of at least 65 pounds a year.[71] The School Commissioners near Markham were held by one teacher to be so incompetent---refusing to visit the school or to supply it with fuel---that the teacher considered suing them.[72]

While some Commissioners of Common Schools were themselves critical of their office, there was certainly no popular consensus as to the means for educational reorganization. Nor were centralized state control or professional teacher's control the only alternatives elaborated. The Commissioners for Gainsborough Township argued that their duties should be limited to the examination of teachers. The Humberstone Commissioners argued that school fees should be set and collected by trustees elected in each school district [i.e.

section], and the Wainfleet Commissioners urged the abolition of both Commissioners and Superintendents and their replacement by elected school section trustees. A return to the *status quo ante* was suggested by many commentators on the Act of 1841.[73]

Gidney and Lawr point out that before the Act of 1841 'all the powers required to administer individual schools were already vested in locally elected trustees. If a system was to be imposed, many of these powers would have to be removed to, or at least shared by, other administrative authorities.'[74] The Act of 1841 aimed precisely to redistribute powers of educational management away from the locality, but local educational control retained its vocal partisans. A person named J. McDonald wrote at length to R.S Jameson, the (titular) Superintendent of Education for Canada, that the key weakness of the Act of 1841 was its abolition of elected local trustees. He stated,

> The trustees were always chosen as the most intelligent men in each School District among them are to be found men of as good intelligence, abilities, and Education, as are to be found in the Townships.... They are better acquainted with the wants of the respective schools to which they belong than the commissioners can be supposed to be, and more interested in their well doing. They have also the advantage of being better acquainted with all the common School Teachers, as to character and education, and consequently better able to Judge of them that are best qualified amongst them.

McDonald added that the 'present Teachers' were entirely 'able to supply the present wants of the common Schools,' that is, if they were 'fairly dealt with' and if 'country female Teacher be excluded.'[75] The Clerk of the Wellington District wrote to Robert Murray that while he personally opposed a return to the system of local trustee management, 'I see a great increasing desire to do so in this District.'[76]

But while elected trustees may well have been the most intelligent local residents, they were still considered incapable by many 'respectable' educational observers, and it was these observers whose views approximated those of educational administrators, with whom in any case they were frequently acquainted. Dr. Craigie of the Ancaster Academy, a personal friend of Robert Murray, whose opinions had been solicited by the Education Commission of 1839, held this view. Craigie opposed the principle of election for school officials, because 'able' men could not be chosen in this way. When 'some well meaning person' at the annual schoolmeeting in Ancaster 'proposed one of our clergymen as a Commissioner,' he wrote, 'a general shout of 'No priest craft' shewed the wisdom of their Royal Highnesses the sovereign people.' Craigie ranted against the dangers of democracy at length.[77]

## The Assistant Superintendent and the School Act of 1841

The views of the Assistant Superintendent on the School Act of 1841 are visible in his Annual Report for 1842 and in his correspondence with groups and individuals in the colony on a range of issues. Robert Murray frequently stressed the political importance of sound educational organization in Canada West. In assuring the members of the Johnstown School Society that his 'greatest earthly ambition' was 'to make Teachers respectable, efficient, & independent,' Murray emphasized that 'much of the civil & religious peace and prosperity of this great country must depend on the education of the young.' Everything done to improve the condition of teachers would tend 'directly to advance...the best interests both civil & religious of this Province.'[78] Education was particularly important in securing the interests of property.

> No man possessed of property in this Province, who would attend for a little to the state of ignorance which pervades the great mass of the many thousands who are annually settling among us, & the ignorance in which our native youth are growing up around us could hesitate for a moment to pay any reasonable tax for the support of education, as he would thereby be increasing the value of his estate, & securing himself & his posterity in possession of it.[79]

In contrast to his successor in office, Murray was remarkable for the encouragement he offered male teachers in their early efforts at professional self-regulation. Under Murray, teaching was conceived much more as a self-regulating profession than as the *corps d'etat* it became under Ryerson. Murray described the suggestion of the Brock District teachers that they should control curriculum and pedagogy as 'reasonable and valuable' and promised to lay it before the executive.[80] He told the Johnstown District teachers that he hoped teachers in all municipal districts would form teachers' societies as a means of close communication with the education office.[81] To teachers in the Gore District he wrote that he 'would be happy to see Teachers invested with the power of judging of the qualifications of those who are to be admitted as Members of their body.' Such powers would 'lead directly to the respectability and usefulness' of teachers as a whole, and Murray promised to 'lay the subject before the Government with some arguments in its favor.'[82]

Murray's position nonetheless meant breaking community control over teachers and meant the separation of teaching from other branches of the division of labour. Murray presented this position quite explicitly in his Annual Report for 1842. Teachers on the whole were reasonably moral and respectable. However, they were rendered incapable of educating the people by their economic and social dependence upon the local community. In this regard their situation was 'most unpropitious.' Their habit of 'boarding for a few days at a time' with the families of their employers meant that 'their minds have become dissipated' and they had no opportunity for 'private study.' If they did not 'board around', their incomes were so low that they were compelled to stay 'in the lowest taverns, and consequently to associate with the lowest and most dissipated characters in the neighbourhood.' 'By this daily intercourse with barroom politicians, and bar-room divines,' teachers were 'insensibly... assimilated to them in their manners, views and habits, and [were] thus rendered utterly disqualified for conducting the education of youth.' For Murray sound education meant 'improving' the dissipated local population, by substituting respectable politics and divinity for the barroom politics and divinity found in the locality. Only teachers who were independent of the community could perform this function. As Murray put it, 'whatever is adverse to the comfort and respectability of Teachers stands directly opposed to the education of youth, and consequently to the power of the Civil Government, and the moral respectability of the people.' Still, Murray argued that teachers generally were in need of Normal School training. Many of them had only 'a very limited education' and this was obtained in schools 'where none of the modern improvements in education had been introduced.' Teachers were thus often unable 'either to communicate instruction, or to exercise discipline to the best advantage.' During his educational tour of 1842, Murray himself attempted to provide some normal training.[83]

In addition to his concerns with teaching as a means of increasing the power of government, and with situating teachers as public officers in an administrative grid, Murray was also interested in the nature of school knowledge. He saw the schools as particularly deficient in this regard. Books were in short supply and of poor quality, and a shortcoming of the School Act in Murray's view was the lack of power it accorded him in this area. Not only did he have 'no legal power to appoint books,' but also he was 'not aware of any in use at present in the Province' which he would have found himself 'at liberty to recommend.' This was not because there were no 'good books, but there is no system of books in use here, besides they are miserably got up, & double the price at which they might be sold under a general Provincial System.'[84] The problem for Murray was a lack of central control over school knowledge. 'The power is so divided in the hands of those who hold it,' he wrote to Patrick Thornton, 'that it cannot be made available to the advancement of any great Provincial Scheme.' The effectiveness of education as political socialization was undercut by local power over the curriculum. Murray noted 'there is in certain quarters a deep rooted jealousy' against centralized control over the content of education, but he was 'thoroughly convinced that unless the appointment of School Books is committed to the Superintendent, more than half of his usefulness will be lost to the public.'[85]

Murray was again remarkable in contrast to his successor, in his insistence on the use of the Bible and Testament as class books. Most school reports for 1842 suggest that these books were very widely used,[86] but opposition to them existed in some quarters. John Treffey, a School Commissioner in Norwich Township, communicated with Murray on this matter. Treffey claimed that when he suggested to his fellow Commissioners that they prescribe the use of the Testament in schools he 'was strongly opposed by all present but one, who appeared indifferent about it.' His opponents argued that such a use for the Testament would be 'the means of teaching the youth to take the sacred Name in a vain Manner & also to Swear, & dislike it on account of being made to labour in it when learning to read.'[87] Murray replied that he could 'see no valid objection to the use of the New Testament in every Protestant School.' The argument that its use might teach young people to take the sacred name in vain could equally be used to stop all 'public & private exercise of religion,' and if students were made to labour in learning to read, the fault lay with their teachers, not with the Testament.[88]

In his Annual Report for 1842, Murray also attacked the control exerted over educational organization by elected School Commissioners. The Act, he noted, required him to encourage educational uniformity in the colony, but gave him no means to do so. As long as Commissioners had 'full power to determine the qualifications of Teachers, the course of study, the books to be used in their respective Townships, and the general rules for the management of schools, all hope of establishing any uniform system of education is utterly in vain.' As things stood, 'more than three hundred different systems of education might be in operation in Canada West.' In order to 'bring about a result so desirable' as educational uniformity, a person of 'judgment and discretion' was needed, and 'his hands should be strengthened by the strong arm of the law.'[89] When revisions to the School Act of 1841 were undertaken by the legislature in 1843, Murray expected the new act to address the matter of uniform schoolbooks.[90] However, the School Act of 1843 did not speak to Murray's concerns. Murray wrote to his friend Dr. Craigie on the day of its passage that he did not 'consider it my duty to express any opinion of the provisions of the Bill, no credit is due to me in the matter, they who are interested therein owe the whole, with one or two slight alterations to the late administration.'[91]

## The School Act of 1843 and Responsible Government

During the winter of 1841-2 the efforts of Reformers to create a uniform party came to fruition. The Reform party was founded on an alliance of diverse interests over the question of responsible government. While Sydenham was able to manipulate an Assembly in which party affiliation was only slightly developed, his successor as Governor-General, Sir Charles Bagot, confronted a situation in which he was forced to choose between a majority Reform party and a small minority conservative party. The majority of the Assembly was increasingly opposed to the Draper-Harrison ministry formed by Sydenham. Compact Tories opposed its liberal bent, French Canadian members opposed its chauvinism and the bulk of the Reformers had abandoned it because of its failure to actively support their version of responsible government. Faced with this parliamentary situation, and in direct contravention of his official instructions, Bagot admitted the two leading Reformers, Robert Baldwin and L.-H. Lafontaine, into the ministry. These two joined the moderate Reformer Francis Hincks, who had accepted the position of Inspector-General (finance minister) earlier in 1842.

In fact, Bagot's concessions to responsible government were slight, and the Colonial Office agreed after the fact that he had had no choice but to act as he did. His only real concession was to admit some French members into cabinet. He retained the power of the executive intact.[92] However, the inclusion of Baldwin and Lafontaine in the ministry hardened party lines and placed members of the Tory party in a particularly ambiguous position. Tories had consistently presented themselves as the party of loyalty and had supported the Governor as the champion of good non-factional government. Bagot, however, seemed to be rewarding the rebels of 1837 and to be pursuing a dangerously republican course. As the old compact Tory J.S. Cartwright wrote to Bagot in 1842,

> On the question of Responsible Government I have already explained to your Excellency my views of its dangerous tendency; and the more I reflect upon it the more I feel convinced of its incompatibility with our position as a colony---particularly in a country where almost universal suffrage prevails; where the great mass of the people are uneducated, and where there is little of that salutary influence which hereditary rank and great wealth exercise in Great Britain.[93]

This opinion seems to have been shared by the Colonial Office, and

Bagot was recalled in mid-1843.

A new school bill was drafted by the Baldwin-Lafontaine ministry and guided through the Assembly by Francis Hincks. We know little of the bill's origins in detail. It seems to have had the support of the Assembly generally; at least most members agreed that major amendments to the Act of 1841 were necessary and the Act was passed even after the resignation of the Baldwin-Lafontaine ministry.

The School Act of 1843 attempted to overcome the administrative confusion provoked by the Act of 1841, and was responsive to the kinds of concerns articulated by teachers' organizations.[94] The Act applied only to Canada West, and from this period the educational history of Canada West again diverged from that of Canada East. The Act also abolished the office of Township School Commissioner, and increased the powers of the central education office.

Under the Act, educational organization was to be coordinated by an appointed Assistant Superintendent of Common Schools. Acting under the nominal direction of the Chief Superintendent of Common Schools for both the Canadas, this official was to prepare the forms of educational information-gathering and reporting, and was to instruct other educational officers in such measures as he deemed 'necessary and proper for the better Organization and Government of Common Schools.' However, the Assistant Superintendent had limited powers of enforcement in these matters. While he could withhold educational funds from areas which refused to tax for school purposes, or which did not deliver adequate reports, lower level officials in the system were not appointed by and could not be removed by him. Nonetheless, the Chief Superintendent gave the Assistant Superintendent (Robert Murray) broad administrative discretion, and at the same time, educational correspondence increasingly was directed to the education office itself.[95]

The Act envisaged two levels of educational administrative regulation. At the township and city or town level, superintendents of common schools appointed by municipal councils were created. These officers were to manage local educational monies, to visit schools regularly and to examine and certify candidates for teaching. They were also empowered to annul teachers' certificates with cause. However, because the municipal bill of 1843 on which the operation of these officials was also dependent failed to become law, their role in educational administration in the period was slight.

County or district superintendents played a more central role. These officers were appointed by the district councils and were to hold office during pleasure.[96] They were salaried officials and they were compelled to post a performance bond before entering office. County superintendents were to examine all prospective teachers with respect to 'moral character, learning and ability.' They could grant teaching certificates valid either throughout the county or limited to a particular area. The Act also empowered them to re-examine practicing teachers when they saw fit. While township, town and city superintendents were charged with the routine administrative work of educational management, county superintendents were clearly intended to function as morally forceful educational inspectors. They were charged with visiting all district schools at least once a year, and in the course of these visits, they were to 'examine into the state and condition of the Schools, both as respects the progress of the scholars in learning, and the good order of the Schools.' They were also instructed to give 'advice and direction to the Trustees and Teachers as to the government' of their schools and as to 'the course of studies to be pursued therein.'

The administration of the Act of 1843 produced a marked shift in the relations of knowledge/power between the central authority and local schools. The volume of educational 'intelligence' increased substantially, and was increasingly concentrated in the central office. At the same time, the quality of educational 'intelligence' changed. The central office increasingly had a corps of paid and 'respectable' educational investigators in the field. While many teachers and other local educational participants continued to correspond with the central office, their conceptions of and interests in educational organization could, from 1843, be counterposed by central administrators to those of respectable men of character. This altered the class nature of educational intelligence.

As we have seen, to Robert Murray's disgust, the Act did not grant the Assistant Superintendent effective control over pedagogy or curriculum. The Act recreated the three elected trustees of common schools in each local school unit, and in addition to keeping the schoolhouse, calculating local school rate bills and arranging for their collection, and exempting indigent persons from payment of school taxes, these officials were 'to regulate ... the course of study, and the books to be used.' This was 'subject, nevertheless, to the approval of the Township, Town, or City Superintendent,' but in practice, local trustees, teachers and school supporters controlled curriculum and pedagogy.

The Act also increased the public funds available to local schools. The receipt of the state school fund in any locality was dependent upon the raising of matching funds by municipal councils, and these were now permitted to tax to raise as much as double the state fund. Schools needed to be open only for three months to be eligible for the school fund, union schools were permitted and city or town councils were permitted to establish free schools (that is, schools supported entirely out of property taxation).

The Act spoke directly to the concerns of many teachers' organizations by allowing for the creation of District Model Schools. District Councils could raise two hundred pounds by taxation for this purpose, provided that they would raise at least an additional forty pounds each year for the payment of a model school teacher and for furnishing the school. The Act provided for the granting of matching funds for these local efforts. The trustees of Model Schools were to be strictly supervised by the county superintendent in all matters, and the Model Schools were to offer free instruction to all county teachers who sought it. Similar provisions existed for the creation of town, township, or city model schools.

Again, the Act attempted to address the problems of payment which so irritated teachers under the Act of 1841. Trustees were to determine the amount of parents' contributions to teachers in the form of Rate Bills, and could exempt indigent parents. Trustees could then appoint collectors to secure payment of the rate bill, and the Act gave them the power to distrain the property of defaulters. Parents or guardians were still enabled to pay the teacher directly if they wished. Trustees were also to arrange for the heating of the schools.

While this Act did not result in a radically increased educational centralization, it was by no means a populist enactment. Educational organization in Canada West became much more enmeshed in public administrative structures under this Act than it had been formerly. While the Act did not contain any specification of duties of 'pupils and teachers', it did place educational organization more directly in developing structures of public construction and administration. This is immediately obvious with respect to general property taxation for educational finance, but it operated as well, although less visibly, with respect to the office of school trustee.

Trustees under the Act of 1843 were quite clearly public officials. While trustees were not yet required to post a performance bond, nor yet liable to penalties for non-performance of duties, their election was nonetheless a condition of local school finance. Their power over local property in general locates them structurally as state administrators.

Leading Reformers in Canada West publicly presented the School Act of 1843 as a triumph for 'the people' and as a populist enactment. Francis Hincks, for instance, the author of the Act, declared,

> that the late Ministry had divested the Grant of all local patronage. Everything has been left to the people themselves, and I feel perfectly convinced that they will prove themselves capable of managing their own affairs in a more satisfactory manner than any Government Boards of Education or visiting Superintendents could do for them.[97]

Yet these kinds of descriptions should be taken particularly cautiously. Hincks, like other Reformers, was not unambiguously the champion of popular character and culture. What the 'people themselves' could do educationally under the Act of 1843 was firmly situated in public administrative structures and subjected to the supervision of members of local elites. This kind of remark is best interpreted in light of the prevailing political situation. The contest for 'responsible government' in the Reform sense was in full swing in this period, and Reformers were quite willing to draw upon popular support for their position. Their opposition to the powers of the Governor-General and the imperial state in the colony made Reformers particularly reluctant to support a radical educational centralization. Without 'responsible government', centralized education might simply be another means of despotic imperialism. As we shall see, however, Reformers lost their fear of centralized education after the coming of responsible government.

## The Act of 1843 in Practice

Local reaction to the Act of 1843 was varied. Some educational correspondents claimed that the Act failed miserably, some parliamentary petitioners objected strenuously to the existence of separate school clauses in the Act and called for a return to the voluntary educational organization of the period before 1841. Nonetheless, the Act markedly increased the availability of educational funds and led to an increased enrollment in the schools. Some District Councils raised more than the legal minimum school matching grants, and at least three district Model Schools came into operation.[98]

In many parts of the colony, district superintendents of education conducted tours of inspection, which contributed to the accumulation of educational intelligence in the central office, and undertook the policing of the occupation of teacher. It was quickly apparent that teachers considered able by local school supporters did not approximate the model sought by educational supervisors. Samuel Hart, the superintendent of education for the Eastern District, was more tolerant than most.

> I have also found in remote parts teachers who altho fairly qualified in other respects do not profess to be perfect in Syntax and as the neighbourhoods in which they are engaged are well satisfied with them and do not consider much grammatical accuracy essential I imagine they might be allowed to teach but should be limited to such neighbourhoods.[99]

More typical was Patrick Thornton of the Gore District. Thornton wrote of his examinination of two teachers,

> The one was so ignorant of the English language that he blundered every two or three words in pronouncing to a pupil the words in a column of Mavor's Sp book. He could write tolerably. The other could neither read accurately nor write legibly. I declared them both unqualified.[100]

The superintendent of the Western District, Charles Eliot, 'found some of the teachers very deficient, ignorant wholly of Grammar, able indeed only to read & write, & comprehending Arithmetic hardly as far as the rule of Three.' Eliot suggested that teachers be classified and paid differently according to qualifications.[101]

The superintendents generally agitated against the remaining powers of school trustees and repeatedly stressed the ignorance of the rural population. Hamnett Pinhey of the Dalhousie District claimed that there was no systematic education given in his district, and described 'parents' as exceptionally ignorant. Pinhey was active in pressing for the establishment of the Dalhousie District Model School.[102] Many of the district superintendents claimed that the control exerted by school supporters and trustees over school books was the most serious barrier to efficient educational organization. This control was inextricably bound up with individualistic methods of instruction, and these in turn allowed for many of the other 'evils' of popular educational organization: irregular and unpunctual attendance, 'uninstructed' teachers, and so forth. 'The selection of Schools books being placed in the power of the Trustees, has been an impediment to my superintendence, as books published in the united states owing to their cheapness have been adopted, which are for many reasons totally unsuited to the British constitution,' complained S. B. Ardagh, the superintendent of education for the Simcoe District.[103] William Hutton of the Victoria District was a particularly active proponent of the Irish Readers later adopted under the Act of 1846. He wrote,

> The greatest evil under which we labor in our Common Schools in this district is decidedly the want of a universal adoption of a uniform set of School Books---- I have hitherto strongly recommended the use of the Irish National Books but from many of the Parents already being in possession of (objectionable) publications & being unwilling to purchase new ones I find it uphill work....[104]

Other district superintendents articulated plans for educational 'improvement'. Newton Bosworth, the superintendent for the Brock district, secured a collection of books from the British and Foreign School Society and publicized them in his district. He urged the Assistant Superintendent to agitate for the appointment of an official colonial school book committee to design a series of schoolbooks which would be published and whose sale would be subsidized by the government.[105] Jacob Keefer, the district superintendent for

Niagara, inspected the nationality and political loyalty of teachers in his district. He found that there were 30 'alien' teachers out of the 128 active, but this number was 'not so great as to justify any apprehension for the safety of the country.'[106] The activities of superintendents in the local schools, and the information they generated about local conditions which accumulated at the centre were key elements in the development of knowledge/power relations.

Finally, as I have noted, the Act of 1843 also encouraged the organization of several model schools, and a fragmentary report from one of these survives. The Johnstown District Model School opened in January 1846. The school was directed by Johnston Neilson, a teacher who claimed to have a classical education, and who had taught earlier in Carleton Place. Neilson was

> assisted by a Mr. Carroll, who has been trained under Bell's system of Education, and also under that of the Kildare Street Society. The systematic course adopted in this School is Bell's.

In later correspondence, Carroll himself claimed to have been trained in the Dublin model schools. The Johnstown District Model School trained 43 teachers in the first months of its operation.[107]

## Conclusion

By the middle 1840s, a thriving and diverse educational market in Canada West was increasingly subject to administrative and moral discipline in a developing educational state. Colonial governments reconstructed educational organization progressively in a set of public adminstrative structures. Educational actors became public actors, parts of a developing administrative grid which was superimposed on the colony. They came to partake of and to be implicated in the general power structures of bourgeois property.

Still, in the first half of this decade, substantial practical powers of educational self-management remained with local educational consumers. The reforms of 1841 and 1843 did not effectively touch pedagogy, curriculum, or much of day-to-day school management.

Partly this was because the Reform party itself still supported the efforts of respectable proprietors in the locality to organize local government. Partly this position itself was shaped by the more general struggles over responsible government and the form of the colonial state. However, the political crisis of 1843-4 and the rise of Egerton Ryerson led to a radical transformation of educational organization.

## Notes to Chapter 2

1. John Garner, *The Franchise and Politics in British North America, 1755-1867*. (Toronto: University of Toronto Press, 1969) pp.98-9. See more generally Bruce Curtis, 'The Political Economy of Educational Development,' unpublished Ph.D. diss., University of Toronto, 1980.
2. I.M. Abella, 'The Sydenham Election of 1841,' *Canadian Historical Review*, XLVII:326-43; J.M.S. Careless, *The Union of The Canadas, 1841-1857*. (Toronto: McClelland and Stewart, 1967): 14; D.G. Creighton, *The Empire of the St. Lawrence*. (Toronto: Macmillan, 1970):338; Garner, *The Franchise and Politics,*: 98-9; Stanley Ryerson, *Unequal Union*. (New York:International, 1968): 145. As Poulett Thompson, Sydenham served as President of the Board of Trade before being sent out to manage the Canadas.
3. Garner, *The Franchise and Politics;* Ryerson, *Unequal Union.*
4. J.C. Dent, *The Last Forty Years*. (Toronto: George Virtue, 1881) I:128n.
5. Dent, *The Last Forty Years.* I:136.
6. J.G. Hodgins, *Documentary History of Education in Upper Canada.* (Toronto: L.K. Cameron, 1894-1910) IV:18.
7. Hodgins, *Documentary History.* IV:17-18
8. The text of the draft act is in Hodgins, *Documentary History* IV:41-8.
9. The text of the School Act of 1841 is in Hodgins, *Documentary History.*

10. R.D. Gidney and D.A. Lawr, 'The Development of an Administrative System for the Public Schools: The First Stage, 1841-1850,' in N. McDonald and A. Chaiton (eds.), *Egerton Ryerson and His Times*. (Toronto: Macmillan, 1978):164-5.

11. This material exists as PAO RG2 F3A. The forms for reporting delivered to district councils are surprisingly detailed, and include questions about the general condition of education in the district and the means to its improvement. The questions posed included: 'Have any of the Teachers in your Township been removed by the Commissioners during the year? If so, give their School number, name, and cause of removal. Have there been any other matters of dispute respecting Common Schools in your Township, and how have they been settled? Have any School Districts within your Township been exempted from paying the School Tax, and what are the grounds of such exemption?' After several similar queries, the report form concludes, 'State also what alterations you conceive necessary in the Common School Bill, to insure its efficient operation, for the best interests of education in the Province.'

12. This material exists especially as PAO, RG2, F2, although the general incoming correspondence (C6C) also contains teachers' reports.

13. PAO RG2, F2, 'Rules and Regulations,' Charlotteville, 1842.

14. PAO RG2, F2, 'Rules and Regulations,' Fredericksburgh, April 1842.

15. PAO RG2, F2, 'Report of the Committee of Rules for the Common Schools,' Fitzroy, n.d.[1842]

16. PAO RG2, F2, 'Regulations,' Township of Smith, n.d. [1842]

17. PAO RG2, F2, Comm'rs. Pakenham to Mr. And. Dickson, section no. 4, 7 June 1842.

18. PAO RG2, F2, 'Rules and Regulations of the District Common School Established in Queenston,' 23 May 1842.

19. PAO RG2, F2, 'Regulations of Common Schools,' Township of Ekfried, [1842]; 'Copy of rules communicated to me as teacher of Common School in Burgess, James Fowler,' 1842; 'Report of the Common School, no.2, N. Sherbrooke,' n.d. [1842]

20. PAO RG2, F2, 'School Regulations adopted by the CSC of the Township of Dumfries,' n.d. [1842]

21. PAO RG2, F2, 'Report of the Common School, no.2, N. Sherbrooke,' n.d. [1842];'Copy of the rules...James Fowler,' 1842

22. PAO RG2, F2, 'Rules for Common Schools in Gainsborough,' n.d.

[1842]
23. PAO RG2, F2, 'Commissioners, Wellington,' 1842.
24. I discuss this in the following chapter, with respect to Egerton Ryerson's educational reforms. The point is important. First, of course, one must remark the radical edge to bourgeois educational reform: an education which would not be brutal, which would draw upon the students' capacity for pleasure, interest, enjoyment and so forth. Second, these elected officials were participants, to some extent at least, in the progressive discourse of bourgeois reform. Consistently denounced by teachers and educational administrators, and later historians, Commissioners might well have operated very differently in more congenial historical circumstances. As well, fragmentary evidence suggests a considerable continuity between Boards of Commissioners and Superintendents of Schools. Alexander Mann, chairman of the Pakenham Commissioners, for instance, became Bathurst District Superintendent. See for contemporary popular school manuals, Henry Dunn, *Principles of Teaching*. (London: Sunday School Union, 10th ed. c.1847); D.P. Page, *Theory and Practice of Teaching*. (New York: A.S. Barnes, 14th ed. 1852)
25. PAO RG2, F2, 'School Regulations adopted by the CSC of the Township of Dumfries,' n.d. [1842]
26. 'Copy of Rules....' 1842.
27. PAO RG2, F2, 'Rules and Regulations,' Gosfield Township, 1842
28. PAO RG2, F2, 'Regulations,' Township of Smith, 1842.
29. PAO RG2, F2, 'Comm'rs....' 1842.
30. PAO RG2, F2, 'Rules for Yarmouth,' 1842.
31. Phil Gardner's important study, *Lost Elementary Schools of Victorian England* (Kent: Croom Helm, 1984) speaks directly to the points I wish to make here. Gardner examines in detail the organization of private working class schooling in England. He reveals that the schools existed because they satisfied the practical and cultural needs of the communities which supported them. Gardner also points out that market forces ensured teachers who were 'incompetent' in the popular sense of the term did not remain in business. But of course the key issue here is precisely that to middle class reformers, popular educators were 'incompetent' in principle, politically and morally, whatever their 'technical' instructional skills. One cannot treat the concept of 'education' as neutral and understand educational history.

32. For instance, PAO RG2, F3A; the annual reports of district boards of education for 1842 included a space for classifying teachers in four administrative categories, according to their 'abilities to teach'. In the lowest category, '1', teachers were able to teach reading, writing, grammar, arithmetic for commerce, geography and book-keeping. In the highest, '4', teachers were to be 'able to prepare young men for entering the University'. Of 250 teachers classified by five district boards, less than 20% were female, and all of these were categorized as '1', '1/2', '0', or the space was left blank.
33. See Curtis, 'Schoolbooks and the Myth of Curricular Republicanism: The State and the Curriculum in Canada West, 1820-1850' *histoire sociale/Social History,* 16(32):322n.71.
34. PAO RG2, F2, Donald Mac Dermid, Teacher, Cornwall Twp., 'Report for 1842'; C6C, Donald Mc Dermid, Cornwall, 20 September 1843.
35. PAO RG2, F2, William M. Edward, Cornwall, 22 July 1842.
36. PAO RG2, F2, George Elmslie, Bon Accord, Nichol, 10 November 1842; also A. W. Wright (ed), *Pioneer Days in Nichol.* (Mount Forest:1932):257. The Annual Report of the Wellington District Council, PAO RG2, F3A, provides an account of Elmslie's school which differs from the information Elmslie wrote to Murray. Here Elmslie is said to have kept a school for 12 months with an average attendance of 22 students. He earned eighteen pounds and seven shillings in fees. For the Edinburgh Sessional School see John Wood, *Account of the Edinburgh Sessional School.* (Edinburgh: Windlaw, 1829).
37. PAO RG2, C6C, Walter Thomson, Raleigh, 14 October 1842.
38. PAO RG2, F2, Luke Wallis, President, Picton Board of Police, 3 November 1842; 'Report of a School taught by Sarah Mitchell in Picton from February 1842 to February 1843'; 'Report of a School taught by Eliza Bradford in the town of Picton district of Prince Edward from Jany 1842 until September ditto'; 'Report of Common School kept in the Town of Picton from the 1st of Jan 1842 to the 1st of Jan 1843 by Louisa C Ingersoll'; 'Report of a Common School taught in St Johns Hall in the Town of Picton by Ahira H. Blake, 1842'; 'Report of a common School taught in St John's Hall in the Town of Picton, from Jan 1 to Dec 31st 1842 by A.H. Blake'; 'Report of a Common School being taught in the town of Picton commencing January the first, 1842,' John O' Donnele, Teacher, 10 October 1842;

'Report of a Common School taught in Picton commencing January the first 1842 and ending December the 31st 1842', John O'Donnele, Teacher. The total enrollment for 1842 would have been 341, or 53 more than the population aged 5-16. Notice also that the Annual Report, Board of Examiners, town of Picton (F2), 20 February 1844 lists Blake, O'Donnele and Mitchell with three others. Blake is said to make 78 pounds per year, O'Donnele 50, and Mitchell 18 pounds 8 shillings and 9 pence. In Annual Report of the Board of Trustees, Picton, 1848 (F2) there are only three schools in the town, all run by men. All of the teachers listed in 1842 have disappeared, and this report includes a 'private school'.

Schooling in either Picton or Brockville could be examined in more detail using archival material.

39. PAO RG2 C6C, Thomas Smyth, Matilda, 17 April 1843.
40. PAO RG2 C6C, Edward Lane, Brockville, 20 July 1842.
41. PAO RG2 C6C, D.R. Macleod, Vaughan, 1 July 1843.
42. PAO RG2 C6C, Samuel Goshe, Drummond, 17 April 1843.
43. PAO RG2 C6C, Thomas Graffe, Merrickville, 27 March 1843.
44. PAO RG2 C1A, Murray to John Tilt, Cooksville, 19 April 1843.
45. PAO RG2 C6C, Wm. H. McGuire, Elisabethtown, 8 October 1842.
46. PAO RG2 C6C, Nicholas Wilson, Cobourg, 26 December 1842.
47. PAO RG2 C6C, Ahira H. Blake, Picton, 16 October 1843.
48. PAO RG2 C6C, W.H. McGuire, Brockville, 25 November 1843.
49. PAO RG2 C6C, John Brown, Binbrook, 17 April 1843.
50. PAO RG2 C6C, R.R. Mackie, Richmond, 1 November 1842.
51. PAO RG2 C6C, John Flood, Richmond, 15 May 1843.
52. PAO RG2 C6C, Geo. Tiffany, Hamilton, 20 February 1843.
53. PAO RG2 C6C, Rev. J. Flanagan, Binbrook, November 1842. This may well be a response to John Brown's letter note 49 above.
54. PAO RG2 C1A, Murray to Luke Wallis, Picton Board of Police, 17 February 1843.
55. PAO RG2 C1A, Murray to George Tiffany, Hamilton, 23 February 1843.
56. PAO RG2 C1A, Murray to William Reid, Grafton, 20 June 1843.
57. PAO RG2 C1A, Murray to F. M. Annany, Board of Police, Belleville, 26 June 1843.
58. PAO RG2 C1A, Murray to John Brown, Hamilton, 25 April 1843.
59. PAO RG2 C1A, Murray to Mr. John Breather, Oakville, 21 April

1843. This is the central administrative initiative. It replaces the market with an administrative grid in practice. The initiative provokes some resistance, but this soon disappears from the correspondence. See also C1B, McNab to Rob't Boyd, Superintendent of Schools, Prescott, 4 December 1844: 'A School district in the eye of the law is a locality, in which one School is taught, and no more than one can be legally included.' Later, separate male and female schools are permitted in the same school section.

60. PAO RG2 C1A, Murray to William Erskine, Smithtown, 19 January 1843.

61. PAO RG2 C1A, Murray to William Poole, Carleton Place, 28 April 1843.

62. PAO RG2 C6C, John Tuft, 5th Concession York Township, 16 June 1843; C1A, Murray to Tuft, 20 June 1843.

63. Hodgins, *Documentary History* IV:223-4.

64. PAO RG2 C6C, Henry Livesly, Simcoe, 27 May 1843; 3 October 1843.

65. PAO RG2 C6C, Robert Spence, Dundas, 1 April 1843. Spence presents another possibility which calls for investigation: the existence of nascent professional self-organization by teachers and the existence of fledging educational *systems* in localities before the School Acts of the 1840s. One wonders to what extent educational reformers knew of and were concerned about these more systematic forms of educational organization.

66. PAO RG2 C6C, Nicol Nicholson and John Ross, Woodstock, 17 June 1843.

67. PAO RG2 C6C, Teachers of Common Schools in the Township of Sidney, Sidney, 26 June 1842.

68. PAO RG2 C6C, D.R. Macleod, Whitechurch Bay, Newmarket, 27 May 1842.

69. PAO RG2 C6C, Johnston Neilson, Carleton Place, 16 August 1843.

70. PAO RG2 C6C, Patrick Wood, Smith Township, 2 June 1843.

71. PAO RG2 C6C, Robert Mowbray, Aldborough, 1 December 1842.

72. PAO RG2 C6C, A.B., Teacher, Markham, 4 February 1843.

73. PAO RG2 C6C, 'Remarks made by the School Commissioners.... not inserted in the Annual Return,' Niagara District, 22 June 1843. The methodological implications of the title of this communication are interesting.

74. Gidney and Lawr, 'Development of an Administrative System,'

162.
75. PAO RG2 C6C, J. McDonald, Victoria District, 24 June 1842.
76. PAO RG2 C6C, R.F. Budd, Clerk of the Wellington District, Guelph, 25 February 1843.
77. PAO RG2 C6C, Dr. Craigie, Ancaster, 7 October 1843.
78. PAO RG2 C1A, Murray to Edward Lane, Brockville, 14 March 1843.
79. PAO RG2 C1A, Murray to the Warden, Bathurst District, 12 April 1843.
80. PAO RG2 C1A, Murray to Nicol Nicholson, Embro, 20 June 1843.
81. PAO RG2 C1A, Murray to Edward Lane, Brockville, 14 March 1843.
82. PAO RG2 C1A, Murray to Rob't Spence, Dundas, 13 April 1843.
83. Legislative Assembly *Journals,* Third Session, 1843. Appendix 2, Annual Report of the Deputy Superintendent of Education.
84. PAO RG2 C1A, Murray to W. Boultbee, Ancaster, 22 March 1843.
85. PAO RG2 C1A, Murray to Patrick Thornton, Hamilton [?February 1843].
86. PAO RG2 F2, In the Commissioners' reports for 1842, 28 of 36 prescribe the use of the Bible or Testament. In the 128 accounts of schoolbooks from teachers, 104 report the use of the Bible or Testament as classbooks.
87. PAO RG2 C6C, John Treffey, Norwich, 4 July 1842.
88. PAO RG2 C1A, Murray to John Treffey, 13 July 1842.
89. *Journals,* Annual Report, 1842.
90. PAO RG2 C1A, Murray to David Walker, Vaughan, 28 February 1843.
91. PAO RG2 C1A, Murray to Dr. Craigie, Ancaster, 5 December 1843.
92. P.G. Cornell, *The Alignment of Political Groups in Canada, 1841-1867.* (Toronto; U. of Toronto Press, 1962):11-12; Creighton, *Empire:* 351; Dent, *Last Forty Years* I:224-56; Ryerson, *Unequal Union:* 150.
93. Dent, *Last Forty Years* I:223.
94. This is speculation on my part, but notice the abolition of Commissioners, the return of control of curriculum and pedagogy to the local school section, the reform of measures for payment and the provisions for model schools.

95. Gidney and Lawr, 'The Development of an Administrative System,':169.

96. Gidney and Lawr, 'The Development of an Administrative System,':170. 'The township superintendents, however, never did play a significant role under the Act, for they were shorn of many of their responsibilities when the municipal bill of 1843 failed to become law, and in 1846 the office was formally abolished.'

In the Act as passed, superintendents were to be appointed by the courts of wardens at the county level. With the failure of Baldwin's Municipal Bill of 1843, however, these courts of wardens did not come into existence, and their powers devolved upon the district councils.

97. Sir Francis Hincks, cited in Hodgins, *Documentary History*, IV:241. See also Hincks, *Reminiscences of his Public Life*. (Montreal: William Drysdale). Hincks' remarks about patronage should be read in context. This speech was delivered to the Toronto Reform Association after the resignation of the Reform ministry and at the height of the political crisis of 1843-4. 'Patronage' was a loaded concept, given that the ministry resigned over the Governor-General's insistence that the Crown retain the right to overrule the ministry on the distribution of offices. Perhaps to teachers like Henry Lively, who claimed that the local Commissioners gave jobs to their friends, Hincks' words would have struck a responsive note. However, patronage remained central to the system. The office of District Superintendent of Schools was a local political appointment. This can be seen quite clearly in the discussions of William Hutton's appointments, cf. C.E. Boyce, *Hutton of Hastings: The Life and Letters of William Hutton, 1801-61*. (Belleville: Hastings County Council,1972). Notice also the cursory character of the 'examinations' of teachers revealed in Hutton's activities. He examined W.R. Biggs while walking home from his field by asking him to spell four phrases and to parse a sentence with nine 'thats' in it. Boyce, *Hutton*:116. This by one of the more influential Superintendents.

98. In addition to the Johnstown District Model School discussed below (see note 107), see PAO RG2 C6C, W. Eliot, District Superintendent, London, 1 November 1845 for a discussion of the St. Thomas Model School; Hamnett Pinhey, Superintendent for Dalhousie, Horaceville, 20 November 1844, for the Dalhousie District Model School. We know nothing about these schools.

99. PAO RG2 C6C, Samuel Hart, Superintendent of Education, Cornwall, 29 May 1844.

100. PAO RG2 C6C, Patrick Thornton, Superintendent, Gore District, Hamilton, 21 August 1844.

101. PAO RG2 C6C, Charles Eliot, Superintendent, Western District, Sandwich, 20 August 1844.

102. PAO RG2 C6C, Hamnett Pinhey, Horaceville, 20 September 1845.

103. PAO RG2 C6C, S.B. Ardagh, Superintendent of Education, Simcoe District West, Barrie, 5 May 1845.

104. PAO RG2 C6C, William Hutton, District Superintendent, Belleville, 25 December 1845. More information about Hutton's first tour of inspection is in Boyce, *Hutton of Hastings*.

105. PAO RG2 C6C, Newton Bosworth, C.S.C.S. Brock, Woodstock, 5 October 1844; 8 April 1845.

106 PAO RG2 C6C, Jacob Keefer, Thorold, 25 August 1845. Also, 19 November 1844.

107. PAO RG2 F2, 'Report on the Model School of the Johnstown District for 1846'. There are two of these, the first signed by the Warden (?) Ogle R. Gowan, who was active in the Orange Order, and who noted that 'the popular clamour, which arose upon its establishment is now hushed....'

# Chapter Three:
# Public Construction and Educational Reform, 1846-50

Late in 1843, the Reform ministry led by Baldwin and Lafontaine resigned from office. The ministry claimed that the Governor-General, Sir Charles Metcalfe, was actively opposed to the principle of 'responsible government'. Matters were brought to a head by the Metcalfe's appointment of the Clerk of the Peace of the Bathurst District, and by his reservation of the Secret Societies Bill. The ministry claimed that the first action violated the right of the representatives of the parliamentary majority to distribute patronage, and that the second was interference by the Crown in a purely colonial matter.

The ministry expected a call for fresh elections, but Metcalfe refused. He attempted unsucessfully during the winter and early summer of 1844 to construct a ministry of 'conservative men of business', but with the exception of three--- William Henry Draper, Dominique Daly (the 'perpetual secretary') and Denis Benjamin Viger--- no members would serve. The colony was ruled largely from the office of the Governor-General for a period of nearly nine months. Finally, Metcalfe succeeded in assembling a ministry in the late summer of 1844, and elections were called for October. The ministry won a small majority, centred in Canada West, and a nominally Tory ministry remained in office, despite repeated minor parliamentary defeats, until 1848.[1]

The election results were in part due to an intense propaganda campaign conducted by allies of the Crown, especially in Canada West. The organized public agitation of the Toronto Reform Association in favour of colonial political autonomy was countered by the creation of a 'loyalty scare'. The Reverend Egerton Ryerson was particularly active on the side of the Governor-General.

Ryerson was a well-known public figure. A Methodist minister, first principal of Victoria College, and a long-time editor of the influential Methodist newspaper the *Christian Guardian,* he was admired by some Reformers for his defence of Marshall Spring Bidwell, a Reformer persecuted by the colonial executive after the Rebellion. Ryerson had flirted with radical reform in the late 1820s and early 1830s, before the Methodist church was accorded official recognition. However, the funding of the Methodist Church and a visit to English Radical circles convinced him of the infidelity of political radicalism. He became a particularly staunch supporter of 'responsible government' in the sense of impartial administration by able men, and an active proponent of public education as a means to this end.[2]

Ryerson communicated with successive Governors-General about the possible contribution of public education to political stability. In correspondence with Sydenham, Ryerson suggested that 'the publication of a monthly periodical' might work 'to mould the thinking of public men and the views of the country in harmony with the principles of the new Constitution.' Such a publication might create support for the Governor's policy and 'secure a rational and permanent appreciation of its objects and merits'.[3] Ryerson later claimed that Sydenham had been about to appoint him Superintendent of Education. This office, Ryerson thought, could produce social peace and loyalty 'upon high moral principles'. However, other interests intervened to secure the appointment of Robert Murray (of whom Ryerson was almost contemptuous) in his place.[4]

Before engaging in political debate in 1844, Ryerson wrote to Metcalfe outlining the sufferings he had endured in the service of public justice in the past. He concluded,

> I have adverted...to these unpleasant details, that Your Excellency may fully understand and appreciate my present position, and my caution in embarking in another conflict without reasonable hope that I will not be made a victim of abandonment and of oppression, after I have employed the utmost of my humbler efforts in support of the principles of the constitution and prerogatives of the Crown. In the present crisis, the Government must of course first be placed upon a strong foundation, and then must the youthful mind of Canada be instructed and moulded in the way I have had the honor of stating to your Excellency, if this country is long to remain an appendage to the British Crown.[5]

In a series of letters published by the *Colonist* newspaper, and again in pamphlet form as *Sir Charles Metcalfe Defended Against The Attacks of His Late Counsellors,* Ryerson undertook the defence of the Crown early in 1844. These letters were widely read and may well have influenced the outcome of the October elections.[6] Ryerson himself claimed that he had 'scarcely heard of an individual who has read all my letters who does not adopt the sentiments of them--- how strong soever his feelings might be against the Governor-General.'[7]

Already in *Sir Charles Metcalfe Defended* Ryerson's plans for 'public instruction' ---plans translated into practice only in the course of two and a half decades--- were clearly articulated. In his discussion of the conditions under which he had decided to defend the Crown, Ryerson referred to the fact that he had already been offered the position of Superintendent of Education, and that he had been on the point of creating

> a fabric of Provincial Common School Education--- of endeavouring to stud the land with appropriate school houses--- of supplying them with appropriate books and teachers--- of raising a wretched employment to an honourable profession--- of giving uniformity, simplicity and efficiency to a general system of elementary educational instruction--- of bringing appropriate books for the improvement of his profession within the reach of every schoolmaster, and increasing the facilities for the attainment of his stipulated remuneration--- of establishing a library in every district, and extending branches of it into every township--- of striving to develope, by writing and discourses in towns, villages and neighbourhoods, the latent intellect of the country....[8]

In most of its details this was the system of 'public instruction' outlined in Ryerson's *Report on a System of Public Elementary Instruction* of 1846 and enacted in legislation from 1846 as well. Ryerson was also clear that 'public instruction' was not simply confined to 'schools' narrowly conceived. The generation of public 'intelligence' in whatever form was seen to be 'public instruction'. The Toronto Reform Association, for instance, was described as 'a school of public instruction'. Even before his educational tour, then, Ryerson's concern with the political instruction of the 'public' was clear, and he saw 'education' as a matter which extended far beyond the school room itself.

Again, *Sir Charles Metcalfe Defended* is particularly interesting for the grounds upon which Ryerson (successfully, it would seem) supported the Crown. These grounds were primarily *procedural*. Over and over, Ryerson argued that Metcalfe had acted in keeping with established governmental procedures in making appointments and in dealing with legislation, and for that reason deserved the support and approbation of citizens of Canada West. His procedural correctness was counterposed to the Reformers' overwhelming preoccupation with 'partyism'.

The political crisis of 1843 was about power and the organization of power in the colonial state. The Reformers agitated consistently for the parliamentary organization and administration of the central sources of political power. Metcalfe was concerned to retain these sources of power as much as possible under the tutelage of the Crown. By counterposing procedure to partyism, Ryerson supported the power of the Crown against that of the colonial parliament, while appearing to defend a politically neutral position.

More generally, his defence of Metcalfe illustrates a political position asserted by Ryerson throughout his educational career: the primacy of 'neutral' procedure over 'party' conflict. This position was at least internally contradictory, if not actually disingenuous. Procedure is always substance; form is always the form of its content. However, the continual assertion that bureaucratic forms were powerless, were neutral, fair, correct, just and so forth, was an essential element in the construction and legitimation of a bureaucratic educational administration. The legitimation of a particular form of education and of educational power, involved the normalization of power as procedure. In this way one form of education could come to appear as the only possible or reasonable or 'efficient' form.

At the same time, Ryerson connected *procedure* and *christianity* in his defence of Metcalfe. To follow procedure, in his account, was to adopt the elements of christianity. To violate procedure was to violate those elements. As Ryerson asked the reader after claiming that the Reformers did not reveal all the facts of which they were aware, 'Is this doing as they would be done by? Is this fair? Is this telling the whole truth?'[10] Ryerson's work throughout the 1840s involved efforts at state building in which the transition from religion to citizenship was effected, and in which religion in fact justified citizenship. More important, while the notion of 'neutral procedure' contributed to the construction and legitimation of bureaucratic administration, that same notion disguised the very real and substantive power relations at issue in state administration. Educational administration was in fact later elaborated only through violent and durable social conflict. In these conflicts, as we shall see, the education office consistently asserted the primacy of the force of its procedures over the substance of educational struggles.

## Ryerson's Tour and Report

After accepting the office of Assistant Superintendent of Common Schools for Canada West in October of 1844, Ryerson was granted leave for an educational tour of up to one year's duration. He departed early in November, leaving the day-to-day administration of the education office in the hands of Rev. Alexander McNab, and returned late in 1845. His tour took him through most of Europe, including England, Ireland, Scotland, France, Belgium, Holland, Switzerland, Prussia and the other German states, and Italy.

Like Horace Mann before him, Ryerson was especially impressed with the pedagogical practice of the Prussian schools. The 'humanistic' pedagogy of these schools was inspired by the work of the Swiss educational reformer J. Pestalozzi. Like many of his contemporaries, Ryerson believed that Prussian practices could produce the well disciplined bourgeois individual through means that were gentle, popular with students, and effective. The individual school which impressed him the most, however, was the Edinburgh Normal School--- although the practice of 'taking places' did not meet with his approval--- and the school *system* which he saw as most desirable was that organized by the Commissioners of National Education in Ireland.

After his return, Ryerson wrote *A Report on a System of Public Elementary Instruction for Upper Canada* and drafted a major revision of the educational legislation. The *Report* presented a summary of the most progressive propositions of bourgeois political theory, with respect to both the social importance of education, and pedagogical method.

Ryerson was especially concerned with the elaboration of practices for the selective development of the forces of the self. Some of the potential forces of the self were to be developed in such a way that they would govern the others. The techniques of self-construction were the province of pedagogical practice. Underlying Ryerson's analysis was a typical bourgeois anatomy of the forces of the self---a 'psychology' --- which both specified the order of development of the self, and ranked its parts. Education, if successful, would strengthen the individual's forces and structure them such that 'reason' and 'intelligence' rather than 'passion' would be dominant. Intellect and reason were to dominate the passions. The 'higher' tastes were to dominate the lower; the spiritual nature was to dominate the animal nature. The delicate senses were to be cultivated and the base impulses starved. The individual whose self was developed in this way was said to be in a state of 'self--government'.

Self-government as individual self-discipline, and self-government as representative democracy were seen to be sides of the same coin. With the French educational inspector M. Girardin, and with Archbishop Whately of Dublin---- a Commissioner of Irish National Education--- Ryerson argued that representative governments were imperilled by popular ignorance. The exercise of 'rights' in the absence of 'discernment' menaced the representative state; 'when a people know their rights, there is but one way to govern them, to educate them.' If people were to be 'governed as rational beings,' then 'the more rational they are made the better subjects they will be.'[11] Education was centrally concerned with the making of political subjects, with *subjectification*. But these political subjects were not seen as self-creating. They were to be made by their governors after the image of an easily governed population. This was a different version of what other writers called the creation of 'willing and cheerful' obedience. Self-government was social subordination.

The successful training of the forces of the individual would create habits of mind and body conducive to productive labour, Christian religion and political order. Ryerson's concern was to make education *practical*, not in the sense of transmitting particular productive skills, but rather in the sense of constructing habits, predispositions, loyalties, and sentiments in the individual which

would then *practically* and *effectively* guide action. Ryerson argued,
> Now, education thus practical, includes religion and morality; secondly, the development to a certain extent of all our faculties; thirdly, an acquaintance with the several branches of elementary education.[12]

As we shall see below, the essence of educational practice was a sort of public religion. The method of education was the development of the faculties, and these faculties were expanded, exercised and applied in several subject areas.

The progressive dimension of Ryerson's proposed educational reform was contained particularly in his analysis of the development of 'all our faculties'. In part, Ryerson merely elaborated a well-developed critique of the initial attempts at collective instruction conducted in monitorial schools, echoing James Pillans of the High School of Edinburgh, David Stow, Horace Mann and others.[13] These writers argued that the rote learning common in monitorial schools was ineffective because it could not form the forces of the self. Enriched and expanded instructional activity was seen to be a necessary component, in theory at least, of the sound education of the masses. Ryerson wrote,
> The great object of an efficient system of instruction should be, not... a mere word knowledge learned by rote, which has no existence in the mind apart from the words in which it is acquired, and which vanishes as they are forgotten, --which often spreads over a large surface, but has neither depth nor fertility, ---which grows up as it were in a night and disappears in a day....[14]

Such 'word knowledge', Ryerson argued, was commonly transmitted in American schools. This 'superficial and pernicious system' addressed only the memory. Such an education could not affect conduct, because it never penetrated the surface of the individual; it never made contact with 'the heart' or 'character'. Students educated in this way, could produce a 'showy' or superficial display of learning, but when asked to apply their education to practical matters, or to explain the 'significance' of their lessons, they were ridiculous.

An 'efficient' education, by contrast, would involve the 'cultivation of all our mental, moral, and physical powers'.[15] Such an education would not content itself with exercising the memory, but would engage all the human faculties.

> Our senses are so many inlets of knowledge; the more of them used in conveying instruction to the mind the better; the more of them addressed, the deeper and more permanent the impression produced.[16]

Efficient education would penetrate to the core of the student's self, and would organize the fundamental forms of social experience. Of course, Ryerson never planned the development of 'all' our faculties: some human capacities were systematically repressed, especially those for sexual expression and for critical thought. Still, his pedagogical method anticipated a development, a deepening and expansion of the forces of its subjects. In some ways, this was in sharp contrast to the earlier attempts on the part of European ruling classes at the instruction of the masses. Ryerson took the superiority of collective modes of instruction as given.

Ryerson called his productive education 'humanistic', and he frequently stressed its 'humanizing result'.[17] Humanizing education based itself on the emotional susceptibility of the student, the student's capacity for emotional pleasure and pain. Teachers were to create an emotional dependency upon the part of their students, such that they could govern them in the schoolroom with the utmost economy, by means of looks, gestures, expressions and qualities of voice. The schoolroom was to be an emotionally forceful terrain. Once the emotional dependence of the student on the teacher was established, the ideal teacher by virtue of *his*[18] display and deployment of his own energy, could draw out the forces of his students in an economical and pleasing manner. Good teachers were never still and were never seated. They did not rely heavily on books, because they had completely mastered course material. 'The Prussian teacher', whom Ryerson took as a model, 'has no book; he needs none, he teaches from a full mind.'[19] At the same time, this teacher could instantly connect the content of even the most abstruse school lessons to the practical existence of 'the most ignorant man.'[20]

In the sense of creating human forces, Ryerson's pedagogical proposals were positive (i.e., they posited). The progressive moment of his proposals lay particularly in their claim to base instruction upon the capacity for *pleasure,* to the exclusion of *pain and fear.*

In the Prussian schools taken by Ryerson as models of

pedagogical practice, the process of instruction generated joy on the part of the students. This joy or pleasure stemmed from the skill of the teacher, the soundness of method, and the 'sympathy'[21] between teacher and student. For example, in their geography lessons the Prussian teachers, who were all masters of drawing, could make whole worlds appear on the blackboards with which all their classes were equipped.[22] This delighted their students.

> ... the children [became] as much excited as though they had been present at a world making. They rose in their seats, they flung out both hands, their eyes kindled, and their voices became almost vociferous as they cried out the names of the different places....[23]

The generalization of pleasure in learning eliminated the need for corporal punishment or terror as instruments of schoolroom governance. Ryerson quoted Horace Mann on his visit to the Prussian schools,

> I never saw a blow struck, I never heard a sharp rebuke given, I never saw a child in tears, nor arraigned at the Teacher's bar for any alleged misconduct....The Teacher's manner was better than parental, for it had a parent's tenderness and vigilance, without the foolish doatings or indulgences, to which parental affection is prone....No child was disconcerted, disabled, or bereft of his senses through fear....[24]

The foundation of pedagogy upon student pleasure was to eliminate all conflict in education. Bourgeois school reform elaborated a psychology or moral economy of the self and claimed to have unlocked the secrets of individual self-development once and for all. Educational practice would follow the 'natural' path of the faculties, strenghtening the 'higher' parts of the self as these were unfolded. This natural process would be experienced by students as pleasurable. The absence of fear and punishment meant that no negative educational experiences would take place; no desire to oppose the process of instruction would arise, and there were no grounds upon which the student would be able to do so in any case. This education would effectively produce moral individuals.

The harmony between teacher and student in the pursuit of instruction was so complete in the model schools of Prussia, that

Ryerson could write of the teacher who, when a student solved a difficult problem, would 'catch up the child in his arms, and embrace him, as though he were not able to contain his joy.'[25]

Humanization was a process of subjectification, of the development of the forces of the self. But for Ryerson this process was not simply an aesthetic; it was also a politics. Humanization aimed to develop the forces of the self as a means of promoting self-government and self-regulation. Social order, in his view, came increasingly to depend upon the organization of the individual subject. Education was about self-formation and the moral regulation of the population. Only with effective self-regulation, self-constraint, self-discipline, self-repression, could the political rights and privileges associated with 'representative' government be exerted 'responsibly'— in ways which would not menace the security of the state and religion. Educational practice would resolve the contradiction between the formal equality of citizenship and the social subordination of the mass of the population demanded by bourgeois civilization. It would create social subjects who enjoyed and actively embraced their social subordination, who experienced subordination as equality and liberty.

The content of 'humanization' is well illustrated by Ryerson's treatment of the teaching of vocal music. Ryerson argued that this subject should be introduced into all the common schools of Canada West. 'All men,' wrote the American educational commentator Dr. Potter, 'have been endowed with a susceptibility to the influence of music'.[26] The state educational administrators of Britain were unanimous in their contention that vocal music 'facilitates rather than impedes the pupils in their other studies.'[27] For Ryerson, vocal music was an important avenue to the faculties, since all students enjoyed it, and its enlistment in educational endeavours could connect morality with pleasure. In David Stow's view, which Ryerson cited, vocal music would train students to 'worship God in the family' and in the 'public sanctuary', and by 'furnishing the young people with interesting moral songs,' the educator could 'displace in their social amusements many of at least a questionable character.'[28] Vocal music would allow the transformation of the leisure of students into a period of instruction. Music could then 'refine and humanize' students. As the Boston School Committee urged,

> The great point to be considered in reference to the introduction of vocal music into popular elementary instruction, is, that thereby you set in motion a *mighty power which silently but surely in the end, will humanize, refine and elevate a whole community.*[29]

The generalization of vocal music instruction in Germany was reported to have produced a sober working class.[30]

Power and pleasure, then, were interwoven in Ryerson's pedagogical conceptions. Just as bureaucratic procedure was presented as politically neutral, pedagogical practices were presented as 'natural', as in perfect accord with a pre-social human nature. As we shall see, however, in practice this pedagogy was 'intrusive.'[31] It was not experienced by real students as pleasant in many cases. It provoked resistance, and in the face of resistance, the education office abandoned its theoretical concern with the pleasure of students to bolster the integrity of its authority structures.

## 'Several branches of elementary education'

There were to be fifteen branches, or subjects, taught in the best elementary educational system. Ryerson presented a careful outline of the place of each of these subjects, and the manner in which they were to be taught. This in itself is remarkable; subject specialties were relatively little developed in the common schools of the Canadas in the 1840s, and specialized texts did not figure in the education of many people. At the same time, as we have seen above, pedagogical practices varied with the qualifications of particular teachers. The vast majority of schools, at least in the country, were also taught by individualistic methods.[32] Most students learned at a pace determined by their particular needs and interests. The necessity of participating in the domestic economy, the availability of particular kinds of books, religious preferences, and so forth, all influenced the progress of students at school. Ryerson consistently wrote of collective instruction, arguing that it was both more effective and more efficient as a pedagogical method. He proposed both a systematization of course materials and methods, and a real differentiation of subject matters.

After physical training, which was a necessary element in the strengthening of the forces of the self, Ryerson proposed the following elements of a 'common school education', in this order: Reading, Spelling, Writing, Arithmetic, Grammar, Geography, Linear Drawing, Music, History, Natural history, Natural philosophy, Agriculture, Civil Government, and Political Economy. With *Christian Instruction,* (about which more below), this was the curriculum taught in the Irish national schools, and published in the Irish National Series of schoolbooks.

Ryerson did not expect all Canadian common school students to be exposed to all of these subjects, at least not initially. The core of common school training was to be instruction in reading, writing and arithmetic. As Ryerson put it,

> The great object of our Common Schools is to teach the whole population how to read, to write and to calculate,— to make a good reader, writer and calculator of every boy and girl in Canada; and the other studies in the elementary Schools are important, as they teach how to employ these arts upon proper principles and in the most useful manner.[33]

However, reading, writing, spelling and arithmetic were not simply neutral or 'technical' skills. The method of teaching these subjects was particularly important, and Ryerson argued that by following the proper method, one would produce sound moral character in the student. Of course, one always learns to read *something,* and Ryerson argued that if one learned to read a particular kind of thing, then the application of the capacity to read (and by implication to write and calculate as well) would be governed by solid moral and political principles. 'The *intellectual* part of teaching is the most important' in the area of reading, wrote Ryerson, 'though the most neglected. It consists in teaching children to understand what they read— and the meaning of the words used, the facts narrated, the principles involved, the lessons inculcated.'[34] As I have argued elsewhere,[35] reading instruction in particular was designed as a process of subjectification, in which the acquisition of the capacity to read was tied to texts containing 'useful knowledge', and in which the correct application of this capacity was constantly verified by the process of interrogation.

The course of studies for the schools was to be uniform on a province-wide basis and also graded. Students were to progress through a course of studies, with the higher branches providing safe, interesting and improving domains for the application of skills learned in the lower.

This education was to be the same for both male and female students, and for members of all social classes, races, and religious groups. Ryerson was silent, in the *Report,* on gender and class differences in the content of education. The series of textbooks adopted in Canada West---the Irish Readers--- did contain a separate reading book for girls' schools, and Ryerson did not expect that most Canadians would require more than a 'good common school education', but the language of universality and commonality predominated in this *Report.* Later, the establishment of separate schools for boys and girls at local option was allowed, common and grammar school courses diverged, and separate schools for different religious and racial groups were established.

## Our Common Christianity

Educational reform, in Ryerson's view, was 'justified by considerations of economy as well as of patriotism and humanity'.[36] By forming the habits and attitudes of individuals, education would eliminate poverty and crime. It would prepare individuals for their 'duties and employments of life, as Christians, as persons of business, and also as members of the civil community in which they live.'[37] The basis of the new system, however, was to be what Ryerson called 'our Common Christianity.' The *Report on a System of Public Elementary Instruction* devoted thirty pages to this question, and repeatedly stressed the *'absolute necessity of making Christianity the basis and the cement of the structure of public education.*[38] Canadians, Ryerson argued, generally were Christians, and so should their educational system be.

> The creed of our Government, as representing a Christian people of various forms of religious

worship, is Christianity, in the broadest and most comprehensive sense of the term. The practice of the Government should correspond to this creed.[39]

This was simply the 'popular principles of Government' in practice. This public or governmental Christianity was Christianity 'in the broadest and most comprehensive sense of the term.'

In one sense, the notion of a Common Christianity was difficult to sustain. In church practice and structure, no common ground existed amongst different Christian sects, and in civil matters a similar condition prevailed. Orange and green regularly smashed each other's heads in the streets. The Clergy Reserves and Separate Schools were contentious political issues, not to mention the religious affiliation of the universities. As we have seen, cries of 'no priestcraft' were heard when clergy stood for election as common school commissioners, and denunciations of any form of religion were not unknown.[40] While Ryerson's *Report* did replicate Archbishop Whately's list of common beliefs of all Christians, it was not directly in the domain of creed that Ryerson sought to establish the content of the 'Common Christianity' at the basis of education.

In practice, 'our Common Christianity' referred to a set of behavioural traits. Ryerson abstracted from Christian religion one of its moral regulatory dimensions, and sought through educational practice to embody moral regulation in the student population. 'Our Common Christianity' meant a form of self-development or subjectification whereby people in Canadian society would *govern* themselves rationally in keeping with certain moral/political postulates. Education, for Ryerson was not a *means* to government; education *was* government: government of the self. The development of representative institutions demanded the development of individual self-government.

Following what he took to be the successful example of Ireland, and to a certain extent of France and Prussia as well, Ryerson attempted to articulate a conception of social and political universality which would be generalized through education. All Canadians would be educated to some of the habits contained in the Bible: toleration, meekness, charity, respect for others, and the acceptance of established authority. The reciprocal principles of an eye for an eye and a tooth for a tooth were not included here, nor were struggles against slavery and debt. 'Our Common Christianity' involved meekly accepting the abuses one received from others, of being kind to those in error, and of refusing to actively oppose those who harmed one. This education would overcome the political strife, 'partyism', and sectarian violence present in Canadian society.

Ryerson was part witness to, part proponent of a process of state building. He himself engaged in the practical activity of translating principles of moral regulation from the religious to the civil arena. He sought to establish the domain of public education as a systematically organized and rationally administered domain of universality, harmony and classlessness. This was a key element in nineteenth century state-building, moreso, as we have seen above, since Ryerson sanctified bureaucratic procedure.

The universality of the domain of public schooling was also presented in part as political-economic reality. The meaning of the term 'common' schooling shifted in the 1840s in Canada West, from 'rudimentary' or 'ordinary' to 'in common' or 'collective'. Ryerson followed Horace Mann of Massachusetts to advocate common schooling as 'the great equalizer of the conditions of men,-- the balance wheel of the social machinery.'[41] Common schooling meant placing the 'poor man on a level with the rich man' (women were nowhere mentioned),[42] it implied social contact between members of potentially antagonistic social classes. Direct contact between different classes at school would create harmony, mutual respect and social peace in later life. All members of Canadian society were to be provided with a common moral/intellectual property. This property was to be distributed in state institutions, and through its appropriation, all members of society would share a common national heritage and a common relation to the state. With Brougham, Kay-Shuttleworth and the other Radical educators, Ryerson conceived the appropriation of intellectual property as part compensation to the propertyless for their material condition.

In other words, an essential part of the public educational project was a process of public *construction*. Ryerson in effect urged the creation of a new terrain of universality and classlessness in Canadian society, a domain 'above politics', as he liked to call it. This was to be a domain of government; education was government, both as subjectification and as embodiment. Students were to contain in themselves, in the planned development of their capacities, in their social bodies, the basic elements of government. Pedagogical practice, planned by the central authority, aimed at the development of political subjects as forceful and willing. 'Our common Christianity' provided a moral grid through which the potential forces of the self were to be filtered, and some of them strengthened and solidified. The rational administration of the public realm was a powerful process. The means of administration, and the capacity to specify, identify and define the content of moral behaviour— the means of morality— in Ryerson's plan were to rest with the central educational authority and its local representatives and allies. The public which educational practice would construct would allow for the practical mediation of social conflict. The formation of a public was a project for political rule.

## The School Act of 1846

The School Act of 1843 contained several practical flaws, from the point of view of central administrators. New schools could not be funded in the first year of their operation. Township superintendents of schools had to post large bonds to perform their functions, and since most of them were paid no more than ten pounds a year, many refused to serve. In the Dalhousie District, for instance, none of the superintendents at the township level accepted their appointments, and their functions devolved upon the district superintendent. In some places, superintendents were paid from local school monies, and this, combined with the fees charged by township treasurers, reduced the funds paid to teachers. None of the state grant could be paid to teachers before the first of August in any case, and some superintendents pointed out that this was difficult, since summer teachers were hired in May. Many superintendents objected to the financing of schools through the rate-bill system. Again, the annual election of all three local school trustees was problematic. The law did not provide a workable means of publicising such elections in the first place, and newly elected trustees often found themselves committed to teachers in whose hiring they had had no hand.

Egerton Ryerson's proposed school legislation, however, did not content itself with adjusting existing law. In presenting his draft of the School Act of 1846 to Secretary Hopkirk, Ryerson attacked the organizational principles of the School Act of 1843. This Act, he claimed, had been borrowed entirely from the state of New York, and did not take into account 'the differences between the workings of a democratic republic, and those of a responsible system of Government under a Constitutional Monarchy.' The Canadian law contained 'no provision for the exercise of the same executive authority' which attached to the New York Board of Regents, and this was its key weakness. The autonomy of different educational authorities under the Act of 1843 was for Ryerson its greatest flaw. This autonomy prevented the use of the schools as organs of systematic national political socialization.

> The Government has no authority whatsoever to interfere with the doings of any County, Township or School district in Upper Canada....There can be no Provincial System of Education....where there is a completely independent power in each of the Schools in regard to both the books and regulations of the School--- a subject over which the Government is not authorized to say one word.

Books in particular, Ryerson objected, 'were under the inspection of the Township & County Superintendents who again are not responsible to the Government for any thing they do.' This dispersion of authority meant that *public* education was impossible. Ryerson insisted that *responsible* government meant the administration of society by able men who would be independent of sectarian or party conflicts. 'One chief aim of a Monarchical System of responsible government,' as he put it, 'is to stamp the sentiments and spirit of the public mind upon the administration as well as the legislation of the Country, and to secure the collective acts of the Country against the antagonist or selfish Acts of individuals or isolated Sections.'[43]

Ryerson argued here and elsewhere that the most important part of education was *administrative practice*. Legislation by itself was insufficient. Given that the government was 'responsible'--- that the state spoke for the general interests of society--- what was crucial in educational organization was effective administration. Only such organization and *practices* could both set in motion and secure sound educational activity in the locality. As he remarked in his *Report*, 'it is now generally admitted, that the education of the people is more dependent upon the *administration,* than upon the provisions of the laws relating to Public Instruction.'[44] The key point was not simply to legislate educational organization and then leave administration in the hands of local authorities. If the central authority were effectively to govern through educational means, then what actually went on in the schoolroom itself--- and local reaction to these activities--- was crucially important. In Ryerson's words, without effective local administration, 'there may be *one* law, but the *systems,* or rather *practices,* may be as various as the smallest Municipal divisions. To be a State system of Public Instruction, there must be a State controul as well as a State law.'[45]

This political interest was to be secured by the construction of an educational system in which effective authority was centralized. The central authority was to be empowered to regulate local educational activity in principle, and principles were to be secured in practice through the construction of administrative circuits of knowledge/power and moral regulation. In Ryerson's plan, all educational authorities were to be 'responsible': that is, they were to be informed by a central authority, and educational duties imposed upon them were to be enforced by definite legal penalties. At the same time, all subordinate educational authorities were to report to the centre about their activities. And the chief superintendent himself would be authorized to by-pass all intermediate channels to intervene directly in educational matters at the lowest level of the system.

Just as practice in the schoolroom was to preoccupy itself with processes of self-formation, was to penetrate to the core of the consciousness of the subject of education, to seize, shape, sculpt and solidify forms of human energy, so educational administration was to 'stamp the sentiments and spirit of the public mind'--- a mind defined by the central authority--- on all educational practices. This was a proposal for the saturation of civil society with procedures and practices of a regulatory nature. *Education* was indeed *governance.*

The School Act of 1846 completely transformed the principles of educational organization at the elementary level in Canada West. It removed in principle most of the educational autonomy enjoyed by local educational consumers and put in place a set of administrative structures in which respectable members of local elites would be charged with much of educational management. These officials were situated in largely bureaucratic authority structures.

The Governor-General was to appoint a chief superintendent of education who would hold office during pleasure and who would receive a maximum salary of 500 pounds per annum.[46] The chief superintendent was to be aided by a paid clerk, and to be advised by a General Board of Education, to consist of six members in addition to himself. His powers were extensive. He was to apportion the provincial school monies, but could withhold them from any school district violating his instructions. He was empowered to specify forms and regulations for reporting educational intelligence, and to frame such regulations as he thought necessary for the 'better Organization and Government of Common Schools.' He could hear and decide upon any complaint originating anywhere in the system, and he could take measures to ensure that school monies were properly expended. He had discretionary powers over the expenditure of unappropriated school monies. He was to publish and recommend plans for school architecture. He was to encourage the establishment of school libraries, to discourage the use of 'unsuitable and improper' books in schools or libraries, and 'to employ all lawful means in his power to collect and diffuse information on the subject of Education generally, among the people of Upper Canada.' He was to be general superintendent of the Normal School as well.

The chief superintendent was also a member of a General Board of Education appointed by the Governor-General. This body was to consider and recommend books for the use of schools, and to prohibit the use of unacceptable books as well. The General Board was to organize and manage a Normal School and to give the superintendent 'counsel and advice on all questions, and on all measures which he may submit to them for the promotion of the interests of Schools, and for the diffusion of useful knowledge.' However, it was the chief superintendent who was to convene the Board initially, and he also could call a special meeting of the Board at any subsequent time. In fact, for much of its first year of operation, the General Board met in Ryerson's house, and Ryerson suggested potential members to the Attorney-General.

The Act abolished the office of township superintendent of common schools. District superintendents were to be appointed by district councils and any vacancy in that office could be filled by the Governor. In addition to apportioning money and paying teachers, in place of the township superintendent and treasurer under the Act of 1843, the district superintendents now examined and lisenced all candidates for teaching and could re-examine any candidate whenever it was 'expedient'. District superintendents were charged with the active and detailed supervision of local educational activity. They were to visit all common and model schools at least once a year, and until the establishment of a Normal School they were to approve all matters having to do with the local model schools. They were charged with the collection of a detailed educational intelligence, now specified in part by law, which was to include such things as the number and ages of students in each school section, the qualifications of teachers, the branches taught, the state of the schools themselves, the existence of school libraries and private schools, and other things as well.

The Act envisaged the creation of a Normal School for the training of teachers. Fifteen hundred pounds were appropriated for the construction of such a school with one or more attached model schools. After the establishment of the School, no master of any district model school could hold office without a certificate granted from the Normal School headmaster. Autonomous regional teacher training institutes would not exist under the Act.

For the first time the Act of 1846 also contained clauses granting special regulatory powers to members of local elites. The senior Justice of the Peace was to have charge of the annual school meeting in each school section. 'School Visitors' were created. In the draft bill, these visitors were to have been only legally recognized clergyman, but an amendment added 'Ministers, recognized by law, of whatever Religious Denomination....the Justices of the District Court, the Warden of the District, and the Councillor, or Councillors ...also all Resident Justices of the Peace.' School visitors individually or collectively could visit schools in their district at any time they chose and could 'examine the progress of the pupils, and the state and management of the School.' They could advise teachers, and report individually or collectively to the district or chief superintendent.

Crucially, the right formerly enjoyed by all local residents to assemble at will for school purposes now devolved only upon these respectable persons. School visitors under the Act could meet at any time the senior Justice of the Peace or any two other visitors sought to do so. They were empowered to formulate plans for the organization of school libraries and for the 'diffusion of useful knowledge'. They were empowered to examine any candidate for a teaching job and to give a certificate valid for one year in a specific school to any such candidate.

The limitations to the taxation powers of both District Councils and local trustees were removed by the Act of 1846 (but quickly reasserted by the courts). Both bodies could now raise any amount of taxation for educational purposes by a rate on property. Trustees, however, were severely limited in other areas by the Act. They could no longer determine the books to be used in the school; they were to choose from a list published by the General Board. Rules and regulations for school management were now published by the chief superintendent and the General Board. Pedagogical method rested in principle with the teacher, and not with the trustees, although as we shall see, teachers were instructed by the chief superintendent and policed by superintendents of schools. Trustees were subjected to fines if they refused to serve, and were charged with extensive technical duties of school organization, furnishing, heating and information-reporting. The Act made no mention of educational participation on the part of the population at large beyond its spectatorship at the public school examinations, and the voting by resident householders and freeholders at the annual public meeting.

The Act also contained several 'housekeeping' provisions, with respect to such matters as funding for schools in their first year of operation and the organization of separate schools. The rate-bill system, viewed by the chief superintendent and many district superintendents as an educational impediment, was abolished in draft legislation, but reinstated by Reformers in the Assembly.

An amended School Act of 1847 allowed for the municipal organization of educational administration. Urban schools were to be managed by a town or city Board of Trustees, composed of six members appointed by city councils or town boards of police. Urban councils were to have all the taxation and other powers of District Councils, and were to appoint a town or city superintendent of schools. Boards of trustees were to appoint management committees for each urban school.

In principle at least, the key powers of educational organization and administration lay with the central authority. Degrees of autonomy for lower-level officials were closely graded, and all officials were practically instructed by the chief superintendent, the General Board of Education, or both.[47]

## Reaction to the School Act of 1846

Both Ryerson's *Report* and his educational legislation were produced in a period of 'irresponsible' government. The conservative parliamentary ministry suffered repeated defeats over minor matters and just as repeatedly refused to resign, with the support of the Governor and the Colonial Office. Some people, like Joseph Wiltse of the Johnstown District Council, were prepared to believe that if the School Act 'was fairly acted on by the inhabitants it would prove to be of grate Servis in the province for when Reduced to practice its faults Can be Remedied by the Legislature.'[48] However, opposition to the Act was general and vocal.

The Reform party and press were violently antagonistic to the Act, and some District Councils and teachers' organizations responded in a similar fashion.

> The principle of the new school Act is to increase the power of the superintendent. No one could doubt that the framer of the Act would have given us the Prussian system if he had dared to so outrage public opinion. He went as far in depriving the people of power as he deemed prudent. The spirit of the new Act is to centralize power in the hands of the superintendent--- that of the old, to leave it with the people.[49]

That was Francis Hincks' opinion, and while he underplayed the disciplinary dimensions of the Act of 1843, the new Act certainly centralized educational authority. Robert Spence, the editor of the Dundas *Warder,* called for the abolition of the office of chief superintendent. He described the School Act of 1846 as 'notoriously calculated to wrest the education of the youth of the Country from the people, and to vest it in the hands of the executive.'[50]

Several District Councils reacted similarly. The Gore District Council sent a memorial to the legislature calling for the repeal of the Act and a return to the Act of 1843, or even to that of 1816. The Council objected to the onerous duties required of school trustees, who were confronted with a plethora of useless forms produced by the education office. The Council also objected to the payment of educational bureaucrats and to the public funding of the Normal School which, it claimed, would train people at public expense for occupations other than teaching. This memorial was endorsed by the Newcastle District Council which added its own criticisms of the chief superintendent. The Home District Council, in an address to the legislature, claimed that its members,

> especially object to that prominent feature in the existing School Act of 1846, which runs throughout the whole of it, the concentration of so much power upon one individual,--- the Chief Superintendent of Schools--- that Officer being the nominee of the Governor-in-Council, and in no way responsible to the people. They submit that any enactment which places so much power in the hands of an Officer, over whom the people have no control, directly, or indirectly, either in making the appointment, or with regard to the manner in which that power is exercised, and the duties of the Office discharged, is not congenial to the feelings of a free people nor compatible with the institutions of a free country.

This Council suggested the subordination of the Chief Superintendent to the General Board of Education and the abolition of school visitors. The Western District Council took a similar position, although at least one District Council came out in favor of the Act.[51]

The teachers of the Gore District (who had made the greatest strides towards stable and independent professional organization in the late 1830s and early 1840s) opposed the Act in at least two public resolutions. In 1848 they denounced the Act as 'cumbersome' and 'sectarian in its tendency'. They argued that it had been framed by a person who had no practical experience of teaching, and called for the establishment of a Commission to draw up a new bill. In 1849, the same group of teachers again passed a resolution opposing the Act.[52] Cries of 'Prussian despotism' and of the 'lynx-eyed' state abounded in the press. District superintendents reported the existence of opposition to different sections of the Act, especially to the textbook clauses.[53]

The chief superintendent was not idle in the face of this onslaught. He toured the colony delivering public speeches on the importance of education, stressing that education would make people prosperous, keep the boys home on the farm, make the girls the charms of the domestic circle and increase the power of the people.[54] He defended himself and his policy in the press.[55] Circulars were sent to superintendents, trustees and district councils stressing the importance of the School Acts. District councils were provided with free sample sets of school books. Plans went forward for the publication of an educational periodical, to be distributed to all educational officials. The first number of the *Journal of Education for Upper Canada* appeared in 1848. Ryerson also began to adopt a political position less closely identified with that of the conservative ministry.

## The Educational Crisis

Despite Ryerson's efforts to circumvent opposition by putting the educational system into practical operation, his position was seriously threatened in 1849. There were several forces at work in this matter. One set of events led to the closing of the schools of Toronto from June 1848 to June 1849.

The School Act of 1847 consolidated the management of urban schools under a central Board of Trustees. Ryerson had two particular interests in framing this Act. He sought the establishment of urban central schools in which the approved practices of collective instruction, such as classification, instruction in the gallery, and gradation, could be put in place. At the same time, the Act created the possibility of eliminating the rate-bill system in the urban schools. Ryerson and most district superintendents particularly objected to the latter aspect of educational organization. They claimed that parents used their discretion in school finance to cheat the teacher of its salary. When parents suspected that the rate-bill would be high, they withdrew their children from the schools which often ground to a halt, it was claimed, from this cause.[56] The School Act of 1847 seemed to make property taxation for educational finance the only means possible in towns and cities.

Under the Act, the city superintendent of common schools was to prepare estimates of the funds needed for local school purposes beyond those contained in the legislative school grant and in the local matching grants. The Act did not seem to bind trustees to accept these educational estimates, nor to specify any means whereby the funds should be raised. However, in a circular to municipalities distributed in January 1848, the chief superintendent referred to municipal taxation as the only means of local school finance under the Act.

The city superintendent for Toronto drew up a plan for the consolidation of the city schools and for the construction of large permanent schools to replace the rented schools then in use. A budget of 2000 pounds was placed before the city council late in 1847. Council asked the Tory ministry in January 1848, and the Reform ministry in February 1848, for clarification of the taxation clauses of the Act. Both ministries replied that taxation was the only means of urban school finance and stated that council was obligated to raise all the funds demanded by the Board of Common School Trustees. Council's Education Committee reported that the educational estimates would necessitate an additional tax of 4 1/2d. on the pound, and refused to levy a rate. A lower estimate submitted in June of 1848 was also rejected, and the city schools closed for the year.[57]

Council argued that the rate-bill system, or some other means, should be employed to raise educational revenues. The Reform press concurred in this position. The Dundas *Warder* printed an editorial arguing that without the rate-bill, 'the tie, which, heretofore existed between the Teacher and the parent of the taught, is severed.' This would lead to 'irresponsibility'--- the word was probably not accidentally employed--- and 'it becomes a matter of total indifference how Schools be conducted so long as the Teachers' salaries be provided.'[58] If parents and guardians had no control over teachers' salaries, Reformers emphasized, they would have no control over what was taught. This was precisely the situation Ryerson sought, at least for the majority of the population.

While the debate over free schools in Toronto progressed, a Reform ministry came to power in the province. With the triumph of the free trade party in England, the Canada policy of the Colonial Office shifted dramatically. Lord Elgin, the Governor dispatched to Canada late in 1847, was instructed to support whatever colonial government enjoyed a majority position in parliament. The Sherwood-Daly ministry, the last attempt of colonial Tories to organize a working government, was exceptionally weak. During the last session of 1847-8, this ministry was increasingly incapable of conducting government business.

> The weakness of the Ministry... was made manifest from day to day, and there was no chance for them to carry any measure as to which there was a serious divergence of opinion. They were repeatedly defeated, and there were again indications of internal disorganization.[59]

When elections were held, the Reformers won a large majority, and the second Baldwin-Lafontaine ministry took office early in 1848. Rural opposition to property taxation for education figured in the elections, and it seemed a major educational reorganization was at hand. However, Ryerson had remained on close personal terms with some Reformers, and even during his framing of the Act of 1847 he was moving away from the Tory ministry. He came to be seen increasingly in Reform circles as a 'loose fish', rather than as a committed supporter of the executive, and he took pains in his role of chief superintendent to present himself as 'above politics'.[60]

In an effort to show his willingness to follow parliamentary opinion, Ryerson presented a set of amendments to the School Acts in May of 1848 and again in the autumn. He disclaimed any responsibility for the taxation clauses in the Acts, and denied any desire to reduce local educational financial autonomy. He proposed to allow Boards of Trustees to determine the method of local school finance. He proposed to invest the powers of certifying teachers in the hands of District or County Boards of Education created for that purpose, instead of confiding these powers to district superintendents alone.[61]

By early 1849, sections of the Reform party were becoming disenchanted with the pace at which political reform was proceeding.

The leaders of the ministry seemed content with the form of political democracy. Other sections of the party were increasingly pushing for the substance of reform, and they were pressured by the depression provoked by the repeal of the Corn Laws and the Navigation Acts, as well as by the popular excitement surrounding the news of the risings in France, Germany, Ireland and elsewhere. Malcolm Cameron, the Assistant Commissioner of Public Works and a spokesperson for radical Reform, presented a school bill of his own which passed the house in May of 1849.

The Cameron School Act of 1849 was badly drafted and would likely have proven unworkable. It introduced new provisions into the School Act without repealing the provisions which already existed. Still, the Act struck at several of the principles of education-as-government contained in the earlier acts. The chief superintendent was subordinated to the General Board of Education, and was made explicitly responsible to the ministry, rather than to the Governor alone. He was to post a performance bond as a condition of holding office. District superintendents of schools were to be replaced by township superintendents, and the surprise school inspections encouraged by Ryerson were made illegal. All teachers were to be notified at least three days in advance of any inspection of their schools. County Boards of Education were to be named by the Governor-in-Council. These Boards were to examine and certify candidates for teaching positions. The powers exerted by the General Board of Education under the Act of 1846 with respect to schoolbooks now devolved upon County Boards as well. County Boards were to define the local school curriculum, but the Act insisted that no student be required to study any 'controverted theological dogmas, or doctrines, or to join in any exercise of Devotion, or Religion, which shall be objected to by him.' The Act abolished the school visitors.

The independent taxation powers of trustees were sharply curtailed by the Cameron School Act of 1849. No tax could be levied by trustees for school maintenance or construction, unless the majority of landholders and householders in the school section agreed. The measures taken for school maintenance were to be defined by an open school meeting. The collection of rate-bills was to be facilitated, and local schools could be supported by a rate on property at local option.

The Act of 1849 was internally contradictory. Yet, generally speaking, it strengthened the powers of local organs of government in educational matters at the expense of the central office. Those offices which placed such broad powers in the hands of the 'respectable' did not appear in it. Justices of the Peace had no special status at the annual school meeting; school visitors would not exist; the district superintendent was eliminated, and teachers were not prone to be visited at any moment by an official instructed by the central office.[62]

Ryerson apparently learned of the Act's existence only after it had been passed. He quickly denounced it as the product of personal malice against him on the part of Malcolm Cameron. He criticized the Act for lessening educational uniformity and for lessening the power of the General Board of Education to produce a rational school curriculum. His own efforts to build a school system, he claimed, had always embodied the principle of local educational autonomy. 'It has been my endeavour, from the beginning,' wrote Ryerson, 'to increase the powers, and render more simple and easy the duties of the Trustees.'[63] The 'loose fish' could swim against the educational currents he had set in motion.

Ryerson claimed that the Cameron School Act would undo the progress made in various towns and cities towards the establishment of graded free schools. It would place the selection of books in the hands of local bodies which had no interest in educational uniformity and which would be at the mercy of itinerant book dealers. The only way uniform educational organization could exist was by the creation of an executive authority capable of framing and enforcing regulations for the school system as a whole.

> The only way in which a State, or National, System of Schools can be established and maintained in connection with local popular institutions, is, by the Executive authority making the General Regulations, and being able to secure their observance by means of the distribution and the veto power in the application of the legislative School Grant, or State Fund, in aid of Schools.[64]

Ryerson offered his resignation if the Cameron Act was to remain in force.

In an unusual move, the Provincial Secretary informed Ryerson in December of 1849 that the School Act was under consideration by the Executive Council, and that he should do whatever he must to keep the Act of 1847 in force in towns and cities.⁶⁵

## Disintegration of the Reform Alliance

The fate of the Cameron School Act, and of educational organization in Canada West generally, was determined by the disintegration of the Reform alliance which had existed since 1842. Through 1848 and early 1849, the left and middle wings of the party remained solidary in the pursuit of an ambitious program of civil reform. In addition to attacking the School Acts, the party passed an Amnesty Bill which allowed the exiled rebels of 1837 to return to the colony.

The breakup of the imperial economic system with the coming of Free Trade, the repeal of the Corn Laws and the Navigation Acts, exacerbated class divisions in the Canadas. The depression of 1848-9 threatened merchant capital centred on the trade in staples and on the canal system. Conservative sections of the population were politically disaffected by this and by the perception that the colonial state had been given to the 'French rebels'. The Irish famine migration of 1847 placed a substantial proletariat in the colonial towns, and political excitement surrounded the news of revolution in Europe.⁶⁶

In April of 1849, the Baldwin-Lafontaine ministry secured imperial assent to the Rebellion Losses Bill. This Bill sought to compensate property owners who suffered damage during the Rebellion of 1837. It applied especially to people in Lower Canada, where British troops had engaged in extensive looting and pillage. Despite Tory agitation, the Reform party refused to include in the Bill any strong measure to differentiate participants in the Rebellion from non-participants. To the Tory opposition and its supporters outside parliament, the Bill was simply a reward for disloyalty and republicanism.

As Lord Elgin left the parliament buildings in Montreal after giving assent to the Rebellion Losses Bill, he was attacked by an angry mob and pelted with stones and rotten eggs. The mob invaded the parliament buildings, which were sacked and burned. The leaders of the Reform party were assaulted by the mob in the streets, their houses were besieged and in some cases burned. Mob violence, inspired by the Tory party, broke out sporadically in Montreal and in many other Canadian towns in the ensuing months, and the sentiments of the mob were echoed in the Tory press in Canada West. A section of the merchant capitalist class published an Annexation Manifesto calling for the annexation of the Canadas to the United States.[67]

At the same time, the Reform party was riven internally by factional division. The left of the party pressed increasingly for what it took to be the substance of Reform: secularization of the Clergy Reserves, judicial reform and 'poor man's law', financial retrenchment, and the adoption of the electoral principle for all governmental offices.[68] The agrarian radicalism of the 1830s was resurging, but Canadian radicals now had links with European socialist movements.

The moderate Reformers and the Governor-General were particularly concerned with the possibilities of an alliance between the left of the Reform party representing agrarian radicalism and militant Irish canal workers.[69] Faced with the double menace of mob violence from the right and agrarian radicalism from the left, moderate Reformers sought to consolidate a centrist alliance. Ryerson occupied a strategic position, and the social significance of centralised education appeared in a different light. Before 1848, moderate Reformers could join with more radical currents in the party to oppose centralized education as imperial despotism. After 1848, centralized education was increasingly seen by moderate Reformers as the salvation of the 'responsible' state. Ryerson came to seem a valuable ally for the centre in the crisis of 1849, where political alliances in the colony were shifting. The Governor wrote to the Colonial Secretary late in December of 1849 that,

> ...we have, steady to the connexion, that portion of the reforming Party which is attached (as Baldwin is) to constitutional Monarchy, and that portion of the Tory Party which is sincere in its detestation of Republicanism---- It is not easy to say what may be the relative strength of these parties in the

Country--- probably at present they vary considerably from day to day.[70]

Elgin himself claimed that Ryerson ---a man 'accused by many of being somewhat cunning which is not altogether improbable' --- was threatened by the Reform party at first, and that he [Elgin] 'had to do some battle for him when they first came in.'[71] Late in 1849, moderate Reformers moved to sustain Ryerson, and the left of the party seceded to form a new party of agrarian radicalism. Ryerson was invited to draft a replacement bill for the Cameron School Act.[72]

## The School Act of 1850

The School Act of 1850 was drafted by Ryerson while the opposition from the left consolidated its political organization. Peter Perry, a radical democrat who had held a seat in the Upper Canadian Assembly in 1834-6, re-entered politics and attracted a wide rural support.[73] In March of 1850, a convention was held in Markham, Canada West, and the political platform of the 'Clear Grit' party was laid down. The platform drew heavily on the principles of the English People's Charter.[74] In the spring elections, the party gained several seats.

The School of Act 1850--- declared on the 12th of July--- moved away from the strictly subordinate 'responsibility' of the Acts of 1846-7 and towards the principle of electoral self-government. Educational power structures were to be managed in substantially different ways, but many key powers remained in principle at the centre.

Unlike the earlier acts, which had begun with the duties and powers of the chief superintendent and which then enunciated the powers and duties of inferior officers, the School Act of 1850 proceeded in the opposite direction: from school trustees upwards. The powers, duties and procedures surrounding local trustee organization were closely specified by the Act. The principle of representative democracy was solidified, and the range of plebiscitarian democracy formalised (and of course, limited).

Definite procedures for giving notice of the annual school meeting, for determining the eligibility of voters, and for the selection of the chairman of a school meeting were now specified. The chairman was no longer the senior Justice present, but anyone elected by the majority of voters. The duties and powers of the annual school meeting were specified. Householders and landholders resident in the section could elect school trustees and decide the *manner* (rate-bill or property tax) but not the *level* of school finance. At other school meetings convened by the trustees, local property and householders could appoint an arbitrator to represent their interests in disputes over school sites. They could vote to unite their section school with another to form a union section, and they could vote to decide how to dispose of superfluous school property. Voters and other local residents could also attend the annual public school examination. At the same time, anyone disturbing a school meeting was subject to a fine of five pounds on the evidence of one credible witness.

Trustees were to be a corporation. Individual trustees could be fined for refusing to serve, and for acting illegally became personally liable. One of the trustees, rather than the teacher, was to serve as Secretary, and all the acts of the trustees were to bear their corporate seal. Trustees could determine the level, but not the method of local school finance. They could enforce the collection of school rates or taxes by distraining property. They hired certified teachers, and agreed with them as to salary. They could establish a separate school for males and females in the school district, but part-time schools for both sexes in different parts of the district were not mentioned as they had been under the 1849 Act. The autonomy of the trustees extended particularly to the physical management of the local school. Without consulting any school meeting, they could undertake whatever arrangements they chose with respect to 'building, repairing, renting, warming, furnishing, and keeping in order the section school house, and its appendages, wood house, privies, enclosures, lands, and moveable property...and for procuring apparatus and text-books for their school.'

These provisions were the object of local struggle and conflict in later years. They constituted the trustees as powerful public educational figures, but other sections of the Act attempted to specify the mode of operation of these powers. For instance, the trustees could buy books and rate or tax for them. But they could not buy any 'Foreign books in the English branches' without permission from the centre. Activities in the market place and propaganda by the central office made the Irish Readers both cheaper and easier to obtain than other books. Trustees were required to receive an educational periodical in their section. The most readily available was the *Journal of Education* in which the centre also instructed trustees, ---in a less binding fashion, but nonetheless. Trustees were locally elected. Their office embodied the electoral principle of the 'Clear Grit' party. However, they were *centrally instructed* and *bureaucratically incorporated*.

The School Act of 1850 also created a novel device designed to 'resolve' and contain local educational disputes. All matters of contention between teachers and trustees, touching not only salaries but also 'any other matter in dispute', were to be settled by binding arbitration. A representative of the teacher, of the trustees, and the township superintendent were to meet to discuss contentious issues, and were to have 'full authority to make an award between them, and such award shall be final.'

The powers of township councils to form school districts, to unite school districts and to consolidate school districts were also made subject to the consent of householders and freeholders. Town and city councils were accorded the same powers as municipal councils. School trustees were to be elected on a ward basis in towns and cities, and were collectively to form a corporation. Unlike rural school trustees, however, urban trustees possessed taxation powers not subject to the approval of local proprietors. The town or city council was explicitly enjoined to raise all the sums deemed necessary for school construction and furnishing by the trustees.

County councils were to tax to raise an amount at least equivalent to the county's share of the school fund, and no upper limit to the council's taxation powers were specified. Councils which failed to collect the school tax on or before the fourteenth of December in any year were nonetheless to pay teachers with lawful orders on demand. County councils were also to appoint local superintendents, either one for each township, or one for several townships. No superintendent, however was to be charged with supervising more than one hundred schools, and superintendents were to be paid by the county councils. No deductions from school monies were to be allowed to county treasurers.

The Act abolished the office of District Superintendent of schools and placed the power of examining teachers with newly created County Boards of Public Instruction. These Boards were to be occupied by the trustees of the county grammar school and the superintendents of schools. The county council could establish one such Board for the county as a whole, or circuit boards for particular parts of the county if there was more than one county grammar school. These Boards were to meet quarterly to examine candidates for teaching certificates. All candidates were to present 'satisfactory proof of good moral character' and were to be British subjects before taking the Board's exam.[75] The Boards were to classify teachers 'into three classes, according to their attainments and ability, as shall be prescribed in a programme of examination and instructions to be provided by law.' Teachers could be re-examined at the discretion of the Board. The Act did not empower County Boards to determine the curriculum of the schools, or to exercise any other substantial powers of school management. A vaguely worded clause allowed Boards to take measures to 'advance the interests and usefulness of Common Schools' and to promote libraries, but the substantial powers accorded to them under the Cameron Act of 1849 were removed.

The nature of educational inspection was also altered by the Act of 1850. Local superintendents appointed by Township Councils were now required to visit all schools in their jurisdictions at least four times a year and to deliver a public lecture on educational subjects. They were explicitly enjoined to enforce the law as this was interpreted in regulations from the Council of Public Instruction. They were to do everything they could 'to persuade and animate parents, guardians, trustees and teachers, to improve the character and efficiency of the Common Schools, and secure the universal and sound education of the young'. They were to encourage the use of authorized books, and 'for any cause which shall appear to...require it,' superintendents could annul the certificate of any teacher until the next meeting of the County Board. The Act specified the form of reporting to be followed by superintendents.

The school visitors created under the Act of 1846 and abolished by the Act of 1849 reappeared in the Act of 1850. Once again, clergy, judges, members of parliament, magistrates, and now also members of county councils and aldermen could enter the schools at will, examine teachers and pupils, investigate the condition of the school, and give advice to teachers. Visitors were again empowered to meet and plan educational 'improvement'.

Finally, the Act specified and slightly reorganized the powers of the Chief Superintendent and the General Board of Education, which now was to be known as the Council of Public Instruction. The chief superintendent was now to be responsible to a 'Department of Her Majesty's Provincial Government'. His powers with respect to the management of the Normal School, and with respect to the key administrative functions of framing and publishing forms for educational reporting remained intact. Now, however, the Council of Public Instruction, and not the chief superintendent was to formulate and publish the regulations for school organization and management, which retained the force of statute law. The Council retained the powers of the General Board with respect to the books used in schools.[76]

## Conclusion

The School Act of 1850 created the basis of a broad educational agreement among the governing classes in Canada West; the basis for the construction of a particular form of hegemony. Although this educational settlement provoked persistent local opposition, and although more general attacks were made upon it in the decades which followed, it proved to be remarkably durable. The peculiar mix of local election of trustees, appointed and semi-autonomous County Boards, and a strong central authority with broad regulatory powers and well-developed information- gathering procedures provided both for the local containment of educational conflict and for disciplinary initiatives from the centre. Education under the Act indeed became public education, and from one point of view, the educational system became astonishingly large, and surprisingly centralized as well. Hundreds of thousands of students, over five thousand teachers, fifteen thousand school trustees, hundreds of township school superintendents, members of county, town, city, village and township councils, justices of the peace, clergy and others in Canada West were implicated in educational organization and practice by the time of the first systematic revision of the Act in 1871. Much of this educational activity was framed and regulated by less than ten people working out of the education office in Toronto, in conjunction with the nine members of the Council of Public Instruction and the staff of the Normal School. The educational system acquired a solidity and an internal administrative dynamic-- a life--- in this period.

The Act resolved those educational disputes which preoccupied the propertyholding classes from the 1830s. The disputes over local versus centralized educational management, over the autonomy of propertyholders in each school section as against the authority of the centre--- these were settled by the Act. With this settlement, the dynamic of educational development in Canada West was transformed. A particular form of *public* education was accepted by the property holding classes. Educational conflict now came to surround the management and administration of this form. What Ryerson had seen as the central aspect of educational organization--- *local practice* --- now became the locus of educational conflict.

An Amendment Act of 1853 made minor adjustments to more effectively allow for the local management of educational disputes.[77] A key clause was one which proposed fines for school 'disturbers', defined by one 'credible witness'--- the teacher in practice--- as anyone disrupting the conduct of the school either inside it or in its vicinity. The clause, of course, was not directed at respectable school visitors, whose disruption was regarded as 'intelligent'. It was directed rather at local educational consumers and participants who opposed local educational *practices:* parents, students, even in certain cases, trustees themselves. It is the practice, the administration and management of public education which will concern us in what follows. Public education was administered into dominance only through a myriad of local struggles.

## Notes

1. J.C. Dent, *The Last Forty Years*, (Toronto: George Virtue, 1881), I:324-6; 350. For an account of the Orange Order, the target of the Secret Societies Bill, see Hereward Senior, 'The Genesis of Ontario Orangeism' in J.K. Johnson (ed) *Historical Essays on Upper Canada*, (Toronto: McClelland and Stewart,1975):241-261. Stanley Ryerson, *Unequal Union*, (New York: International, 1968): 153-5.
2. There are many biographies of Egerton Ryerson. R.D. Gidney's account in *The Dictionary of Canadian Biography* (Toronto: University of Toronto Press, 1981) is quite useful.
3. Egerton Ryerson, *The Story of My Life*. (Toronto: William Briggs, 1883) edited by J.G. Hodgins:284.
4. R.D. Gidney, 'The Rev. Robert Murray: Ontario's First Superintendent of Schools,' *Ontario History*, LXIII (4):191-204.
5. Ryerson, *Story of My Life* :321.
6. Ryerson feared the ministry would lose elections called for the fall of 1844. This was because the facilities for 'public' education in the colony were not well developed. He wrote to Draper in mid-September that 'the facilities for circulating knowledge amongst the mass of the people are so very imperfect, that it takes a long time, and great exertions, even out of the ordinary channel, to inform the body of the people on any subject.' *Story of My Life*, :338. The question of Ryerson's role in the elections has been debated at length. See C.B. Sissions, 'Ryerson and the Elections of 1844,' *Canadian Historical Review*, 23(2) 1942:157-76; J.M.S. Careless, *The Union of the Canadas* (Toronto: McClelland and Stewart, 1967):86-8; P.G. Cornell, *The Alignment of Political Groups in Canada, 1841-1867*, (Toronto: University of Toronto Press, 1962):14-5; Gidney, 'Robert Murray'.
7. Ryerson, *Story of My Life*, :338.
8. Egerton Ryerson, *Sir Charles Metcalfe Defended Against the Attacks of the His Late Counsellors*, (Toronto: British Colonist, 1844):7-8.
9. *Sir Charles Metcalfe Defended*, :38.
10. *Sir Charles Metcalfe Defended*, :93.

11. Egerton Ryerson, *Report on a System of Public Elementary Instruction for Upper Canada,* (Montreal: Lovell and Gibson, 1847): 20. Parts of this analysis are a reworking of material that appears in my 'Preconditions of the Canadian State: Educational Reform and the Construction of a Public in Upper Canada, 1837-1846,' *Studies in Political Economy,* 10, 1983: 99-121.

12. Ryerson, *Report* :22.

13. It is James Pillans of the High School of Edinburgh who produces the most important initial criticism of monitorial education. This appears in his *Principles of Elementary Teaching* (Edinburgh: 1828). However, Pillans held the system of rote learning, so inappropriate for the developing mind, to be the most effective in the higher grades. In *The Rationale of Discipline: as exemplified in the High School of Edinburgh,* (Edinburgh: Maclachlan & Stewart, 1852), Pillans argues for monitorial instruction, particularly in the languages where memory work is unavoidable. In his earlier work, Pillans also strenuously opposed physical punishment as an ineffective pedagogical instrument. The criticism of monitorial education was by no means restricted to middle class educational writers. Radical writers, such as William Thompson, produced sharp critiques in the 1820s. See Brian Simon (ed) *The Radical Tradition in Education in Britain* (London: Lawrence and Wishart, 1972).

14. Ryerson, *Report on a System* :52.

15. Ryerson, *Report* :57.

16. Ryerson, *Report* :75.

17. Ryerson, *Report* :131.

18. The masculine pronoun is used throughout the report in reference to the teacher.

19. Ryerson, *Report* :55.

20. Ryerson, *Report* :55.

21. Nineteenth century middle class educational theory is pervaded by conceptions drawn from the philosophy of mind/ moral philosophy/ political economy of the Scottish Enlightenment. 'Sympathy' is a case in point. This essential proposition of the efficacy of collective instruction can be traced to Adam Smith's *Theory of Moral Sentiments* as David Hamilton shows in his very instructive 'Adam Smith and the moral economy of the classroom system,' *Journal of Curriculum Studies,* 12(1981):281-91.

22. A central component of educational reform in Canada West was

the generalization of the technology of instruction: books, slates, blackboards, globes, desks, maps, pointers, schoolrooms, waterclosets, swings, and so on. Relatively little attention has been paid to these matters for the formative period in Canada West, despite the formation of the Educational Depository and despite the purely economic importance of school manufactures. With respect to the generalization of blackboards, which were an indispensable
component of collective instruction, see Alison Prentice's 'From Household to School House: The Emergence of the Teacher as Servant of the State,' *Material History Bulletin,* 20:19-29. My 'The playground in nineteenth century Ontario: theory and practice,' *Material History Bulletin* , Fall 1985:21-30, examines the place of the playground in educational reform.

23. Ryerson, *Report,* :120.
24. Ryerson, *Report,* :168.
25. Ryerson, *Report,* :169.
26. Ryerson, *Report,* :129.
27. Ryerson, *Report,* :125.
28. Ryerson, *Report,* :126.
29. Ryerson, *Report,* :130. emphasis in the original.
30. Ryerson, *Report,* :131.
31. Barbara Finkelstein, 'Pedagogy as Intrusion: Teaching Values in Popular Primary Schools in Nineteenth-Century America,' *History of Childhood Quarterly,* 2, Winter 1975;349-78. The acquisition of 'good moral character' in schools run by the middle classes for the rest of the population invariably entailed attempts to construct selves through the undeviating repetition of rituals which regulated standing, sitting, speaking, moving and so forth. At the least, these assumed a uniform character and a uniform pace of development of the self in the schooled population.
32. See my 'Schoolbooks and the Myth of Curricular Republicanism: The State and the Curriculum in Canada West, 1820-1850,' *Histoire Sociale/Social History,* 16(32) 1983:305-29.
33. Ryerson, *Report,* :107.
34. Ryerson, *Report,* :78.
35.'The Speller Expelled: Disciplining the Common Reader in Canada West,' *Canadian Review of Sociology and Anthropology,* 23(2) 1985:346-68.
36. Ryerson, *Report,* :10.

37. Ryerson, *Report,* :11-14.
38. Ryerson, *Report,* :32 original emphasis.
39. Ryerson, *Report,* :50.
40. C.R. Sanderson,(ed) *The Arthur Papers* (Toronto: University of Toronto Press and Toronto Public Libraries,1942) III:1-2. Arthur reports that the insurgents along the frontier in 1839 when asked what their religion was, responded 'None!'
41. Quoted in H.S. Commager, *The Era of Reform,1830-1860,* (Toronto: D. Van Nostrand,1960):134.
42. J.G. Hodgins(ed) *Documentary History of Education in Upper Canada,* (Toronto: L.K. Cameron,1894-1910) VII:192.
43. PAO RG2 C1C, Ryerson to Hopkirk, 3 March 1846. Ryerson outlines the amendments he proposed in this letter. Notice also that correspondents to the education office under Alexander MacNab revealed several flaws in the Act of 1843. The 'alien' clause prevented teachers from various ethnic communities from teaching; cf. C1C, Ryerson to Alex. Allan, Preston, 29 January 1846. No one was named in the Act to give notice of the first meeting in a school section; cf.C1B, MacNab to Francis Kent, 20 September 1845. No section without a school for at least three months in a given year could claim the school fund for the following year;cf. C1C, MacNab to D. McKenzie, 10 October 1845 and also to R.F. Percy, 10 October 1845, 'The law on this point as well as many others is exceedingly lame....' No compulsion existed with respect to the collection of taxes levied for schoolhouse construction; cf. C6C, Wm. Elliot, London, 17 August 1845.
44. Ryerson, *Report* :176. Philip Corrigan pointed out the importance of this passage.
45. Ryerson, *Report* :175. I wish to stress that these are Ryerson's emphases. I think his conviction here is genuine, and it probably helps one understand how he could reconcile himself to the changing educational currents in the period 1844-50. Whatever the law in its general provisions, as long as it enabled the centre to regulate local *practices* it was important.
46. As we have seen above in chapter two, this was about ten times the wage of a teacher.
47. The Act is reproduced in Hodgins, *Documentary History:* VI:58-70. The draft bill also contained a clause abolishing the rate bill as a means of school finance. This clause was defeated in the

house on an amendment proposed by Robert Baldwin, and supported, Ryerson claimed, by a few wealthy members of the government.
48. PAO RG2 C6C, Joseph Wiltse, Farmersville, Yonge Township, 7 January 1846. Wiltse expressed a sentiment common to many local school consumers in the 1840s. By the end of the decade, many rural residents especially wanted a school act that would actually work and that would stay in force for more than two years without being completely reconstructed.
49. R.D. Gidney, 'Centralization and education: the origins of an Ontario Tradition,' *Journal of Canadian Studies*, VII,1972:40.
50. Hodgins, *Documentary History* VII:198.
51. Hodgins, *Documentary History* VII:120.
52. PAO RG2 E2, Dundas *Warder*, 18 August 1848, 'Resolutions by Qualified Teachers of the Gore District'; also 'Meeting of Parliament' 22 September 1848. Hamilton *Provincialist*, 13 December 1849, 'Minutes of Meeting of Teachers of Gore District'; see also 'Schools in the Brock District'.
53. See 'Schoolbooks and the Myth of Curricular Republicanism: The State and the Curriculum in Canada West, 1820-1850' *Histoire Sociale/Social History* 16(32):305-29.
54. E.Ryerson, 'On the Importance of Education to an Agricultural, and a Manufacturing Population', *Documentary History of Education*, VII:141-50.
55. For examples, *Documentary History*, VII:214-5.
56. Cf. PAO RG2 C6C, S.D. Ardagh, Simcoe, 11 April 1846: 'the parent having to pay only for the actual number of days the Children are in attendance, they are kept at home for the most trivial purposes...'
57. Hodgins, *Documentary History,* VIII:68-74. P.N. Ross, 'The Free School Controversy in Toronto, 1848-1852' in M.B. Katz and P.H. Mattingly (eds) *Education and Social Change: Themes from Ontario's Past* (New York: New York University Press, 1975):57-80.
58. Hodgins, *Documentary History:* VIII:61.
59. Dent, *Last Forty Years* II:93.
60. R.D. Gidney, 'Centralization and education.'
61. Hodgins, *Documentary History* VIII:88-90.
62. Hodgins, *Documentary History* VIII:167-185, for the complete text of the Act.
63. Hodgins, *Documentary History* VIII:235.

64. Hodgins, *Documentary History* VIII:236.
65. PAO RG2 C6C, Leslie to Ryerson, 15 December 1849.
66. Dent, *Last Forty Years* II:128-9; Kenneth Duncan, 'The Irish Famine Immigration and the Social Structure of Canada West' *Canadian Review of Sociology and Anthropology* 1965.
67. Dent, *Last Forty Years* II:156-70.
68. G.M. Jones, 'The Peter Perry Election and the Rise of the Clear Grit Party,' *Ontario History*, XII, 1914:164-75.
69. S. Ryerson, *Unequal Union* :165.
70. Sir A.G. Doughty, (ed) *The Elgin-Grey Papers, 1846-1852*. (Ottawa:The King's Printer, 1937). II:565, Elgin to Grey, 24 December 1849.
71. *Elgin-Grey Papers*. II:724, Elgin to Grey, 11 October 1850.
72. Gidney, 'Robert Murray':41-6
73. Jones, 'Peter Perry':169.
74. Careless, *Union of the Canadas* :168; Dent, *Last Forty* II:186; Jones, 'Peter Perry':173.
75. However, aliens could teach if they agreed to take the oath of allegiance. With central control over curriculum and method, Ryerson regarded the alien clauses as of much lesser significance than they were before 1846.
76. The text of the Act of 1850 is in *Annual Report of the Chief Superintendent on the Normal, Model and Common Schools for the Year 1850*.
77. The text of the Act of 1853 is in *Annual Report of the Chief Superintendent on the Normal, Model and Common Schools for the Year 1852*. As far as I know, this is the first instance of binding arbitration in Canadian public administration.

# Part II:

## The conscience is an infinitely better disciplinarian than the rod.'

### Educational Administration, 1850-1871.

# Chapter Four:
# Contestation of Pedagogical Space

In his essay, 'Politics as a vocation,' Max Weber repeats Leon Trotsky's conception of the state as monopolized violence. 'A state,' he wrote, 'is a human community that (successfully) claims the *monopoly of the legitimate use of physical force* within a given territory.' He added the following important qualification: 'Of course, [physical] force is certainly not the normal or the only means of the state...but force is a means specific to the state.'[1]

A leading preoccupation of Weber's political thought is precisely the translation of the state's monopoly over the means of violence into the effective operation of administration. Class power in the bourgeois era increasingly appears as bureaucratic administration. Bureaucratic administration, in turn, is itself legitimated practically through the establishment of authority relations based on a mixture of rational conviction and habitual obedience.[2] And, of course, for Weber, legitimate authority is authority legitimated by the activities of those subject to it: legitimate authority is recognizable because it is obeyed.

In addition for Weber, one of the characteristics of bureaucratic administration is the specification for bureaux of definite and limited jurisdictions. The rational administration of civil society by the state is conducted through the application of definite rules by a specific personnel within a functionally delimited sphere of authority.[3]

In the construction of bureaucratic educational administration in Canada West, the specification of the educational sphere according to a bureaucratic model was problematic in theory and practice. In theory, the difficulty stemmed from the fact that the educational sphere was intended in a very real sense to be co-extensive with civil society. In practice, the difficulty stemmed from real and persistent struggles over the extent of the pedagogical domain, over its temporal duration, and over the character of the relations it contained.

While the propertyholding classes agreed on the necessity of social education, then, the translation of this agreement into effective practices was accomplished only through persistent struggles, whose echoes remain with us. Even after questions of the locus of educational power had been decided in principle, it remained to make this power real and legitimate--- in Weber's sense, to dispose educational practices and power relations, and to secure obedience to them. Continual conflict surrounded these initiatives.

## Persons and Occasions

The opening of any novel sphere of political force in civil society involves a number of processes. These include the definition of boundaries, the creation of categories of persons, the specification of occasions, the recruitment of personnel, as well as the definition of the content of relations in the sphere in question.

The construction of the educational state in Canada West involved the disposition of at least four kinds of persons, and the recruitment of personnel to function as these persons. The most obvious kinds of educational persons are teachers and students. The pedagogical sphere could not operate without persons charged directly with pedagogical practice in the schoolroom, and without human subjects of that practice. The history of the construction of these persons and more especially of the recruitment of this personnel is treated later in chapters on school attendance and on the production of teachers. In addition to these two groups, the successful operation of pedagogical practice demanded the creation and disposition of elected and appointed public actors. These persons included township or county superintendents of schools, members of county boards of public instruction, school trustees, and particularly as well, school electors. The organization of the pedagogical sphere involved the social production of those directly engaged in it, and of those performing necessary functions for its management.

The production of participants in school elections and in more general processes of school administration was a conscious objective of educational reformers. These persons were to occupy newly created administrative structures and were to follow definite administrative procedures. Participation in administrative activity was intended as a practical exercise in self-government----and all government for nineteenth century state reformers was ultimately self-government (i.e., government of the self, or moral regulation).

This tends to be underemphasized in much educational history. The 'educational' is customarily seen to lie in relations between teachers and students. However, just as the process of education was intended to embrace all of the student's self, so the process of school government was intended to implicate all adult male subjects in a different process of education. The administrative structures of education were intended to educate civil society. The educational *state* points to a general *condition of discipline* for society as a whole, and educational reformers and administrators were well aware of this. As the chief superintendent pointed out in a circular to county clerks in 1852, the administrative procedures of education were crucially important.

> These are not mere arbitrary provisions; they are means to a great end---the social elevation of the whole population of the land. And *this elevation is not effected merely by schools,* but by teaching and habituating the people at large to transact all their public affairs,---from the school section to the county municipality,---in a business-like manner. The accuracy, punctuality, and method observed in such proceedings, will soon be extended to all the transactions of domestic and private life, and thus exert a salutary influence upon all the social relations and personal habits of the whole people.[4]

Throughout the discourse of mid-nineteenth century educational reform, the centrality of local administrative structures as themselves key organs of 'civilization' is evident. The chief superintendent engaged in various kinds of administrative activity which sought to frame or structure local educational activity. He and other central officers produced standardized instruments for reporting and evaluating local practices: attendance registers, daybooks, forms of accounting. Attempts were made even to standardize the form of educational correspondence, with letter-writers at times instructed to use particular kinds of paper, and to organize their letters in particular ways. Procedures were specified for the local acquisition of educational equipment such as maps and prize books. The chief superintendent distributed circulars on various subjects to local administrators, circulars which specified practices to be followed locally, or which sought to collect from localities particular ways of dealing with 'educational problems'.

In addition to framing educational knowledge and practice in these general ways, the central authority consistently intervened in particular localities to enforce compliance with official procedure. Individual County Clerks, for instance, who were slow, sloppy, or inadequate in school accounting were exhorted by central administrators to follow standard procedures more closely. The Clerk for Hastings County in 1853, for instance, was warned that his procedures were sufficiently inept 'to bring down any Public Department of the Government.' The chief superintendent added,

> Though it is not the duty of this Department to instruct county clerks in their duties as prescribed in the School Act, much less to provide them with forms of their accounts, I have undertaken no little pains in successive Circulars to point out to them the kind of returns required, to call their attention to the several defects occurring in their returns, & even in providing them with blank returns....My circular to you last year on this subject, was so explicit & minute as to leave no justification for the errors & defects in the returns of this year.[5]

Looking back on his efforts at the construction of an educational administration before 1867, the chief superintendent wrote:

> ...I have sought...so to frame the whole school system as to make its local administration an instrument of practical education to the people, in the election of representatives, and the corporate management of their affairs---embracing most of the elementary principles and practice of civil government, and doing so to a greater extent than is done in the school system of any country in Europe, or of any state in America.[6]

Educational practice was directed at the enfranchised male propertyholder and through him to domestic or 'private' life generally. It sought to make that person an active participant in civil government.

The central office sought to abolish the traditional powers of the local school meeting to decide almost all matters of educational import. The Education Acts envisaged the creation of a body of public officials known as school trustees. These adult male propertyholders in the local school section were elected by other adult male proprietors. Specific administrative functions were enjoined upon them, and they were subject to legal penalties for inadequate performance. Once in office, trustees were independent of local opinion and interest in principle in all matters except the method of paying the school tax and the selection of a new site, should the schoolhouse be moved.

In practice, trustees were in a contradictory position which subjected them to diverse and often conflicting demands. They were situated locally and hence constrained to interact with friends and neighbours, to live as members of the local community. In many instances, they defined their interests in ways congenial to the majority of people in the locality, and against those of the education office. The local interest in economy, to which many trustees were responsive, for instance, led trustees to engage teachers considered incompetent by the education office. Other trustees in the same interests allowed banned books to be used in schools, or conspired to exclude some local residents from access to the school. There was a good deal of truth in the position of the trustees in section no.4 of Logan Township in 1866 with respect to proposed changes in the School Act which would have replaced local section trustees with Township School Boards. The trustees in Logan Township wrote that their office should be preserved because,

> ...the parents and guardians who mainly support the school, and who have the main care of their children, and who shall be once accountable for them, should have the management of their school in their own hands.[7]

On the other hand and at the same time, the Education Acts removed the powers of the local school meeting, in the main, and trustees were interposed between community members and teachers. As the chief superintendent wrote to Edward Roberts of Smith Town in 1852,

> The teacher is not responsible to the parents of the Children he teaches. He is alone responsible to the Trustees, to whom the parents can state their complaints.[8]

While local residents repeatedly attempted to assert their right to directly determine educational questions in a democratic forum, the education office as repeatedly refused to accept the existence or proceedings of any school meeting outside the narrow compass defined by the law. The *Educational Manual* for 1856 noted that,

> All that an annual school meeting has power to do, is enumerated in the....act. All else that an annual school meeting may resolve to do is null and void, as if it had not been done....The trustees are not required to refer to any public meeting whatever, as to the nature or amount of any expenses they may judge it expedient to raise, to promote the interests of the school under their charge....[9]

The School Act of 1850 also explicitly removed from local residents the powers they had enjoyed under the Act of 1816 to assemble at will for school purposes. As the *Educational Manual* again emphasized, 'No other parties than the trustees of a school section have authority to call a legal meeting of the voters of each section, except the local superintendent....'[10]

## Parents and Children

In addition to this kind of incorporation, the educational initiatives sought to create two less immediately obvious categories of persons, called 'parents' and 'children', who collectively were to constitute 'families'. The School Acts and the practice of school administration posited the existence of such entities, and attributed particular kinds of characteristics to them. To parents was imputed 'authority' over 'schoolchildren' while the latter were not at school (more or less as we shall see). 'Good' and 'responsible' parents exerted this authority successfully and in perfect harmony with the characterological thrust of schooling. These parents ensured that what went on in school was replicated at home. They 'accustomed their children to discipline' so that teachers could easily govern them at school. They trusted implicitly in the process of schooling and in teachers and willingly abdicated their authority over 'children' at school.

'Bad' or —as they were usually taxed—'indifferent' parents did not exert this authority at all or at all effectively. They countered the efforts of the school at home by practices such as criticizing the teacher in their child's hearing. They were not content to relinquish their authority during school hours. They were likely to be 'school disturbers'; that is, to intervene in the sphere of direct pedagogical practice. They were not content, if voters, to restrict their educational participation to those approved official occasions and activities: voting at the annual school meeting, spectating at the quarterly public examination.

While parents are less immediately visible as products of the state's activities, it is clear that they are necessarily posited by the operation of educational administration. That political process, in which schooling is centrally implicated, of disciplining the population, involved the creation of 'due parental authority', and also involved the obverse process: 'infantilization'. As the adult members of households were posited as authoritative in relation to juvenile members, the latter were posited as lacking in authority. The noun used to refer to these last changed with the establishment of public schooling, from the neutral 'scholar' to the laden 'schoolchild' or 'pupil'. As Alison Prentice has shown, this paralleled another linguistic change from 'friends' to 'family'; from 'friends' to 'parents'.[11] The linguistic change signals a political change. Prentice has explored the ways in which the discourse of schooling presented the school as continuous with 'the family',[12] but this may be somewhat misleading. Bourgeois reformers generally regarded existing domestic organization in the population at large to be socially dangerous. Vehement denunciations of domestic organization were widespread, and plans for the reorganization of domestic relations amongst the 'lower orders' were widely publicized.

E.A. Talbot's *Five Years' Residence in the Canadas* (1824) presented a view of social organization which, if somewhat exaggerated to titillate its British audience, was nonetheless characteristic of middle class reaction to Canadian social organization. In the Canadas, according to Talbot, the lower orders were 'indefatigable in acquiring a knowledge of THE RIGHTS OF MAN, THE JUST PRINCIPLES OF EQUALITY AND THE TRUE NATURE OF INDEPENDENCE.'[13] While the 'first class' of society, composed of 'professional men, merchants, civil and military officers,' was a feeble but acceptable version of polite society in Britain, the 'second class', consisting of 'farmers, mechanics, and labourers, who associate together on all occasions without any distinction,'[14] was extremely degraded. In this class, marriages were early and thoughtless and the conditions of economic independence were easy. Sexual intercourse before marriage was ordinary and after marriage 'UNIVERSAL LOVE' was the 'order of the day; and heaven have mercy on the man who is married, and is not willing to recognize this as sound doctrine!'[15] Women raised children out of wedlock with no apparent dishonor, widows with children were the most desirable marriage partners and men were expected to do household labour.[16]

In addition to the absence of sexual property in women, Talbot claimed that books in Upper Canada were more scarce than 'pine-apples on the summit of Snowdon'. The people were 'utterly devoid of all relish for reading' and 'gain' was 'their god, at whose shrine they sacrifice all principle and truth.' Swearing and gambling were universal and Talbot quoted his predecessor, Dr. Howison:

> A lawless and unprincipled rabble, consisting of the refuse of mankind, recently emancipated from the subordination that exists in an advanced state of society, all equal in point of right and possessions, compose of course a democracy of the most revolting kind.[17]

As for the members of the juvenile population, they quickly 'imbibe[d] the same absurd notions of equality and independence.' The boys were total strangers to 'every thing like subordination' and considered themselves 'free as the mountain air, and independent as the sun of heaven.' These young people tended to 'hold in the most sovereign contempt the opinions and approbation of the better part of society,' and Talbot insisted that it was very unlikely that any such person 'can make a very valuable member of civil society.'[18]

Again, while Talbot's prose is likely hyperbolic, the political thrust of his discourse is clear: sound social organization was seen to involve an overlapping complex of authority relations. These were centred on the authority of men over women, of parents over children, and of the 'first class' over the 'second'. Public educational reform was situated in this discourse---both during the period in which it was initially organized, and in its later self-reflection on its origins. Talbot's text appears in the official history of education in

Canada West as an accurate empirical description.

School reformers and administrators in Canada West were also well acquainted with the efforts of middle class reformers in Britain and France to reconstruct popular domestic organization. The plans of Thomas Chalmers to reconstruct the 'civic economy' were particularly widely publicized, and the education department library seems to have contained a copy of the Paris prefect of police's scheme for the creation of sound families.[19]

The educational project, then, aimed far beyond the walls of the schoolroom. 'Due relations of authority' were posited throughout the relations of educational administration, and educational historians have tended to overlook the extent to which the process of educational reform involved the construction of now-ordinary social categories and authority structures.

This point can be illustrated by looking at the practices which public schooling attempted to make normal. Consider the rules of the Hamilton Central School, published in 1853. This school was the first to put the 'Normal School system' in practice outside of Toronto. It organized graded instruction in a central school, conducted largely by female Normal School graduates under the direction of male administrators. The Hamilton Board of Trustees published a lengthy and precise list of rules and regulations designed to govern the behaviour of students at the school, and these included claims on the part of the school to determine who might attend and under what conditions. In particular, the trustees demanded notes from the parents of absent students. This practice was sufficiently novel that the trustees felt compelled to explain it in a lengthy postscript, in which they claimed to,

> feel that in conducting a large school of 1000 or 1200 children it is essentially necessary that the Principal should be able to ascertain what children are *voluntarily* absenting themselves, and which are detained at home by their parents. They have therefore authorised him to require a note upon all occasions when a child is absent or arrives late at school. Should any parent, however, object to the trouble of writing these excuses, they can, by calling upon the principal and stating their wishes to him, have their children exempted from the requirements

of this regulation. But it must at the same time be remembered, that, as it is impossible for the teachers to call upon the parents of all the absent children, the authorities of the school cannot be responsible for the regular attendance of these exempted pupils.[20]

Elsewhere, the trustees pointed out that students voluntarily absent from school would be exposed to various 'micro-penalties', such as demotion, loss of standing in a class and so on.

One might be tempted simply to view this is an instance of the emergence of bureaucratic procedure out of the increasing scale of relations in education. As the school grows larger, teachers are unable to verify attendance personally, so note-writing becomes the necessary instrument. However, as we shall see in the following chapter, 'parents' often refused to write notes at all and insisted that their 'children' could come to school whenever they [the 'children'] pleased.

The trustees' postscript is more accurately seen as an instance of the imputation of authority over 'children' to 'parents' outside the school. The postscript contains the proposition that parents must write notes for children. If they do not wish to, they must go through a definite procedure---coming to the school, having a desire for an *exemption,* (not for the abolition of the regulations) expressing that wish, and being willing to accept the 'responsibility' that the school will thereby forfeit. 'Children', of course, can't write notes, determine when they want to come to school, or be responsible for themselves.

The construction of civil administration involved the elaboration of new patterns of authority in society generally, and the redistribution of authority relations. As a disciplinary process it involved the imputation of powers and obligations to some members of civil society, and a practical disempowering of others. State building was inevitably a process of subjectification, as Philip Corrigan and Derek Sayer so eloquently demonstrate.[21] It involved the multi-faceted construction of gendered and authoritative selves and the formation and populating of social categories. However, these processes of state building and self-construction did not go forward silently or smoothly. There were no smooth, anonymous, structurally homogeneous social transformations involved. Rather, selves were built and forms implanted only through a process of struggle and resistance, a process which remains continually with us.

## Opposition to Pedagogical Space

Opposition to the creation and development of state pedagogical spaces in general was common in Canada West in the formative period from 1850 to 1871. This resistance took different forms. The most public forms of resistance will concern us least here. They include the highly organized opposition to public education which came from the hierarchy of the Catholic church. Beginning in 1852, Bishop de Charbonnel of Toronto began an intense agitation against public schooling, publishing a pastoral letter which threatened excommunication to all Catholics who attended or patronized such schools. While this activity was effective in enshrining or strengthening separate school clauses in the School Acts, and while the question of sectarian education was repeatedly debated in parliament, its consequences were limited. Perhaps eighty or a hundred separate schools were organized during the period under investigation, out of a total of over three thousand. For all the political furor the question generated, its history is written and need not concern us here.[22]

Other and less well-known forms of opposition to the existence of pedagogical space as such also existed. Local opponents of pedagogical space acted directly to counter its organization or operation. Schools were burned or otherwise destroyed, unpopular teachers were beaten or harrassed, school taxes were evaded or avoided, and so forth. These forms of opposition were highly localized. They did not result in the organization of stable groups or movements, and indeed rarely did they attract any attention outside the particular school section. Of course, the central educational office knew about them, but did not generally address them publicly. Nonetheless, these and other forms of opposition existed in virtually all parts of the province throughout the period 1850-1871. If this opposition was often inarticulate and incohate, it was also irrepressible.

No systematic research of the history of school burning has yet been written, and I do not presume to present one here. Such a history would involve detailed investigation of sources not touched upon here: the local press, court records, traces of popular memory. While school-burning was perhaps not the popular activity in Canada West that it was in Ireland[23] or even Canada East, many reports of schools being burned exist in the archival records. The motives of school burners varied, and in many cases remain unknown. Still, the education office received numerous accounts of schools burned 'by design', through 'the work of an incendiary', of school fires whose origin seemed to local residents 'a mystery', and of schools robbed and then burned.[24] The circumstances sometimes pointed to local taxpayers, as when the school register---- used to calculate the school tax--- was burned before the house was set alight.[25] In other instances, opposition to the conduct of trustees or of the teacher led to direct action in the locality which might include burning or otherwise destroying the schoolhouse. In union section no. 20 of Toronto and Trafalgar Townships in 1856, the trustees complained there existed 'a riotous group of people whose conduct publicly declares their aversion to the improvement of education.' These people attempted to have a resolution abolishing the section school passed at the annual school meeting, and when the resolution failed they burned the school to the ground. When the trustees attempted to continue the school in a rented house, the opponents of the school elected one of their number a trustee and banned the teacher from the school.[26]

This sort of activity was not simply the action of a 'disgruntled' section of the local school population. Some of it was clearly related to the political transformations in school organization provoked by the School Acts. The latter ended in principle and increasingly in practice the direct or plebiscitarian democracy in school matters which had prevailed before 1846. In particular, the Acts empowered the elected representatives of adult male propertyholders to determine the educational will of the school section. Where these representative school trustees decided to define the educational interests of the section in ways the majority of the population found unacceptable, they were nonetheless supported in principle by the education office.

In this situation, local school participants were left either to abdicate their right to participate actively in the pedagogical sphere, or to intervene directly and extra-legally. Their traditional right to be present in the schoolhouse during lessons---a right formally stated by some school commissioners under the Act of 1841[27]-as removed by the Acts of 1846-53. Under the Act of 1853, they were subject to fines or imprisonment as 'school disturbers'. While it seems that in the long run, practice in the educational state has largely succeeded in neutralizing the direct intervention of the adult sections of the population in schools, this was achieved only through struggle. In the formative period of educational administration unpopular initiatives by trustees or teachers were often countered directly.

In section no.24 of Sidney Township in 1858, the school trustees decided to build new schools on new sites against the wishes of the majority of section residents. They began construction, only to have the partially-completed school levelled twice by its opponents. They were successful in a third attempt at construction, levied a school rate and distrained the property of one defaulting taxpayer, only to find themselves served with a writ from the local magistrate.[28]

Both 'improving' trustees and 'improving' teachers who attempted to carry out the letter of central educational policy found themselves the victims of direct and sometimes violent opposition. David Linn, the Secretary Treasurer of section no.4 in Storrington Township, decided in 1866 that affairs in his section should be reorganized to more closely follow the school law. To him this meant, among other things, that parents should no longer be allowed to enter the schoolhouse and tell the teacher what and how they wanted their children taught, nor should they refuse to allow the teacher to punish their children. He attempted to have parents charged as 'school disturbers', but the local magistrate refused to do so, because the parents began disrupting the school before and after legal school hours.[29]

James Bruce, a public advocate of temperance and a public opponent of the Orange Order, was told by some residents of section no.7 Mulmur Township that if he came to teach in their section, they would burn the school. He came anyway, and two days later the school was burned.[30] Francis Naylor was trained at the teacher's college maintained by the British and Foreign School Society in London--- the Borough Road School.[31] He came to Canada in 1856 and took a school in Oneida Township, neglecting, however, to sign an agreement with his trustees according to the form of the law.

When his trustees decided to 'turn him out' of his position, he took the matter to arbitration and won the right to remain. The Trustees vowed to appeal, but the School Act of 1850 specified that all local school arbitrations were binding, and no appeal from their rulings was possible. Soon after the arbitration decision, Naylor found that,

> ...large numbers of children were kept at home. The windows & door of the School house were nailed up then dung was placed on my seat & writing desk & the boards over head were pulled up & thrown over the room in all directions.[32]

Mr. Donoghue in Hillsburg was fired in December of 1857 by his trustees removing the school stove and stovepipes.[33] John Carroll claimed that residents in Oakville were harrassing him, and that his trustees refused to protect him.

> From the commencement of my teaching some party or parties unknown to me began a series of depredations against the schoolhouse: such as breaking the windows, filling the stovepipe with rubbish so as to prevent the smoke from passing out, and compelling me sometimes to vacate the house....[34]

Similar activities took place throughout the formative period from 1850 to 1871. In section no.3 of Arthur Township in 1854, the trustees complained that people who opposed free schooling tore down the school house and sold the furniture. However, here an arbitrator's report described the school as a 'hog pen' and the trustees as incompetent.[35] In no.6 of Beverly Township in 1855, students were withdrawn from the school after the teacher punished a boy over sixteen. The teacher was forced to quit and someone broke into the school house and stole the register to prevent the collection of the school tax.[36] Alex M'Kee claimed he was fired by his trustees for no reason whatsoever, except that he had reported the conduct of one trustee's son for 'firing stones at me in school.'[37] A.J. Keillor claimed to have been forced out of his school 'by reason of the continual interference of one of the Trustees regarding my duties as a Teacher publicly in the S. Room, an individual who cannot sign his own name.'[38] The trustees in this case claimed Keillor was continually drunk.[39] In Oakwood, a person was fined as a school disturber by John Jacobs, J.P., because he attempted to prevent the teacher from teaching by not letting him in the school door.[40] Hugh

Gunn, the Teacher in section no.5 of Puslinch Township in 1868, claimed that his trustees offered him no protection from three men armed with clubs who continually attempted to disturb his school.[41]

Students themselves acted against certain teachers. In section no. 9 of Saltfleet Township in 1859, a young teacher was locked in the school house for an hour by his students, after unsuccessfully attempting to punish some of them. When they released him, 'they threw mud and mire into his face and over his clothes.' The students were said to be encouraged by their parents.[42]

A far more notorious set of events took place in section no.7 of Brantford in the 1860s. Here a teacher named W. Young taught in 1863. Young was highly qualified, in the terms of the education office. Among other things he had been an Assistant Teacher under Ryerson himself at Victoria College in 1840, and had also attended one of the training sessions at the short-lived Model Grammar School in Toronto. He wrote to the chief superintendent in April of 1863,

> In my efforts to introduce good order & discipline I have been so thwarted by the trustees & parents of the children, that I have been under the necessity of seeking the protection of the Magistrate & have had some of the scholars fined for disorderly conduct.

Young had been assaulted by one of his students, a trustee's son, who was twenty years of age and who, Young claimed, was encouraged by his father. The student, Young wrote, 'knocked me down, repeatedly kicking me & striking me on the head, & cutting me severely.'[43] Young's successor claimed that 'Mr. Young's head, face, and body was, if I understand rightly, pounded literally to jelly.'[44]

Eighteen months later, Timothy Slee began teaching in the same section. One of his twenty year old students tried, in Slee's words 'to set at defiance all authority to govern and keep discipline.' When Slee 'suggested the propriety of his leaving the school,' the student offered to fight. Slee grabbed him by the collar and was about to throw him out of the school when the older male students 'as if by premeditation' pounced on Slee, threw him to the floor and began punching his head. Remembering what had happened to Young, Slee, by his own account, fought to his feet and dismissed everyone from the school. Slee vowed to leave the section at once, but the trustees promised to expell the offending students and any others who disturbed him in the future. With the exception of a visit to the school by 'a young man of over 20 years of age...for no good purpose' who contented himself with throwing bread, paper and snow at the girls, and with spitting tobacco juice into the drinking water on his way out, Slee continued teaching peacefully the following day.

However, one night soon after, as Slee and his family were asleep in the school house, a group of young men disturbed them by throwing stove wood onto the roof. This continued for four nights and when Slee threatened to inform on those responsible, he was told that their friends would provide them with alibis. Three weeks later, Slee was awakened in the dead of night by 'a sudden dreadful crash' and found that one of the schoolhouse windows had been smashed, sash and all. He protested to his trustees, who refused to act. The very next night, the schoolhouse was surrounded by a crowd of about 'twenty roughs of the neighbourhood' who passed in front 'humming a doleful dirge' and then began pelting the house with broken bricks and gravel, laughing and talking the while.

Slee maintained that he was not about to be driven out by a gang of roughs, nor would he abandon a school which everyone in the neighbourhood agreed was a success. Yet soon after, two of the trustees served him with a month's notice to leave the school. Slee claimed that they found no fault with him as a teacher, but wished to prevent 'serious consequences, as parties outside of the school had some kind of grudge against me.' Slee then announced to his scholars that he was closing the school. The following night, an armed party marched around the school in quasi-military formation, whistling the 'Rogue's march' and at midnight, Slee was disturbed by 'a low whistling and dodging.' He resolved to move his family to the safety of Brantford village, but as a wagon was being loaded with his possessions, shots were fired and 'threats were made to have satisfaction out of the master if he returned.' Slee claimed that he was determined 'upon no consideration' to teach 'in so treacherous a neighbourhood.' Yet two weeks later, the trustees 'and patrons' had Slee arrested for breach of contract. He was arraigned, a prosecution was begun and plans were made to commit him to trial, when the local justice, 'Squire Mathews', refused to continue. The trustees and Slee settled through 'an equitable adjustment in financial matters.'[45]

No other archival material exists with respect to this particular case. It is not possible to determine the motivations or interests of those opposed to Slee, nor to resolve the contradictory and ambiguous elements in his account. It is not necessary, in any case, to champion populist violence (which I do not) to appreciate that where democratic local educational self-government was abolished and where the education office encouraged the placing of missionary teachers in local schools, educational participants might resort to direct action to alter educational practices, or to remove offensive teachers. Many teachers did accept teaching as a mission, as John Thomas Tuthill, who saw teaching as 'to instruct the young, to elevate the masses, and refine public taste', attests. The education office attempted to give to such teachers greater security of employment, by specifying legal forms for teachers' contracts, and by making such contracts binding on trustees.

Where oppositional activities came from students, many teachers claimed they were encouraged by others in the community. 'I find that the bad conduct of many of the pupils has been upheld by the parents,' complained Hiram Maloy.[46] As the superintendent of schools for Thurlow Township put it, parents

> ...too frequently fault the Teacher in presence of their Children, ---The child listens to the parents, and forms the same opinion of the Teacher---In this case his influence is lost with that child.[47]

The opposition of students, this suggests, is not best seen as the 'deviance' of a few people incapable of achieving desired community standards. Rather, in cases where students had the support of other community members, opposition may more usefully be seen as resistance in the face of political initiatives directed against popular character and popular culture.

## The Limits of the Pedagogical Sphere

While there were many instances of opposition in localities which one may interpret as statements about the existence of a state pedagogical sphere as such, other forms of opposition conceded the existence of this sphere but attempted to limit its extent or to control relations in it. The distinction often cannot be finely drawn, for some counter-definitions of schooling in effect called state schooling as such into question. For example, opponents of a particular element in the curriculum may have accepted that there should be a school and that the school should have a curriculum, only that consumers should determine some items in it. Yet, given that state schooling was about improving the 'ignorant' masses, even such limited forms of opposition implicitly defined educational consumers in ways unacceptable to the operation of state education. Still, some forms of local opposition seem to be particularly concerned with the extent and duration of the pedagogical sphere and of pedagogical activity.

In the nature of the case the limits, both temporal and spatial, to the pedagogical sphere were problematic. On the one hand, education was intended to be limitless in its consequences. The student adequately formed at school was to live its principles at all times. In this way, schools were seen by state officials as a means of diffusing useful habits throughout civil society. Yet, on the other hand, educational administration claimed to be governed by universalistic bureaucratic norms. Schooling was to be a distinct sphere, in which teachers would govern according to principles specified in advance by the central authority. The limitless thrust of schooling and the limited jurisdiction of educational bureaucracy frequently conflicted in practice. The participants in schooling struggled continually and at times violently over these matters.

The School Act of 1850 by no means created the problem of defining the limits of the pedagogical sphere. In the transitional period of the 1840s various attempts were made by school authorities to specify workable limits. The township Commissioners of Common Schools under the School Act of 1841 were empowered to specify rules for the management of township schools. Many of these Commissioners concerned themselves with the temporal and spatial limits of the authority of the teacher. In most townships, the Commissioners were content merely to specify the hours of 'keeping school', the timing of 'intermissions' or recesses, and to inform teachers that they were responsible for the conduct of their scholars during these periods.[48]

The main impetus for the attempts by Township Commissioners to extend the authority of the school teacher outwards seems to have come from an interest in separating the genders. In this period, where school toilets were largely unknown, some Commissioners were particularly concerned with enforcing the separation of the genders during recesses. Thus, for example, the Commissioners for Dumfries Township specified that the school day would be from 9 am to 4 pm in summer and from 9 am to 3 pm in winter with an hour's intermission at noon. Students were not to leave the schoolroom without permission, and 'Boys and girls shall not be allowed to leave at the same time.'[49] In Huntly Township, the teachers were required to 'provide an instrument called a pass to prevent more than one child to be out at a time and that for only five minutes each time.'[50] In Cornwall Township, the Commissioners sought to prevent 'the practice so prevalent in schools of children running out and in during school hours' by specifying a ten minute break at 11 am and at 3 pm where teachers were to 'allow the Female and Male scholars to go out alternately.'[51] The rules for Gainsborough Township sought to prevent the scholars from leaving the schoolroom without permission, and to prevent them from 'loitering in the road' on their way to and from school.[52]

Some Township Commissioners and some teachers were also concerned to extend the authority of the school further outwards. In the second division of Dunnville, for instance, the Commissioners requested the Teacher to 'inculcate on the minds of his Pupils, that on all Occasions they do show a proper respect to their Superiours and all aged persons.'[53] Similar rules were made by individual teachers. James Brenan, the teacher in section no.5 of Emily Township, presented a list of rules to his students which included this:

> It is required that all children coming to school, will have their hands and face cleaned, and head combed, that they will come to, and go from school quietly and mannerly, saluting every person they meet by the way, without either shouting or hollowing or loitering their time on the road.[54]

In Cobourg village, Nicholas Wilson insisted that the students were 'to come to and go from the School as <u>Decent</u> and <u>Well</u> conducted <u>Children</u>.'[55] Some Township Commissions specifically required teachers to correct 'improper' behaviour by students outside the school. In Cornwall Township, the teachers were to 'take Cognizance of any disorderly or indecorous conduct of any of the scholars when going to or returning from the school.'[56] Teachers in Sidney Township were instructed to appoint student monitors to watch students on their way to and from school, and to report any misconduct.[57] In Charlotteville, where the Commissioners elaborated and published a comprehensive set of school 'Rules and Regulations', the second 'duty of teachers' was,

> To take charge of the scholars as far as practicable from the time they leave home for school, until their return from school; to require them to make no unnecessary call at any house, shop, or other place, during said time—to remain at, or within calling distance of the school-room, during intermission, and to avoid all unnecessary noise, and dangerous and improper diversions.[58]

No means of doing this were specified.

The expectation that norms of scholarly behaviour would prevail beyond the walls of the schoolhouse clearly existed in some quarters before 1850, and in some places teachers were expected to enforce behavioural patterns outside as well as inside the school. In this matter, as in many others, the policy of the central office after 1850 drew upon earlier practices. However, the educational interventions of 1846-50 sharply changed the importance of the matter. It was one thing for scattered and locally elected Township Commissioners to regulate particular aspects of pedagogical practice in given areas, and quite another for a centralized administration to attempt to create uniform practice throughout the province. As well, of course, the nature of pedagogical activity itself increasingly changed. What went on the schoolroom ceased to be determined in principle (although less so in practice) by local consumers of education, and instead was specified by a central authority in keeping with definite political objectives. As a course of 'civilizing' and 'improving' local populations, pedagogical activity was radically different after 1850 than before. Pedagogical authority was transformed, and with it the significance of its limits.

The School Act of 1850 gave the Council of Public Instruction the capacity to formulate such rules and regulations for the government of public schools as it saw fit. In none of the School Acts passed in the period 1850-1871 was any mention made of the authority of teachers extending to the activities of students outside the schoolroom and outside definite schoolhours. Omnibus clauses did exist which allowed teachers to enforce general behavioural demands--- the clause instructing teachers to enforce any rules of school governance specified either by their own trustees or by the Council of Public Instruction is a case in point--- but law was significantly vague on the precise limitation of the pedagogical sphere. In practice, these limits were defined through local negotiation, struggle and conflict. This is an area in which attempts were made to transform law into administration; an instance of what Foucault has called 'normalizing power'.[59] Here power was constituted through practice, through habituation, through enforced repetition to the point where repetition became a force in its own right.

The correspondence of the education office during the period 1850-1871 abounds with letters dealing with the question of the limits of teachers' authority. The sheer weight of the correspondence points both to the existence of a great deal of local activity in this area, and to the existence of struggles which could not be resolved in local school units. It is remarkable that the education office itself was unable to specify a set of effective limits to the pedagogical sphere during this period. Questions posed in one school section and addressed by the education office reappear again and again in other school sections. Published opinions from the education office do not halt the flow of local reports of conflict over the question.[60]

J.C. Misener of Troy wrote in April of 1866 wondering if he could punish students for offenses they committed on Saturdays and Sundays. He was told he could only punish for offenses committed at school.[61] Other teachers complained that their authority in the schoolroom was severely limited because trustees would not allow them to punish students for offenses committed outside school hours.[62] The question posed by the Teacher in Hullsville in 1868 appeared again and again: precisely at 'what time a teachers authority begins and ends over a pupil attending school?'[63]

Teachers attempted to enforce the patterns of behaviour they taught in the school upon students outside the schoolroom, either from a conviction that 'sound morality' was their charge at all times, or simply because they were instructed to do so by their employers. J.B. Rogers, one of the trustees of a school in Tecumseh, found that his son had been fighting with another boy on his way to school, and informed the teacher, who then punished both boys. Other people in the school section complained to him that he had no business interfering in this matter, and that teachers had no power over students on their way to and from the school.[64] In Hagersville, the trustees were disturbed by the refusal of their teacher to stop students beating one another on their way to and from school. Here the teacher claimed he had no jurisdiction in the matter.[65] A teacher in Springford encountered opposition when he wanted to suspend one of his students who had been drunk and swearing in a local tavern.[66] For her part, Anne E. Jackson was told by her trustees to stop the schoolboys from hitching rides on the log sleighs which travelled the road near the school, for fear one of them would be killed. When she suspended one boy for doing so, some of the parents claimed she had exceeded her authority.[67] Ellen Bowes of Strathroy attempted to oversee the behaviour of students on their way home from school, but encountered opposition from parents. She asked,

> May I not appoint a committee of any of the Pupils to report to me every day the conduct of the children on the road going home without the consent of the parents?[68]

She was told by the education office that she could do whatever her trustees said she could.[69]

The principal of the Johnson Street School in Kingston complained of a boy who ran outside the school gate and mocked him, claiming that the principal's authority did not exist off the school grounds.[70] E. Brokovski of Medonte Township discovered that some of his students were stealing from local gardens after school and wondered if he could suspend them and inform the victims.[71] When Martha Pepper attempted to punish a boy for some misdemeanour committed on the road to school he 'stoutly resisted'. When she expelled him, his parents said she had no right to punish him in the first place.[72] Could teachers whip students for offenses committed on the way home, wondered the magistrate for Blanchard?[73] 'At what time or when does the Teacher's authority cease?' enquired J.P. Flanagan of Paris.[74]

## Administrative Vagueness

Initially, in this matter as in several others, the education office attempted to lay claim to a large domain of comportment in civil society. The office clearly considered the educational state to extend well beyond the schoolroom, but this initial position was abandoned in the face of local conflict and struggle.

The Hamilton Central School claimed from the outset the right to regulate the activities of students on their way to and from school. The institution's seventh rule read:

> Pupils who are known to conduct themselves improperly on their way to or from school will be debarred for a time from the privilege of attending the school, or otherwise punished according to the nature of the offense.[75]

(Note here the translation of rights into privileges.) The education office supported this position on the question in the early 1850s, and encouraged local trustees to adopt it as well. The chief superintendent wrote to a trustee in section no.1 of Trafalgar Township in 1855,

> ...the Discipline of the School, and therefore the authority of the teacher, extends to all pupils from the time they leave their parents or guardians until their return to them. Pupils are as responsible to the authority of the School for wrongs they do their fellow pupils, or other improprieties they commit on their way to and from School, as if they did such things on the School premises or in the School. If pupils were not responsible to the School authorities for their conduct going to and from school, endless irregularities might be committed with impunity by pupils.[76]

The journey between household and school was problematic to the education office precisely because 'due relations of authority' had not been established there. Ideally, 'children' would be under authority in the household and in the school, but how to ensure their 'just

# Contestation of Pedagogical Space 163

subordination' in between the two? The position the education office wanted to establish is clear.

> ....a teacher has the same right to punish a child for committing an impropriety in going from or coming to school as he has to punish a pupil for committing an impropriety in school.[77]

The authority of the teacher was to expand to cover this social and physical terrain. Civil society was to be colonized by educational forces and saturated with authority relations--- pedagogical and parental.

Yet the attempts by teachers to govern students outside of schoolhours and off the school grounds generated such consistent and persistent local resistance, that the education office itself was forced to retreat from its initial position. By 1862, the chief superintendent was writing that 'a teacher can exercise none but a moral influence over his pupils going to or returning from school,'[78] and he increasingly left the resolution of this question to what local teachers and trustees could and would enforce:

> ...a Teacher can lawfully carry out any rules adopted by the Trustees in regard to the conduct of the pupils in going to & returning from school; but she cannot of herself make any such rules.[79]

In the later 1860s, the chief superintendent recognized that this question could not be resolved by statute law, and attempted to invoke 'usage'. 'Properly speaking,' he wrote to Wm. Mackintosh, a teacher in Brock, 'a teacher has only control over a pupil while on or near the School premises, but usage gives him a certain control over them especially when going from School; but no general law can be laid down upon the subject.'[80] Increasingly the education office attempted to articulate a conception in which power was related to physical distance, the limits of vision, and the consciousness of the teacher. For instance, in a letter to J.G. Armstrong, the teacher in Hullsville, Ryerson wrote that 'a teacher's authority over a pupil begins when the pupil is near the school premises & terminates when he is out of sight of them.'[81] In 1868, the former superintendent of schools for Brantford wrote to the chief superintendent for aid and guidance with respect to 'two cases of severe punishment for trifling offenses' which 'agitated' his neighbourhood. He asked if teachers had jurisdiction over students going to and from school, 'and if so, how far from the School grounds does the Teacher's jurisdiction extend, and within what hours?'[82] Here again the education office attempt to invoke usage in support of extending pedagogical space beyond the physical limits of the school, and here again no clear limits to this extended authority could be specified.

> ...it has been held by this Dept. that as a general rule the jurisdiction of the teacher over a pupil extends to the whole of the school hours of the day provided the pupil does not go home during the noon recess. In that case (as well as in coming to & going from school) it has been held that a pupil is amenable to the teacher for his conduct while on or near the school grounds or premises. In coming home in the morning or afternoon a pupil (having been last under his parents' control) is responsible to those parents for his conduct until he comes within sight of, or to within a reasonable distance from, the Sch. house. In going from School the pupil is in like manner responsible to the teacher until he passes out of sight of the School house.[83]

A notably different version of the same position appeared in a letter from the chief superintendent to a teacher in Berlin in 1870. Here the teacher's knowledge was implicated in defining the limits of pedagogical authority. Ryerson wrote in part,

> ...it is considered...but right and proper in itself that the master of a Sch. should be responsible for the acts of his pupils while on or near the school premises, as they are under his control & are amenable to his dicipline. That control by analogy may be assumed to be kept up so long as the pupils in going hom are within sight of the sch premises or within ken of the Teacher. It would scarcely be fair to hold the master responsible for the conduct of the pupils as they near their houses, for then the responsibility & jurisdiction of the parent or guardian fairly commences.[84]

The usage the education office attempted to invoke here had no clear existence. 'Usage' was a discursive entity which attempted to cloak whatever local trustees and teachers could successfully enforce with the trappings of tradition. Clearly the limits of pedagogical authority could not be specified in a model of purely bureaucratic administration. The increasing distance between law and administration is particularly evident in this matter. Educational administration was a set of practices of a moral regulatory character.

The parallel between Foucault's analysis analysis of 'panopticism' as a mode of disciplinary power and the education office's conception of pedagogical authority is striking. Increasingly, the limits to authority were defined by the physical arrangement of school and community. 'Sight' of the schoolhouse, 'ken' of the teacher jointly were a form of knowledge/power designed to induce in students a sense of visibility and vulnerability to pedagogical authority. Ideally, for educational administrators, students would internalize this sense and the school would function effectively as a moral authority. The sight of the school, the consciousness that one was drawing near to the school, would induce certain kinds of behaviour, of self-regulation. Pedagogical authority would become effective and legitimate by being implanted in the selves of students. Power creates subjectivities, to recall Foucault once again. The actual physical presence of the school---a presence planned by the education office, which repeatedly published works on school architecture---ideally would influence the behaviour of members of the community.

In any case, the vagueness of administrative initiatives in this regard is not simply accidental. 'Positive' law in fact allowed for the specification of limits to pedagogical authority which would have only counteracted the political principles of social education. By its nature this education could not cease at the schoolroom door or at the schoolyard fence. It was to be implanted in students, and for that reason to be, eventually at least, co-extensive with civil society. A limitless power could only be imperfectly contained in bureaucratic forms; it spilled over their limits, just as those exposed to it sought to specify and contain it.

The education office regarded plans for the extension of pedagogical authority with favor, if these did not provoke serious resistance. This can be seen in the office's support of the plan of the school trustees in Portsmouth village in 1864 to require teachers to visit the parents of all schoolchildren absent for more than three days, to determine the reasons for their absence.[85] Again, in response to the departmental circular of 1863 which sought local suggestions for preventing 'vagrancy and truancy', a member of the Board of Trustees for Kingston suggested the taking of an annual census of all children not attending school. From this census, a secret list of vagrant children would be compiled and circulated to members of the churches to which these children belonged. The Board of Trustees also recommended that the education office enlist charitable organizations for aid in 'watching over families.' [86] 'These are very valuable and practical suggestions,' noted the chief superintendent. [87]

## The Schoolday

Through all these attempts and plans to specify the pedagogical sphere, local struggles over the limits of the schoolday, the organization of activities in it, and the management of its intermissions persisted. As we shall see below, many struggles centred directly on the capacity of teachers to organize the activities of people at school at all---to determine when they would attend and in what condition, and to determine what they would learn. But parallel and persistent conflicts surrounded attempts by teachers to organize the limits of the schoolday, to enlist students in school tasks, to keep them in during the period of noon recess or after school, and so forth.

From this remove, some of this opposition to the activities of teachers seems relatively unproblematic. For instance, a group of parents from Oil Springs complained in 1869 of an incompetent teacher who kept her students from going to the toilet. As one resident wrote, 'my children was compelled to stay in the School by Miss Sefton after requesting to be let out to obey a call of nature until they was obliged to a buse their Clothes most Shamfully.' [88] Still, where teachers had successfully ended the practice of 'children running in and out' at any time during the schoolday, such possibilities were generally present. As well, as a process of self-formation, educational practice involved the shaping of the eliminatory functions in particular ways. A certain kind of self-regulation was one of the capacities posited in the 'schoolchild'

# Contestation of Pedagogical Space 167

by official practice.

Other struggles surrounded attempts by teachers to keep students in after legal school hours or to exclude or suspend them for limited periods. Teachers often attempted to use 'detention' and 'suspension' as disciplinary tactics in place of corporal punishment. The trustees of section no.3 of Wolfe Island thus asked the education office in 1870 if a teacher could 'keep children in after 4 O'clock to learn their lessons,.... Corporal punishment not being allowed; a Teacher has no other alternative.'[89] While the education office here supported the practice,[90] students and parents often refused to accept it.

R.H. Gilbert of Baden told his son to come straight home after school. The teacher insisted the boy remain to sweep the schoolroom, but the boy informed him of his father's instructions and left the school. He was suspended by the teacher and the teacher in turn was supported by the trustees.[91] Other parents intervened directly to prevent teachers from detaining children in the school after hours. H. Turner, the teacher in Millbrook in 1861, locked a group of students in the schoolhouse for an hour at the end of the day as a punishment for not learning their lessons, and went home. When he was gone, someone came and broke down the schoolhouse door to release the students.[92] 'On account of misconduct and neglect of lessons,' wrote John Austin, the teacher in Clark's Mills, 'I kept a number of children in, yesterday evening.' Austin went home, and when he returned to release his prisoners he found 'one person during my absence came and took his little daughter away home.'[93] William Ramine complained in 1870,

> Last evening I had occasion to detain a boy belonging to one of my trustees on account of a misdemeanour which he committed. His father came in, ordered the boy home, accusing me of punishing his boy for the faults of others, using threatening language &c....[94]

A teacher in Walkerton wondered if he could do anything to such parents.

> If the father of the child so detained comes to the school-house and makes a forcible entrance, and in opposition to the teacher orders his child home, and takes him away, does he render himself liable to any punishment for the same.[95]

In this matter, as in many others, the pedagogical theory to which central educational administrators adhered contradicted the reality of practical local administration. By 1850, state school promoters argued routinely in principle that detention was an unsound practice. Yet where teachers were prevented from using corporal punishment--as in many places they were-- detention was an important instrument in the arsenal of school government. The force of this contradiction can be seen in the inconsistent advice directed by the central office to local correspondents. Thus, for example, while the trustees in section no. 3 of Wolfe Island were informed that detention was well within the powers of teachers, a teacher named Peter McDonald from section no.3 of Tuckersmith Township was informed that,

> ...to detain pupils to learn lessons is calculated in the opinion of the best educationists, to make a child hate rather than love his book. To deprive a child of play, or of what he loves, as a punishment for neglect of his lessons, is better than to detain after school hours either to learn or recite his lessons.[96]

In this instance, as in many others, the progressive thrust of bourgeois pedagogy---its attempt to discover and anchor itself in pleasure and the 'true nature' of the student---was blunted by the practice of schooling a reluctant and antagonistic population. Educational administrators frequently wandered in their correspondence with local educational managers between two positions: one specified by bourgeois educational theory, and one required by the struggle to subordinate resistant populations. This often meant that, so long as system principles were not put in question, local teachers and trustees were left to make do, to solve local disputes as best they could. Central policy could not create educational harmony; it settled for the local containment of conflict.

Many of the conflicts in the schoolroom during this formative period of educational administration surrounded the question of freedom of movement on the part of students. Before 1871, no compulsory attendance provisions existed in the School Act. Still, the Council of Public Instruction ruled that students were under the authority of teachers at all times of the school day. Having set foot inside the school, they abdicated the right to leave as they pleased, or to study what they pleased. Local struggles frequently revolved around attempts by teachers to prevent students from leaving the schoolroom once they had entered there. As a chapter eight shows, many of the most violent schoolroom struggles surrounded attempts by students to leave the schoolroom rather than to be beaten by the teacher, and attempts by teachers to force students to remain in the schoolroom and to accept a beating. The education office usually supported these efforts by teachers.[97]

Teachers particularly encountered resistance from older students in regard to detentions and suspensions, and in addition to their own considerable physical capacities, older students were often supported by trustees and local residents in their activities. William Anderson, for instance, who taught in section no. 5 of Pakenham Township, complained in 1859 of 'two young men' in his school 'who think because they are 'young men' that they will do as they please.' Their offenses consisted, among other things, of simply getting up and leaving the schoolroom when they felt like having a stroll and a chat.[98] John Hannah complained of the impossibility of maintaining order in a school with between eighty and ninety students, where the young men hissed and groaned at his precepts, where those he attempted to discipline offered to fight him, and where both trustees and parents refused to allow him to punish older boys.[99] A boy William Beattie attempted to keep in after school for having been late at noon simply pushed Beattie out of his way and left the school.[100] When W.H. McCurdy punished a sixteen year old boy 'with a small wooden rod', the student and three of his friends gathered up their books and left the school. Soon after, McCurdy complained,

> ...five or six pupils <u>bluntly refused</u> to prepare an exercise in composition...I detained them three quarters of an hour....Complaints are now being made that I have violated the law and 'must be expelled'....[101]

Despite the assurance of the education office that McCurdy could discipline his older students----Ryerson wrote, 'It is a great mistake on the part of some boys or girls over sixteen years of age to suppose that they can take liberties in a school,'[102] ---McCurdy's troubles continued. When he tried to make one of his students serve as a monitor the student refused, and the education office this time did not support him.[103]

Both teachers and trustees also frequently encountered refusals by students, often with the support of parents, to accept suspensions, and to perform school maintenance tasks. G.M. Priest, the teacher in section no. 9 of Walpas Township, attempted to govern in the schoolroom in the approved Normal School manner, which involved a repertoire of looks, glances, gestures, and postures, but without success.

> A boy about 13 years of age was reproved by me for laughing and talking in School. I called him up and reprimanded him...[after] a week when he resorted to his former habits I reproved him several times by looks and notions of the head which he regarded but little ....

Priest then expelled the boy for two hours, but his parents described this as insulting behaviour and claimed that the teacher had no right to expell their son.[105] A magistrate in Arkana in 1861 sought information from the education office in a case where

> ...some large boys has thought that they can set the Masters authority at defiance...they resist and in one or two cases clinch him and even strike him several blows. Parents appear to uphold them and say he the (Teacher) has no right to put them out....[106]

In the 1850s, the education office counseled teachers to employ the physical force necessary to remove disobedient students. For instance, Ryerson wrote to Lewis Allen, the teacher in section no.17 of Ernesttown Township,

> ....if a Master finds it necessary to suspend a pupil for gross misconduct, he must of course, use the necessary force to give effect to his orders. If the pupil should resist, and commit an assault, then the Civil Authority should be applied to ....[107]

However, unsuccessful attempts by teachers to remove large students who resisted were so common that by 1864 the education office was counseling them not to attempt it. While the office held that teachers had the legal authority to expell students, where the latter resisted it was more 'dignified' for the teacher to threaten them with the charge of disturbing the school.[108]

Again, many students refused to perform such tasks as sweeping the school house, lighting fires or cleaning the yard.[109] Vina Root, who taught the village school in Plum Hollow in 1868, asked one of her students to split some wood for the school. When he refused, she told him to take off his coat and be punished. He refused again, and then told his father who supported him. When Root expelled a seventeen year old girl for inattention, one of her trustees came into the schoolroom and berated her before the class, calling her too independent in her attitude towards the students.[110] Abraham Shortland's attempts to make his students spy on each other at noon hour were opposed by them, and they complained to the trustees. Shortland also had difficulty making the students write in the manner he wanted. 'Some conceited fellows,' he complained, 'will not write after me in school. Have I a right to compell them to write large text hand, or such hand as I think will benefit them?'[111]

Attempts by the education office to extend the authority of the teacher to periods not closely specified in the School Act met constant resistance from students and parents, but also from reluctant teachers. For example, in a school section near Camden East in 1867,

> The teacher...ordered a boy out of the school room while it was being swept out, he went out, but not as fast as the teacher thought he should, he therefore followed him out an struck him three or four time with a pointer....[112]

Here people in the school section claimed that the teacher's jurisdiction over the student had ended the moment he ordered him out of the school. The teacher in turn demanded of the education office, 'Has a School teacher jurisdiction to keep order within the limits of the School premises during the intermissions allowed by law....'[113] But while the education office here argued that 'the authority of the master over his pupils is paramount at all times of the day during which the pupil is in his charge---including the dinner hour,'[114] teachers themselves were not always prepared to exercise a continuous authority.

Where teachers did not live in the schoolhouse, as was more often the case after 1860, they customarily went home to eat dinner at noon. This often meant that students were left alone in the schoolhouse, and many of those who supported 'due order' in the school---or who regarded this as laxness on the part of their employees--- objected. Could the teacher, Thomas Henry asked, leave at noon for dinner and 'leave the Children to practice all evil and immoral actions, beat and abuse each other?' Would it not be better that he stay and 'hinder the evil corruption and watch over them?'[115] Initially the education office advised local administrators to follow established practices in their area,[116] but by the later 1850s the chief superintendent urged teachers to change their eating habits and to stay in the school at noon. Ryerson warned the teacher in section no.2 of Dereham Township that he could not delegate his authority over students to a monitor during the noon hour, but should stay in the school at noon and dine in the evening.[117] Later, while agreeing that a teacher might 'appoint a trusty pupil to observe and report irregularities in his momentary absence during the schoolday,' Ryerson nonetheless urged teachers to imitate the behaviour of urban government and clerical workers.

> In nearly all public departments, & I believe in many of the City & town shops, the officers do not get their dinners till their day's work is done. They take but a cold luncheon at noon if they take anything at all, as do pupils at School.[118]

This matter also illustrates the extent to which the successful peopling of the public sphere involved the formation of selves. Here the 'appetite' of teachers was posited in a particular way by the operation of schooling.

Parents and local residents, as well as some school administrators, in a similar vein, opposed attempts by teachers to allow school recesses or 'intermissions'. The education office supported the practice of granting intermissions on the grounds of sound pedagogy. The practice was general in the model schools which most impressed Egerton Ryerson on his educational tour of 1844-5, and in some ----David Stow's Glasgow Normal Training Seminary, for instance--- intermissions of as much as ten minutes every hour or more were allowed.[119] Thus, when the trustees of the village of Meaford attempted to prevent D.R. Grey's sister from giving her students a morning and afternoon intermission, the chief superintendent wrote to defend her right to grant intermissions of a few minutes an hour up to five times a day.[120] Still, the Board of Trustees in St. Thomas opposed recesses on the grounds of the noise they generated, and when a teacher named McLachlin defended the pedagogical necessity of the practice they fired him.[121] Parents in Newcastle opposed recesses because their children tore their clothes and wet their feet.[122]

Some people, like Mr. Mac Farland of Grimsby, regarded recesses as a dereliction of duty on the part of teachers and as an affliction produced by the education office. He wrote,

> ...may the Teacher take them in at 9 O clock Ceep theme in all for a fiew minutes and then let a part or what he cales a class out on what he cals intermitian, not on the School or play grounds of the School, as he says the make rather much nois for him to stand that is paid for it, but to let them run at large Jump yeal and Screame like the Demans raund the Streets of the Village to the terror and annoyance of those that are grievously Taxed to pay for their education and not their annoyance and newsence....[123]

Urban 'terror and annoyance' were unintended consequences of the organization of 'children' into large groups at school. It was schooling that gathered the people Mr. Mac Farland complained of together, and it was undoubtedly the experience of schooling which in large part constructed their desire to 'Jump yeal and Screame like the Demans.' Schooling in fact generated the very characteristics it posited in categories of persons. But those intended to occupy the categorical spaces of schooling often did so only reluctantly. This will be shown again in the matter of school attendance, which the next chapter investigates.

## Notes to Chapter Four

1. Max Weber, *Essays in Sociology,* (C.W. Mills and H.H. Gerth, eds) (New York: Oxford,1958:)78.
2. Max Weber, 'The Social Psychology of the Great Religions,' in *Essays in Sociology,* :293ff.
3. Max Weber, 'Bureaucracy', in *Essays in Sociology:* 196-244.
4. PAO RG2 C1G, Circular to Clerks of County Councils, 10 July 1852.
5. PAO RG2 C2, Ryerson to County Clerk, Hastings, Belleville, 29

July 1853. A similar point is made by Alison Prentice, 'The Public Instructor,' in McDonald and Chaiton (eds) *Egerton Ryerson and His Times:* 132. Prentice is rather more concerned with Ryerson and his role than with the more general political impact of administrative structures. It is interesting to compare the other essays in *Egerton Ryerson and His Times* on administration and political socialization. In neither Gidney and Lawr's 'The Development of an Administrative System for the Public Schools,' nor in Neil McDonald's 'Egerton Ryerson and the School as an Agent of Political Socialization,' is the connection made between politics and administration. In the first, administration is seen largely as technique; in the second, political socialization does not have an administrative dimension.

6. Egerton Ryerson, *The New Canadian Dominion: Dangers and Duties of the People in Regard to their Government.* (Toronto: Lovell and Gibson, 1867):3.

7. PAO RG2 C6C, Trustees, no.4 Logan Township, 12 April 1866. Also, C6C, Joseph Garner, Trustee, section no.9 Pelham Township, 3 December 1861. There are dozens of similar letters; here a trustee seeks official approval for the established practice in the section of using unauthorized books. In C6C, Trustees, section no.7 Tecumseh Township, 9 November 1854, the trustees object to the action of the Municipal Council in re-drawing the school section boundaries, forcing them to abandon the schools built 'so long ago by mutual consent.'

8. PAO RG2 C1G, Ryerson to Edward Roberts, Smith Town, 9 November 1852. Roberts had written, in C6C, 30 October 1852, 'Is it judicious or even admissible to take the evidence of children either pro or con in reference to any difficulty that may arise between a teacher and the parents of a child as to their Teacher's mode or instruction or correction, or have parents a right to come to the school on such matters to the annoyance of the Teacher and the hindrance of his duties,—should they not rather apply to the Trustees and if necessary the Trustees apply to the Superintendent.' The modern reader is tempted most likely to imagine how difficult it would be to teach with interruptions from parents, but these administrative changes, as we shall see in more detail in chapter six, were an essential part of 'elevating' the teacher so that the teacher could in turn 'elevate' the population. Notice also the practical

decision to treat the reactions of 'children' to schooling as suspect in principle.
9. *The Educational Manual for Upper Canada*, (Toronto: Thompson & Co., 1856):131.
10. *The Educational Manual for Upper Canada,:* 135. This ruling and practice is crucial in understanding the extent to which the School Acts changed local educational organization. The Supplementary School Act of 1853, the first adjustment in law to administrative practice, specified that only trustees could call meetings. Lots of 'illegal' school meetings were held according to the pre-1846 practice during the 1850s, and 'improving' trustees were often faced with unified opposition around particular local issues. Educational power is particularly visible in the practice of trustees who overrule such meetings, and who go so far as to distrain the property of educational opponents. Other trustees simply exercized their powers at law without consulting local residents in school meetings. For instance, in C6C, T. Freeman, Trustee, section no.6 Loughborough Township, 7 June 1858, the trustees ask if they can build a new schoolhouse and levy a rate for it without calling any meeting, since they know most residents would vote against such a proposition.
11. Alison Prentice, 'Education and the Metaphor of the Family: An Upper Canadian Example,' in M.B. Katz and P.H. Mattingly (eds) *Education and Social Change* (New York: University Press, 1975) 112-3.
12. Prentice, 'Education and the Metaphor of the Family;' also, *The School Promoters*, (Toronto:McClelland and Stewart, 1977). There is little or no 'evidence' for this position, as Prentice herself points out. How else to make sense of the 'campaign against the family' so visible here?
13. E.A. Talbot, *Five Years' Residence in the Canadas,* (London,1824), II:10-11.
14. Talbot, *Five Years,* II:20-1.
15. Talbot, *Five Years,* II:27.
16. Talbot, *Five Years,* II:35-41.
17. Talbot, *Five Years,* II:69;77.
18. Talbot, *Five Years,* II:95-99. Talbot's book is certainly not the only work one could adduce in support of the view that the propertied classes generally regarded popular culture and domestic

organization with disdain and discomfort. For instance, the popular *Roughing it in the Bush,* by Susannah Moodie [1851] recounts repeatedly the author's discomfort at living in the 'bush' amongst a largely American population. Here the sense of private property was so little developed that to Moodie's horror, people would freely enter her house and borrow her things. Again, however hyperbolic Moodie's account, it points to a critical reaction amongst the propertied and respectable classes to popular culture and to authority relations in the population at large.

19. Thomas Chalmers, *The Christian and Civic Economy of Large Towns,* (Glasgow,1821); H.A. Fregier, *Des classes dangereuses.... et des moyens de les rendre meilleures* (Paris,1840); for some discussion of Fregier's important text see also Alain Corbin, *Les filles de noce* (Paris: Aubier, 1982) passim. Fregier attempts to devise what he calls a 'moral topography of civil society' and his work deals at length the salutary political consequences which would result from popular marriage. See also, Jacques Donzelot, *The Policing of Families* (New York, 1978) and Philippe Meyer, *L'enfant et la raison d'etat* (Paris, 1980).

20. PAO RG2 G4, 'General Rules and Regulations to be observed by the pupils attending the Hamilton Central School' undated (c.1853).

21. Philip Corrigan and Derek Sayer, *The Great Arch: English State Formation as Cultural Revolution.* (Oxford: Blackwell,1985).

22. For the general legislative outline, J.G. Hodgins, *The Legislation and History of Separate Schools in Upper Canada,* (Toronto,1897). Also, F.A. Walker, *Catholic Education and Politics in Upper Canada.* (Toronto: 1956.) The struggles over separate schooling are interesting not simply for their durability, but also for the lie they give to the conceptions of a 'universal' public and a 'Common Christianity.'

23. For Ireland especially see D.H. Akenson, *The Irish Educational Experiment* (Toronto, 1971).

24. PAO RG2 C6C, Trustee, section no. 4 Manvers, 22 March 1865; Trustee, section no. 2 Maidstone, 15 October 1866; Trustee, section no. 5 North Elmsley, 1 December 1866; Trustee, section no. 9, Normanby, 4 March 1870. I suspect that a systematic search would unearth a considerably larger number of cases of what Ian Davey has dubbed 'the burning question.'

25. For example, PAO RG2 C6C, Superintendent of Common Schools, North Wellington, 8 June 1857.

26. PAO RG2 C6C, Trustees, union section no. 20, Toronto and Trafalgar, 25 April 1856.
27. For example, RG2 F2, Rules and Regulations for Adelaide Township, 1842. We read in part, 'The Parents of the scholars may be present during schoolhours to witness the proceedings...the parents will not be permitted to interfere with the Authority of the Master.' The rules for the management of schools published by the Commissioners of National Education in Ireland explicitly permitted the presence of parents in the schoolroom during lessons.
28. PAO RG2 C6C, Thomas Eggleton, Trustee, section no.24 Sidney Township, 5 July 1858.
29. PAO RG2 C6C, David Linn, Secretary Treasurer, section no. 4 Storrington Township, 6 February 1866.
30. PAO RG2 C6C, James Bruce, section no.7 Mulmur Township, 2 February 1866.
31. For a contemporary evaluation and discussion of the Borough Road School, see the 'British and Foreign School Society,' *Quarterly Journal of Education,* V, 1833, 52-71. Ryerson visited this school during his European tour of 1844-5 and was favourably impressed, despite its use of monitorial methods. For a detailed account of the methods of the BFSS see the textbook by the master of the Borough Road School, Henry Dunn, *Principles of Teaching,* (London, c.1847 [10th ed.]).
32. PAO RG2 C6C, Fras. Naylor, Teacher, section no.5 Oneida Township, 30 August 1856.
33. PAO RG2 C6C, P. Donoghue, Hillsburg, 4 December 1857.
34. PAO RG2 C6C, John Carroll, Teacher, Oakville, 4 September 1870.
35. PAO RG2 C6C, Trustees, section no. 3, Arthur Township, 4 September 1854; Arbitrators, section no.3, Arthur Township, 20 April 1854.
36. PAO RG2 C6C, Trustees, section no.6 Beverly, 13 July 1855; C10, Hodgins to Trustees, 17 July 1855.
37. PAO RG2 C6C, Alex M'Kee, Teacher, section no. 1, Toronto Township, 1 July 1858.
38. PAO RG2 C6C, A.J. Keillor, Mornington, 6 July 1858.
39. PAO RG2 C6C, Thomas Commel, Trustee, section no.2 Mornington, 24 July 1858.
40. PAO RG2 C6C, John Jacobs, J.P., Oakwood, 27 July 1858.

41. PAO RG2 C6C, Hugh Gunn, Teacher, section no.5 Puslinch Township, 11 March 1868.
42. PAO RG2 C6C, Alexander Gallan, section no.9, Saltfleet, 19 February 1859.
43. PAO RG2 C6C, W. Young, Brantford, 28 April 1863.
44. PAO RG2 C6C, no. 4091, 1865; contains letter by Timothy Slee clipped from the Brantford *Expositor*, 31 May 1865.
45. PAO RG2 C6C, no. 4091, 1865. One wonders, for instance, how Slee 'dismissed the school' while being beaten by these young men, and why they left. Also, it would be interesting to know if Slee was teaching military drill.
46. PAO RG2 C6C, Thomas Tuthill, Monroe, New York, 26 August 1859; Hiram Maloy, Maple, 28 February 1870.
47. PAO RG2 C6C, W. Sells, Superintendent, Thurlow Township, 24 March 1857.
48. For example, PAO RG2 F2, Rules and Regulations, Township of Grantham, 1842; Common School Commissioners, Township of Goderich, n.d.[1842]; Rules, Gore District, 1842; Trafalgar Rules, 1842; Rules and Regulations, Demorestville, 7 May 1842; Rules and Regulations, Township of Erin,1842.
49. PAO RG2 F2, School Regulations, Township of Dumfries, n.d. [1842].
50. PAO RG2 F2, Rules, Huntly, 1842.
51. PAO RG2 F2, Common School Commissioners Township of Cornwall to Mr. W.J. Hamilton, Teacher, School--Mille Roches, n.d. [1842].
52. PAO RG2 F2, Rules for Common Schools, in Gainsborough, n.d.[1842].
53. PAO RG2 F2, Second Division of the Common School in Dunnville, 4 July 1842.
54. PAO RG2 F2, Rules and Regulations to be observed by the Scholars of this School, no.5 of Emily, n.d. [1842].
55. PAO RG2 F2, The Course of Study pursued in the Common School taught in Division Street Cobourg by Nicholas Wilson, n.d. [1842].
56. PAO RG2 F2, Common School Commissioners, Township of Cornwall, n.d. [1842].
57. PAO RG2 F2, Rules, Sidney Township, July 1842.
58. PAO RG2 F2, Rules and Regulations to be observed in the several

Schools in the Township of Charlotteville, in the Talbot District, from the Commissioners, n.d. [1842].
59. I have found the discussions in M. Foucault, *Discipline and Punish*, (New York, 1977), especially 'Panopticism,' and *The History of Sexuality, Part I*, (New York,1978) most useful. See also, M. Foucault, *Knowledge/Power* (New York, 1980).
60. After the mainly formulaic part of the correspondence (order forms, especially for prize books and maps), after demands for guidance in disputes over school sites, it seems this question occupies the next largest set of letters from localities addressed to the central office. I think the fact that the question reappears continually, despite published responses from the chief superintendent, is an index of struggle against the extension of pedagogical space.
61. PAO RG2 C6C, J.C. Misener, Troy, 7 April 1866; C2, Ryerson to Misener, 19 April 1866.
62. For example, PAO RG2 C6C, Teacher, Charlotteville, 5 December 1866.
63. PAO RG2 C6C, Teacher, Hullsville, 19 February 1868. For others at the end of the period under study, see nos. 7185, 1868; 1537; 1567; 2657; 4525, 1869; 3677; 3819, 1870.
64. PAO RG2 C6C, J.B. Rogers, Tecumseh, 19 April 1851.
65. PAO RG2 C6C, Trustees, Hagersville, 12 March 1861.
66. PAO RG2 C6C, P. Lyon, Springfield, 27 March 1861.
67. PAO RG2 C6C, Anne E. Jackson, Balsam, 22 March 1862.
68. PAO RG2 C6C, Ellen Bowes, Strathroy, 21 July 1862.
69. PAO RG2 C2, Ryerson to Bowes, 2 August 1862.
70. PAO RG2 C6C, Principal, Johnson Street School, Kingston, 7 March 1865. This letter seems quite amusing, with a detailed account of the student's activities as soon as he reached the comparative freedom of the outside of the school gates.
71. PAO RG2 C6C, E. Brokovski, Medonte Township, 19 September, 1865; in C-2 Ryerson to Brokovski, 30 September 1865, the education office said that suspension was not possible, and while there was no rule concerning what the teacher should do, Ryerson thought it permissible that he inform the victims.
72. PAO RG2 C6C, Mrs. Martha Pepper, Teacher, Lunenburg, 3 February 1870.
73. PAO RG2 C6C, Chas. Bellamy, J.P., Blanchard, 22 February 1869. The correspondence between the education office and local

magistrates is particularly significant in this period. Not only is administrative practice established in schools and their vicinity on the basis of formal law, but the opposite also increasingly happens: local justices seek information on which to base legal decisions from those charged with administrative practice. This is in part an instance of what I call the 'density' of the educational state, and which I discuss below at more length.
74. PAO RG2 C6C, J.P. Flanagan, Paris, 28 February 1868.
75. PAO RG2 G-4, General Rules and Regulations to be observed by the pupils attending the Hamilton Central School.
76. PAO RG2 C1O, Ryerson to Levi Wilson, Trustee, section no.1, Trafalgar Township, 1 June 1855.
77. PAO RG2 C1T, Ryerson to James Williams, Teacher, Pelham, 31 January 1857.
78. PAO RG2 C2, Ryerson to Alex Goulet, Teacher, Harwich, 24 January 1862.
79. PAO RG2 C2, Ryerson to Anne E. Jackson, Teacher, Balsam, 2 April 1862.
80. PAO RG2 C2, Ryerson to Wm. Mackintosh, Teacher, Brock, 28 April 1866.
81. PAO RG2 C2, Ryerson to J.G. Armstrong, Teacher, Hullsville, 25 February 1868.
82. PAO RG2 C6C, John Wood, Brantford, 24 February 1868.
83. PAO RG2 C2, Ryerson to John Wood, Brantford, 27 February 1868.
84. PAO RG2 C2, Ryerson to George Smith, Teacher, Berlin, 25 April 1870. This is draft correspondence & Ryerson scribbles.
85. PAO RG2 C6C, Wm. Graham, Board of School Trustees, Portsmouth, 6 February 1864.
86. PAO RG2 C6C, Wm. Ford Jr., Board of School Trustees, Kingston, 11 March 1863.
87. PAO RG2 Ryerson's notes on the original above n. 86.
88. PAO RG2 C6C, L. Sims and others, Oil Springs, 22 January 1869.
89. PAO RG2 C6C, Trustees, section no. 3, Wolfe Island, no.6661, September 1870.
90. PAO RG2 C2, Ryerson to Trustees, section no. 3, Wolfe Island, 27 September 1870.
91. PAO RG2 C6C, R.H. Gilbert, Baden, 20 March 1861.
92. PAO RG2 C6C, H. Turner, Trustee, Millbrook, 27 May 1861.

93. PAO RG2 C6C, John Austin, Clark's Mills, 22 June 1869.
94. PAO RG2 C6C, William Ramine, Teacher, McGillivray, 20 April 1870.
95. PAO RG2 C6C, Nathaniel Smith, Teacher, Walkerton, 7 July 1865.
96. PAO RG2 C-2 Ryerson to Peter McDonald, section no.3 Tuckersmith, 30 December 1865; this is in reply to C6C, McDonald to Ryerson, 26 December 1865.
97. In this regard in particular one sees the breakdown of pedagogical theory which claimed to make the process of education pleasant. The response of the education office in the face of opposition was not, as we shall see, to seek the flaws in its practice which generated opposition, but rather to attempt to suppress that opposition—and violently if necessary.
98. PAO RG2 C6C, William Anderson, Teacher, section no.5 Pakenham, 11 March 1859; Ryerson outlined the powers of suspension in C2, Ryerson to Anderson, 17 March 1859.
99. PAO RG2 C6C, John Hannah, Adelaide 11 March 1857.
100. PAO RG2 C6C, William Beattie, Teacher, Hornby, 10 April 1863.
101. PAO RG2 C6C, W. H. McCurdy, Teacher, section no. 7, Malahide, 12 March 1864.
102. PAO RG2 C2, Ryerson to McCurdy, 17 March 1864.
103. PAO RG2 C2, Ryerson to McCurdy, 12 May 1864.
104. PAO RG2 C6C, G.M. Priest, Teacher, section no.9, Walpas, 15 March 1869.
105. As I suggest at more length in the following chapter, the opposition of parents to expulsion points to a popular conception of school attendance as a literal public right.
106. PAO RG2 C6C, Niel Eastman, J.P., Arkana, 17 December, 1861.
107. PAO RG2 C2, Ryerson to Lewis Allen, section no.17, Ernestown, 9 October 1856.
108. PAO RG2 C2, Ryerson to George Wright, Teacher, section no. 5, Hay, 9 March 1864.
109. For example, PAO RG2 C6C, William Armstrong, Clerk, Euphemia, 18 October 1856.
110. PAO RG2 C6C, Vina Root, Teacher, Plum Hollow, 30 April 1868.
111. PAO RG2 C6C, Abraham Shorland, section no.2 Deneham, 15

February 1868.
112. PAO RG2 C6C, John Clancy, Trustee, section no.13, Camden East, 15 February 1867.
113. PAO RG2 C6C, Martin Pomery, Teacher, section no.13, Camden East, 14 February 1867.
114. PAO RG2 C2, Ryerson to Clancy, 19 February 1867.
115. PAO RG2 C6C, Thomas Henry, Chairman, Board of Public Instruction, Sandhill, 9 March 1852; also, David Wylie, Chairman, Board of School Trustees, Brockville, 25 June 1862.
116. PAO RG2 C1F, Ryerson to Henry, 17 March 1852.
117. PAO RG2 C1X, Ryerson to A.S. Harris, Teacher, section no.2 Dereham, 18 February 1858.
118. PAO RG2 C2, Ryerson to D.B. Gordon, Blandford, 23 February 1864.
119. David Stow *The Training System,* (Glasgow, 1840).
120. PAO RG2 C1X, Ryerson to D.R. Grey, Meaford, 30 June 1858; in response to C6C, D.R. Grey, Meaford, 26 June 1858. It was already somewhat archaic for Grey to write *for* his sister. In the 1840s especially, women teachers approached the education office only through male sponsors, or only with letters of introduction from respectable male figures. By the 1860s, a considerable correspondence was taking place directly between the education office and female teachers. Nonetheless, the vast majority of correspondents throughout this period are male. This probably means that the troubles female teachers had with their employers were more effectively contained locally. However, the archive itself clearly contains this gender bias, and I cannot see how one might control for it.
121. PAO RG2 C6C, 2 November 1854 contains extracts from the St. Thomas *Dispatch* of 6 & 10 October outlining the case.
122. PAO RG2 C6C, George Shaw, Board of School Trustees, Newcastle, 21 December 1861.
123. PAO RG2 C6C, A. Mac Farland, Grimsby, 6 August 1866.

# Chapter Five:
# Struggles over School Attendance

In his lectures on the science of education delivered at the Sorbonne in 1902-3, the French educator and sociologist Emile Durkheim stressed the dependence of morality on regularity of conduct.
> Morality is basically a constant thing, and so long as we are not considering an excessively long time span, it remains ever the same. A moral act ought to be the same tomorrow as today, whatever the personal predispositions of the actor. Morality thus presupposes a certain capacity for behaving similarly under like circumstances, and consequently it implies a certain ability to develop habits, a certain need for regularity.[1]

As he does so often in his *Moral Education,* Durkheim here states the position of nineteenth century state school administrators as an abstract imperative. Writing after public education had acquired the status of the normal educational form, Durkheim could present its moral regulatory dimensions in terms of abstract universals. For the proponents of public schooling in the first half of the nineteenth century, however, the moral imperatives of schooling were immediately connected to desired transformations to be wrought on the body politic, on popular character and culture. Regularity in school attendance was to produce regularity and stability in more general behavioural patterns, particularly in political behaviour. Regularity fostered a condition in which the schooled population would be 'insulated' from 'subject[ion] to momentary impulses'.[2] The schooled population, in the regularity of its habits, would naturally resist the inflammatory phrases of revolutionary demagogues, the immoral temptations of salacious print, the momentary anger resulting from social injustice.

School administrators and planners in the formative period of educational organization in Canada West attempted to secure regularity of behaviour in the schooled population by enforcing norms of regular and punctual school attendance. They attempted to institute pedagogical practices and plans in which regular and punctual attendance were systematic imperatives. Collective instruction was to replace individual instruction: the student was to learn at the pace of the group, not at a pace determined by its own needs or desires. School administrators in towns and villages increasingly attempted to organize a 'lock-step' model of sequenced learning, in which students moved through a set curriculum in homogeneous achievement (but not yet age-graded) classes. School administrators attempted to specify closely the occasions for learning, with set and homogeneous school days, through the institution of timetables, and again through classification. Nor were administrators content when they secured the physical presence of students—however punctual and regular. Attendance was valued as pedagogically productive presence; students were not only to attend, but to attend bearing the marks of receptivity to the pedagogical process. These marks typically involved manner of dress, 'cleanliness' 'neatness', and other types of comportment.

However, throughout the 1850s and 1860s, school managers in Canada West were plagued by irregular attendance. Ian Davey has shown that while average enrollments in the common school system increased consistently during these two decades, average school attendance did not. By 1871, when the first compulsory attendance clause appeared in the Ontario School Act, a large majority of the population between the ages of five and twelve was enrolled in school. Yet at no time between 1850 and 1871 did *average* attendance approach enrollment figures. Throughout these two decades a majority of the enrolled population actually attended school for less than one hundred days a year. The 'want of discipline' of the population in the eyes of the middle class school administrator was clearly visible in low average attendance rates, and in irregular attendance patterns.[3]

## Structural Causes of Non-Attendance

Research by critical writers in the late 1960s and early 1970s produced structural interpretations of patterns of school attendance. Ian Davey's important work has pointed to the sharply different realities embodied in working and going to public school in nineteenth century Canada West. Drawing upon E.P. Thompson's perceptive essay 'Time, Work-discipline and Industrial Capitalism',[4] Davey contrasts the public school's demands for regular and punctual attendance to the seasonal demands of petty agriculture for labour power. The production process in mid-nineteenth century Canada West, especially in the countryside, demanded what Thompson calls a task-work orientation. The demand for labour power was determined by the presence of definite tasks--in agriculture, by such things a haying, harvesting, planting and so forth. As active participants in the rural economy, school attenders had, in addition to regular daily tasks, such as wood gathering and milking, to be responsive to the appearance of seasonal tasks.

The public school, by contrast, embodied the same orientation to labour and time as the factory: uniform time work. Schooling was a uniform and regular process, occupying definite hours of the day, with little or no variation in principle due to seasonal differences in the supply of raw materials or motive power. The school always, in principle, had teachers to teach and tasks to learn throughout the school day. Furthermore, as collective instruction was increasingly enforced, the school became more dependent upon industrial time. Non-attendance, Davey suggests then, is intelligible historically as the product of a structural conflict between the temporal organization of schooling and work.

There is ample material in the archival records of schooling in Canada West to support Davey's position. Robert McKee Moore and Luke Maxwell Dally taught in turn in a common school in West Gwillimbury Township in the late 1840s. Until Dally was fired for insisting upon teaching grammar to the son of one of his subscribers, they kept a day book in which they not only recorded daily attendance at the school, but also attempted to explain its variations. The entries in the daybook relate school attendance to the variations in the agricultural labour cycle and to weather conditions. For instance, one reads,

> Wednesday, 13 August, 1845. The School with the exception of two pupils, is composed of a few little children: All that are able for any farm work are engaged at it.
> 
> Thursday, 16 October, 1845. Children are assisting at taking out Potatoes.

> Thursday, 23rd October, 1845. Very fine day. The children all engaged at Potatoes.
> Monday, 23 February, 1846. A good many of the grown boys today at Mr. Landerken's thrashing.
> Monday, 9 March, 1846. Some of the big boys are withdrawn preparing for sugar making.
> Wednesday, 6 May, 1846. Potatoe planting commenced.
> Tuesday, 16 June, 1846. a few kept at home burning stumps.
> Tuesday, 21 July, 1846. Wheat cutting commenced.
> Monday, 26 October, 1846. Every child who can pick up potatoes is now engaged. I think I will follow the example set & stop at home tommorrow and take up mine.
> April 5, 1847. Sugar Making has taken every child (able to carry a pail) away from School.
> 7 July, 1847. Haymaking commenced. Big boys now withdrawn from School.[5]

On the 23rd of October in 1846 attendance at the school was very small because it was 'freezing great guns and Snowing Ammunition.'[6]

Young people in the towns were engaged in labour processes necessary to the survival of the urban household which produced parallel pressures on their capacity for school attendance.

Yet, for all the insight they generate about the structural organization of school and work, such explanations of non-attendance at school do not pay sufficient attention to other kinds of activity on the part of local community members. They suggest that we have understood the phenomenon of non-attendance at school by pointing to this formal structural conflict. Such an assumption leaves unexamined and unquestioned the practices and content of schooling itself. If one argues that students did not attend regularly because their labour power was indispensable for the reproduction of households, one may implicitly also be assuming that such students would have attended school-- and existing schools-- if only they could have done so. One may implicitly assume that students viewed existing schools as a superior alternative to participation in production. The archival evidence suggests that in many cases students did not attend because the existing organization of schooling was itself obnoxious, inadequate or less attractive than a range of alternative activities. The empirical reality of schooling in mid-nineteenth century Canada West is in fact much richer than a structural account suggests. At a lower level of abstraction, one notices that these structural conflicts do not exhaust the range of subjective responses to schooling.

In part this can be seen by looking at the causes of non-attendance identified by school administrators themselves. In the case of Canada West, school superintendents were frequently canvassed by the central office with respect to the reasons for low rates of school attendance. While many routinely parroted the official view that non-attendance was due to 'parental indifference', other informants made it clear that this was not the only force at work. J. Fletcher of Mono Township claimed that 'distance from the Schoolhouse & want of clothes or shoes' were important causes of non-attendance.[7] John Flood, writing in 1860, identified six forces governing non-attendance at school. These point to some of the lacunae in the structural analysis of time discipline. Flood wrote,

> One thing from which most of this evil arises is parents' taking a dislike to the teacher often when they have scarcely any reason. Another cause is that parents, being poor and hurried, keep their children at home to work. A third cause is indifference or drunkeness of parents. A fourth cause is a swamp or a large wood running between the schoolhouse and some of the inhabitants. A fifth is poverty: some cannot procure clothes for their children. And a sixth cause is that some of the families are of a different class of society from the rest. These families are not willing that their children, while learning the branches taught in the school, should be falling into the use of vulgar expressions, and into such habits as that of spitting and wiping the nose with the sleeve or the back of the hand.[8]

Difficulties of travel, poverty--- both as the necessity for child labour and inadequate clothing--- and cultural conflict kept people out of school in Flood's judgement. Cultural poverty, it should be noted, points not so much to a complete absence of cover--- although there were undoubtedly many instances where potential students had insufficient clothing to protect them during the long winter walk to school--- but to an absence of 'acceptable' or 'decent' cover. Cultural poverty points to a conflict between the economic condition of the population and the moral demands of regulated schooling.

Apart from scattered and indirect references, the archival records contain little information about the non-attendance of the students from 'respectable' households because of the 'incivility' of the bulk of the student population. The 'respectable' sections of the population probably kept away from the common school in some cases for these reasons, and patronized private schools. The case of William Hutton, a District Superintendent of Schools for Victoria is illustrative. Hutton was sufficiently concerned that his son avoid exposure to the students 'of a vulgar cast' at the common school that he kept him at home. Gidney and Millar document the existence of a large private sector for middle class schooling. This type of schooling declined in the 1860s, as members of the middle class obtained publicly-funded grammar schools, but grammar schooling was at times explicitly conceived as a means for 'respectable' education away from the 'lower orders'.[9]

Still, it is clear that many students, often with the support of their parents and friends, did not attend school during the formative period of the school system from preference for alternative activity and for distaste or dislike for schooling or for a particular teacher. Attendance was seen quite differently by the central education office, by teachers, and by students and school supporters. For the central office, as I have indicated, punctual and regular attendance was moral activity in itself, and also a precondition of 'efficient' instruction.

For teachers, the matter was somewhat more ambiguous. Teachers had a direct pecuniary interest in a high and regular attendance at their schools, since the school fund was distributed according to average attendance. Where schools were supported in part out of rate-bills on parents as well, teachers had a further pecuniary interest in regular attendance. The central office attempted to limit variations in attendance under the rate-bill system by insisting that the rate-bill be levied by the month, however many days a student might actually attend. But teachers generally had an immediate interest in encouraging regular attendance and in reporting a high attendance. Many teachers regularly falsified their registers of attendance— upon which central grants and rate-bills were calculated— and a considerable number of them were detected in this activity.[10]

From a technical pedagogical point of view as well, regular attendance simplified the labour of any teacher adopting the practices of collective instruction. Regular and punctual attendance facilitated classification and stopped the interruptions caused by students irregularly entering or leaving the schoolroom. Many teachers supported regularity in attendance for these reasons. At the same time, it should constantly be borne in mind that enrollments increased enormously in the period from 1846 to 1871. In 1850 for the province as a whole, there were 43 students enrolled in the common schools for every teacher. In 1865, there were over 81 students enrolled for every teacher. In free school sections, teachers sometimes faced groups of over a hundred students, and to these teachers a lesser attendance would likely have been welcome.[11]

However, the teachers' interest in uniform, regular and punctual attendance was also determined by their social position in the community and their orientation to the model of teaching promoted by the central education office. Clearly not all—if even the majority— of teachers in the 1850s and 1860s approximated the model of professional dignity and loyalty to the public sphere sought by leading school administrators. The erudite male teacher in his comfortable residence, with its private study, collection of books, and decorative garden, was a rural rarity. Teachers in many schools remained very highly integrated in community relations, despite the best efforts of educational reformers to 'elevate' them.

Despite a legislative prohibition of the practice— a prohibition sustained in the Court of Queen's Bench and publicized in the *Educational Manual,* — some local school sections persisted in the custom of 'boarding the teacher', that is, paying part of the teacher's salary in the form of room and board in the households of school supporters. In section 1 of Yonge Township in 1856, for instance, the female teacher hired refused to board around, but one of the trustees boarded her himself in his own house for $8 per month, and then attempted to pay her board out of the school tax. Despite the consent of a school meeting to this activity, the Education Office ruled that no teacher's living expenses could be paid out of the school tax,[12] but school supporters in the 1850s frequently attempted to preserve the custom. Furthermore, male school teachers were compelled to perform annual statute labour on the roads with all other adult males. This form of community participation continued despite the bitter complaints of teachers such as J. O'Shanahan, who protested the 'injustice of compelling men, who devote their time to the civilization of the present and future generations, to labour at what they are not accustomed.'[13] In addition, given the lowness of teachers' pay, many of them were compelled to practice marginal forms of agriculture. For these, the seasonal demands of agriculture were similar to those faced by their students, and such teachers can have had little interest in uniform attendance.[14]

Again, some teachers were so closely identified with their students that they had little desire for 'civilizing' or 'improving' them at all. Access to the occupation was still quite easy, and many teachers were the former fellow-students of their own students. In 1870, for instance, the magistrate in section 4 of King Township complained to the education office that the school teacher, himself a former student, spent his time playing cards with his older pupils.[14] A resident of Canning complained in 1860 of another teacher who tried to 'make a gambling hell of a public school house' by playing at cards with the students.[15] Other teachers found it more pleasurable to read the newspaper than to teach anything, and these also seem to have shown no active interest in enforcing official attendance norms.[16]

## Overcrowding

While a great many new schools were constructed during the first decade after the passage of the School Act of 1850, school buildings were often unable to accommodate all the students seeking to attend. Especially where 'free' schools were established, overcrowding became common, and the physical conditions of schooling then made school attendance undesirable to many school supporters. In Port Sarnia, the schoolhouse was described in 1852 as 'a miserable, smoky Shantie, scarcely fit, for a pigery. Its size is only 16 by 18 feet. And this is the only sanctuary for the training of 86 children, in intelligence, & moral principle.'[17] A resident of Plympton described the local school house ceiling as 'being so low' he 'could not stand in the house with my hat on', the floor 'as should not be in a pigpen' since the teacher and students were in continual danger of 'falling through', and 'as for the desks and seats, they are worse than none at all.'[18] In Innerkip, students were described as 'huddled up in a pen not fit for the shelter of their horses or cattle.'[19] In Wellesley, 'there were sometimes last winter as many as 90 children packed away in a miserable place about 18 by 24 and not more than 7 1/2 feet between the floor and ceiling'.[20] The village school in Whitby was twenty seven feet square and had seats for 45 students. There were sometimes 100 present.[21] As the local superintendent for Chatham, Harwick, Howard & Oxford Townships put it, in many places the school was 'a dreary prison.'[22]

Conditions in the official Model Schools of Toronto were only somewhat better. In the late 1850s, the chief superintendent claimed that 'one teacher cannot efficiently teach more than fifty or sixty pupils.'[23] In the mid-1860s, he wrote that 'about 50 pupils are as many as any single teacher should be obliged to teach. That is the number of pupils assigned to each of our Model Sch. teachers even where they have other helps which are not available in ordinary Schools.'[24] In this matter Ryerson was either badly informed, or disingenuous. The Boys' Model School master had declared in 1855 that he would be 'satisfied if we have one teacher for 70 scholars, instead of one for 85 as at present.'[25] And in 1866, the Normal School master was seeking more space for the Model Schools so that class sizes could be reduced to 65.[26]

With this level of crowding, school supporters complained that students were continually ill. W.J. Anderson went to the Boys' Model School in April 1858 to discover why two of his four children were continually ill.

> In going into one of the rooms, being the Gallery in which my youngest boy was, I found him sitting with upwards of fifty other boys, in a room not exceeding fifteen feet square by twelve high--- not heated with pure warm air, but from imperfect construction or disorder of the heating apparatus, poisoned by an atmosphere redolent of smoke, and as no other means of ventilation existed, the window

had been opened and a strong current of cold air, was poured down on the bare heads of the boys.²⁷

In summer, the heat in the Model School made J.M. Vancock's son too ill to attend, and one February Louis Sabbati Ullman discovered that his daughter 'with some other Scholars has to set during school hours in wett & water, floor, I mean her seat is situated in that manner, she suffers now nearly every day with sore throat, cold &c.'²⁸ Indeed, the Normal School master himself argued that the school rooms were so 'imperfectly heated, badly lighted, and inadequately ventilated' that the institution was setting a bad example.²⁹

## Unpopular Teachers

While Superintendent Flood may have been correct in asserting that many parents kept their children at home after taking a dislike to the teacher for 'scarcely any reason', in a large number of cases dislike for the teacher was well-founded. Drunkenness, brutality, incompetence, cruelty and sexual assaults were common characteristics of and activities by teachers which limited school attendance.

There was a considerable local variation in the kinds of behaviour school supporters were inclined to accept from teachers. The 'strictly temperate habits' demanded by the central education office were reinterpreted locally, and were themselves sites of cultural conflict. For instance, the attempts of the local superintendent in Mariposa Township in 1855 to suspend the teaching certificate of James Adam, a shoemaker-turned-teacher accused of drunkenness, immorality, swearing and ridiculing the Bible, were constantly defeated by local rate payers and by his school trustees. While Adams' trustees admitted that he was occasionally drunk, they did not take that as evidence of immorality, and argued on the contrary that his behaviour towards the 'female sect' was generally correct.³⁰

At the other extreme, Hugh Lamont, who taught in Georgetown, was 'called to task' by his trustees for cursing in the schoolroom. He

wrote,
> In teaching a class in the Elements of Eng. Composition, in this school which I now have charge of, I made use of the word 'blasted'....[31]

The chief superintendent advised Lamont that while words such as 'blasted', or 'bloated' or 'polluted' were not objectionable in and of themselves, they might well be so in certain contexts.[32] This moral vagueness, of course allowed both the central office and local residents room for manoeuvre, and points to attempts by participants to chart the terrain of conflict.

The aura of moral regulation through good example which the central office attempted to attach to the teacher, as the agent of civilization in the moral wilderness of popular culture, tended to subject teachers to close moral scrutiny in the locality. Frequent complaints to the education office resulted, and frequent demands for the specification of the exact behavioural constituents of 'strictly temperate habits' were made. The trustees of section 3 Sunnidale, for instance, wrote in May 1861 to complain of a teacher who drank and gambled. The teacher from the same section wrote in turn to the office in October 1862 to enquire what 'strictly temperate' meant. Could he, he wondered, drink one drink? lodge in a respectable tavern? listen to music? go to a social party and dance?[33]

In many other instances, however, the behaviour of teachers caused a falling off of school attendance. Students refused to attend, and school supporters to patronize, schools where teachers were brutal. 'I had an orphan brother and sister attending School,' wrote John Cameron of Beaverton. 'The teacher was in the habit of chalking the faces of children giving any offence whatever and also tying the children to a pin and and causing them to stand on a Bench for the most part of the day....I cannot get the children to go to School for fear of Being Chalked.'[34] John Montgomery of Headford complained that the school trustees had re-hired a teacher earlier 'suspended for gross misconduct in the school.' Montgomery's son would not attend this teacher's school.[35] A trustee from Glammis wondered how to act in a situation where 'the Teacher has inflicted so much corporal punishment on one of his pupils that the parents of said pupil dont feel at liberty to send him any more to the school.'[36] In section 1 Westminster, the trustees hired a graduate of the 18th and 19th sessions of the Normal School named Joseph Boag.

School supporters soon complained of Boag's maltreatment of the students, which included 'having beaten' one student 'about the head to such a degree that he had to be attended during the night'. When one of his female students had her hair cut short, Boag 'asked her aloud if she had just come out of Jail---this he did merely to get the child laughed at.'[37] In section 6 of Williams, the teacher, with the support of the trustees, pinned names on the students, made them cross dress, put stove pipes on their heads and blackened their faces with soot as means of correction. The trustees claimed this did no harm, and they 'thought better way to shame them than flogging them. the stovepip on ther head and go on ther knees would do them no harm &c.' Attendance declined.[38]

The capacity of school supporters to oppose these and other forms of brutality was limited by the authority structures of public educational administration. Non-attendance was one of the few options available to school supporters, where intervention might lead to legal penalty. For example, William Parrish of section 4 Fenelon claimed that the female teacher 'took my youngest son tying his hands and feet with a rope and unlawfully beating him with a stick another son sitting close by caught hold of the rod which stopped her from beating him any more.' The latter boy was fined in court under the 'school disturbers' clause.[39] In section 11 Pickering, the trustees supported a teacher who threatened 'that he would Thresh any child who related anything that might occur at School.'[40] When J. McKilligan of section 1 East Zorra complained to a teacher who had beaten the students (including McKilligan's daughter) 'in such a manner that some of the grown up lads expressed surprise that some of the little ones ribs were not broken,' the teacher 'sent a warning to me ...to keep out of his way or he would give me worse than he gave the boys in school.'[41] In this situation, non-attendance was one of the few tactics available to students and school supporters.

Other school supporters and students kept away from schools where teachers could not or would not teach. John Green of Fitzroy complained of conditions in his school section where there was,

> neglect of teaching and neglect of discipline allowing
> the Children to scuffle and drag each other club into
> fours and sixes confabing and running for and
> aft....Clubbing up tearing each others books lifting the

boards of the floor and soiling under them boys exposing themselves to the Girls and watering through the chinks of the house....

Here as well it was impossible for passersby to avoid being assailed by the students.[42]

Drunkenness was a common complaint against male teachers and a common cause for non-attendance. J.S. Glyne of Wawanash wrote in 1857 of,

a School Teacher named Charles Black who has been repeatedly drunk and fiting and has taught with a Black Eye and on the 16th of this month Came from Goderich to the School drunk and in that drunken stupid State lay round the School among the Children all day....[43]

John Buchannan from Tilbury West Township revealed in 1859 that the teacher in his section drank and lost control of himself in the schoolroom.

...on opening the School with prair he at some slite offence of some of the children got up in A pashion and in anger said it showed their D...breeding he would tell the girls to go out and watter their colts tell them they acted like two year old bulls or stud horses called bitches and little sows he called some of the boys little scrubby mangy boars and said he must get a Negro wench to sit along side of them.[44]

The section trustees claimed that Buchannan simply wanted to get rid of the existing teacher so that one of his relatives could have the job.

Other such instances abound in the official correspondence. George Hamilton of Esquissing Township wrote in 1861 of a teacher who was drunk in school and who swore at his students, 'you ass you stupid ass you jackass you Scoundrel etc' which Hamilton 'with a Good many of my Neighbours [thought] it calculated to corrupt the morals of youth.' Hamilton complained that the trustees refused to act against the teacher.[45] The trustees of section 5 Oxford Township sought to rid themselves of a teacher who was guilty of 'gross uncleannes about the School House door and indecent and grossly immoral language in the School House among the Scholars.'[46] Their counterparts in section 11 Puslinch Township were saddled with a teacher whom they had hired for ten months at $20 per month without board, but who had been drinking steadily for three weeks and had the 'Delearam tremmenes'.⁴⁷ This kind of behaviour on the part of teachers often led to a direct decline in attendance,⁴⁸ although teachers sometimes resorted to expedients such as paying their students to attend in an effort to preserve their employment agreements.⁴⁹

Religious non-conformity on the part of teachers, or their violation of local norms of piety, sometimes led to non-attendance and to attempts by residents to remove teachers. Mr. Fletcher of section 5 Harwich Township kept his children out of school because the teacher said to one of his students,

> ...there was once on Earth a fellow called Jesus and he had twelve followers called Apostles one of which was called Peter, a long nosed fellow, and he was always putting his nose into other peoples business and you are like him.⁵⁰

A trustee in section 13 Yarmouth Township lamented his misfortune at living 'in a neighbourhood where infidelity and spiritualism abound.' He and some of his neighbours had 'resolved that we cannot send' our children to school because his brother trustees had hired one 'Lydia Oill, who is a spiritual medium!! She has been known to practice her system before the scholars....'⁵¹

Single female teachers were particularly subject to close moral scrutiny---in addition to especially low pay and insecurity of employment. The trustees in Pembroke attempted to break their agreement with a female teacher in 1861 because they alleged she,

> broke the Sabbath day by dancing in that day in the bar room of Belfeuille's tavern, where two of your petitioners sa[w] her rolling in the ball alley and playing cards on Sunday night---that the teacher does not keep regular hours....[they] saw her after nights several times walking in the woods with a young man who lately robbed his father...⁵²

The trustees of section 12 Roxborough Township claimed their teacher had violated her agreement with them.

> She when employed aggred to avoid all frolicks & Dances but attends all within reach of her also swears in the presance of the Scholars allso refused to

give the schoolars a Lesson morning and Evening in the Bible and and Testament and dont say prayers...[53] Female teachers were also accused of maltreating students, although such accusations were less frequent than in the case of male teachers.[54]

On the other hand, many parents refused to send to, and many students to attend, schools were teachers engaged in various forms of sexual activity, from exposure and fondling to 'seduction' and rape. After complaints of drunkenness, the official correspondence abounds with charges of sexual misconduct on the part of male teachers. This was an activity not complained of on the part of female teachers. Male teachers were repeatedly accused of 'gross immorality',[55] 'Impertinent freedom with females,'[56] 'visits to houses of illfame ...such as to require medical treatment for v---l complaints,'[57] bigamy and seduction,[58] and others.

James Byrns of North Crosby Township claimed that the tendency of the local teacher to be 'grossly immoral, especially towards the female Schollars,' had reduced the average attendance in the section school to only eight.[59] A teacher in the vicinity of Penetanguishene was found guilty at a public investigation of bigamy, joining in charivaris, fighting, telling his students about his love affairs, going to 'houses of pleasure' and trying 'at different times to seduce one of his pupils, a Girl of about 15 years of age,' whom he 'afterwards expelled' from the school.[60] Anne Cameron, who went to school in Lobo Township in the 1850s, complained that when she was walking to and from school 'the Teacher would on the highway turn round to her and piss before her face.'[61] This claim was discounted in principle by the chief superintendent, who knew the teacher in question personally.[62]

The teachers involved in complaints of sexual misconduct were by no means entirely the old, dissipated, or marginal members of the occupation. Normal School graduates, highly 'respectable' teachers and those often regarded as the best by the central office were frequently implicated as well, and a number of highly sensational and widely publicized cases took place during the 1850s and 1860s. The entire domain of sexuality and schooling---and of Normal School training and sexuality---deserves systematic treatment. I propose to do so elsewhere, but at least one of these cases may be mentioned here.

In April and May of 1864, a number of parents in section 1 of

Minto Township complained of the persistent sexual misconduct of the teacher and of the refusal of either the elected trustees, or the local superintendent to intervene. They wrote:
> The charges are such as lifting up girls clothes and handling their persons---or taking their hands and putting them into his pants to feel his nuts and when they would go up with their slates for information he would generally take the slate and draw some most disgraceful figures of Men & Women in such a stile as is too disgraceful for polite ears---and that he would have no control of boys or girls above eleven or twelve years of age---when they misbehave in any improper manner in our out of school....[63]

The chief superintendent refused to believe the parents involved, maintaining that the local superintendent had investigated and found the teacher innocent. Ryerson knew this teacher personally, as well as the teacher's son, who was then a Normal School student.[64] Whatever this teacher's actual conduct, the charges undoubtedly led to a reduced school attendance.

Students and parents then, avoided going or sending to school not simply out of economic necessity; their resistance and opposition was active. It was based on custom, and also on particular conceptions of the process, occasions and content of education which conflicted with those, at times, held by central educational administrators. Far from being evidence of 'parental indifference', non-attendance was often based upon alternative educational principles. While these were not always clearly articulated nor consistently progressive, the regularization of school attendance involved their suppression.

## Securing Attendance

For those teachers who attempted to enforce official norms of attendance, teaching was a continual struggle. Official norms conflicted not only with the reality of production processes in both town and country, but also with prevailing community conceptions of schooling. For teachers who supported the official view, the school was a politically and morally productive space, where definite habits of mind and body would be inculcated, where an official body of knowledge was to be administered, and where punctuality and regularity were both moral habits in themselves and means to the other official ends of education. Here, furthermore, students were to attend bearing the marks of 'willingness' to learn, bearing the visible behavioural signs of an acceptance of the legitimacy of the process of public schooling. To students and local residents, an earlier reality of schooling was still in play, a reality in which the school was a locally-controlled convenience, adapted both to community needs and to community desire. Many students, furthermore, existed as full-fledged and largely independent members of the local community: actively engaged in labour processes as soon as their physical capacities permitted. The reality of schooling, by contrast, was one in which they appeared as 'children' to be governed by an alien 'necessity', determined by anonymous others, and imposed upon them for their 'own good'. Such a conception of themselves was one they frequently refused, and their refusals were broadly supported at times by parents and friends.

Teachers learned at the Normal School, at school conventions, County Board examinations and in the educational press, a number of tactics and manoeuvres designed to aid them in securing regular and punctual attendance. These tactics and manoeuvres were the locus of struggles. Teachers, for instance, were increasingly encouraged by the education office to exclude latecomers from the schoolroom, to lock the school door after nine o'clock in the morning, to require notes from late students, and to employ systems of merit and demerit marks. The Education Acts defined the school day in an uniform manner for the province as a whole, and attempted to end the considerable local variation in the time of schooling which had existed in the 1840s and earlier.[65] In correspondence with local teachers, the chief superintendent frequently invoked Normal School practice in matters of attendance as a precedent to be followed locally. In the official Model Schools, latecomers were commonly excluded from school for the day or half day. However, the chief superintendent rarely remarked that the Model Schools were heavily over-subscribed, with waiting periods of up to a year for admittance, which undoubtedly facilitated the application of sanctions against the violators of many school rules.[66] The attempt to apply Normal School practice outside Toronto was often doomed to failure because the technical conditions of schooling in the countryside were markedly different from those of the towns. For instance, William Gunn, the school superintendent for the 1st division of Bruce County, commented in 1857 that the practice of locking the school door against latecomers was cruel.

> Such conduct in a Scattered Section of poor people of large extent in which probably there is not half a dozen time pieces in use is to say the least, cruel.[67]

However, the attempt to apply Normal School practice in the countryside and towns also provoked active opposition and resistance.

John Neelands, a Normal School graduate teaching in section 16 of Chinguacousy Township, attempted to force two teenaged boys to write an explanation for lateness during January of 1861. They refused, and Neelands suspended them from the school. Their father then charged Neelands before the local magistrate with abusing his children, and told Neelands 'when his boys went home that he was displeased with them for not pulling me out of the school house and kicking me.'[68] The Board of Common School Trustees for the village of Newmarket complained to the education office that while the rule they had adopted in 1862 requiring punctual attendance worked admirably, 'one man thinks his dignity is affected because his children come under such a law and is instituting legal proceedings.'[69]

Some Boards of Trustees simply refused to allow teachers to employ any such measures against lateness. J.B. Newman, who taught in the village of Bell Ewart, for instance, was so troubled by students 'coming in late when classes have been on the floor' that he began to lock the school door at ten past nine. His students protested against this practice to the trustees, who in turn instructed Newman to stop it.[70] The education office counseled Newman that while 'the practise itself is followed in our model schools,' he could not enforce rules opposed by his trustees.[71] For his part, Henry Steinson of Columbus village attempted to follow the Normal School practice of minimizing corporal punishment. For lateness, and other 'offences' he offered students a choice between a black mark and a flogging. The accumulation of six black marks was to result in suspension, but the trustees refused to suspend the accumulators of black marks. In this case, by contrast,[72] the education office urged Steinson to suspend whom he chose.

Parents and students frequently asserted their customary right to make use of the school at their convenience. These were matters of sometimes violent struggle. After John Agnew, who taught in Sydenham village, began locking the school house door at twenty past nine in the morning, attendance generally improved (from his viewpoint) but,

> the parents of a few of the rest have become indignant...& have said that the children can come to school at anytime of the day they choose, one parent especially came to the school this afternoon & abused me most shamefully, blaspheming at a fearful rate before the school and threatening todo me serious bodily harm, if I should ever dare lock his children out again.[73]

While this particular incident took place in the summer, the practice of locking the school door in winter was potentially dangerous to students, many of whom might travel several miles to school wearing inadequate clothing.

The assertion of students' capacity to determine themselves when they wanted to attend school recurred frequently. Educational administrators viewed this as a lamentable lack of 'parental authority', but it is more intelligible as a statement of the customary position of young student/workers in town and country. Students were not in household or community the flawed subjectivities defined as 'schoolchildren' by educational reform. They were rather 'scholars': people attending school. This was an activity which in the views of many should continue to be largely voluntary. Furthermore, the definition of scholars as children was accompanied by the imputation of authority over them to parents---especially fathers. Resistance by parents to the initiatives of public schooling then, were not simply jurisdictional disputes, with the school *replacing* the family. Schooling attempted to transform the authority structure of the household as well: to place 'children' under control. Parents often seem to have had no desire to engage in the authoritative activity required of them by public schooling.

Teachers frequently reported that parents encouraged their children to attend at school as the latter saw fit. Walter Bell of

Chesley complained that 'the parents encourage the children in their conduct. They think I have no authority to demand their attendance at 9 a.m.'[74] A parent in section 16 of Wolford Township kept his son at home every day until 10 o'clock in direct defiance of the teacher's practice of locking the door and, according to the local trustees, said 'that he has a perfect right to send to school at just what hour he pleases'.[75] Other teachers encountered real or threatened violence from parents and students for attempting to exclude latecomers.[76] A teacher named M.E. Bell from St. Catherines who attempted to stop latecomers from interrupting his morning prayers by locking the door until they were finished found his attendance rates drop off rapidly.[77]

Teachers who attempted to secure regular attendance by demanding notes from the parents of latecomers encountered similar difficulties. One of the school trustees in section 12 of Bathurst Township claimed that this practice was bound to fail anyway, since most parents couldn't write.[78] But other parents and students simply opposed this claim to authority on the part of teachers. Robert Dunn, another Normal School graduate teaching in a rural school, attempted to make late students bring notes. One of his trustees' children-- a twelve year old boy--came late without a note and as a punishment Dunn made him and several others 'stand for a short time with their face to the wall.' When the boy began swearing at him, Dunn ordered him out of the room. 'I did not attempt to whip the boy,' Dunn wrote, 'for I knew I would have to abuse him so as to conquer him.' Soon after, boy's father came into the school and denounced Dunn for his treatment of his son.[79]

Some teachers used their statutory powers under the School Act of 1853 to counter attempts by parents and students to determine attendance patterns. Thus in section 4 of Culross Township,

> The Teacher...suspended a couple of boys for being late suspended them untill the forenoon recess after which the Father of the Boys came with them into the school and ordered them to take their seats and told the Teacher to 'put them out if you dare'...the Teacher summonded the Father before a Magistrates Court charging him with disturbing the School at which Court he was fined.[80]

However, as we shall see, the local magistrate was by no means always prepared to enforce the School Act, and in any case teachers who took legal action against ratepayers might easily find their contracts not renewed. Many other teachers in like circumstances sought advice from the education office and attempted to use the written opinions of central administrators as authoritative communications in the locality.

Struggles and conflicts surrounded attempts by teachers to enforce the marks of cleanliness, health and neatness upon students. Parents and students objected particularly strenuously to all school practices which differentiated individual students from the rest. In section 4 of Whitby, the trustees found their 1st class teacher threatened with a law suit from an outraged father whose child the teacher had sent home for being dirty. One of the trustees wrote,

> Our teacher calls the scholars in a line every morning by ringing a bell---Any boy neglecting to get in his line before the bell quits ringing has to stand on one side until the rest are seated in the school room---A boy was so placed with others one morning---and allowed to come to his seat after the rest had entered---after he came in it was discovered by the teacher that he was very dirty about his boots and coat and of course he was sent home to clean himself---after he returned---his father came to the schol room and abused the teacher for setting him on one side and sending him home to clean himself.[81]

In this case the education office responded that the trustees should threaten the parent in question with prosecution under the School Act.

> Cleanliness and punctuality being two of even general school regulations, a teacher has discretionary power to do what your teacher did in sending the boy home; and his father coming and abusing the teacher has rendered himself liable to imprisonment or a fine of five pounds under the provisions of the 9th section of the Supplementary School Act.[82]

Clearly the matter of the teacher's discretionary power over the habits of students was important to the central authority. At the same, time, however, local residents struggled against attempts by teachers to redefine cultural standards of 'cleanliness' and 'decency'.

Samuel Daniels of Georgina Township was grossly offended when his children were expelled for being dirty, since they did not have the complaint known as 'the itch' (scrofula). 'We as common people,' he wrote, 'suppose that the words neat and clean extend to power of the Teacher when they had that filthy complaint.'[83] His children clearly did not. Other parents objected to having their children inspected for lice.[84] In their zeal to enforce 'sound moral habits', teachers often were threatened with violence. N.K. Nesbitt, the teacher in section 8 of Nelson Township, for instance, wrote to the education office in 1863 wondering, 'As Pupils are in the habit of coming to School Barefoot....whether a teacher cannot inflict some punishment on them.' Attending school barefoot, to this teacher, was a clear violation of sound morality, and he countered the habit in one case by beating a barefoot boy on his feet. The boy's father came into the school and warned him, 'I am going to send my boy Barefoot, and if you touch him I shall thrash you for it severely.'[85]

In addition to conflicts over exclusions, attendance struggles also involved local opposition to attempts by teachers to keep students in after school hours, and to assess such other 'micro-penalties' as demotions. Many of these struggles involved questions of the jurisdiction of teachers discussed elsewhere in this study. Still, H.T. Crossley, for example, kept a student in after school as a punishment for irregular attendance in April of 1870, even though he knew that the student's father was aware of the student's absence. The parent came into the school while the detention was underway and told the teacher 'he had no right to keep his child in after telling him that he [the father] had given him [the student] liberty.' Crossley claimed that he could keep children after school if he saw fit, but the father dared him to do it again. The following day, Crossley attempted to make the boy sit with the younger students and suspended him when he refused. At recess, the boy's father again came 'greatly enraged at the conduct of the Teacher', swore at him in front of the class and ordered his son to take his usual seat. Crossley sought advice from the education office.[86]

School supporters frequently asserted a customary right of access to the school under conditions they found convenient. They treated public schooling not as a general 'public' right, to be administered to the population in practice as school administrators saw fit, but rather as a substantive right of access to schooling which they themselves would define in terms of structure, content, and occasion. The reality of this assertion is replicated again and again in the archival accounts.

For example, scholars and parents frequently asserted a claim to be schooled not only when they saw fit, but under congenial conditions. These conditions extended even to such things as where scholars would sit, and with whom they would learn or be taught. In 1868, for instance, Mr. Durnion's son was absent from school for two days. When the boy
> ...left the School he was in the middle of his Class, after two days he was sent to the School again and the Teacher put him back into the next lower Class. It appears that Mr Durnion sent word to the School that he wished his Child to go into his former Class..

In this case the teacher responded by sending the boy 'home and with instruction that his father was to teach him at home.' This dispute could not be settled locally, although it is not clear what intervention the central office made.[87]

The question of the age of the population which could have access to the school was also contested locally. The School Acts attempted to define a section of the population as 'capable of profiting from instruction'. In the Act of 1843, schooling was aimed at those between the ages of five and sixteen. The Act of 1846, after much popular pressure, extended the limits of official schooling to include all those between five and twenty-one years of age. Here again administrative uniformity conflicted with custom and local interest. Before the School Acts, age-specific attendance patterns were quite directly linked to production cycles. Children too young to work attended school in the busy summer season---particularly in the countryside---and the winter schools were filled with older students, including people in their late twenties and early thirties.[88] Female teachers were commonly hired in the summer, and male teachers in the winter. The School Acts sought to exclude both the very young and those over twenty-one, and these exclusions generated opposition and attempts at counter-organization.

Those under five were to be excluded entirely from the school. Many parents and older child-minders, however, attempted to use the school as they had customarily done, as a day-care centre. The Woodstock Board of School Trustees in August of 1862 sought information from the central office because 'a few children called by themselves or parents five years of age, but looking younger have been admitted to our schools.'[89] Many school boards produced regulations excluding those underage explicitly. An early example was the specification by the Township School Commissioners for Charlotteville under the Act of 1841 that 'Small children not attending as scholars, shall not be taken by scholars to school.'[90] In the absence of systematic social means for the verification of age categories, such rules were difficult to enforce, and in some instances, trustees attempted to contract with teachers for the continuation of traditional attendance patterns. V.E. Blake, who taught in section 4 of Usborne Township, complained in 1855, for instance, that his trustees attempted to force him to accept those under five and over twenty-one in the school.[91]

With respect to those over the age of twenty-one, as Gidney and Lawr have emphasized,[92] the central office eventually attempted to extend the range of locally available schooling. The Chief Superintendent at times supported the continued attendance of older students, but nonetheless supported their payment of extra fees. To Mr. Pillar of Dickenson's Landing who complained in 1859 that his trustees were charging fees of five shillings a month to students over twenty-one---which they could not pay---the chief superintendent replied,
> I think the attendance of persons over 21 years of age ought to be encouraged as much as possible & the trustees should charge as small a fee as they can.[93]

Again, when a trustee from section 5 of Storrington Township asked if the section's teacher could, 'put away schoolers out of the school for no other reason than that they are over School age, And thus compell them to stop learning,'[94] the chief superintendent affirmed the power of the local trustees to determine the conditions of admission to the common schools.[95]

Here as in many other instances, a particular administrative politics stands out, a politics in which the central office in effect allowed local administrative organs to make out as best they could in the face of local resistance, at least so long as system principles were not at issue.

However, in some locations these powers of trustees were used to exclude some classes and ethnic groups from the school. The attempts by white ratepayers to exclude black children from the common schools throughout the period from 1846 to 1871 are notorious.[96] In 1857, in addition, the local superintendent for Goderich claimed that local trustees were excluding the 'Rail Road' children---- children whose parents worked on railroad construction projects---unless they paid discriminatory fees.[97]

Questions of limiting access to the school tended to be most hotly debated in villages and towns which had established free schools. At one extreme were attempts like those by the Oshawa Board of School Trustees simply to exclude all advanced students from the village schools in the interests of economy.[98] The other extreme was typified by the experience of the village of Dundas. Here the attempts of school trustees to organize schooling according to notions of public efficiency and public economy encountered opposition from school supporters who sought to sustain customary conditions of access to schooling, and customary pedagogical practices.

In 1865, the board of school trustees for the village of Dundas introduced the 'graded system' of instruction. This village was one of those which had established union schools under the School Amendment Act of 1853. Here the grammar and common schools were united under the direction of a single board of trustees. This form of educational administration was regarded, by 1865, as increasingly unsatisfactory by the central education office. Grammar and common schooling were increasingly viewed by the centre as mutually exclusive from the outset. In Dundas, the union of the schools had produced local conflict before 1865. In May and June of 1864, for instance, parents, teachers, trustees and others had engaged in a heated debate about the powers of grammar school teachers over the students in the common schools.[99]

Nonetheless, after the 'graded system' had been in place for a year the trustees were well pleased with it. It increased the 'efficiency' of teachers, and thus reduced expenses. With graded classes, it was possible to increase class size and thus to reduce the number of teachers and classrooms in the system, for a considerable saving. However, the system was predicated upon the conception of the movement of students through classes (i.e., promotions.) Students, supported by their parents, refused to be promoted, particularly where this involved leaving the common schools and attending the grammar schools. In February of 1866, the Secretary of the board of

trustees wrote the education office to remark that,
> A number of the pupils who are fit to enter the highest department rebelled the other day against going away from...their 'own teacher'.... They evidently did this at the instigation of their parents who insist not merely that their children shall have the education provided by law, but that they must have it *in the room* & from the teacher of their choice.[100]

Under its powers to determine the general conditions of admission to the common schools, the board of trustees then refused access to the common schools to students it considered too advanced. Some school supporters protested vehemently. Mr. Rossell, whose children were sent by the trustees to the town grammar school, insisted 'I do not wish my children to learn classics, and desire them to have such an Education as the law provides is to be given in the Common School.'[101] Mr. Strathan complained of the uselessness and expense of a grammar school education for his daughter.
> I suppose that in that school she would have to study Latin, and Greek and other branches of knowledge that would be of no advantage to her in the sphere she has to move, besides---entailing on me a canciderable expence for books, which I cannot afford, being but a working man.[102]

While it is not clear what happened in these cases, the matter did not die in Dundas. Two years later further complaints were made about the school board attempting to force students from the '4th division' to go on to the grammar school.[103] While the debate over promotions raged in Dundas, it reappeared in the village of Guelph. Here the students promoted to the grammar school,
> ...decline going and say they cannot be compelled referring to a Letter once written from your Department to the effect that Pupils could not be compelled to avail themselves of a Grammar School Education if they only wished a Common School education.[104]

This was indeed the position of the central office by the late 1860s. Central educational administrators increasingly supported a limited and distinct common school education for the bulk of the population, extended after 1871 by the creation of 'continuation' schools for advanced but still 'elementary' education. It was their contention increasingly in the decades after the organization of public education that class differences in provision were good and necessary, and this contention underlay their increasing dissatisfaction with the organization of union schools. Interestingly, the attempts by local administrators to establish the 'lock-step' model of schooling in the interests of 'efficiency' and 'public economy' were limited by the central office's support for two distinct educational streams.

In this situation, the administrative problems created for local agencies by opposition to grading and promotions were simply left by the central office to local solution. Thus, when George Bradshaw complained that the trustees of the local union school in Metcalfe sought to send his children to the grammar school against his wishes, the chief superintendent assured him that,

> Every ratepayer is entitled to the privileges of the Common School for his children so long as the rules are observed, and no pupils can be compelled to enter the grammar school department of a united grammar and common school unless the parents desire that they should receive a higher English education not taught in the Common School.[105]

In addition to the difficulty local school administrators faced in establishing a bureaucratically rational public educational system in the area of curriculum and promotions, urban school supporters attempted to preserve another pattern of school attendance which had characterized market-determined schooling. On the urban educational market, attendance was determined in part according to the perceived competence of teachers. 'Good' teachers--however defined--attracted large numbers of scholars, while unpopular teachers had the opposite experience. Town and village school administrators found themselves plagued by the attempts of students to continue these patterns of school selection and school attendance after the organization of public schooling. The superintendent of schools for Ottawa wrote to the education office in 1870 that,

> The Teachers of our Schools complain that their authority over the pupils is very much interfered with ---in consequence of the pupils of their own whims----leaving one Public School and entering

another. they (the Teachers) request that some rule be established to prevent this state of things.[106]
The superintendent wondered if the town board of trustees could make rules to force children to attend a particular school. With characteristic vagueness, the education office replied that parents had every right to choose where their children would be schooled, but stated that this right must not interfere with the school board's reasonable rules for school organization.[107] The answer, of course, left the matter to local solution, but the importance of the matter should be stressed. The capacity of school supporters to learn from the teacher whom they found most attractive--- for whatever reason--- was an important component of their power in the educational domain. The establishment of a public educational domain involved the removal of these traditional powers, and the subjection of both school supporters and teachers to a logic of public administration.

## Conclusion

Educational administrators and partisans of the public educational project viewed popular opposition to public schooling as inherently irrational, at least for the most part. Irregular attendance was seen as parental 'negligence' and 'indifference' or 'ignorance'. Yet a closer scrutiny of the activities of school supporters reveals that this opposition was quite intelligible in terms of the reality of structures of production and in terms of the quality of the schooling offered. The overwhelming concern of school administrators at the centre with 'catchment' produced a distorted view of local educational reality. 'Parental indifference' was in reality an intelligible and at times progressive response to the project of centrally controlled schooling. This 'indifference' was overcome only by unceasing attempts to normalize the conditions and practices of state schooling.

## Notes to Chapter Five

1. Emile Durkheim, *Moral Education*. (Glencoe: Free Press, 1961), 27.
2. Durkheim, *Moral Education:* 27. Compare the discussion of regularity in D. Stow, *The Training System.* (Glasgow: Blackie, 1845): passim, or virtually any other mid-nineteenth century work.
3. Ian Davey, 'The Rhythm of Work and the Rhythm of School' in A. Chaiton and N. McDonald eds. *Egerton Ryerson and His Times.* (Toronto: Macmillan, 1978):225; 235.
4. E.P. Thompson, 'Time, work-discipline and industrial capitalism,' *Past and Present* 38, 1967. For Davey, see also 'School Reform and School Attendance: The Hamilton Central School, 1853-1861' in M.B. Katz and P.H. Mattingly, (eds) *Education and Social Change.* (New York: University Press), 246-70.
5. PAO MU972, Education Papers Collection, 1840-1849. Robert McKee Moore's Register & Day Book, West Gwillimbury Township.
6. PAO, MU972, Robert McKee Moore... (see note 5).
7. PAO RG2 C6C, J. Fletcher, Superintendent, Mono Township, 24 February 1855.
8. PAO RG2 C6C, John Flood, Superintendent, Dunn, 26 January 1860.
9. G.E. Boyce, *Hutton of Hastings* (Belleville: Hastings County Council, 1972),50.
10. There are dozens of instances. For example, PAO RG2 C-6-C, no. 5613; 7306, 1867; no.6460, 1869.
11. *Annual Reports of the Chief Superintendent of Education, 1846-70.*
12. PAO RG2 C6C, Wm. Heather, no.1 Yonge, 12 January 1856; C1Q, Hodgins to Heather, 21 January 1856.
13. PAO RG2 C6C, J. O'Shanahan, Teacher, Lafontaine, 24 June 1859.
14. PAO RG2 C6C, J. Wood, J.P., no.4 King, 20 January 1870.
15. PAO RG2 C6C, W. Kilty, Canning, 29 May 1860.
16. PAO MU2109, Miscellaneous Papers Collection, Memoirs of Eliza Blair Keyes, 1844, no. 14. Keyes remembers a teacher in the 1850s who 'Between classes' would read novels or the newspaper and 'would give her ruler to a boy and tell him to stand on the floor and watch the others. If he saw anyone talking he was to give that one the ruler. This pupil had to bring the ruler to the teacher and

hold out his hand for the stroke of the ruler.'
17. PAO RG2 C6C, J. Armour, Pt. Sarnia, 9 March 1852.
18. PAO RG2 C6C, C. Blunden, Plympton, 22 August 1853.
19. PAO RG2 C6C, A. McMillan, Innerkip, 11 April 1856.
20. PAO RG2 C6C, James Sim, superintendent, Wellesley, 7 May 1856.
21. PAO RG2 C6C, A.A. Clarke, teacher, Whitby, 22 March 1860.
22. PAO RG2 C6C, A. Campbell, superintendent, Chatham, Harwick, Howard & Oxford, 7 February 1855.
23. PAO RG2 C1X, Ryerson to Secretary, Board of Union School Trustees, Bond Head, 2 March 1858.
24. PAO RG2 C2, Ryerson to John Soules, teacher, East Gwillimbury, 8 March 1865.
25. PAO RG2 C6C, A. Macallum, Model School, 20 March 1855.
26. PAO RG2 C6C, J.H. Sangster, Normal School, 16 November 1866.
27. PAO RG2 C6C, W.J. Anderson, Toronto, 16 April 1858.
28. PAO RG2 C6C, J. M. Vancock, Toronto, 30 June 1858; Louis Sabatti Ullman, Toronto, 4 February 1864.
29. PAO RG2 C6C, J.H. Sangster, Normal School, 16 November 1866.
30. PAO RG2 C6C, P.W. Clarke, Superintendent, Mariposa, 18 June 1855; Board of Public Instruction, Victoria, Lindsay, 26 June 1855; Gilbert Tweedie, Lindsay, 3 July 1855; C2, Hodgins to Tweedie, 11 July 1855.
31. PAO RG2 C6C, Hugh Lamont, Georgetown, 8 February 1858.
32. PAO RG2 C2, Ryerson to Lamont, Esquissing, 15 February 1858.
33. PAO RG2 C6C, Trustees, no.3 Sunnidale, 13 May 1861; Edward Allen, Teacher, no.3. Sunnidale, 13 October 1862.
34. PAO RG2 C6C, John Cameron, Beaverton, 19 January 1858.
35. PAO RG2 C6C, John Montgomery, Headford, 1 March 1861.
36. PAO RG2 C6C, D. McLennan, Trustee, Glammis, 30 October 1870.
37. PAO RG2 C6C, T. Smith, Trustee, section 1 Westminster, 23 June 1862; C2, Ryerson to Smith, 5 July 1862; C6C, J. Armstrong superintendent, Westminster, 15 August 1862; J. Boag, Teacher, Westminster, 29 August; C2, Ryerson to Armstrong, 21 August 1862.
38. PAO RG2 C6C, Trustees, section 6 Williams, 12 December 1859; Alexander Campbell, Williams, 7 December 1859; Alexander Levie, superintendent, Williams, 5 December 1859; C1BB, Ryerson to Levie, 14 December 1859.
39. PAO RG2 C6C, William Parrish, section 4 Fenelon, 24 December

1866.
40. PAO RG2 C6C, Wm. Barnes, section 11 Pickering, 8 January 1868.
41. PAO RG2 C6C, J. McKilligan, section 1 East Zorra, 2 November 1861 (in 11 November 1861).
42. PAO RG2 C6C, John Green, Trustee, Fitzroy, 17 February 1855.
43. PAO RG2 C6C, J.S. Glyne, Wawanash, 19 June 1857.
44. PAO RG2 C6C, John Buchannan, Tilbury West, 16 April 1859.
45. PAO RG2 C6C, George Hamilton, Esquissing, 19 January 1861.
46. PAO RG2 C6C, Trustees, no.5 Oxford, 25 March 1855.
47. PAO RG2 C6C, Trustees, no.11 Puslinch, 20 October 1855.
48. As it did in PAO RG2 C6C, A.R. Urquhart, Wardsville, 19 October 1864.
49. As did PAO RG2 C6C, John Wright, Ramsay, 31 October 1860.
50. PAO RG2 C6C, A. Fletcher, no. 5 Harwich, 5 April 1859.
51. PAO RG2 C6C, J. McDiarmid, no.13 Yarmouth, 28 April 1858.
52. PAO RG2 C6C, Superintendent, Pembroke, 24 May 1861.
53. PAO RG2 C6C, Trustees, no.12 Roxborough, Moose Creek, 18 September 1865.
54. For instance in PAO RG2 C6C, E. Thornbury et al, no.15 Sombra, 23 August 1869.
55. PAO RG2 C6C, Local Superintendent, Lindsay 26 November 1862; M. Dingwall et al, no.11 Ancaster, 10 January 1866.
56. PAO RG2 C6C, K.A. Campbell, local superintendent, Mara & Rama, 2 February 1867.
57. PAO RG2 C6C, Alex. Gordon, no.5 Mosa, 19 January 1864.
58. PAO RG2 C6C, F.J. Payne, no.7 Southwold, 8 April 1861; Superintendent, Alice, 30 June 1868.
59. PAO RG2 C6C, James Byrns, North Crosby, 12 February 1864.
60. PAO RG2 C6C, W. Simpson, Superintendent, Tiny & Tay, 17 October 1864.
61. PAO RG2 C6C, J. Skinner, Local Superintendent, Lobo, 21 February 1857.
62. PAO RG2 C1V, Ryerson to J. Skinner, 28 February 1857. 'It appears to me a matter of personal spite rather than a regard to morality.'
63. PAO RG2 C6C, Parents, no.1 Minto, 15 April 1864; also J. Darroch and others, no. 1 Minto, 3 May 1864.
64. PAO RG2 C2, Ryerson to Parents, no.1 Minto, 26 April 1864;

Ryerson to Darroch, 9 May 1864.
65. The miscellaneous school reports collected mainly in 1842 and included in PAO RG2 Miscellaneous School Reports, (F2) point to school days which range in starting times from 8:30 to 9:30 a.m.; in ending times from 3:30 to 6:00 p.m., and in which lunch breaks are also variable.
66. For instance, PAO RG2 C6C, no.6574 reveals that in September of 1868 there were more than fifty names on the waiting list for admission to the third division of the Boys' Model School.
67. PAO RG2 C6C, Wm. Gunn, Superintendent, no. 1 Bruce, 28 October 1857.
68. PAO RG2 C6C, John Neelands, no. 16 Chinguacousy, 28 January 1861.
69. PAO RG2 C6C, Secretary, Board of Trustees, Newmarket, 21 June 1862.
70. PAO RG2 C6C, J.B. Newman, Bell Ewart, 19 February 1862.
71. PAO RG2 C2, Ryerson to Newman, 25 February 1862.
72. PAO RG2 C6C, Henry Steinson, Columbus, 16 December 1862. C2, Ryerson to Steinson, 22 December 1862.
73. PAO RG2 C6C, John Agnew, Sydenham, 22 August 1865.
74. PAO RG2 C6C, Walter Bell, Chesley, 2 April 1869.
75. PAO RG2 C6C, Trustees, no. 16 Wolford, 14 April 1856.
76. PAO RG2 C6C, D.A. Bucknell, no.7 South Norwich, 18 July 1860; William Costin, Holbrook, 24 September 1868; Jno. Pepper, Canboro, 14 January 1864. See in this regard as well 'The Brantford 'School Difficulty', Upper Canada, 1859,' in A. Prentice and S. Houston (eds) *Family, School and Society in Nineteenth-century Canada.* (Toronto:Oxford, 1975): 107-14.
77. PAO RG2 C6C, M.E. Bell, St, Catherines, 16 May 1861.
78. PAO RG2 C6C, Trustee, no.12 Bathurst, 29 March 1869. This shows once again the extent to which the bureaucratic administration of civil society demands the creation of capacities in the population.
79. PAO RG2 C6C, Robert Dunn, Teacher, no.2 Tosorontio, 13 February 1865.
80. PAO RG2 C6C, J.L. Allan, Secretary-treasurer, no.4 Culross, 22 November 1866.
81. PAO RG2 C6C, Isaac French, Trustee, no.4 Whitby 7 May 1855.
82. PAO RG2 C1K, Ryerson to French, 11 May 1855.
83. PAO RG2 C6C, Samuel Daniels, Georgina, 23 May 1864. See also

for medical exclusions, R.D. Gidney and D.A. Lawr, 'Who Ran the Schools? Local Influence on Education Policy in Nineteenth Century Ontario,' *Ontario History,* LXXII,(3): 131-143.
84. PAO RG2 C6C, John King, Teacher, no.6 Barton, 16 January 1865.
85. PAO RG2 C6C, N.K. Nesbitt, Teacher, no.8 Nelson, 4 May 1863. As in many instances, no reply preserved.
86. PAO RG2 C6C, H.T. Crossley, Culloden, 23 April 1870.
87. PAO RG2 C6C, Thomas Farrow, Local Superintendent, Morris, 26 June 1868.
88. More information on age of scholars can be found scattered in PAO RG2 F2; for example, E.M. Griffiths, Lot 11, 12th Con. Burford Township; F.W. Wilmotte, Windsor; Robert S. Aldrich, 7th Concess. Yarmouth Township.
89. PAO RG2 C6C, J.C. Silvester, Board of Trustees, Woodstock, 11 August 1862. Note the summer attendance of those too young to work.
90. PAO RG2 F2, Rules and Regulations, Charlotteville.
91. PAO RG2 C6C, V.E. Blake, Teacher, no.4 Usborne, 12 July 1858.
92. R.D. Gidney and D.A. Lawr, 'Egerton Ryerson and the Origins of the Ontario Secondary School,' *Canadian Historical Review.* LX (4) 1979:442-465.
93. PAO RG2 C2, Ryerson to Pillar, 10 May 1859; E.W. Pillar, Teacher, Dickenson's Landing, 6 May 1859.
94. PAO RG2 C6C, J. Mundell, Trustee, no.5 Storrington, 6 April 1859.
95. PAO RG2 C2, Ryerson to Mundell, 11 April 1859.
96. I propose to make this the subject for a future paper.
97. PAO RG2 C6C, John Nairn, Local Superintendent, Goderich, 18 March 1857.
98. PAO RG2 C6C, R.H. Thornton, Local Superintendent, Oshawa, 20 September 1858. This is one of several on the topic.
99. PAO RG2 C6C, for the 'Dundas School Difficulty', A. Caldwell, Dundas, 18 May 1864; Chairman Board of Trustees, Dundas, 7 June 1864; Caldwell with clippings from the Dundas *True Banner* 6 June 1864; Hugh Fraser, West Flamboro, 8 August 1864; C2, Ryerson to Trustees, 23 May 1864; Ryerson to Fraser, 13 August 1864.
100. PAO RG2 C6C, A. Healdwell, Secretary, Board of Trustees, Dundas, 17 February 1866.
101. PAO RG2 C6C, A. Rossell, Dundas, 19 February 1866.

102. PAO RG2 C6C, E. Strathan, Dundas, 20 February 1866.
103. PAO RG2 C6C, J.W. McLean, Dundas, 6 March 1868.
104. PAO RG2 C6C, Henry Peterson, Guelph, 3 October 1866.
105. PAO RG2 C2, Ryerson to Bradshaw, 19 February 1870; also, C6C, Geo, Bradshaw, Metcalfe, 17 February 1870; relatedly, C2, Ryerson to Naron, Head Master, Scotland Union School, 29 April 1870.
106. PAO RG2 C6C, M. Cousins, Ottawa, 10 March 1870.
107. PAO RG2 C2, Ryerson to Cousins, 21 March 1870.

# Chapter Six:
# Training the 'Good' Teacher.

In the late 1850s, the education office recruited a young Englishman named Watts to be Second Master for Classics and English in the Model Grammar School. The Normal School administrators were seeking an able young teacher who might prove capable of leading the institution. The education office corresponded with Watts and his parents, encouraging him to come to Canada by presenting a bright view of his prospects. Watts came to teach at the Model Grammar School in 1858.

However, it soon became clear to Watts' superiors that his performance was not satisfactory. Before removing him, the Chief Superintendent sought written evaluations from the Normal and Model School masters. What Watts lacked, as far as his fellow teachers were concerned, was not scholarship. Everyone agreed that as a scholar, Watts was highly qualified. Rather, his mastery of pedagogy was defective.

'The master must govern by moral suasion and force of character,' wrote G.R.R. Cockburn, the Rector of the Model Grammar School. 'If he does not possess marked decision of character, and fully understand the young mind, & art of managing it in its manifold phases, he cannot expect his efforts, however well intended, to be crowned with success.'[1] In Cockburn's view, Watts had the misfortune to possess 'that cold, unsympathetic character which deadens instead of exciting to renewed and sustained activity the young & ardent mind.'[2] T.J. Robertson, Principal of the Normal School and himself trained by one of the Prussian schoolmasters, argued that Watts was defective as a classroom manager.
> One of the most essential points in Normal School
> education is the inculcation of a careful system of
> order & regularity, involving many minute circum-
> stances unimportant in institutions of a different
> character. Without such system and order a Normal
> School is a mere school of Instruction.[3]

Watts was incapable of maintaining effective classroom discipline. He did not notice the small elements of disorder in his classes, and this oversight threatened the larger order of the school. 'Some of the female teachers' were reported to 'have brought their sewing into the room & thus occupied themselves during his lectures,' while others were 'occupied in a less useful way.'[5] As the Chief Superintendent added, this failure in classroom discipline was also evident in Watts' failure to exercise his students.

> I do not think Mr Watts possesses the faculty or power of drilling students or pupils in any subject. He expresses himself accurately & readily, but without any energy, or animation, or impressiveness, or point; & does not appear to produce any clear or distinct impressions or conceptions in regard to the subjects of which he treats, much less does he excite any interest in them.[4]

The case of Watts demonstrates the characteristics sought by educational administrators in the ideal teacher. These included a forceful development of the self, a 'watchful eye', attention to detail, enthusiasm, and the ability to develop the capacities of students.

The maxim 'The Teacher makes the School' was a commonplace in nineteenth century educational reform. The teacher was to be the practical embodiment of the moral character sought by educational administrators in the population as a whole. The school was seen to be a constantly productive space: students were formed by the experience of schooling, and all aspects of the experience were educational. Everything the teacher did, all arrangements put in place, all habits of mind and body exhibited, patterns of dress, ways of speaking, everything was educational. Pedagogical practice went beyond this. The teacher was not simply exemplar, but also instructor, governor, manager in the schoolroom. As G.R.R. Cockburn pointed out, education was a forceful process, a relation of governance in which the teacher ruled through a particular kind of knowledge/power. The ideal teacher possessed a practical force--- force of character-- which, combined with knowledge of the 'young mind and the art of managing it' enabled the teacher to develop the forces and form the selves of students.

From the passage of the School Act of 1846, the education office engaged in a range of initiatives designed to construct, reproduce regulate and generalize this knowledgeable, forceful and moral teacher. Central administrators after 1846 sought to transform teachers into a *corps d'etat*. This involved subverting the free market in teaching and precluding the emergence, at the same time, of a relatively independent and self-governing teaching profession. The intimate connection between teacher and local community was to be broken; access to the occupation was to be regulated by the imposition of 'qualifications' specified by the central authority; and ultimately, in the period after 1871, all teachers were to be trained in state institutions. The teacher came to occupy a regulated space in an administrative grid, and over the period 1850-1871, the boundaries of this grid became more clearly defined and the density of controls within it increased. In the same period, the composition of the teaching labour force came to be dominated by women.

## Training the Teacher

In his *Report on a System of Public Elementary Instruction,* Ryerson made three arguments in favour of the organization of a Normal School for the training of teachers in Canada West. First, the regular training of teachers would end itinerance in the occupation. Trained teachers would 'regard it as their vocation' and remain in the occupation for life, the 'infant and youthful mind' would be 'rescued from the ignorance and pernicious examples of incompetent and immoral Teachers' who would no longer have access to the occupation, and 'School-Teachers [would] respect themselves, and be respected as other professional men.' Second, Ryerson argued that Normal School training would ensure higher wages for teachers. The demand for teachers trained in the Normal Schools of Glasgow, Dublin, London and Edinburgh was so great, he argued, that most teachers were employed before completing the training programme. The demand for teachers far outstripped the supply, and trained teachers in consequence were highly paid.[6] Third, trained teachers were cheaper and more effective in a public educational system. Ryerson claimed that

> ...a trained Teacher will, as a general rule, by the superior organization and classification of his School, and by his better method and greater ability for teaching, impart at least twice as much instruction in

any given time, as an untrained one.[7] Even if such teachers were paid twice as much as their untrained counterparts, the pupil would save time and acquire the 'additional advantage of good habits, and accurate views.'[8] The efficiency and effectiveness of the trained teacher consisted also in its capacity to teach without violence. The trained teacher had mastered the secrets of student nature and of pedagogical technique, and so could activate and animate students while making instruction pleasant to them.

Yet these were not the only, or perhaps not even the most important, arguments for the training of teachers by the government. As John Beverly Robinson, Chief Justice of Upper Canada, emphasized, if teachers were not so trained, and if the government did not control the books used in schools,

> There could be little, or no, security for what they might teach, nor any certainty that the good, which might be acquired from their precepts, would not be more than counter-balanced by the ill effects of their example.[9]

The security of the political order demanded that both what teachers *were* and what they might say be regulated by the educational authority.

The debate over the training of teachers was particularly concerned with the question of whose agent the teacher was to be. In the early 1840s, under the direction of Robert Murray, the education office argued that teachers should be their own agents. Murray urged the breaking of the market relations in which teachers were 'at the mercy of the public', dependent upon their employers or upon elected trustees. He agitated for and encouraged the professional self-organization of teachers. After the appointment of Ryerson, however, central policy changed in this regard. Ryerson also sought to break the dependence of teachers upon employers and trustees, but aimed to make teachers subservient to a 'public interest' defined and administered by the education office itself. In sharp contrast to the period of Robert Murray's tenure of office, under Ryerson teachers' self-organization was at best regarded with suspicion, and at worst, actively discouraged.[10]

Like his counterparts in Britain and America, Ryerson consistently argued that untrained and itinerant teachers were immoral and incompetent. These teachers were hired by local school supporters because the latter were ignorant, negligent of education, or the victims of duplicity.[11] Yet while many educational consumers were discontented with some features of the educational market—particularly with itinerance on the part of teachers and with the difficulty of attracting skilled teachers in remote areas, the reality of the educational market was probably not adequately represented by educational administrators in Canada West. There is no evidence to suggest a wholesale, or even a substantial exodus of teachers from the occupation after local educational inspection began in 1844, nor after it became more rigorous from 1850. Some candidates for teaching were disqualified by superintendents, of course, but the educational market seems to have produced and sustained enough teachers who could conduct schools and pass superintendents' examinations.[12]

It is not possible to know exactly how numerous they were, but highly trained teachers were certainly present in Canada West in the late 1840s and 1850s. In addition to George Elmslie of Nichol Township who practiced the 'intellectual' method of the Edinburgh Sessional School, and W.B. Carroll of the Johnstown District Model School, who had been trained in the Dublin model schools, many other teachers were at work who approximated the education office's conception of competence. J.F. Morris of Fort Erie had been trained at the 'Normal School of the Irish Educational Commissioners'. A. Migoleton had been educated at Mareschal College in Aberdeen, and George Wilson of Sydenham had attended King's College in Aberdeen, and then the Edinburgh Normal School for four months.[13] Two of the teachers in Augusta Township in 1855 who held first class certificates from the County Board of Public Instruction had been trained in Dublin Normal school.[14] Teachers, both singly and in groups, considered emigrating to Canada West. John Ireland, a graduate of the Glasgow Normal Seminary, considered doing so, as did a group of his fellow students.[15] The education office's own lists of superannuated teachers contained many European-born and possibly European-educated teachers who stayed in the occupation long enough to qualify for a pension.

But if the education office's claims that the colony was swamped with immoral, incompetent, designing and disloyal teachers were factually incorrect, they nonetheless served to justify policy initiatives which reorganized the occupation.

The School Act of 1850 placed the power of certification of teachers in the hands of County Boards of Public Instruction. These Boards were composed of grammar school trustees and township superintendents of schools. Teachers were required to submit to examination before the County Boards in order to acquire licences to teach, without which local trustees were not permitted to hire them. The County Boards could grant certificates of qualification valid either generally in the County, or limited to a particular period or location. County Boards could also annul certificates and re-examine teachers at their discretion. A condition of entry to the teacher's examination was the possession of a certificate of moral character from a clergyman of a legally recognized religious sect.

While teachers' examinations seem to have been quite cursory at first, many County Boards of Public Instruction began raising the standard of qualification in the late 1850s. After 1858, the central education office began to specify the minimum requirements for each class of teaching certificate, and also agitated for the granting of the lowest class of certificate in exceptional circumstances only. From 1853, the Chief Superintendent was empowered to issue licences valid throughout the colony to graduates of the Normal School. While the practical operation of these and other regulatory measures was the object of local conflict and struggle throughout the period before 1871, they defined the teacher in principle as an agent of the state.

## Breaking Community Control

Three main processes were involved in attempts by the central education office to define the teacher as a legitimately authoritative figure in the locality. The office of teacher was increasingly defined as a cell in a central administrative grid. Access to this cell was increasingly regulated by the examination of candidates as to the possession of definite attributes defined by the central authority. And a relation of knowledge/power was constructed in which the legitimacy of the teacher's authority was based on its possession of 'sound moral character' and on its monopolization and administration of a body of both school knowledge and pedagogical technique. The educational project, the 'civilization', 'humanization' and 'elevation' of the population, this process of government, involved a myriad of small but persistent struggles aimed at separating the teacher from the local community and making that person authoritative. The moral 'elevation' of the teacher involved the separation of teacher and school from direct community control. Teachers had to occupy a position of relative independence and moral authority in relation to the local community, if they were to be capable of 'civilizing' the population. The school had to be defined as an authoritative 'public' institution, rather than as a community institution.

One of the initiatives in this project was an attempt to reconstruct teachers' ordinary living conditions. The central education office acted in the late 1840s and early 1850s to end the practice of 'boarding around' by teachers. Throughout the period before 1846, country teachers were routinely paid the bulk of their salaries in kind, in the form of room and board in the households of school subscribers. As one local historian described it,

> There was also a system of 'boarding round' on the part of a single Teacher. He would board two weeks at one house, where there were two Children attending, three weeks at another house, from which three Pupils would be attending and so on, the Teacher's board being taken in lieu of that much money.[16]

Teachers were immediately embedded in the life of the community; they were employees of school supporters, living like most of those around them without the mediation of cash money until the annual payment of the government grant. Many retired teachers who had boarded around in their youth claimed to have enjoyed the practice. Some argued that they were sought after as resident guests by their scholars, and that a sort of competition with respect to their comfort existed. Others reported that they were expected to participate in household labour processes, and were popular to the degree that they possessed domestic skills. Many teachers who boarded around commented that the knowledge they gained of the lives of their students in this way was useful to them in the schoolroom as well.

While many rural school sections continued the practice in the 1850s, rising living standards in many parts of the colony made boarding around repugnant to many teachers. A teacher from West Hawkesbury, who claimed that township superintendents were providing the education office with a view only of 'the glossy outside representations' of school matters, was particularly disgusted with the practice. This person claimed that he was usually stuffed into the worst corner of the house where he was lucky to find a bed. He often slept in a leaky attic room where his clothes were stained with soot whenever it rained or snowed and where 'his eyes will be melted out of his head with smoke.'[17]

Whether teachers enjoyed the practice or not, however, it did not allow them to occupy the position sought for them by the education office. Teachers could not 'civilize' and 'humanize' a population to which they were socially subordinate, or with which they lived on conditions of moral equality. Effective education, in the eyes of central administrators, entailed the creation of the teacher as a legitimate local authority, and one instructed by the education office, not by local residents. The practice of boarding around was opposed by the education office in correspondence from 1846. A ruling of the Court of Queen's Bench (7 UC Q.B.R.,130) declared it illegal for any portion of school tax to be deducted for the teacher's room and board, and this judgement was reprinted in the *Educational Manual for Upper Canada* of 1856. Attempts to circumvent the ruling were defeated when they came to the attention of the education office, but several superintendents of schools claimed that the practice continued illegally. For instance, Edward Scarlett, the superintendent of schools for Northumberland County, claimed in 1856 that many teachers were still boarding around, and instead of preparing their lessons at night, were 'spending their precious time in joke telling or probably corrupting the manners of the youths about them with tobacco smoking or snuff taking by which means (snuff taking) they often ingratiate themselves in the families with whom they are boarding.'[18]

However, simply outlawing the practice of boarding around did not by itself 'elevate teaching into a profession.' For one thing, many teachers boarded with their employers because of a shortage of other rural accommodation. When precluded from boarding around, many teachers were compelled either to live in taverns---which was generally unsatisfactory to central administrators, or in the school house itself. The latter arrangement also sometimes exposed students to conditions considered improper by the education office. In section no.4 of Kilty Township in 1860, the trustees actually partitioned the schoolroom to provide living quarters for the teacher. The dimensions of the room were 26 x 24 feet, and a space 8 x 14 feet was partitioned off for the teacher, his wife and two children. The school supporters claimed that the trustees had ruined the school. The partition cut through a desk, and the students were compelled to listen to squalling infants and domestic disputes in the course of their lessons.[19] This kind of community embeddedness was resolved only gradually in the province through the increase of living accommodation and through salary increases for teachers.

## Spaces and Qualifications

In his first communication to the education office after his appointment as Township Superintendent for Bastard Township, John Blacksbury complained that many of the teachers he had examined 'strictly speaking could only 'half read half spell.' ' This was because 'ill-educated' people were often hired to teach 'at decent wages on account of their usefulness on sundays and evening meetings as preachers, exhorters or leaders in one or other of the many religious sects to be found in country places.' In other cases, illiterate people were hired as teachers because they also served as secretaries of the local secret society. 'For the reasons given above the local officers could not introduce any new book except such as would be acceptable to the people.'[20]

Blacksbury identified one of the general characteristics of the local reality of teaching which the education office sought to combat: the location of the office of teacher in local structures of power and welfare. Central educational administrators sought to make teaching the 'full-time business' of trained professionals. Teaching was not to be combined with other functions, not with activity in local political or religious structures such as those mentioned by Blacksbury, not with official functions such as postmaster or poundkeeper, and certainly not with other productive activities. The seamstress- or shoemaker-teacher were anathema to central administrators.

As the teacher was to have a purely 'educational' identity, so central administrators frequently sought such an identity for the schoolhouse itself. Local conflicts over central educational initiatives in the 1850s and 1860s involved questions of access to the school house and over questions of the activities to be conducted there. The education office increasingly attempted to redefine the social identity of the school, from multi-purpose community building to the site of public education.

In the period immediately after the passage of the School Act of 1850, many school trustees set about constructing new school houses funded from tax revenue. The education office encouraged this activity, and distributed copies of Barnard's *School Architecture* to County Councils. The work was also reprinted in part in the *Journal of Education*. The education office was concerned that *proper* schools be built: healthy, well-lighted, well-ventilated, heated and spacious schools, with 'conveniences' separated for the sexes, and with treed playgrounds surrounded by a fence. Architecturally, the school was to facilitate the discipline and government of students. The school was to have an overwhelmingly educational identity, both structurally and functionally.

However, this concern frequently conflicted with an older reality in which the schoolhouse, as one of the few community buildings in many areas, served as church, debating room, lecture hall, political meeting room and recreation centre. Local residents and taxpayers repeatedly attempted to preserve these earlier uses for the building financed by local property, and teachers and trustees, with the support of the education office, just as frequently attempted to confine the school house to its strictly educational use. The dynamic of conflict in some localities was rather more complex than this. Some ratepayers, for example, used the fact that the schoolhouse was open to religious meetings to refuse to pay the school tax. Others agreed that non-*educational* activities should be prohibited, and still others attempted to force the school out of buildings used as meeting houses.

In East Nissouri township in 1852, one local resident complained that the trustees had prevented some groups from using the school house for a sunday school, while allowing others to do so. This person was incensed because the trustees 'in order effectually to debar them placed a lock upon the door of the Schoolhouse which hitherto had remained open.'[21] In Arthur township, some residents were concerned that the trustees were allowing the use of the house for purposes of which they disapproved. They wondered 'whether C. School Trustees have any right to Let or hire a School House for any purpose such as to hold a Ball, Montebank Show, or any other public or private parties contrary to the wishes of any Rate payers.'[22] A teacher named J.G. House complained of a group using the school house as a debating room. 'At their 'Debating Assembly,' as they call it, they fumigate the room with tobacco smoke, and scatter their grinds over the floor in a manner highly disagreeable to a person who makes no use of the poisonous weed.'[23] The Corresponding Secretary of the Aldborough Total Abstinence Society wondered whether the Wardsville school trustees could charge his group twenty-five cents for the use of the school house. The teacher had complained after one of the Society's meetings that 'the floor of the School Room was in a scandalous state from the use of tobacco and the ejected 'Cuds' and saliva of the Committee men.'[24] In Markham and Otonabee townships, people complained of the use of the school house by the teacher or by others for a theatre or dance hall.[25]

These debates about the dirtiness of the school room after community use should not be seen simply as neutral questions of hygiene. There is no record of their existence before the increasing development of public schooling. As well, as Prentice has shown, a common conflict between teachers and trustees throughout the period from 1850 to 1871 involved the issue of who should be charged with cleaning the schoolroom. Trustees increasingly attempted to get teachers to undertake school maintenance tasks, teachers tried to impose these on students, or to claim extra pay for them, and all of this may well have been exacerbated where the shortage of *acceptable* local accommodation forced teachers to live in the school.[26]

Debates over the religious and community use of the school and over hygiene emphasize the changing identity of the schoolhouse. The 'public' in which the school was to be situated was to be both a hygenic and non-sectarian domain. Here the state adopted a position of formal neutrality towards all *christian* religion. Here self-respect as hygiene was a sign of respect for authority. However, as a community institution, the school had often been identified with particular religious groups and community organizations. Local conflict over the use of the school house frequently highlighted the changed relationship between trustees and the local community which the School Acts effected.

The educational correspondence of the 1850s contains many references to such conflicts over the schoolhouse. In most of this correspondence, the central issue was the power of the school trustees to determine the purposes to which the schoolhouse would be put. The education office consistently defended their power. George Street of Port Stanley complained that the school trustees closed the schoolhouse against Sunday services, despite the vote of a public meeting to allow such services. 'The practice hitherto has been to permit the use of School houses in rural Sections to religious bodies,' responded the chief superintendent, 'and under certain circumstances I can see no objection to the practice.' However, this practice was becoming 'archaic', and in any case, the power was held to rest with the trustees.[27] In section no. 2 of Sophiasburgh Township in 1855, the trustees had built a new school house for 225 pounds and wanted to move the old school house thirty feet away and use it for a woodshed. They also wondered about their powers with respect to religious meetings. Ryerson replied that they could do anything with school property that they chose to do. 'The law does not authorise trustees to permit the School House to be used as a place of worship,' Ryerson added, 'but custom is in favor of it.'[28] In other instances, religious sects using the schoolhouse were accused of destroying educational apparatus. For example, the deed to one of the school houses in Reach Township contained a clause which stated that the house would be open for religious worship on Sundays. The trustees claimed that the school books were cut and ruined during church services, and sought to close the house against them. The chief superintendent assured them that they could do so and added that 'The only way in which any religious party can proceed to test its right to the house is by a suit in the Court of Chancery--- which probably no party would undertake.'[29] 'Protracted meetings' were said to damage the school house in section no. 15 of Kingston Township, and the trustees in Rockton in Beverly Township claimed that Methodists meeting in the school house destroyed the school's charts of the Lord's Prayer, the Apostle's Creed and so forth.[30]

## Duties of Teachers

If the education office was moderate in its encouragement of the emergence of a strictly educational identity for the school house, its attitude towards the qualifications and behaviour of the teacher was more forceful and direct. The School Act of 1846 for the first time included a list of duties for teachers, taken from a similar statute in the state of Massachusetts. Section XXVIII of the Act specified that teachers were to teach 'diligently and faithfully, all the branches required to be taught in the School' according to their agreements with the trustees and according to the Act. Teachers were required to keep the school Register and to 'maintain proper order and discipline' in the school, 'according to the Regulations and Forms, which shall be prepared by the Superintendent of Schools.' Teachers were required to hold quarterly public examinations of their schools, and to inform parents, guardians, trustees and school visitors of these events. Finally, teachers were required to act as secretaries to the school trustees.[31] This clause reappeared in the School Acts of 1849 and 1850.

The Regulations formulated by the 'Superintendent of Schools' from 1846 to 1850, and afterwards by the Council of Public Instruction, had the force of statute law as well, and here the behaviour and qualifications of teachers were regulated in much greater detail. These regulations were adopted almost entirely from those published by the Irish Commissioners of National Education.

Canadian teachers were to concern themselves particularly with moral behaviour. They were to impress upon the students by their own example 'the great rule of regularity and order--- a time and a place for everything, and everything in its proper time and place.' They were to encourage 'cleanliness, neatness and decency' in their students, and teachers were to do this first by ensuring that they were themselves clean and neat 'in their own persons, and in the state and general appearance of their Schools.' Also to this end, teachers were 'by personal inspection every morning' to ensure that students had their hands and faces washed, their hair combed, their clothes cleaned and mended.

In the same domain, teachers were instructed to pay the 'strictest attention to the morals and general conduct of their pupils.' They were to take every opportunity to teach the principles of 'Truth and Honesty; the duty of respect to superiors, and obedience to all persons placed in authority over them.' The 'kindly and affectionate feelings' were to be encouraged; quarrelling, cruelty to animals, and 'every approach to vice' were to be discouraged. Finally, teachers were to aim to govern their students 'by their affections and reason, rather than by harshness and severity.' The practice of 'humanistic' pedagogy was a statutory requirement for teachers.

Teachers were also instructed as to method in these Regulations, despite the repeated insistence of the chief superintendent in his local correspondence that teachers were autonomous as to their mode of instruction. Throughout most of the period from 1846 to 1871, the Regulations required teachers to 'classify the children according to the National School Books...to study those books themselves; and to teach according to the approved method recommended in their several prefaces.' The Regulations explained how this classification was to be done, and urged the 'intellectual' system of education as the best possible.[32]

In addition to their clerical duties as secretaries to the boards of trustees, teachers were required to keep a visitor's book, which they were to present to the official school visitors. The latter were permitted to write whatever they might choose, and teachers were 'by no means, to alter, or erase' these remarks, but were rather to 'lay them before the District Superintendent of School[s].' In the 1850s, teachers were also required to keep a punishment register, which was to be displayed at the quarterly public examination and then destroyed.[33]

## Policing Teaching

While the education office could legislate and administer certain kinds of behaviour and orientations on the part of teachers in general, the practical policing of the occupation of teaching was rather more difficult. The central office was dependent in this regard on the activities of superintendents of schools and county Boards of Public Instruction, as well as, to a lesser extent, upon school visitors. Persistent conflicts and incessant complaints surrounded the policing process.

In the first place, the Act of 1850 contained a lacuna which threatened the policing process in general: it did not preclude teachers from serving at the same time as superintendents of schools. Several teachers undertook to police their own schools as their own local superintendent, before the School Amendment Act of 1853 prohibited both teachers and trustees from serving as superintendents.

More generally, however, as far as the education office was concerned, some forms of police or regulation were precluded by the necessity of sustaining the authority of the teacher in the locality. In fact, the education office was in a contradictory position with respect to the teaching force. On the one hand, moral regulation of the teacher and control over curriculum by the central authority was seen as a key principle of effective political socialization. On the other hand, the teacher needed considerable practical autonomy and room to manoeuvre in the schoolroom itself. School manuals and official lessons in pedagogy repeatedly stressed that teachers should not be restricted in their schoolroom activities. Teachers were counseled, for instance, not to publish extensive lists of rules for schoolroom governance, because such things would limit their capacity to govern. They were urged repeatedly to have only one rule: DO RIGHT, which would be sufficiently general to allow any teacher to deal with all possible situations.[34]

This contradiction, between strict bureaucratic regulation and necessary personal autonomy, engaged the education office and other educational administrators in ambiguous, inconsistent and confused initiatives in different situations.

On the one hand, the education office attempted to establish, defend and stabilize the office of the teacher as an authoritative local office. This involved a range of initiatives, some of which we have detailed above. 'Parents' were repeatedly urged to do all in their power to sustain a conception of the teacher as an authoritative entity, and trustees and superintendents of schools were urged to do the same. In his first circular letter to school trustees, for instance, Ryerson stressed that while trustees hired the teacher, agreed with 'him' as to pay and hours, 'the <u>mode of teaching</u>' was with the Teacher. He continued,

> On the expiration of the term of agreement, Trustees can dismiss a Teacher if they are not pleased with him; but, subordinate to the general rules and regulations provided by law, the Teacher has a right to exercise his own judgment in teaching the School, and the District Superintendent and Visitors alone have a right to advise him on this subject. The Teacher is not a mere machine, and no Trustee or Parent should attempt to reduce him to that position. His character and his interest alike prompt him to make his instructions as efficient and popular as possible.... While a person is employed as a Teacher, it is essential, both to his character and success, that he, and not others, should be the Teacher of the School. It is, nevertheless, the duty of the Trustees to see that the School is conducted according to the regulations provided for by law.[35]

In a similar circular to District Superintendents, Ryerson again stressed the same points: the teacher was to enjoy a regulated autonomy; superintendents should sustain the teacher against local opposition, but insist on strictly moral comportment.

> It sometimes happens that the best Teacher suffers most from some ignorant and prejudiced person or persons, who, though unacquainted with school-teaching, and perhaps even what is taught in the School, undertake to dictate and interfere with the Teacher, both as to his teaching and discipline.

Such teachers were frequently blamed by parents, Ryerson continued, for the 'dullness, or idleness, or vice and neglected bringing up' of their pupils. However, superintendents should notice that the teacher was legally authorized to teach and his duties were prescribed, 'even the principles and methods of teaching— as recommended in the prefaces of the National School Books.' These prescriptions, however, 'interfere not with individual independence of mind and diversity of talent', and the teacher should 'be maintained in the rights of his office, as well as in its obligations.' The existence of an authoritative teacher was in the interest of the public, but 'the amount of ignorance and prejudice in some neighbourhoods' was 'so large,' that superintendents should realize that 'the intelligent Teacher needs all the support which can be given him.' Here again, however, Ryerson insisted that authority depended on the moral regulation of the teacher, for 'public duty requires that no nuisance should be tolerated in the person of a Teacher.'[36]

Later communications of a similar sort were common. The official *Journal of Education,* the *Educational Manual,* public speeches, and the correspondence of the chief superintendent stressed the same points. Superintendents of Schools were instructed to 'pursue such a line of conduct as will tend to uphold the just influence and authority both of trustees and teachers.' As we shall see in a later chapter, even in cases of extreme violence on the part of the teacher toward students, superintendents were to defend the teacher publicly and exhort the teacher privately. 'The mode of teaching is at the option of the teacher; and the local superintendent and visitors alone have a right to advise him on the subject.' School visitors were instructed to advise the teacher discretely, preferably in private, and to avoid public criticism.[37] The schools were opened to respectable visitors, and these were encouraged to participate actively in local schooling. 'The frequency of visits to the schools by intelligent persons, animates the pupils, and greatly aids the faithful teacher,' argued the *Educational Manual.*[38]

At the same time, the 'school disturbers' clause in the School Amendment Act of 1853 imposed penalties upon anyone other than legal visitors and superintendents who might intervene in the school room. In localities where school supporters attempted to exercise their traditional authority over school matters, these penalities were sometimes invoked. Elsewhere, appeals were made to the education office. For instance, in section no.4 of Brant Township, a trustee complained that parents believed everyone in the section was a legal school visitor, and many people entered the schoolhouse to instruct the teacher. An 'interested parent' in the same section wrote asking if it were indeed true that parents had no rights in the conduct of schooling except to withdraw their children, and demanded the same rights as school visitors.[39] In 1863, Alfred Parrinton of Medonte Township was shocked when the local school trustees refused to let him write in the visitor's book. He wondered if all members of the public were not school visitors.[40]

However, if the teacher as official person was to be supported by other public administrators and protected from 'the interference of the public', the personnel of the teaching force was subjected to detailed and multi-faceted regulatory initiatives. Superintendents were central to the regulatory process, both as inspectors of local schools, and as members of Boards of Public Instruction for the examination of teachers. Although there were instances in which they supported local trustees and teachers against the policy of the education office, superintendents commonly both sought and accepted instructions from the education office. The education office attempted to direct superintendents in the field to the moral regulation of teachers. The teacher's knowledge and skill were to be tested in examinations before County Boards of Public Instruction.

Superintendents of schools were not allowed to remove teachers for pedagogical incompetence, but rather for 'moral' derelictions. While these two sometimes overlapped, the education office attempted to maintain the distinction. The case of John Howee, a teacher in Pelham Township whose teaching certificate was suspended by the local superintendent, J. Brockbill, in 1858, is illustrative. Howee complained to the education office that he had been suspended for incompetence. He claimed to have thirty years' teaching experience, but to be forced to teach quickly because attendance at his school was irregular. He protested that his trustees supplied only American books, with the exception of one copy of the National Arithmetic, and none of the boys in the school would study grammar. The chief superintendent wrote to the local superintendent that only immorality gave cause to suspend a teacher's certificate, and not incompetence in the schoolroom. Brockbill, the superintendent, responded in his own defence that while Howee couldn't teach either mental arithmetic or bookkeeping and let the children be noisy, his faults also included having placed the privy in front of the school and using indecent language.[41]

Throughout the period from 1850-1871, local superintendents acted to suspend the certificates of teachers for 'moral violations'. The Reverend J. Anderson of South Gower suspended a teacher's certificate for 'inefficiency and impudent language' over the opposition of the local trustees.[42] R.J. Williams suspended the certificates of two teachers who had been cursing and swearing.[43] K.A. Cambell, the superintendent of Mara and Rama Townships, suspended a teacher's certificate for drunkenness, lying and 'Impertinent freedom with females.'[44] Several other teachers lost their certificates for fraud or forgery. The school register was frequently forged by teachers who sought higher salaries, and in some instances, teachers also presented forged Normal School certificates to their trustees.[45]

With respect to other questions of 'morality', superintendents sought instruction from the central office. The local superintendent of Oro Township asked about a teacher who also kept a store and sold alcohol.[46] The superintendent of Stamford Township reported a teacher with a 2nd class provincial certificate who had been guilty of public drunkenness and swearing.[47] W. Ferguson, whose jurisdiction was in Grey County, wondered whether a teacher whose wife had a child soon after marriage should have his certificate suspended.[48] Edward Scarlett, a county superintendent, sought advice in April 1858 about a case in his jurisdiction involving a drunken teacher, and sent the chief superintendent a letter of complaint he had received. A school supporter had claimed that the teacher in question was guilty of drunkenness, beating his students, acting as a 'blackguard' toward the girls and ridiculing some of the students as well. Scarlett explained that this teacher had formerly been 'addicted to drink', but had not drunk for two years, except for one occasion at Christmas. The teacher was attempting to reform, and Scarlett sought instructions.[49]

In the case of James Keating, the teacher of section no. 1 in Stamford Township, the chief superintendent sent the local superintendent to hold a public meeting with respect to charges that Keating was a drunkard and prone to profanity. Several students and the trustees as well testified that Keating was often drunk, and he was reported to have said to his students, 'I do not care for the whole damned scrape of you; you may go to hell' and to one boy, 'damn your little soul.' Keating was suspended.[50] In another case, a student swore before a magistrate that the teacher had used 'indecent language by asking an illegal connection with her,' and the local superintendent wondered if the teacher's certificate should be removed.[51]

In section no.11 Ancaster, the chief superintendent ordered the suspension of a teacher's certificate on the strength of the following report:

> ...on a certain morning when the pupils came to school some obscene language was found written upon a desk and also upon a slate. It was read by many of the scholars. When the teacher came he was told of it. He came to the desk and read it for himself. But instead of inquiring who had been the author of the writing, he compelled three girls to write the obscene language upon paper, and then he called up a class, boys and girls and examined them minutely as to the meaning of each word, and what Dictionary they had seen it in....

The teacher was drunk at the time, and the trustees wanted to keep him. Despite petitions from the trustees, several local residents and the teacher himself, Ryerson ordered his suspension.[52]

These instances point to the construction of an effective circuit of knowledge/power connecting the conduct of local education to the central educational authority. Through the educational intelligence generated by local superintendents, and by the active consent of many of the same superintendents to seek instruction from the central office, the chief superintendent was frequently able to intervene in particular school districts. Township superintendents did not always behave in this way; some clearly sought to accommodate the interests of local school consumers in cases where these interests conflicted with those of the central authority. Yet these officials might themselves be exposed by local residents or trustees consulting the education office directly. While the office of teacher was constituted as locally authoritative, then, the office could be policed by the central educational authority. The importance of this process as state building should not be underestimated. With the exception of the centrally-appointed justices, few connections existed between central government bodies and local institutions in Canada West before the 1850s. Not until 1849, indeed, did substantial organs of local electoral government exist in the colony. The organization of educational administration was a serious contribution to the construction of patterns of political authority in the locality responsive to the interests of central government. It involved processes and procedures for making local activities visible to the centre.

## Examinations of Teachers

As we have seen above, all candidates for teaching in any county were to present themselves for examination before a County Board of Public Instruction composed of superintendents of schools and county grammar school trustees. County Boards met quarterly. A certificate of moral character from a legally recognized clergyman was a condition of entry to such an examination, and only teachers possessing certificates of qualification granted by the chief superintendent were exempt from the County Board's examination. All teachers had to possess a certificate of qualification from a County Board (or the chief superintendent) to be hired by school trustees. Teachers hired in the periods between meetings of the County Board could be granted temporary certificates by local superintendents, but even these teachers could not legally teach longer than three months without undergoing an examination, if they were to be paid from public funds.

The County Boards, especially towards the end of the 1850s, became increasingly active and effective in policing the occupation of teacher. The Boards moved to limit entry into the occupation, by restricting access to the teacher's certificate in various ways, and by imposing difficult and time-consuming examinations upon candidates. Written examinations replaced verbal examinations and measures were adopted to prevent cheating. Examination questions began to be changed periodically. Examinations more frequently contained questions about approved pedagogical technique. Many County Boards--and the Council of Public Instruction as well--- periodically annuled all the certificates they granted and required all teachers to undergo re-examination. In the 1860s, the central office urged County Boards to grant the lowest or third class teaching certificate only in exceptional circumstances.

While the central office had intended that the general use of the Irish National schoolbooks would lead to both sound and uniform instruction for the Canadian population, the generalization of the texts had one unintended consequence. The books were to serve not only as texts, but also as teaching manuals. Teachers were enjoined, as we have seen, to study the texts, to classify students according to them, and to teach according to the instructions given in the books' prefaces. County Boards of Public Instruction based their annual examinations largely on the Irish texts as well. However, many students were easily able to learn the material in the Irish texts, to learn the simple teaching instructions they contained, and to present themselves at the County Board for examination as teachers.

A main base for the teacher's authority in the schoolroom-- especially given the official emphasis on 'gentle' pedagogy-- had to be 'force of character' combined with a monopoly over school knowledge. But the Irish curriculum did not obtain a monopoly of official knowledge for the teacher; this knowledge was generally accessible. This meant that the occupation of teacher remained open to a broad section of the population. Teachers frequently found themselves teaching students who were as qualified, and in some cases more qualified, than they were themselves.

Robert Futhey of Stayner reported in 1863 that in his section of the province there were more teachers than schools. Young farmers spent their evenings studying algebra in order to qualify to teach. They preferred teaching to hard farm labour, and could easily pass the standard for the third class certificate. This meant graduates of the Normal School were unemployed, and the youth of the region was subjected to dangerous moral influences.[53] Ease of access to the occupation, one Brockville resident complained, meant that male teachers could not make a living.[54]

The fact that many students could obtain teaching certificates themselves was a matter of debate in many school sections. William Carrich, a school trustee from section no.5 of Plympton Township, sought advice from the chief superintendent in 1858 in this regard. In this school section, two of the trustees had joined to fire a first class teacher, and to replace him with a second class teacher. This threatened the existence of the school, since many of the scholars of school age themselves had second class certificates. Here the trustees wondered if they could not remove students with teaching certificates from the school.[55] A trustee in section no. 14 of Charlottenburgh Township wrote in 1868 for advice in the case of a 16 year old boy who had been teaching for four years, and who had just received a 1A (the highest) certificate from the County Board.[56] John Close of Camden complained that his daughter's second class certificate from the County Board had been suspended by the local superintendent. Elizabeth Close had been hired in a local school for eleven months at $12 per month. The superintendent suspended her on the grounds that she was under age, but Close complained that she was *fifteen* and the County Board had passed a rule allowing girls to begin teaching at *fourteen*.[57]

Many County Boards moved to block the certification of common school students as teachers. One of the first was the Ontario County Board of Public Instruction. A.W. Lauder, a teacher in Oshawa who held a first class certificate himself and who taught 'upon the Normal system', used the annual examinations of the County Board as a sort of proving ground for his best students. Many of them succeeded in getting first class certificates, but in 1855 the Board began demanding a declaration of an intention to teach as a condition of examination for candidates. The Board did not consciously intend to tighten up access to teaching, but sought rather to save itself the labour of examining large numbers of candidates. R.H. Thornton, Chairman of the Board and superintendent of schools, explained that the Board had to deal with candidates as young as fourteen and was swamped with work.[58] Other County Boards adopted similar regulations, and different means of more closely policing candidates for teacher's certificates were also put in place.

Charles Fox, an English immigrant teacher who taught for three months in Amherstburg on a temporary certificate from the local superintendent, was refused admission to the examinations of the County Board on the grounds that he lacked a certificate of moral character. Despite a large number of impressive written testimonials from England, the Board ruled that local residents could not form an adequate estimate of Fox's character in three months.[59] The local superintendent of McKillop uncovered an imposter sitting the Board's exam for an incompetent teacher.[60] Joseph Powley of Peel County suggested the establishment of information channels among different Boards to prevent those whose certificates had been cancelled by one Board from presenting them to another. The Peel Board had accepted the certificate and testimonials of W.C. Anderson, which although 'quite a bundle', were misleading, for 'he proved himself a drunkard, his conduct towards little girls gross and towards the colored children most grossly insulting, we would have paid him to leave he would not.'[61]

Some screening devices particularly incensed teachers. George Thomson, a teacher from section no.11 of Tuckersmith Township, complained in 1859 that John Nairn, county superintendent for Huron, held preparatory classes for teachers before the Board examinations. Nairn charged a fee of $1 for these classes, and Thomson claimed he was particularly hard during the examination on teachers like Thomson who refused to pay.[62] A teacher named James Carswell from Arnprior claimed that the Renfrew County Board of Public Instruction was not competent to examine teachers. The teachers assembled for the annual examination were 'miserable and dejected looking beings...the offscourings of the earth,' and the Board accepted ridiculous answers to easy questions:

What isthmus joins North and South America? Ans. Suez.

What part of speech is 'the'? Ans. a noun.

Carswell claimed that his own certificate was renewed without examination, but he was incensed by the fact that the Board charged a fee for certificates: 12 1/2 cents for a third, 25 cents for second and 50 cents for a first.[63]

Complaints from teachers about the fact and the quality of examinations were continual. Peter Lawson of Windham claimed that the first class programme of the Norfolk County Board took two and a half days to complete.[64] Nathan Bicknell travelled from Camden East to Kingston to sit the teacher's exam before the Frontenac County Board in 1863. He was kept from 10 a.m. until dark and forced to answer improperly posed questions. Bicknell complained that exams favoured fast writers, and argued that the examiners should all be college graduates. He suggested that the County Board was purposely making its exams difficult in an effort to reduce the supply of teachers and thereby increase teachers' pay. This was interference in matters properly left to teachers and trustees.[65] The local superintendent for Perth County remarked,

> There is a natural aversion on the part of many Teachers to submit to frequent examination by the County Board of Public Instruction and in some cases this is encouraged by the trustees who think themselves competent judges of the qualifications of a Teacher for their section which is often decided by them by the rate of remuneration rather than by

litterary attainments.[66]

In the late 1850s, administrators in the education office and at the County Board level sought to remove the lowest stratum of the occupation. Entrance standards for admission to the Normal School were raised in 1859, and in 1860 the headmaster was suggesting the recall of all second class Normal School certificates. The headmaster pointed out that in the first sessions 'the class of students presenting themselves for training was sometimes very inferior, & we occasionally could not avoid giving a low certificate to a person previously legally sanctioned as a teacher.'[67]

County Boards had acted earlier. The clerk of the County Board for Simcoe reported in October 1857,

> We had a Meeting of our County Board of Instruction last Monday--- I moved & carried a Resolution that all Certificates heretofore granted by the Board should be null and void from & after the 10th of Jany next as regarded Male Teachers, and on the 15th April next for Females--- I am of the opinion that we may now venture to raise the Standard a peg higher.[68]

By 1860, many other Boards had followed suit.[69]

This was a serious extension of the bureaucratic policing of the occupation of teaching and it generated opposition. Some teachers, like Duncan Campbell of Lobo Township, objected that the recall of certificates was insulting. The Middlesex County Board recalled all of the certificates it had granted since its formation, and demanded that all teachers present themselves for re-examination. Campbell refused to be re-examined, arguing that his certificate had been granted 'during good Conduct', and hence the call for a re-examination was an attack on his character. Campbell sent the chief superintendent his testimonials and proof of his competence as a teacher. He stated that if the Board had downgraded certificates he would willingly have appeared for re-examination, but, he suggested, the Board was really examining moral character, and his was impeccable. The chief superintendent claimed that the Board had changed the standard of examination, but Campbell insisted that the 'new' examinations used the programme from 1850. Campbell still sought redress a year later, but to no avail.[70]

One of the two examining boards in Victoria County was called the Oakwood County Board. Late in 1858, the Board decided to raise the standard of examination, and to allow the grammar school master, a graduate of the Normal School, to conduct the teachers' examinations. Many teachers were disqualified or downgraded in these exams, and many of them were incensed. Alex. MacGregor claimed his certificate was annuled because his school effectively competed with the local grammar school. MacGregor had spent two sessions at Edinburgh Normal school and had high testimonials. Morgan Barker was a former Normal School student, but the Oakwood Board refused to grant him even a third class certificate, despite his 8 years' experience. The exam was long and difficult, Barker complained, with candidates expected to give the roots of the words 'Migration, Fidelity, Nutritious, Unsealed, Compensate, Corresponding' and to solve arithmetical problems. Barker went to another Board and got a second class certificate. He objected to allowing one teacher examine another. George Coleman had a second class certificate before the examination, but the Board would only give him a certificate to teach for one further month.[71] To all of these teachers, Ryerson responded that he could not intervene, although he did advise George Coleman to go and appear before the main Victoria County Board itself. Ryerson congratulated one of the members of the Oakwood Board, the Reverend A. A. McLauchlin, for the Board's efforts to improve the standard of teaching. 'You are quite right in regard to maintaining [sic] the Standard of Examination. It is now under consideration of the Department to revise the programme of Examination, & thus to raise the Standard.'[72]

These and other initiatives by County Boards, the central office and local superintendents put in play a web of practical administrative controls over the occupation of teaching. The connections in this web became increasingly dense over the period 1850-1871, and in two ways. First, the information-gathering and reporting circuits connecting local and central authorities were made more efficient and regular. Second, centrally defined pedagogical criteria came to regulate both the conditions of entry to and the conditions of labour in the occupation. 'Rising standards' in practice meant that before one could participate in educational administration as a teacher, one first had to be the subject of educational administration oneself. Only those who proved themselves both successful and reliable as students, as members of a congregation and as followers of bureaucratic routine --- the examination--- were to be trusted with the educational administration of students.

One effect of these initiatives was to pressure some teachers out of the occupation altogether, while others attempted to acquire training in the methods approved by the education office. Still others attempted to survive on the margins of the occupation, teaching in isolated sections, or teaching only young children, until some resident complained against their employment or until they were discovered by a superintendent. The superintendent of Augusta Township, for instance, discovered an old teacher who had lost his certificate and who was teaching in a school with young students. He attempted to have the teacher placed on the superannuation list.[73] The superintendent of Charlottenburgh argued in 1852 that many of the teachers in new settlements could not 'come up to the Programme', but were good as teachers of beginners, and were the only teachers available. He was told not to certify such teachers.[74]

J. Lyons of Drummondville sought information about the Normal School in 1851.

> I was teaching a Common School some time ago, but I found it too laborious to attend to eighty schollars, with the old system only, and as there was a general cry for a Normal School Teacher. I resigned... I am considered a very fair Teacher in the old system, but I find that the Normal School plan... is the only popular mode of instruction....[75]

William B. Williams of Dunnville wrote that he was underqualified as a teacher and had managed to find employment only by avoiding the 'populous centres'. However, since Ryerson had been in office, Williams claimed, 'a new era has taken place in Canada--- a spirit of inquiry has sprung up even in these remote regions, which render it necessary for the old (standard) teachers to make proportionate improvements or quit the business.'[76] With the development of urban free schools, many independent teachers were also pushed out of business. As the proprietor of the Kingston Academy complained in 1861, 'no Private Academy can hold its ground against well-organized and skillfully conducted Free Schools.'[77]

The granting of third class certificates--- certificates valid in only one school section for a limited period--- by County boards, and to a lesser extent the granting of temporary certificates— valid until the next sitting of the County board— allowed many marginal teachers to survive in the occupation. The granting of these certificates was a contentious issue among educational administrators at different levels of the system, and at times between local school supporters and trustees as well.[78]

As the education office urged the upgrading of the general standard of teachers' qualifications used by County Boards in the late 1850s, in the mid- and later-1860s it agitated for the severe limitation or abolition of third class certificates. Regulations published by the Council of Public Instruction in 1864 attempted to restrict the granting of third class certificates to exceptional circumstances. This initiative was supported by many educational administrators and by some local school supporters as well. School supporters whose children were well advanced in school were frequently incensed when trustees hired teachers with second or third class certificates in the interests of economy. R.H. Davie of Pakenham complained that the teacher in his section was not qualified to teach his son, and so Davie was compelled to pay for the boy to board in Perth where he could attend the Perth Union School.[79]

The Reeve of the Township of Greenock complained that in one section the parents who had no children, or who had girls, hired a cheap third class female teacher. This led many of the older students to quit, and because the teacher could not maintain order 'the morals of the children are affected.'[80] Patrick Donovan of Campbellford wondered what to do with his children who were too advanced for the third class teacher hired by his trustees, and some residents of Lyndhurst complained that the Leeds County Board was in the habit of 'granting certificates to boys and girls as soon as they are capable of parsing a short sentence in grammar tell the diameter of the globe or do a small sum in vulgar arithmetic.'[81]

At the same time, the third class certificate was used by some teachers as a convenient way of circumventing the tiresome and time-consuming County Board examinations in the higher classes. The Secretary Treasurer of the Berlin Common School Board noted that many teachers who had 'secure schools' and who did not want to 'struggle' routinely got third class certificates. This school board wanted to force these teachers to apply for higher certificates.[82] The chief superintendent counseled the Berlin board to grant third class certificates only in exceptional circumstances, and only for a single year.[83]

However, while many County Boards of Public Instruction voluntarily raised the standard of teacher qualification, and while many took measures to limit the granting of third class certificates, these measures did not always succeed. When one County Board classified teachers and restricted third class certificates, superintendents reported local opposition.[84] When the Hastings County Board raised the third class standard in 1865, so many teachers failed to pass that the Board was forced to grant exceptions.[85] In this situation, the chief superintendent began to advise local trustee boards that they could hire third class teachers if they chose, but any teacher must be capable of teaching all the students in the school section.[86] But while administrative pressure existed to undercut the lowest stratum of the occupation, fragmentary evidence suggests that some teachers did manage to circumvent these measures of occupational police.

It is entirely possible that local superintendents granted temporary certificates to female teachers for the summer season, thereby allowing the continuation of the traditional distinction between summer and winter schools. At least the superintendent of Euphrasia Township complained in June 1862 of one of his colleagues who routinely granted temporary certificates to teachers, none of whom were ever examined.[87] Many teachers taught with forged or outdated certificates for long periods before they were detected, and one can safely assume that not all such teachers were detected. Such teachers were in a vulnerable position, liable to exposure by disgruntled school supporters. Elizabeth Acheson was fired in 1859, for instance, when she dissatisfied her employers. 'Some said I did not whip enough,' she complained, 'and more said I whipped too much.' When she was fired it was discovered that her second class certificate from the Farmersville Circuit Board was invalid and she could not collect the $60 owing to her for six months' teaching.[88]

## Moral Regulation in the Normal School

The Education Acts of 1846-50 provided for the production of a supply of qualified teachers in Canada West through the creation of a Provinical Normal School in Toronto. 'Normal' training — the habituation of teachers —was to diffuse the most effective and efficient techniques of instruction throughout the province and to elevate the occupation into a 'profession'. However, the School never trained more than a small fraction of the teaching labour force. From 1847 to 1870 a total of 6,069 teachers had been admitted to the institution, while in the latter year alone there were 5,165 active teachers in Ontario.[89] Not all graduates of the Normal School entered teaching, and the continuing recall of Normal School certificates pushed others out of the occupation. D.Y. Hoit, one of the most enthusiastic graduates from the School in 1849, taught for several years on his expired certificate and was finally detected in 1869 teaching with a forged certificate.[90] Others were pushed out earlier. A graduate of the eighth session, described by the head master as 'an exceedingly clever young man', had his certificate cancelled by the Wardsville superintendent in 1863 for public drunkenness.[91]

The Normal School subjected students to a process meant to implant in them the habits, skills, and the character structure appropriate to the morally forceful teacher. Normal schooling, as managers of the institution repeatedly stressed, was *training*. The loyalty teachers were to demand of their own students was here practically demanded of nascent teachers themselves. Their active acceptance of their own moral and bureaucratic subordination was a precondition for access to the relative autonomy of the position of teacher.

The atmosphere of the Normal School, organized and enforced by T.J. Robertson, a former chief inspector for the Irish Commissioners of National Education, the first headmaster (1847-1866), and his successor, J.S. Sangster, was one of intense moral regulation. Students were admitted only with a certificate of moral character and after sitting an examination. They worked very long hours in the school itself, lodged only in lisenced boarding houses and were expected to attend church services at least weekly. With varying levels of zeal, the Normal School masters undertook to inspect boarding houses and to enlist boarding house keepers as behavioural 'supervisors'. Students were expected to be at their boarding houses by 9 p.m. at the latest.

Of particular concern was the maintenance of a high level of sexual repression, especially for female students. Ryerson himself wrote,

> On each of the [female teachers] leaving the
> Institution for their destined work of responsibility
> and usefulness, I wish to be able in connection with
> the Masters of the Normal School not only to respect
> and confide in them ourselves, but to recommend
> them to the respect and implicit confidence of all
> parents having children to be instructed,---that they
> should not only be above reproach, but
> above suspicion.[92]

While in his relations with his own daughter Ryerson was prepared to allow a certain liberty,[93] both in and out of the Normal School all forms of 'intercourse' between male and female students, including simple conversation, were prohibited. Ryerson defended the necessity of restricting relations between men and women in the Normal School in the public press in 1853. He explained to the editor of the *North American* that female students were in need of protection since they were usually young, innocent, alone for the first time in a large city and 'peculiarly exposed to intrusions and dangers'. The regulations, he claimed, were in any case only 'a response to the wishes of anxious Parents and friends.'[94]

Unlike the practice of the Scottish and Irish Normal Schools, Toronto Normal did not maintain an official boarding hall, nor did it actively encourage co-education. Despite the warnings of T.C. Young, a friend of the education office clerk and deputy John George Hodgins, that the Irish Commissioners had found a boarding hall necessary to avoid the 'bad results' likely from allowing students to live in different parts of the city, Toronto Normal licensed private boarding house keepers.[95] The reluctance of the chief superintendent to encourage co-education--- although he was forced to allow it in the Normal School--- flew in the face of Scottish practice. David Stow, the Glaswegian reformer, argued that co-education was a question with 'important national, and of course, individual consequences.' In his view, co-education ensured female chastity by teaching girls and young women to deal with men. In France, by contrast, Stow claimed,

> ...of those girls educated in the schools in convents
> apart from boys, the large majority go wrong within
> a month of their being let loose on society, and
> meeting the other sex. They cannot ... resist the

slightest compliment or flattery from the other sex.[96] The managers of Toronto Normal aimed at a much more repressive sexual politics.

Although the pressure of business often prevented the Normal School headmaster from a regular boarding house inspectoral tour, at the beginning of Robertson's tenure and at the beginning of Sangster's, serious efforts were made to police the boarding houses. When Mr. Graham was found in April of 1851 to be 'keeping company' with his landlady's daughter, and to be attempting to enter her bedroom with a view to taking 'improper liberties', he was expelled from the school and the boarding house was struck from the approved list.[97] The head master was concerned by reports of note-sending between male and female boarding houses, and by reports of 'excessive mirth' in the boarding houses as well.[98] While students were required to attend a place of worship at least weekly, excessive attendance at religious services was at times interpreted as a desire for illegitimate social intercourse.[99]

Students continually attempted to bend or violate different aspects of the institution's rules, and the Normal School authorities were required to maintain a constant vigilance. The head master was alarmed to learn in 1860 that 'two of the female students were in the habit of frequently spending the night with each other, instead of each in her own residence.' This practice 'has been made the subject of comment,' T.J. Robertson reported, and 'though it involves no impropriety, I deem it objectionable.'[100] Soon after this, the presence of male and female students in a boarding house became the 'subject of ill natured comment.' The men were asked to move, and thereafter the Council of Public Instruction required that all boarding houses be single-sex institutions. Keepers violating this rule were to be struck from the list.[101]

In 1863, a revised boarding house keeper's application form demanded the participation of boarding house keepers in the regulation of student behaviour. This was in response to the difficulty the headmaster experienced in 'obtaining information from the proprietors' of houses, whose interest lay first in 'maintaining their popularity among the students.'[102] The revised application form specified,

> The teachers-in-training are expected to lead orderly and regular lives, and to be in their respective

lodgings before Half-past nine o'clock P.M., and to attend their respective places of worship with strict regularity. Any improprieties of conduct will be brought under the special notice of the Chief Superintendent of Education.... Female students cannot, moreover, board in any house in which other than Female Boarders are admitted.[103]

The boarding house inspections languished in the latter years of Robertson's tenure of office, but they were renewed with vigor by his successor, J.S. Sangster, in 1866. After two students died of typhoid early in the spring of that year, Sangster noted that

Several of the licensed boarding houses are so filthy in themselves, and others are so objectionable on account of the low and depraved neighbourhood in which they are located, that they ought to be summarily struck off the list.[104]

Of course, as all total institutions do, Toronto Normal produced its own 'underlife'.[105] The harsh role demands of the instructional programme were softened for students by various forms of counter-organization. Students managed to avoid official curfews.[106] Lying and cheating were common, despite the requirement of certificates of moral behavior from prospective students. A number of students found cheating on examinations in the 34th session were allowed to seek re-admission after confessing.[107] At the end of the 30th session, the head master reported that two graduates did not appear on the graduation list.

Two others were recommended... but as it appeared that their 'Composition' papers were verbatim alike, I have written to them for explanation.[108]

In some cases, attempts to circumvent the rules of the institution led to rapid expulsion. In the summer of 1860, for instance, a group of men and women was detected whose members

...were in the habit of walking together in violation of the rules of the institution, & when taxed with the impropriety, denied their guilt with the most blushing effrontery....

These people were refused re-admittance.[109] 'Stringent measures are absolutely necessary in these cases,' noted the head master, 'otherwise we can not keep up the discipline of the class to the high standard to which we have brought it.'[110] As well as punishing offenders, the head master stressed that 'watchfulness & personal influence may do much, as indeed experience has proved.'[111] Care was taken by the authorities of the school to prevent activities which might call the institution into disrepute. Normal School employees were fired for marching in the Toronto Orange parade in 1856.[112] Joseph Hodgson, who was partly deaf, had a speech defect and lacked a leg, was allowed to attend the 15th session, but was refused a teacher's certificate on the grounds that he might 'reflect discredit on that noble Institution.'[113]

The course of Normal School training was to be an emotionally forceful process for the student teachers. Yet the Normal School administrators were continually plagued by their inability to find and retain forceful and competent masters, and by the continual intervention of the local community into the Normal School process. Good music masters were particularly hard to find. In Mr. Cooper's music classes, shortly before he was fired, the head master pointed out

> ...as an instance of the utter want of order therein the fact (acknowledged by the class) that the students were in the habit during lecture hour of throwing 'sweat meals' at each other & sometimes at their teacher.[114]

Evening singing schools open to the public in the Normal School were discontinued when the head master found that 'unseemly tricks' took place there. After these singing classes, the floor of the hall was littered with bits of paper, lozenge wrappers and notes, some of them 'suggesting impropriety', which the head master feared might come to the attention of the female students. The general disorder of the room threatened the 'Aesthetic education' of the future teachers.[115]

The teachers were 'subjected to various annoyances' by having to pass through the Boys' Model School yard on their way to gymnastic exercises.[116] Annual recitations and singing displays were made difficult 'by crowds of children from the streets & city schools' who excluded 'parents and respectable adult visitors from the gallery of the theatre.'[117] The gymnastic exercises of girls were a popular spectacle for 'strangers, young lads and others' and the 'boys off the street' collected on the roof of the Normal School shed to satirize the student teachers' drill association. 'Any attempt to drive them out only calls forth the grossest abuse,' complained Robertson.[118]

The notebooks of Maria Payne, an eighteen year old student of the 41st session, point to the heavy work load carried by the students. Payne copied and undoubtedly memorized reams of material about biblical geography and history as well as arithmetic and other subjects. She was also instructed in 'school management' and in comportment for teachers. The competent teacher, she noted, should 'argue to have everything neat and well kept.' She should be 'dressed with good taste' and attend to the fact that 'over jewelled is not good taste.' Her clothing should be 'well put on, well kept, well kept linen, white' and she should wear 'black boots, well-brushed' and 'well-fitting gloves'.[119]

While the Normal School was intended to be a morally forceful institution for the habituation of teachers, it spawned an underlife and various forms of internal opposition or counter-organization greeted its initiatives---from students and from the larger community. The effects of the course of training were unpredictable. One of those passing through the institution became the socialist union organizer Mother Jones (1830-1930, as Mary Harris in 1848).[120]

Other people wrote of the Normal School course as a quasi-religious experience. William Carlyle, later an inspector of schools for Oxford County, wrote of one of the Normal School masters,

> ...he fired his burning thought into my untutored mind, lodging his instructions there never to be obliterated.
>
> To me he was teacher and text-book. His utterances repeated one day, I could reproduce verbatim the next. He took full possession of me for the time. I was filled with his thought. My imagination kindled at the touch of his....As a man he became my ideal. As a teacher he created within me a thirst for teaching that can never be quenched.[121]

This was undoubtedly the sort of forceful relation sought by the School's managers.

Equally instructive, however, is the case of a student named Jones in 1864. The head master received a number of anonymous letters in the first half of that year which reported Jones for writing notes to a male student in the institution. Robertson investigated and found Jones to be innocent. Something made him suspicious, however, and on further investigation Jones admitted to being herself the author of the anonymous letters. 'Her aim in the matter' Robertson wrote, 'was, eventually to raise herself & her friend Miss Sullivan in our estimation by according an opportunity to disprove a false charge.'[122] Some students were very susceptible to the institution's demands upon themselves. The hunger for official approval created in some students at the Normal School replicated one of the character traits good teachers were said to be able to induce in common school students. Still, the 'humanistic' discourse of Normal training undoubtedly contained contradictory elements which could be turned in different directions by different students---not to mention the possibility of simple dissimulation. Whatever the individual consequences of the process, however, its forcefulness is clear.

**The Feminization of Teaching**

As Table 1 indicates, women came to dominate the occupation of teaching by 1871. According to the official statistics, women were 21.9% of all common school teachers in 1847, and 50.2% of all common school teachers by 1871. This increase continued beyond the period studied here, and by 1901 almost three-quarters of all public school teachers in Ontario were female. However, the official statistics of women's participation in the occupation are conservative. Three dimensions of women's participation in teaching do not appear in the official account.

First, the traditional pattern of male winter teachers and female summer teachers continued in many localities throughout the 1850s and 1860s, but the female teachers were not always counted. Many of these teachers were never certified by the local superintendents, or were granted temporary certificates and then did not appear before the County Boards. Technically, anyone could teach in a public

Table 1
Female as a Percentage of Male and Female Teachers in Ontario Public Schools, 1847-1875

| Year | Teachers | Male | Female | % |
|---|---|---|---|---|
| 1847 | 3,028 | 2,365 | 663 | 21.9 |
| 1848 | 3,177 | 2,507 | 670 | 21.1 |
| 1849 | 3,209 | 2,505 | 704 | 21.9 |
| 1850 | 3,476 | 2,697 | 779 | 22.4 |
| 1851 | 3,277 | 2,551 | 726 | 22.2 |
| 1852 | 3,388 | 2,541 | 847 | 25.0 |
| 1853 | 3,539 | 2,601 | 938 | 26.5 |
| 1854 | 3,539 | 2,508 | 1,031 | 29.1 |
| 1855 | 3,565 | 2,568 | 997 | 28.0 |
| 1856 | 3,689 | 2,622 | 1,067 | 28.9 |
| 1857 | 4,083 | 2,787 | 1,296 | 31.7 |
| 1858 | 4,202 | 2,965 | 1,237 | 29.4 |
| 1859 | 4,235 | 3,115 | 1,120 | 26.4 |
| 1860 | 4,281 | 3,100 | 1,181 | 27.6 |
| 1861 | 4,336 | 3,031 | 1,305 | 30.1 |
| 1862 | 4,406 | 3,115 | 1,291 | 29.3 |
| 1863 | 4,504 | 3,094 | 1,410 | 31.3 |
| 1864 | 4,625 | 3,011 | 1,614 | 34.9 |
| 1865 | 4,721 | 2,930 | 1,791 | 37.9 |
| 1866 | 4,789 | 2,925 | 1,864 | 38.9 |
| 1867 | 4,890 | 2,849 | 2,041 | 41.7 |
| 1868 | 4,996 | 2,777 | 2,219 | 44.4 |
| 1869 | 5,054 | 2,775 | 2,279 | 45.1 |
| 1870 | 5,165 | 2,753 | 2,412 | 46.7 |
| 1871 | 5,306 | 2,641 | 2,665 | 50.2 |
| 1875 | 6,018 | 2,645 | 3,373 | 56.1 |
| (1901 | 8,403 | 2,353 | 6,050 | 72.0) |

Source: *Annual Report of the Normal, Model, High and Public Schools for the Province of Ontario, 1875.* (J.G. Hodgins, ed. *Historical and Other Papers and Documents Illustrative of the Schools of Ontario.*) V:168n.

school and be paid entirely out of private fees, so long as no claim was made upon the school fund. If a legally qualified teacher kept school for at least six months of the year, the school would be classified nonetheless as a 'public' school. Trustees might pay summer teachers out of incidental expenses. In Zorra Township in 1858, two female teachers were hired only for the summer months at $11 per month.[123] George German's daughter taught a summer school without a certificate and was then refused one by the local superintendent.[124] The Trustees of a school section in South Gower complained in 1863 that 'Miss Glenday' had taught all year on a temporary certificate and refused to go before the County Board,[125] and the superintendent for Hawkesbury found a 'girl' teaching in section 1 Caledonia who had never been examined.[126] There were many female teachers in this situation who did not figure in the official statistics.

Again, women and girls taught as assistants in common schools, or as second teachers, and were not counted as such. The practice of hiring assistant teachers was necessitated by the enormous class sizes produced by free schooling, especially in villages and towns. The education office initially ruled that the practice was legitimate, so long as assistant teachers worked as the private employees of certified teachers, and were not paid directly out of school monies. Of course, the practice placed the assistant teacher in a particularly precarious position, with no legal claim on the school fund, and no access to the mechanism of school arbitration. Still, as the superintendent for Gwillimbury East pointed out, large class sizes demanded two teachers, female assistants could be had for little pay, and trustees could sometimes pay them out of the general expenses of the school.[127]

Finally, there was a certain movement of female teachers between the public and private sectors, and it is not clear that such mobile teachers figure in the official statistics. For example, Elizabeth Unsworth of Fergus complained in January 1860 of attempts by the trustees to dislodge her from a school she had formerly run as 'Fergus Female School'. The trustees claimed she was underqualified, but Unsworth complained that she did not earn enough to support herself at the Normal School.[128]

Prentice has argued that the feminization of teaching is to be understood first as a function of the low wages paid to female teachers, which was itself related to the scarcity of 'respectable' employment for urban women. In addition, the feminization of the occupation allowed for the extension of male power and authority by creating urban educational career lines for men. Male teachers could become supervisors of female teachers.[129] As we have seen in chapter one, Charles Duncombe argued in the late 1830s that public education would never pay large numbers of teachers enough to support a family. Female teachers on the whole were certainly not paid enough to do so.

Yet attention should also be paid to the changing rural economy of Canada West, and to the relationship between gender, bureaucracy and political authority. In the first regard, the increasing penetration of capital into the agricultural sector of the economy of Canada West probably affected men and women differently. This can be seen most sharply in the area of dairying, where in the decade after 1864 cheese and butter production changed largely from a women's domestic industry to a factory industry employing men,[130] but other branches of agriculture were also affected. Already in the mid-1850s observers like the Picton school superintendent were pointing to a movement of women out of farm work into teaching.[131] J.E. Barr of Brockville complained in 1860 that men couldn't make a decent living as teachers, 'the schools being so flooded by slips of girls, more fitting to be taught than to teach'.[132] Teaching was one of a few 'respectable' avenues of employment for women, although the pay was often so low that teachers had to supplement their incomes in other ways. Janet Mcullough, for instance, used monitors to watch the school while she knit stockings or made dresses.[133] In 1861, a twenty year old woman named Lenay Vanflooring sought admission to the Normal School. Vanflooring had been self-supporting since the age of nine, and wrote 'I am willing to assist in doing housework, sewing, or any thing that is respectable.'[134] As Prentice has shown, the Normal School itself was an important avenue to higher education and respectable employment for some women.[135]

High levels of female agricultural underemployment contributed to low wage levels. The social and political subordination of women also made them attractive to some employers, and also placed many women teachers in a relatively vulnerable position. On the one hand, the educational correspondence contains relatively few accounts of brutality by women in the schoolroom, and no cases of sexual assault by women teachers. To employers, female teachers may well have appeared superior because of their capacity to use gentle pedagogical means---although complaints of the inability of women to govern large boys were heard. That they were unlikely to assault students sexually may also have recommended them. On the other hand, employers could place certain kinds of moral regulatory demands on female teachers more easily than upon men. 'The Trustees of Caledon School Section No 4,' wrote J.D. Hagerman, 'wish to engage a Female Teacher (she must be single ) for the coming year 1861.'[136] The scarcity of alternative employment made women particularly vulnerable to moral regulation in the locality.

At the same time, many women teachers found themselves in difficult positions as at once relatively independent and single, and as subordinate members of the educational bureaucracy. Tryphena S. Carter, a Normal School graduate, complained that she was subjected to libels on her character and repeated marriage proposals from the men in her first school section.[137] The superintendent of North Hastings described a case in which Margaret Dunn was encouraged to teach in a section by a trustee who had 'improper motives'. Dunn was hired for $12 per month, but her certificate was not legitimate. When she rejected the trustee's advances, she was fired.[138] Ellen Bowes, a teacher from Adelaide, warned the education office of her local superintendent. The superintendent's wife was still living, but he had seduced a young girl, and Bowes herself was very afraid of 'falling'.[139]

Of course, female teachers did not always accede to moral discipline, nor did they passively accept the less salutary aspects of their condition. Pay disputes were common, and many women teachers sought either the support of the education office, or legal redress. While the arbitrator appointed in section 3 of Madoc township could write of a 'young and inexperienced' teacher being cheated out of her pay by the trustees, other teachers--- like Amelia Robertson of Ottawa--- refused to be mistreated.[140] A teacher named Hoit, herself a Normal School graduate, resisted the attempts of the local superintendent---also a Normal School graduate--- to inspect her school. She claimed he was incompetent, and sought to undermine the inspection by encouraging the students to be noisy, by interrupting the superintendent's address to the school, and finally by dismissing the school.[141] School superintendents increasingly encountered highly qualified female teachers who were not in the

Training the 'Good' Teacher    257

least intimidated by the 'bad boys' nor by the superintendents themselves.[142]

However, feminization of the occupation put in place a set of personnel which was perhaps more responsive to the contradictory demands of autonomy and subordination which characterize bureaucratic organization than male teachers, with their history of autonomy in the market place, would have been. In Canada West, the most authoritative and competent male teachers enjoyed a career line which involved the supervision of women teachers. While some women could move to positions of supervision over female teachers, there were no female principals of mixed schools.[143] While women teachers in the schoolroom enjoyed a measure of autonomy, they were supervised and regulated by men---as trustees, superintendents, and central administrators. Educational authority structures were gendered, and were continuous with the pattern of authority relations which pertained in the household, where women were similarly subject to male authority. It should be remarked that the part of E.A. Talbot's concern with political governance, discussed in chapter one, which entailed the dominance of men over women, was partly realized in the educational state. Educational organization contributed practically to the construction of the authority structures sought in Canada West by bourgeois reformers: of the first class over the second, men over women, adults over children.

## Conclusion

Although nascent independent teachers' organizations existed in the 1850s, the significance of the transformation of teaching effected by the education office in Canada West in the period from 1846-1871 should not be underrated. Teaching ceased to be a craft-like occupation regulated entirely by local market forces and was effectively incorporated into a bureaucratic administrative structure. The free market in schooling largely disappeared. Teachers became a *corps d'etat,* a body of workers situated in an administrative grid and subjected to rising levels of controls which embraced not simply skill, but comportment, manners, habits of mind and body. Many teachers came to embody the local political authority sought by central educational administrators. The contradiction between autonomy and authority which characterized the situation of the teacher in an educational bureaucracy came to be mediated through gendered structures of individual character.

**Notes**

1. PAO RG2 C6C, G.R.R. Cockburn, Model Grammar School, 24 September 1858.
2. PAO RG2 C6C, G.R.R. Cockburn, Model Grammar School, 14 October 1858.
3. PAO RG2 C6C, T.J. Robertson, Normal School, 24 September 1858.
4. PAO RG2 C6C, 'Memorandum on the case of Mr Watts,' 24 September 1858; also C1Y, Ryerson to Watts, 30 September 1858.
5. PAO RG2 C6C, 'Memorandum on the case of Mr Watts,' 24 September 1858.
6. Egerton Ryerson, *Special Report on a System of Public Elementary Instruction for Upper Canada.* (Montreal: Lovell and Gibson, 1847):159-162.
7. Ryerson, *Report:162*
8. Ryerson, *Report:162*
9. J.G. Hodgins(ed)*Historical and Other Papers and Documents Illustrative of the Educational System of Ontario.* (Toronto: L.K. Cameron, 1911-12) II:33.
10. I don't propose to detail this here, but two examples may be cited. An itinerant teacher named Sweet toured parts of Canada West in 1858 conducting teachers' institutes. Residents and teachers around Brockville and Delta wrote to the education office pointing to the necessity of having a teachers' association but stating their opposition to Sweet. Ryerson counseled local teachers to wait for an initiative from the education department. PAO RG2 C6C, S.R. Sweet, Delta, 27 April 1858; Brockville, 10 July 1858; W.J. Black, Teacher, Delta, 20 July 1858; C1Y, Ryerson to Black, 26 July 1858. Also in 1858, Robert Alexander informed the education office that the York County Teachers' Association planned to promote a national teachers'

association and inquired about funding for the association's library. Ryerson replied that he did not think a provincial teacher's association could succeed, and offered no encouragement. PAO RG2 C6C, Robert Alexander, New Market, 13 October 1858; C1Y, Ryerson to Alexander, 16 October 1858. Harry Smaller deals with these questions at more length in 'Early Teachers' Associations in Ontario, 1840-1900', Ph.D. in progress, Department of History and Philosophy, Ontario Institute for Studies in Education. The reader might also refer to James Love, 'The Professionalization of Teachers in Mid-Nineteenth-Century Upper Canada', in N. McDonald and A. Chaiton, (eds), *Egerton Ryerson and His Times.* (Toronto: Macmillan, 1978), for quite a different kind of analysis.
11. Phil Gardner, *Lost Elementary Schools of Victorian England.* (Beckenham, Kent: Croom Helm, 1984).
12. PAO RG2 C6C, Hamnett Pinhey, Horaceville, 7 February 1847. Pinhey writes that at the most recent teachers' examinations he passed 56 of 100 candidates. Others were encouraged to study and take the exam again.
13. PAO RG2 C6C, W.B. Carroll, Smith Falls, 4 May 1852; J.F. Morris, Fort Erie, 15 February 1853; A. Migoleton, Albion, 25 February 1853; George Wilson, Sydenham, 7 November 1853.
14. PAO RG2 C6C, James Clapperton, superintendent, Augusta, 22 February 1855.
15. PAO RG2 C6C, John Ireland. Belvedire, New Jersey, 12 August 1851; A.B. Hawke, Emigration Officer, Toronto, 28 August 1854.
16. Hodgins, *Historical and Other Papers,* II:42-3.
17. PAO RG2 C6C, 'A Teacher', West Hawkesbury, 3 April 1852. Most volumes of Hodgins, *Documentary History* contain a section devoted to 'reminiscences' of retired teachers. Many such teachers discuss 'boarding around'. Notice also how common the practice was elsewhere in North America, cf. Carl Kaestle, *Pillars of the Republic.* (New York: Hill and Wang, 1983):passim.
18. PAO RG2 C6C, Edward Scarlett, Report on the State of Education, County of Northumberland, 1855-6, March 1856.
19. PAO RG2 C6C, Trustees section 4 Kilty, 21 February 1860; Residents, section 4 Kilty, 13 February 1860.
20. PAO RG2 C6C, John Blacksbury, superintendent, Bastard Township, 25 March 1854.
21. PAO RG2 C6C, W. McKone, East Nissouri, 18 October 1852.

22. PAO RG2 C6C, J.F. Halsted, Arthur, 14 January 1857.
23. PAO RG2 C6C, J.G. House, Teacher, Boston, C.W, 27 October 1858.
24. PAO RG2 C6C, P. Campbell, Corresponding Secretary, Aldborough Total Abstinence Society, Wardsville, 10 October 1859.
25. PAO RG2 C6C, Thos. Chambers, Otonabee, 1 January 1862.
26. PAO RG2 C6C, A.A. Brodie, Markham, 15 March 1858. Also, Alison Prentice, 'From Household to School House: the Emergence of the Teacher as Servant of the State,' *Material History Bulletin*, 20, 1985.
27. PAO RG2 C6C, George Street, Port Stanley, 27 December 1858.
28. PAO RG2 C6C, N. Greely, Trustee, section 2, Sophiasburgh, 9 September 1855.
29. PAO RG2 C6C A. Eachman, Trustee, Reach, 26 January 1857; Ryerson to Eachman, C1T, 31 January 1857.
30. PAO RG2 C6C, W.J. Clarke, London, 9 December 1851; W. Dairtt, Thurlow, 7 January 1854; Trustees, Rockton, 17 February 1854; Trustee, section 15, Kingston Township, 1 April 1854; T.N. Converse, St. Vincent, 28 August 1854; Trustee, Consecon, 11 January 1855; Secretary, section 17 Westminster, 2 February 1855; J.H. Howlett, Meaford, 28 April 1855; R. Hamilton, section 11 Whitechurch, 25 July 1855; J. McFaul, Cavan, 13 November 1855; Trustees, section 7 Cavan, 8 February 1856; Wm. Gunn, superintendent, district 1, Bruce County, 2 March 1857; J. Brink, St. Mary's, 15 July 1858; See also the report prepared by Thomas Hodgins, 'Re School Property,' 16 July 1858, which traces the legislation at more length in chapter 8. on property in schools from 1816 to 1858.
31. 13 Vic.,c.XLVIII, 'An Act for the Better Establishment and Maintenance of Common Schools in Upper Canada.'
32. J.G. Hodgins, (ed) *Documentary History of Education in Upper Canada*, (Toronto: L.K. Cameron, 1894-1910) VII:302; 'General Regulations and Instructions Framed under the Common School Act of 1846.'
33. 'General Regulations, 1846'; *The Educational Manual for Upper Canada,1856:128*.
34. This position is ubiquitous in the literature and is discussed at more length in chapter 8.
35. Ryerson, *Report,* 'Measures taken for the establishment of a

Normal School':55.
36. Ryerson, 'Measures taken,':71.
37. *The Educational Manual, 1861:143;134.*
38. *The Educational Manual, 1861:127.*
39. PAO RG2 C6C, H. O'Neill, Trustee, section 4 Brant, 23 June 1863; Alex Kerr, section 4 Brant, 23 June 1863.
40. PAO RG2 C6C, Alf. Parrinton, Medonte, 3 November 1863.
41. PAO RG2 C6C, John Howee, Teacher, Pelham Township, 12 March 1858; J. Brockbill, superintendent, Fonthill, 29 March 1858; C1X, Ryerson to Brockbill, 26 March 1858.
42. PAO RG2 C6C, Rev. J. Anderson, South Gower, 17 May 1852.
43. PAO RG2 C6C, R.J. Williams, superintendent, Caledon, 16 October 1856.
44. PAO RG2 C6C, K.A. Campbell, superintendent, Mara & Rama, 2 February 1867.
45. PAO RG2 C6C, no. 6460, 7215, 1869; also in 6802, 1869, a teacher in Durham is caught changing a Normal School certificate from 2B to 2A; also, Local superintendent, Metcalfe, 5 October 1861.
46. PAO RG2 C6C, Local superintendent, Oro, 27 August 1860.
47. PAO RG2 C6C. Local superintendent, Stamford, 22 November 1861.
48. PAO RG2 C6C, W. Ferguson, superintendent district 4, Grey County, 16 December 1862.
49. PAO RG2 C6C, E. Scarlett, superintendent, Castleton, 28 April 1858.
50. PAO RG2 C6C, George Bell, superintendent, Stamford, 2 December 1861.
51. PAO RG2 C6C, F.J. McLean, superintendent, Beamsville, 20 July 1863.
52. PAO RG2 C6C, John Lees, Ancaster, 13 February 1866.
53. PAO RG2 C6C, Robert Futhey, Stayner, 17 December 1863.
54. PAO RG2 C6C, J.E. Barr, Brockville, 4 December 1860.
55. PAO RG2 C6C, W. Carrich, section 5 Plympton, 24 December 1858.
56. PAO RG2 C6C, Trustee, section 14 Charlottenburgh, 13 January 1868.
57. PAO RG2 C6C, John Close, Camden, 12 March 1861.
58. PAO RG2 C6C, A.W. Lauder, Oshawa, 22 December 1855.
59. PAO RG2 C6C, Charles Fox, Teacher, Amherstburg, 1 January

1862.
60. PAO RG2 C6C, Local superintendent McKillop, no. 353 1866.
61. PAO RG2 C6C, Joseph Powley, Peel, 15 January 1858.
62. PAO RG2 C6C, George Thomson, section 11 Tuckersmith, 11 November 1859.
63. PAO RG2 C6C, James Carswell, Arnprior, 25 January 1859.
64. PAO RG2 C6C, Peter Lawson, Windham, 9 January 1863.
65. PAO RG2 C6C, Nathan Bicknell, Camden East, 1 September 1863.
66. PAO RG2 C6C, T. Macpherson, superintendent, Perth County, 21 August 1857.
67. PAO RG2 C6C, T.J. Robertson, Normal School, 20 June 1860; 29 June 1860.
68. PAO RG2 C6C, W. Wilson, Simcoe, 21 October 1857.
69. PAO RG2 C6C, G.A. Bull, superintendent, Barton, 10 February 1859;local superintendent North Hastings, 21 July 1859; James Skinner, Secretary, County Board of Public Instruction, London, 30 December 1859; E. Scarlett, superintendent, Northumberland, 1 February 1860.
70. PAO RG2 C6C, E. Sullivan, superintendent, Lobo & London, 12 July 1860; Duncan Campbell, Teacher, Warwick, 28 July 1861; See also H3, Minutes of the Middlesex County Board of Public Instruction. Campbell submitted to re-examination once, but when the Board attempted to re-examine him again, he organized his school supporters in opposition. This was influential in leading the Middlesex Board to begin offering 'life' certificates to some teachers.
71. PAO RG2 C6C, George Coleman, Mariposa, 16&28 November 1858; 15 October 1858; Alex. Mac Gregor, Mariposa, 8 October 1858; 15 November 1858; Morgan Barber, Little Britain, 14 October 1858; C1Y, Ryerson to Coleman, 22 October 1858; Ryerson to Barber, 22 October; Ryerson to Cameron, 8 & 15 October 1858; C2, Ryerson to Coleman, 2 December 1858.
72. PAO RG2 C6C, A.A. McLauchlin, Mariposa, 28 October 1858; C1Y, Ryerson to McLauchlin 8 November 1858.
73. PAO RG2 C6C, Superintendent, Augusta, 23 September 1861.
74. PAO RG2 C6C, D. Clarke, Charlottenburgh, 2 September 1852.
75. PAO RG2 C6C, J. Lyons, Drummondville, 1 August 1851.
76. PAO RG2 C6C, Wm. B. Williams, Dunnville, 8 January 1851.
77. PAO RG2 C6C, Proprietor, Kingston Academy, 14 September 1861.

78. PAO RG2 C2, for example, Ryerson to Jno. Stewart, J.P.,
79. PAO RG2 C6C, R.H. Davie, Pakenham, 1 December 1856.
80. PAO RG2 C6C, Reeve, Township of Greenock, 12 November 1858.
81. PAO RG2 C6C, Patrick Donovan, Campbellford, 7 March 1864; Residents, Lyndhurst, 17 June 1862.
82. PAO RG2 C6C, J.M. Mechum, Berlin, 26 November 1863.
83. PAO RG2 C6C, Ryerson to Mechum 7 December 1863 (in no. 491 1864).
84. PAO RG2 C6C, Superintendent, North Oxford, 29 June 1863.
85. PAO RG2 C6C, G.H. Boulton, BPI Hastings, 27 February 1865.
86. PAO RG2 C2, Ryerson to W. Price, Trustee, section 11 Toronto, 21 January 1864.
87. PAO RG2 C6C, Superintendent, Euphrasia, 11 June 1862.
88. PAO RG2 C6C, Eleanor Acheson, Elizabethtown, 1 July 1859.
89. *Annual Report of the Chief Superintendent on the Normal, Model and Common Schools for the Year 1870.*
90. PAO RG2 C6C, D.Y. Hoit, Elgin Field, London Township, 15 December 1849; London, 28 December 1856; no 7616, 1866; no 6935, 1869.
91. O.E. Bush, Wardsville, 20 October 1863.
92. Hodgins, *Historical Documents and other Papers* III:274.
93. See C.B. Sissons(ed) *My Dearest Sophie.* (Toronto:Ryerson, 1955.) By contemporary Methodist standards, Ryerson was liberal, allowing Sophie to go ice skating on the lake and sending her to a convent in Quebec to learn French.
94. Hodgins, *Historical Documents,* II:24. But notice also PAO RG2 C6C, J. Burns, Chinguacousy 30 May 1853, asks that her daughter be exempted from the rule precluding social intercourse with men in part from a desire that she not be lonely.
95. PAO RG2 C6C, T.C. Young Secretary, Irish National Board of Education, Dublin, 3 June 1847. This person was probably related to the infant educator Samuel Wilderspin.
96. David Stow, *The Training System.* (Glasgow: Blackie, 1840): 136.
97. PAO RG2 C6C, T.J. Robertson, Normal School, 27 April; 30 April; 1 May; 5 May; 11 May 1851; Mr. Graham, Toronto, 1 May; 24 May 1851.
98. PAO RG2 C6C, T.J. Robertson, Normal School, 7 January 1853; 18 January 1853; 9 June 1853; 15 September 1853; also, T.S.

Bowerman, Normal School, 15 June 1853.
99. PAO RG2 C6C, T.J. Robertson, Normal School, 18 January 1853.
100. PAO RG2 C6C, T.J. Robertson, Normal School, 13 April 1860.
101. PAO RG2 C6C, T.J. Robertson, Normal School, 15 May 1860. Alison Prentice provides an important analysis of relations in the Normal School in 'Women and Men at Toronto Normal School', paper presented to the Canadian History of Education Association, Vancouver, 1983.
102. PAO RG2 C6C, T.J. Robertson, Normal School, 30 December 1862.
103. PAO RG2 C6C, passim 1863, 'Application for License as Keeper of a Boarding House.'
104. PAO RG2 C6C. J.S. Sangster, 9 June 1866.
105. For the concept 'total institution', Erving Goffman, *Asylums: Essays on the Situation of Mental Patients and Other Inmates.* (New Jersey:Anchor Press, 1961).
106. *Toronto Normal School Jubilee Celebration.* (Toronto:Warwick, 1898). A former female student remembers a certain selective blindness on the part of administrators to some minor forms of misbehaviour.
107. PAO RG2 C6C, nos.25, 2790, 3667 1866; C2, 26 April 1866.
108. PAO RG2 C6C, T.J. Robertson, Normal School, 28 December 1863.
109. PAO RG2 C6C, T.J. Robertson, Normal School, 28 July 1860.
110. PAO RG2 C6C, T.J. Robertson, Normal School, 20 October 1863.
111. PAO RG2 C6C, T.J. Robertson, Normal School, 23 March 1863.
112. PAO RG2 C6C, S.P. May, Normal School, 19 July 1856.
113. PAO RG2 C6C, Joseph Hodgson, Ratho, 9 November 1863.
114. PAO RG2 C6C, T.J. Robertson, Normal School, 24 August 1858.
115. PAO RG2 C6C, T.J. Robertson, Normal School, 27 January 1860.
116. PAO RG2 C6C, Committee of Normal School Students, 1 November 1859.
117. PAO RG2 C6C, J.S. Sangster, Normal School, 2 June 1868.
118. PAO RG2 C6C, T.J. Robertson, Normal School, 23 March 1858; 9 May 1864.
119. PAO, MU975, Education Papers Collection, 1860-69, Notebooks of Maria Payne.
120. Mary Harris appears on the graduation list for 1848.
121. *Toronto Normal School Jubilee:27*.

122. PAO RG2 C6C, T.J. Robertson, Normal School, 1 June 1864.
123. PAO RG2 C6C, J. Carroll, Zorra, 5 January 1858.
124. PAO RG2 C6C, George German, Wellington, 12 August 1862.
125. PAO RG2 C6C, Trustees, South Gower, 20 January 1863.
126. PAO RG2 C6C, J. Armstrong, Hawkesbury, 24 January 1863. In addition to this instance, cases of uncertified female teachers may be seen in Trustees, no.18 Percy, 9 November 1859; Trustee, no.6 Wainfleet, 27 December 1859; Trustees, S. Gower, 20 January 1863; J. Armstrong, Superintendent, Hawkesbury, 24 January 1863; Trustee, no.5 Townsend, 4 February 1863; Trustee, nos.1&13 Crosby, 20 January 1862; George German, Wellington, 12 August 1862; Arbitrator, no.3 Madoc, 3 December 1862; Trustee, no.8 Woodhouse, 3 May 1861; Trustees, no.4 Georgina, 25 January 1857. There are others.
127. PAO RG2 C6C, Superintendent, Gwillimbury East, 8 January 1866; also, R. Aitken, Brampton, 7 February 1865; Egerton Young, Teacher, Madoc, 6 January 1862.
128. PAO RG2 C6C, Eliz. Unsworth, 13 January 1860.
129. Alison Prentice, 'The Feminization of Teaching' in S. Trofimenkoff and A. Prentice (eds), *The Neglected Majority*. (Toronto: McClelland and Stewart, 1977):52; 60.
130. R.L. Jones, *History of Agriculture in Ontario, 1613-1880*. (Toronto:University of Toronto Press, 1977): passim; J.A. Ruddick, 'The dairy industry in Canada,' in H.A. Innis (ed), *The Dairy Industry in Canada*. (Toronto: Ryerson, 1937).
131. PAO RG2 C6C, Superintendent, Picton, 18 March 1857.
132. PAO RG2 C6C, J.E. Barr, Brockville, 4 December 1860.
133. PAO RG2 C6C, W. Mary (np), 30 June 1857.
134. PAO RG2 C6C, Lenay Vanflooring, Scotland, 4 December 1861.
135. see Prentice 'Women and Men'.
136. PAO RG2 C6C, J.D. Hagerman, Caledon, 30 October 1860.
137. PAO RG2 C6C, Tryphenia S. Carter (np), 21 July 1865.
138. PAO RG2 C6C, Superintendent, North Hastings, 11 August 1860.
139. PAO RG2 C6C, Ellen Bowers, Adelaide, 27 June 1864.
140. PAO RG2 C6C, Amelia Robertson, Ottawa, 12 December 1860; Arbitrator, section 3 Madoc, 3 December 1862.
141 PAO RG2 C6C, for Hoit see nos. 3116, 3298, 3523 1866; also, C2, 14 April 1866.
142. PAO RG2 C6C, for example, nos.2684, 2983, 3176, 3179, 1867.

143. Prentice, 'Feminization of Teaching'.

# Chapter Seven:
# Defining School Knowledge

School reformers from John Strachan in the 1810s to Egerton Ryerson in the 1840s campaigned for central control over books used in common schools. The schools were repeatedly denounced as hotbeds of 'Americanism' --- a synonym for democracy and sedition--- because of popular control over books. Elsewhere,[1] I have shown that these claims were factually dubious. Scattered information suggests that most schools used British books in most subjects in the 1830s, and more systematic information from school reports for 1842 bolsters this suggestion. School reformers may well have believed that local common schools used republican schoolbooks, but they were probably mistaken.

The School Acts of 1846-50 nonetheless gave the General Board of Education, the Council of Public Instruction and the Chief Superintendent of Education very broad powers over the books used in schools. All 'foreign' books in the English branches of education were banned from schools supported out of public funds, and the school grant could be withheld from schools violating this rule. The education office sanctioned the series of reading books produced by the Commissioners of National Education in Ireland for use in the common schools. An American grammar by Samuel Kirkham, and the American Morse's *Geography* were also authorized.

Many educational historians have tended to regard the generalization of educational apparatus ---especially school books ---- as benchmarks of educational progress. Earlier commentators on the changes in the curriculum provoked through the Acts of 1846-50 have seen these developments as an 'improvement.'[2] The Irish texts were certainly remarkable. They were graded in a series which took readers from the alphabet through a vast array of factual, moral, political, and economic material. The *Fifth Book of Lessons,* intended for thirteen year olds, in its 400-odd pages contained material on physical geography and geology, ancient and modern history, vegetable and animal physiology, astronomy, hydrostatics, pneumatics, optics, electricity, chemistry, and also had a concluding section of poetry. The book was illustrated.[3] The Irish texts were better printed, cheaper, and physically easier to read than Murray's *English Readers,* which predominated in the common schools before

1846 and which were not graded.

Yet to regard the curricular reforms of 1846-50 simply as an improvement is to overlook the transformations these reforms provoked. At least four changes in the organization and administration of school knowledge were directly involved. First, the introduction of the Irish series constituted a movement in the organizing principles of school knowledge away from sacred and directly religious literature towards 'science' and 'useful knowledge'. The Irish series embodied the results of the 'natural theology' movement of the late eighteenth and early nineteenth centuries, and was also very much the product of European attempts to provide 'sound intellectual aliment' to the 'lower orders,'--- to discipline a growing working class.

Second, the texts assumed the introduction of novel pedagogical practices such as 'interrogation' and evaluation. Reading in the Irish series was explicitly promoted as a 'meaningful' activity. In most of the books, for instance, lessons were headed with a list of important words, and teachers were to examine students repeatedly to evaluate their acquisition of 'correct' meanings. This method was conceived quite explicitly as a means of forming 'sound views on political questions' in the student body,[4] but one must also notice that it involved an orientation to the text rather different from that which was implied for earlier readers. Murray's *Readers*, for example, contained large amounts of material intended for oral recitation. The Irish series represented a shift in reading objectives. While the distinction cannot be rigidly drawn, reading tended to be seen much more as a 'useful' than as a 'decorative' art. At the same time, what teachers could do to and demand of students changed in principle.

Third, the generalization of a uniform set of texts was seen by educational reformers as a means to collective instruction. The Irish series demanded the classification of students by providing graded reading lessons. The generalization of the Irish series was bound up with a movement from individual to collective methods of instruction. Rather than each student proceeding at its own pace through lesson material, aided by direct individual attention from the teacher, 'classes' were to move at a uniform rate and to be instructed together. Pedagogical practice moved from a preoccupation with the development and interest of the individual reader to a concern with the administration of a population of potential readers.

Fourth, and not least, control over curriculum in principle, and increasingly in practice, moved away from parents, scholars and teachers and towards the central authority. The purposes of instruction in the educational state were much more 'societal' than individualistic (although, nonetheless, 'societal' goals were to be achieved through a process of political *individuation*).

## Generalizing the Irish Texts

The control accorded the central education office over schoolbooks was one of the 'despotic' aspects of the Act of 1846 in the eyes of Reformers and of some local school supporters as well. Dexter D'Everardo, District Superintendent for Niagara, reported widespread opposition to the textbook clauses of the Act in his district. There, he argued, parents were used to buying American books, not because parents were disloyal, but because American books were cheap and of good quality. D'Everardo counseled Ryerson to proceed cautiously with respect to the introduction of new texts.[5]

A minute of the General Board of Education, formulated largely in response to D'Everardo's concerns, urged a moderate policy. The Superintendent of Schools was ordered to 'recommend a delicate treatment of the subject' in all his official communications, and to let unauthorized books rather 'fall into disuse, than exclude them all together, when they come into competition with those School Books already sanctioned.'[6] Ryerson himself replied to D'Everardo that his initial objective was not to have a uniform series of books in the province as a whole, but to have one series only in each school. Regulations published by the Council of Public Instruction in 1850 reasserted official support for uniformity in schoolbooks. 'Heterogeneous school books (however good each book may be in itself)' insisted the Council, 'render classification impossible, increase the labour and waste the time of the teacher, and retard the progress of the pupils. But the teacher and pupils labour at the greatest disadvantage, when they are compelled to use books which are as various as the scholars' names.'[7]

The financial powers of the Council of Public Instruction were not directed against schools using offending books, although occasional threats to do so were made. The generalization of the Irish texts was promoted rather through attempts to make them cheap and easily available, on the one hand, and on the other hand by propaganda efforts, and by measures designed to implicate them in routine administrative activity.

Initially, the General Board of Education proposed to seek competitive bids from Canadian publishers for the Irish series, and to grant to the successful bidder an exclusive monopoly for a five year period. However, there were so many interested publishers that the Board decided to leave the reprinting of the texts to the market, with the stipulation that books would be officially authorized only if sold below a specified maximum price and only if they met definite standards of quality.[8]

Sample sets of the Irish texts were shipped to District Councils in 1846, and Councils were encouraged to promote their adoption. An Educational Depository was established in Toronto to facilitate the distribution of books and other apparatus for schools. District superintendents of schools urged the adoption of the books during their tours of inspection. William Hutton was particularly active in this regard, and S.D. Ardagh, Rector of Barrie and Simcoe District superintendent, recommended the Irish texts in notes he wrote in school logbooks.[9] The *Journal of Education* encouraged the use of the books repeatedly. More important, from 1850 County Boards of Public Instruction used the Irish texts as the basis for teachers' examinations. Finally, as we have seen in chapter six, the regulations for teaching specified by the Council of Public Instruction enjoined the use of the Irish texts upon teachers.

These initiatives were remarkably successful. In his annual report for 1850, the chief superintendent claimed that the Irish texts were 'used' in 2,593 of the 3,059 schools (84.7%) which made returns to the education office. In 1856, the comparable figure was 3,054 of 3,472 (85.6%); in 1860, 3,843 of 3,969 schools (96.6%), and in 1865, shortly before the next major revision of the curriculum, the Irish books were said to be used in 4,223 out of 4,303 of the schools (98.0%). Ryerson himself commented on this widespread adoption of the Irish texts,

> I question whether there is an example in any
> Country, --- certainly none in America,--- where

there is such a complete uniformity in the Text Book Readers of the Public Schools; and that without any compulsion, from the excellence and truly national character of the Books, and the absence of all monopoly in the publication and sale of them.[10]

**Table 1**
**Students in Reading Classes in Public Schools, Canada West, 1850-1865**

| Year | Students aged 5-16 | Enrolled aged 5-16 |
|---|---|---|
| 1850 | 259,258 | 151,891 |
| 1855 | 297,623 | 211,629 |
| 1861 | 384,980 | 309,895 |
| 1865 | 426,757 | 361,617 |

| | Reading Classes | | | | |
|---|---|---|---|---|---|
| Year | 1st | 2nd | 3rd | 4th | 5th |
| 1850 | 24,551 | 27,537 | 31,805 | 27,874 | 13,268 |
| 1855 | 42,151 | 44,502 | 49,656 | 42,350 | 31,903 |
| 1861 | 63,973 | 63,688 | 67,129 | 57,889 | 58,090 |
| 1865 | 73,944 | 76,912 | 77,770 | 67,526 | 70,254 |

Source:*Annual Reports of the Chief Superintendent of Education.*

Table 1 demonstrates the distribution of the members of the schoolage population enrolled in the common schools among the different reading classes. There were five main readers in the Irish series, with supplements and with a *Reading Book for Girls' Schools* which was not widely used. By 1865, the schoolage population would seem to have been evenly distributed into five reading classes.

While Superintendent Ryerson suggested that no official compulsion existed to make teachers adopt the Irish system, many teachers were compelled by the material conditions of their work to insist upon uniform texts. Some sense of the receptivity of teachers to labour-saving devices can be gathered from the description of his work presented by Thomas Marshall, the teacher of Union section 6 in Ellice & Logan Townships in 1870. Marshall wrote,

> At present, I have 130 pupils on the Register, and a daily attendance from 90 to 100.... this section is purely R.C. and I have to hear every morning three or more classes in the Catechism, 4 classes in the Spelling Book, Super. 3 classes in E. grammar, three classes in geography. then I am compelled to teach three reading lessons daily to the 1st 2nd 3rd 4th and 2 lessons to 5th readers, then set copies for 72 who are writing besides assisting those who are studying Arithmetic from addition up to the most difficult exercises in Sangster's National Arithmetic, also exercise on the map those who are studying geography and in the black-board those who are reading E. grammar, all for the wonderful large salary of $300 p. annum.

Administrators claimed that uniformity in system and text books produced more efficient teaching. The superintendent for the Newcastle District gave the example of a 'Mr Alexander' who, he claimed, 'instructs from 70 to 90 Children of all ages--- his classes are managed like-clock-work,'[11] something made possible by his use of the Irish texts.

While teachers may have liked the Irish texts as such, may have approved of their content and methods, and may have adopted them for these reasons, they may equally have adopted the Irish schoolbooks because the books were generally available to those faced with large schools and because they contained the material upon which teachers' examinations were based. Relatively little discussion of the content of the series seems to have existed in the 1850s, although objections to the method of teaching were more noticeable. However, by the middle 1860s, many Canadian educational administrators regarded the series as badly outdated. Most of the books, it should be recalled, had been produced in the 1830s, and some of them probably earlier. They also had no Canadian content.

Many teachers in the 1840s taught in schools where there were very few books of any kind. Some of these wrote to the education office that they would gladly use any books whatever in their schools if they were simply numerous and durable.[12] Luke Maxwell Dally, who taught a school in West Gwillimbury Township in the late 1840s, not only had so few seats for students that he found it 'impossible to get on with comfort,' but was also continually short of books, particularly in geography. In 1847, he waited until the end of June before one parent 'sent books with his children today for the first time this year.'[13] Although boards of trustees had the legal ability to tax the school section to provide books, relatively few did so before 1871. Most books were supplied by parents and scholars directly, and the cheapness of the Irish series probably made them relatively popular with parents.

Once the supply of books improved through the efforts of the education office, teachers were particularly concerned with the physical quality of the reprints available. Teachers complained repeatedly in the 1850s that publishers were 'flooding the country with badly bound books' which 'fall to pieces before the eyes'.[14] John Hughes of Brantford complained that in his school 'hundreds of books have gone to pieces in this way before they have become in the least worn or soiled.' Worse still, he argued, the books were riddled with errors which frustrated students and discouraged teachers. Page 92 of the 1849 Brewer & McPhail edition of the arithmetic book contained 21 questions but gave at least 5 wrong answers, and this page was not unusual. Indeed, Hughes remarked, 'the small arithmetic is so full of errors and misprints of every kind that with many it has got the book into such disrepute that teachers do all they can to keep it out of their schools.'[15] Many similar complaints were made.[16]

## From Religion to Practice

The School Acts of 1846-50 aimed at the expulsion of the Bible and Testament as classbooks. This was a major shift in educational policy, for these books had been very widely used. Records for 1842 reveal that the Bible and/or Testaments were used in 104 of the 128 schools for which information exists.[17] Many students learned to read in a primer and then moved directly to the study of the Bible. As we have seen in chapter two, under the administration of Robert Murray, the use of the Bible and Testaments in schools was explicitly sanctioned and encouraged.

However, in the Irish system the exclusion of the Bible from the schoolroom was seen as a precondition for successful non-sectarian schooling. 'Common' schooling was to draw upon the 'Common Christianity' of natural theology and political economy, bolstered by lessons abstracted from the Scriptures. This was seen as a means of Christian schooling which would not incite the opposition of the Catholic hierarchy to lay reading of the Bible. The exclusion of the Bible and Testament in Canada West was supported by some local educational administrators as the only means to limit the spread of separate schools.

For instance, the school trustees in Goderich sought to prevent the emergence of separate schools in the town by forbidding all forms of prayer in the common schools.[18] The superintendent of schools in Chatham wrote in 1852 that the reading of the Bible and Testament in the Chatham schools had been abandoned and replaced by the use of the Irish series of books.

> This was done principally at my suggestion as I considered the introduction of this Series to the exclusion of the Scriptures would tend to have a beneficial effect in doing away with that sectarian spirit which unfortunately still prevails to some extent in our Common Schools.....[19]

The Board of School Trustees for the village of Preston passed a resolution in 1853 banning the reading of the Bible in the village schools because of the religious strife it produced. No books were to be used in the Preston schools which teachers could not explain to students in non-sectarian terms.[20] A Catholic teacher of a common school on Wolfe Island refused to teach the catechism during school hours, despite the demands of Catholic parents. A resident of this school section wrote,

> For the last four years the majority of the inhabitants are Roman Catholics and claim the right of haveing the Catechism of that faith taught in the School contrary in my opinion to the school act and to the great annoyance of those who hold a contrary opinion.[21]

Sectarian conflict was common on Wolfe Island in the 1850s.[22]

In 1856, W.D. Donaldson, a trustee in section 4 of West Flamboro Township, revealed that he and his fellow trustees administered a 'mixed' school section, and that in consequence they had instructed their teacher to use only the Irish series in the school and to avoid all sectarian remarks. However, not only did the teacher insist on using the Bible and Testament as class books, but he also insisted on singing hymns in school. The deputy superintendent of education, John George Hodgins, wrote to Donaldson to affirm that the trustees had full authority to forbid Bible-reading and hymn-singing in the school. Indeed, Hodgins added, 'the Bible and Testament are not text books, and cannot be used as such in any School.'[23] The teacher in section 3, North Norwich Township also insisted on religious activity in the schoolroom. This person was so enthusiastic in prayer and scripture lesson, and so long winded, that his students were continually given to restlessness and whispering--- for which offences he expelled them. Here the education office encouraged local residents to stop the teacher's activity.[24] J.M. Mechum, the superintendent of schools for the village of Berlin, failed in his attempt to be re-appointed in 1862. Mechum had been encouraging the study of the scriptures and of grammar in the village schools. Local residents, especially the 'Pennsylvania Dutch' opposed him, claiming he was trying to make 'rogues' of their children.[25]

The use of the Bible, Testaments and prayer in schools was not something demanded only by unusually fervent teachers against the wishes of local school supporters, however. The opponents of centralized educational organization frequently pointed to the absence of the Bible from the schools as evidence of the 'godlessness' of the state system. In the middle 1850s, Ryerson was compelled to authorize school prayers, and the education office published several model prayers. Many local school supporters insisted upon the continuation of directly religious teaching in the schools. The school trustees in the village of Simcoe, for instance, passed a resolution in 1852 'making it compulsory upon teachers to open & close the schools with prayer & requiring that a Chapter or two of the New Testament be occasionally read in School.'[26] The local superintendent of Morris and Grey Townships reported in 1858 that trustees in some school sections insisted upon the use of the Bible as text-book.[27] The superintendent of East Williams Township noted that in one section the parents all insisted upon the reading of the Bible and the use of the catechism during school hours.[28] When a new teacher in section 3 of Usborne Township attempted to stop students reading the scriptures in school, parents assembled and passed a resolution requiring him to hear the students read them three times a week.[29]

Other teachers, however, found themselves simply unable to carry out even officially sanctioned religious exercises. A teacher named David Williams, for instance, complained in 1857 of 'Roman Catholic families who are violently opposed to and determined to prevent me from' conducting the official school prayers. He was infuriated by his students,

> ...all of whom are over twenty years of age attend my school and they combine together to make a disturbance during the closing prayer and they do it in such a way that they think they evade the law. that is they will pray aloud groan shout Amen & pretending to be sincere.[30]

Rational, non-sectarian schooling, in which the glories of God were revealed in natural science, rather than in direct study of the scriptures or in other religious exercises, was a central proposition of public schooling on the Irish model. It undoubtedly appealed to Ryerson and some other Canadian educational administrators as a means to civic harmony and political order. The system never achieved this goal in Ireland---by 1850, indeed, most Irish schools were under denominational control,[31] although it was more successful in Canada West. Still, from 1852 the education office was involved in a dispute with the Catholic hierarchy, which led to the strengthening of the separate school clauses of the School Acts.[32] Religious texts were used in Catholic separate schools.

In addition to attempts to prevent the use of the Bible as a school text, the education office moved against classical instruction in the common schools. Instruction in Latin, in particular, was declared impermissible on the grounds that it took time away from the more 'important' branches of study. Latin could be taught in the schools only 'by a private engagement with the parents of the pupils concerned' and such instruction was to be given after regular school hours.[33] This policy was quite popular. While some school supporters opposed the ban on Latin because they sought a classical education but could not afford grammar schooling,[34] many others regarded Latin as an extravagance or as a distraction in school teaching. James Gibson withdrew his child from a common school in Markham

Township on the grounds that the teacher spent part of the school day teaching Latin to non-residents.[35] Even private arrangements for Latin instruction outside school hours were at times vehemently opposed.[36]

However, official opposition to Latin also spoke to a different sentiment present in many localities. School supporters were accustomed to measure the value of teaching according to the amount of individual instruction accorded to students, especially to young students. In most community-controlled common schools, teachers were preoccupied with teaching young students to read, while older students who had acquired this skill occupied themselves. People accustomed to this kind of educational practice regarded instruction in Latin as suspicious, but also adopted the same attitude to much of the official curriculum. The disciplinary demands of the Normal School method upon older students were often seen locally as aberrant or insulting. Scholars did not readily accept a definition of themselves as schoolchildren.

Robert Brown of Cornwall complained that both Latin instruction and the official method generally took time away from young students.

> I wish to know how far it is consistent with the law to teach Lattin in [the school]---in the nixt Place I wish to know how far it is consistent with the law for the younger Portion of the Schollers to be taught only two lessons in the day, with a Teacher having a first Class sertifocate, when the [old] Teachers having a second and third Class sertifecate would give our younger schollers four lessons in the day.[37]

Other school suporters regarded the attempt to increase the supply of books and apparatus in schools in much the same light. Edward Clegg, a trustee in section 9 of Wellesley Township, complained that his teacher, with the support of the local superintendent tended,

> ...to make use of Every Trash of Books and newspapers in the corse of them three ours & onley afew small children confined I think to Two lessons in whole day.[38]

The same sentiment addressed the superintendent of Etobicoke as 'a very unreasonable man, as he wishes the children to have too much learning, more than will ever be of any good to them.'[39] School administrators commonly equated popular opposition to the official curriculum with popular opposition to learning in general. In some cases the equation obtained, but this was certainly not always the case. Robert Brown, quoted above, did not oppose *learning;* he insisted upon it. He opposed rather the official methods of instruction which seemed to him to result in less teaching for those most in need of instruction. Opposition to 'fancy teaching' was partly opposition to the disciplinary elements of official instructional methods and materials. Knowledge and power intertwined in the construction of the educational state.

Some forms of instruction received official approval, however, because they were both 'useful' to the student and 'useful' to the teacher as a means of occupying students. Instruction in needlework for girls and young women was a case in point. The chief superintendent explicitly supported the teaching of both needlework and embroidery in the common schools.

> Both are taught in our Provincial female Model School; and I think it very desireable that girls should learn how to do them--- which, in many cases they can only do at school.[40]

Elsewhere, Ryerson qualified this position, suggesting that sewing could be taught in female free schools so long as the majority of parents did not oppose it and so long as it did not interfere with other subjects.[41]

As Table 2 indicates, a considerable section of the population enrolled in the schools by 1865 was also enrolled in classes for geography, grammar and vocal music. Enrollment, of course, is not attendance, and the large majority of students who attended school less than one hundred days per year may well have spent their time in the schoolroom engaged in less advanced subjects. Even in the formative period, there is some basis to the official claim that public schooling would generate enriched instructional activity, but it would be more accurate to regard state schooling as having involved a *specification* of school knowledge. If the curriculum expanded under the direction of the central authority, it also contracted. Many of the kinds of instruction formerly offered by teachers in particular schools ceased to be given. Navigation, surveying, dialing, Greek, and band music, for

## Table 2
### Students enrolled in 'higher' subjects in Canada West, 1850-65

| Year | Total Enrollment | Studying Grammar | Studying Geography |
|---|---|---|---|
| 1850 | 151891 | 19741 | 21584 |
| 1855 | 211629 | 40660 | 58291 |
| 1861 | 309895 | 85766 | 114982 |
| 1865 | 361617 | 106798 | 137903 |

| Year | Studying Music | Studying Drawing | Studying Needlework |
|---|---|---|---|
| 1850 | 5745 | | |
| 1855 | 18243 | | |
| 1861 | 31533 | 6644 | 6196 |
| 1865 | 50663 | 6155 | 7860 |

Source:

*Annual Reports of the Chief Superintendent of Education*

example, were forms of instruction given in schools in Canada West in the late 1830s and early 1840s which vanished after 1846. The specification of school knowledge eliminated the (unreliable) variety offered under the market determination of curriculum.

## From Decoration to Interrogation

Reading instruction in the common schools of Canada West in the 1840s was based on a 'letters-to-words' approach. Students learned to read by sounding letters, combinations of letters, and then whole words. Spelling books and primers were their first schoolbooks. Reading instruction centred upon reading aloud. Popular reading books, such as Murray's *English Readers,* presented public speeches, poetry and other material that was meant to be read aloud. Reading was closely allied to the study of rhetoric. Reading was primarily a decorative art and an oral activity. Pronouncing dictionaries were widely used, and meanings were provided in definitional form.[42]

In the Irish series, the methods and objectives of reading instruction were quite different. Here a 'words-to-letters' approach was used in which reading was tied to visual memory. The 'unmeaning and enslaving columns' of the spelling book were to be removed from schools, and in their place the Irish series proposed Sullivan's *Spelling Book Superseded*.[43] Reading instruction focused on the ordered transmission of approved meaning. Reading lessons were headed with the new words they contained, and these words were placed in context in these lessons. Teachers were to 'interrogate' students with respect to the appreciation of correct meanings. Reading was closely allied with writing, which itself focused on the transmission of meaning. Students were to be taught 'a plain round hand' in place of decorative penmanship, and the written examination increasingly figured in the school programme.

**Table 3**
**The spread of educational apparatus in Canada West, 1850-66**

| Year | Schools | with Bb | with G | with M |
|------|---------|---------|--------|--------|
| 1850 | 3,059   | 1649    | 168    | 1814   |
| 1861 | 4,019   | 3342    | 926    | 2820   |
| 1866 | 4,303   | 3964    | 1136   | 3265   |

Key: Bb=blackboards; G= globes or scientific apparatus; M=maps.

**Source:** *Annual Reports of the Chief Superintendent of Education*

Some measure of the spread of 'meaningful' reading and enriched instructional activity can be taken from the spread of educational apparatus, indicated in Table 3. Blackboards are particularly important in this regard, since the connection of reading to writing and visual memory involved 'exercising students on the blackboard'. Grammar was also taught using blackboards. By 1866, more than 92% of the common schools were equipped with blackboards, many of them probably locally made from a recipe supplied by the education office itself. More than three-quarters of the schools also had maps by 1866 and more than a quarter had some other item of apparatus— a globe most commonly, although the educational depository also supplied scientific equipment and magic lanterns. These supplies are not inherently signs of 'educational progress'. They point to the reorientation of educational activity. These new methods and devices involved the systematic gradation and evaluation of students by teachers. A key part of 'making education practical' involved methods designed to regulate the processes of deriving meaning, of 'making sense', on the part of students. These methods can be traced directly to attempts by ruling classes in Europe to control the development of socially menacing ways of 'making sense' on the part of working classes.[44]

The Irish texts demanded from teachers, students and parents a new orientation to reading activity. They demanded participation on the part of students and teachers in new pedagogical relations: interrogation and written examinations. They presented a new set of contents for reading activity. These aspects of the curricular reforms generated local opposition and resistance. Local reaction was also shaped by the rising numbers in the schoolroom itself and by the methods of collective instructive, which challenged existing conceptions of both learning and a fair day's labour on the part of a teacher.

Normal School graduates, those most adept at the Irish methods, frequently encountered resistance to new methods from school supporters and students. The 'intrusive' pedagogy to which these teachers were trained was regarded as an intrusion indeed by some school supporters, and denunciations of arrogant Normal School graduates were common. The village school in Stratford declined because parents withdrew scholars after the trustees hired what the local superintendent described as,

> a little inexperienced, ignorant girl, who had got a few weeks whitewashing at your Normal School, & under whose tuition the time of the pupils was wholly lost.[45]

The superintendent of schools for Huron County observed that parents generally opposed the practice of teaching students meanings, roots and origins of words.[46] John Carson attempted to replace the 'memory-work' system of his predecessor in section 2 of Tecumseh Township with the Irish curriculum and drill, only to encounter serious opposition from school supporters.[47] William McCullough complained that even though his school had 80 to 90 students in attendance in winter, many of them young, and even though he had no assistant, nonetheless school supporters were known to 'favour the introduction of the learning of dialogues by the Pupils in our Common Schools for the purpose of recitation.'[48] 'Let me assure you' wrote T.W. Lillie, a teacher from South Crosby Township in 1854, to Ryerson, 'that the English Reader is preferable to learn to read, except for Beginners, to any book that I have noticed except a good Rhetorical Reader.' While 'the 1st and 2nd of the National may suffice for Beginners,' Lillie urged the education office to abandon the National books.[49]

Like their European and American counterparts, local school supporters in Canada West tended to regard the purpose of schooling as to teach young students to read as quickly and as well as possible. Anything else might be seen as extraneous, frivolous, or insulting. Students who had learned how to read were left to pursue their own interests (more or less).

This kind of reaction alarmed many educational administrators. The superintendent of schools for the village of Ingersoll, for instance, lamented in 1854 that despite the best efforts of the 'leading educationists' of the village the people,

> blamed the teacher for not keeping a sort of military order in the school--- for not compelling the pupils to stand with hands behind them, or at their sides, all the time of lessons without moving muscle or limb; second for teaching spelling acc.- to the system of classbooks (& by written exercises in addition) & not as they desired in long columns after Mavor or Cobb; third & especially for teaching 'what did not belong to a Common School'--- namely, 'Nat'l Philosophy' & 'Physiology'--- Geometry & 'Mensuration' 'Algebra' & the 'nonsense of Gymnastics--- In short all that our wisemen require [is] the mechanical part of the merest elementary education, without mental culture & developmt & attention to the formation of the

habits & character--- & that large amount of valuable real instruction and information....⁵⁰

Many local school supporters claimed that students simply did not progress as rapidly under the Normal school system as they had done formerly. The trustees in section 12 of Vaughan Township had two Normal School graduates in their section, one with a first class certificate and one with a second. However, during the year these teachers taught, 'the progress of the younger Scholars has been observed not only by us but by Parents & Visitors to be in a marked degree slower than it was during the previous six years and a half when we had teachers who had not enjoyed the advantages of being taught at the Normal School.' The trustees argued that there were two reasons for this decline. 'The one is the throwing aside of every spelling book adapted to the capacities of young children. The other is the withdrawal to the extent of three fourths or at least of two thirds from the younger children, of the number of daily lessons formerly taught them by the Master.'⁵¹ Many other correspondents to the education office argued the same point. A trustee from section 10 of Caledon Township remarked in 1862 that there were 'two points which for years past has caused some dissatisfaction' in his section. First, 'the doing away of the Mavor Spelling Books' and second abolition of 'the sistem of rhyming the Spelling over without sylableing.' The latter especially, he claimed, 'is believed to be a grievous error as the children does not improve in spelling as heretofore when the other system was practiced.'⁵² William Galt of Scarborough made a similar point.⁵³

In the method of reading instruction prevalent in the province before the public school reforms, students learned to sound the letters in the alphabet, and approached spelling by sounding letters in combination. 'Sylableing' referred to the practice of pronouncing each set of syllables in a word while spelling the whole. For instance, the student faced with the word 'barber' would typically say 'b, a, ba, b-a-r, bar, b-e-r, ber, b-a-r-b-e-r, bar-ber.' In the Irish method by contrast, this 'rhyming over' was prohibited, precisely because it was held to produce 'unmeaning' combinations of sounds which would distract the student from the proper object of reading: the measurable acquisition of correct meaning. In the Irish method, the student learned to recognize the letters of the alphabet, and then saw the word to be spelled on the printed page or blackboard. The image of the word implanted in visual memory was then decomposed into its letters, spelled, and its meaning explained. So, 'barber' would be written on the blackboard and defined by the teacher. Its etymology would be given and other information about it supplied. It would then be erased. The teacher would ask students to spell it, and they would simply say from memory 'b-a-r-b-e-r'. The process of interrogation would then begin. 'What is a barber?' 'A barber is a person who practices the profession of cutting people's hair, a modern development in a group which formerly performed surgical operations. The word comes from the Latin *barba* for beard. The red and white pole displayed by barbers points to their earlier vocation as surgeons and bloodletters. In our town there are four barbers......'etc. The trustee from Caledon claimed the first method to be more effective and efficient in teaching people to read. Not only was the teacher's time spent largely with the younger scholars, but older students probably had greater autonomy in the schoolroom.

Feelings in these matters ran high. John Barker, an Irish-trained teacher, claimed that in his neighbourhood an old 'hedge school' teacher was

> ...doing all he can to annoy us by prejudicing the minds of the people against the new System.... his objection seems chiefly to spelling the words without pronouncing the Syllables until the word is all spelled.[54]

Herbert Armstrong, who regarded the Irish books and methods to be by far the best, complained that school supporters and the local superintendent all insisted that he use Mavor's *Spelling Book*, the common speller in the country since the 1830s.[55] T.N. Wright of Fenelon Falls was fired for refusing to require a trustee's child to use the dictionary as a spelling book.[56]

## Limits

While Teachers who adopted the official methods of reading instruction encountered opposition based on conventional conceptions of teaching and learning, many teachers simply did not follow such methods. The weight of numbers under free schooling undoubtedly prevented rural teachers from undertaking the processes of interrogation and exposition necessary for the adoption of the Normal

School method. For a teacher with over 80 students to make each of the classes spell the words at the top of a reading lesson, explain their meanings, read the lesson and then respond to a close interrogation on that lesson would have taken all of the school day. Many teachers continued to be oriented to the Irish texts in much the same way as they had been to early readers. Readers were meant to be 'read through'. Joseph Collins, for instance, bought a copy of Murray's *English Reader* in York in 1824. He had 'read this book through three times' by 'August 28th 1826', and was sufficiently proud of the fact to have 'Frederic Stephens, Newmarket, Tutor,' attest to it on the flyleaf.[57] Probably no attempt was made by Frederic Stephens to compell Joseph Collins to demonstrate, in competition with his fellows, the meaning of what he had read.

George Grafftley, an English teacher with fourteen years' experience, was astounded that Canadian teachers made no effort to explain lessons, nor to make students understand.[58] Superintendents of schools repeatedly complained that teachers made no effort to develop meaning. Edward Scarlett claimed that Northumberland County teachers uniformly adopted the practice of

> pressing children in a hurried superficial manner from book to book without reference to age capacity or the future wellbeing of the pupils....Words are learned without meaning sentences are stammered over without knowing the ideas the contain rules are committed without understanding them.[59]

The superintendent of Reach & Scugog Townships lamented that 'scholars have been occupied with Books far too difficult for them.' This was 'altogether unwise, unwise for the Teacher and unwise for his Scholars.'[60] The Charlottenburgh Township superintendent

> ...found Severals of the pupils who could read and Spell distinctly and correctly although I met with but few who could give me the definition of a single word or who seemed to comprehend the subject in their reading lessons.[61]

At the Oshawa Central School— where the weight of numbers was so great that the Board of Trustees had contemplated removing all advanced students— there were 'perpetual complaints that children are advanced from class to class and Book to Book without having mastered any thing.' One trustee observed that at a quarterly examination students studying Natural Philosophy and Geometry were unable to spell the word 'always'.[62] The capacity of the education office to actually put in place reading practices aimed at developing a meaningful relation to 'useful knowledge' was undoubtedly limited by the material conditions of public schooling. Yet this official definition of reading established a system which called into question and eventually marginalized earlier conceptions and uses of reading.

## Pleasure and the Irish Series

As we have seen, the educational reforms of 1846-50 were intended at once to develop the moral capacities of the population and to draw upon the capacity for pleasure. Reading, like schooling generally, was intended to be pleasurable. Aesthetics and politics were inextricably connected in the discourse of reform. However, the archival evidence suggests, the Irish readers were not pleasurable to the student population and were ineffective in the eyes of teachers and administrators for that reason. The use of the Irish series came under attack from the middle 1850s, and with increasing frequency in the 1860s.

The reaction of the education office to attacks on the Irish curriculum was identical to its reaction to attacks on other parts of the educational project. Far from accepting that the Irish texts might be moral *and* unpleasant, and seeking new policies that would be really pleasant, the office rather supported its moral politics over the pleasure of students and teachers. Again and again the education office acted in this way; if authority and pleasure could not be combined, the office consistently opted for authority over pleasure. In the 1850s, critics were simply insulted or disregarded. In the 1860s, this became impossible.

T.W. Lillie, who complained about the Irish series in 1854, received this salvo from Ryerson in reply:

>...on both sides of the Atlantic, numerous and more learned and experienced teachers than you are have had to do in preparing and using the School books to

which you refer; nor is it likely that the decisions [about the worth of the books] you so oracularly pronounce in half a page of letter paper will change regulations which are founded on the largest practical experience of the ablest teachers and educationists of the present century.[62]

John C. Butts criticized the Irish series for failing to instruct students in oral reading and denounced the fifth reader for offering a 'visionary knowledge' of the sciences and 'no clear knowledge of any' particular science. Reading, in his view, should be pleasing as well as instructive and 'reading books should contain select pieces to interest both teacher and learner and call out all the energy of the mind.' Furthermore, he concluded, 'as children are fond of variety, the pieces selected should be calculated to please as well as instruct.'[63]

Ryerson suggested that Butts must be incompetent, for 'a teacher properly trained will find the National Series the greatest help in his work.' In his defense of the readers, Ryerson assumed Butts had begun with the end of the series.

There are four Readers before you come to the fifth, and in these, especially the third and fourth, there is a great variety of interesting and useful Selections.

The fifth reader gave an elementary, not a 'visionary', view of the sciences, 'and a very sound one too, if the teacher is acquainted with them & knows how to teach them.'[64]

Yet it was not simply 'incompetent' teachers who were complaining. The local superintendent of Woodstock wrote that the fourth reader was 'very heavy with an over abundance of hard names'. One of the Woodstock schools had adopted a different series of books in the 'hope of improving the reading of the pupils & cultivating a taste for good reading'. In Woodstock, there was 'nothing of which the Parents complain more than of' the fourth reader.[65] William Gunn from Bruce County, where 'the original tongue of a large proportion of the children' was 'Gallic', noted that the 'lessons in the National Books are found to be very 'dry'. Some of us have thought that the introduction of a more interesting work would be of service.'[66] Not so, replied Ryerson. 'The Second and third books and Sequels of the National Board are amusing as well as instructive for children,' and in any case he could not 'deviate from the catalogue so well considered and so long tried and used (and very extensively in Scotland also).'[67]

Respectable educational opinion in the 1860s began to echo the sentiments of local school supporters and students. Normal School graduates claimed they had long felt the Irish texts to be 'deficient and unsuitable'.[68] County School Conventions began to call for textbook revision.[69] Even the Hamilton Central School —flagship of the Normal school system— had to use spelling books in reading instruction.[70] Local school administrators began to abandon the Irish texts.[71] One correspondent claimed, in a chauvinist vein, that many American books were

> much more sensible and better adapted to the understanding of Children of Canada than your great National Series, for instance in the 1st Book of lessons we find such as this 'Jack rode a mule or a fine ass. Pat or Sam and Ned & Bog' &c now such trash might suit to learn young Irish but but we do not want such teaching in Canada...[72]

The conflict which finally led to textbook revision took place between the education office and Otto Klotz, the school superintendent for Preston. Klotz was an active proponent of public schooling. He had earlier been (and later was again) chairman of the Preston Board of School Trustees, and as such was instrumental in securing free schooling in the village in 1849. In 1852, the Preston trustees constructed a central school on the 'best principles', including separated and fenced playgrounds for boys and girls, desks and chairs, etc., at a cost of 400 pounds.

In 1865, while Klotz was superintendent of schools, the Preston trustees moved to introduce the American Sanders' Series of schoolbooks into the schools. This was done explicitly in opposition to the Irish series. Klotz wrote to Ryerson at length.

> I cannot withhold expressing my surprise that notwithstanding the unparalleled progress which Canada during the last twenty years, has made in her System of education...no Canadian Reading Books have yet been introduced and the public is bound by law to use books which in respect to geography and science are out of date, void of interest in reference to subjects they contain,... that have many paragraphs

> which instead of being instructive tend to mislead the pupils; that speak contemptuously of Canada and its present inhabitants, that are entirely silent on the history of Canada, but abound in a multitude of names of persons notorious for their vices and that even in point of morality are not pure.

Klotz stressed the dullness of the Irish books.

> And since it is a well known fact that books which contain an abundance of stale articles and are barren of interest and of spirit, cannot either instill life or vigor nor give pleasure while reading them; but will produce apathy and displeasure, it follows as a natural consequence that such books as the Irish National Readers are only read...,because the School Act makes it compulsory to read them....

Of course, Klotz was on solid ground. Even the authors of the Irish texts had justified them on the basis of their supposed ability to instruct *and* please.[73] But Klotz observed, 'children very seldom and voluntarily read in the Irish national readers while at home, though they frequently take up and study such other books within their reach.'[74] However, this initiative by the Preston Board provoked an unexpected reaction from the education office. Ryerson had successfully threatened the Guelph school board in 1859 with legal penalties for the use of unauthorized books.[75] To Klotz he wrote in March 1865 with a lengthy defense of the Irish texts and with a threat to withhold the school grant if the Preston trustees persisted in adopting American books.[76]

Klotz was not cowed. He replied with a detailed criticism of the Irish texts, in which he reproduced and dissected several passages which proved his points. Klotz remarked that it was ridiculous for Ryerson to suppose that the loss of the staggering sum of $13--- the Preston school grant--- would seriously influence the Board of Trustees. He went further. At his urging the Waterloo County Board of Public Instruction passed and published a resolution in April 1865 calling for a systematic textbook revision.[77]

Ryerson again attempted to defend the Irish Readers in his *Annual Report for 1865*. The Irish books were not really 'behind the times' or outdated. On the contrary, in England and Scotland, where a free market in schoolbooks obtained, they were by far the most popular. Even if the books did contain a few trivial errors in scientific subjects,

> a reader is not intended as a book of science, any more than the Holy Scriptures, which would be regarded on some matters of science, 'quite behind the times' by certain publishers of new books and their agents. The object of a school reader is not to teach science, but to teach the pupil to <u>read</u> — and the less the learner is diverted from that one object, while learning to read, the better.

'Diversity in the readers of a school,' Ryerson concluded, 'is inadmissible as much as diversity of text-books in a military school.'[78]

This position contradicted the basis of one aspect of the official politics of literacy. The argument that content was insignificant, since really 'reading' was at issue discounted the education office's preoccupation with the Irish texts as a means to 'sound' and 'meaningful' reading. The entire logic of curricular reform in the late 1840s was predicated upon the necessity of controlling meanings in schoolbooks and regulating their acquisition by students. Moreover, Ryerson was well aware of the inadequacies of the Irish texts. Late in 1859, for instance, he wrote to the President of McGill College describing the plans of the Council for Public Instruction to revise the Irish texts. 'We propose to proceed from one book to another until we get the whole Series <u>Canadianized</u>, and I hope improved.'[79] Education office employees were busy throughout the 1850s and 1860s attempting to produce works to fill gaps in the Irish series.[80]

Ryerson's debate with Klotz was about educational power. Here again the education office abandoned its progressive stance with respect to education as pleasure when pleasure threatened the structure of educational authority. In this instance, the education office suffered a minor defeat, and was forced to speed up its plans for textbook revisions. A new series appeared in 1868, and the shift was justified by the education office as a response to the demands of bodies such as the Waterloo County Board of Public Instruction.

While I do not propose to pursue this matter at length here, one should at least note the kinds of shifts in political organization, institutional structure and economic development taking place in the British empire and in capitalist nations more generally during this period. The Irish texts embodied the social politics of the rising and radical bourgeoisie. Capitalist industrialization was viewed as inherently rational and universally beneficial. Radical reformers argued that direct education in the theory of bourgeois civilization-- political economy and 'useful knowledge'-- would appeal to the intrinsic intelligence of all members of society, especially the masses. Reading these evident truths of bourgeois science would be pleasant to the popular reader. Simon has shown that the growing intensity of class struggle in England and elsewhere in the 1830s and 1840s gave the lie to these hopes, and blunted the radical edge of bourgeois reform.

By the 1860s, the basic relations of industrial capitalist production had been stabilized and normalized to a certain degree and bourgeois hegemony solidified. Political economy itself disintegrated into 'economics' and 'social science', bodies of thought which took bourgeois relations of production as given. In schoolbooks, direct lessons in the worth of bourgeois relations of production increasingly gave way to 'apolitical' lessons in 'universal literature and culture'. This was also the period in which the first books containing advice as to personal progress in bourgeois social structures achieved wide (and startling) circulation. Smiles' *Self-Help* is the obvious example. The organization and administration of popular political ignorance by states came increasingly to centre upon 'apolitical' teaching, and moved away from the rational refutation of 'obnoxious doctrines'. The shift from the Irish to the Canadian Readers embodied this more general transformation and demands an attention which is beyond the scope of the present study. A similar attention to gender socialization and to lessons on nationality and ethnicity is also necessary.[81]

## Control over Curriculum

The general process of empowering and making authoritative trustees and teachers was at once a process of removing power and authority in educational matters from students and 'parents' in the decades after 1850. Students and school supporters increasingly lost the power to determine what they would study at school, both individually and collectively. Local conflicts surrounded control over the curriculum.

One issue was the power of trustees under the School Act to tax the school section for the provision of school supplies. Scholars and school supporters before 1850 had themselves largely supplied books and apparatus to the schools, and after 1850 many continued to do so. This practice typically resulted in the provision of books and supplies at a level considered inadequate by many teachers and by the central office, especially as collective methods of instruction were adopted which demanded that each student have its own book. It did, however, give scholars and school supporters a large measure of control over what was taught and learned at school.

The School Act of 1850 empowered trustees to tax for the provision of school supplies, and until an Act of 1874 limited their taxation power to 20 cents per month per student, trustees had formally unlimited discretionary powers in this regard. Local ratepayers frequently opposed trustees who taxed the section for books and apparatus without first consulting them. However, the education office, as we have already seen, consistently defended the powers of trustees as *public* actors to define the the educational interests of the school section in ways which might be unpopular. The central office certainly attempted to ensure that trustees would behave as 'friends of education,' but where the activities of trustees accorded with central educational objectives, trustees were supported by the education office against the school section.

Although the residents of a school section in North Oxford Township had voted for the establishment of a free school, they opposed trustees who purchased a set of Holbrook's Apparatus from the education office on the grounds that 'the Children are not far enough advanced to be benefited by the use of them.' The trustees levied a rate-bill to pay for the Apparatus, but rate-payers objected 'because the Trustees procured them before consulting us.'[82] The trustees in section 11 of Mountain Township wrote that they 'felt ourselves in duty bound to get a set of books and slates &c for the whole school' after the teacher complained repeatedly of his inability to teach without them. 'There were a number of books in the school but not sufficient to classify the pupils properly.' Rate-payers complained of the trustees' exhorbitance in spending $20 (two months' salary for many female teachers) for books, but the education office assured the trustees that they had discretionary taxation powers in this area.[83] Again, in Palermo, when the trustees spent $24 for maps, an annual schoolmeeting voted that no expenditure should be made in excess of $4 without the approval of a public meeting of rate-payers. The education office assured the Palermo trustees that the power to make expenditures for school supplies was theirs alone, and was not subject to local approval.[84] This was an area in which the 'public' interest of education asserted itself against the collectively expressed interests of local proprietors.[85]

The education office also instructed trustees that they were legally bound to provide for the local delivery of the official curriculum in its entirety. A resident in Haldimand complained that the trustees had hired a teacher who could not teach his son Algebra, Geometry and Book-keeping. This person refused to pay his school rates, since he supported the boy outside the section. Ryerson insisted that school trustees 'ought certainly to employ a teacher qualified to teach all children whose parents' were taxed.[86] At other times, trustees were informed that they could hire whomever they pleased, but that the teacher must be qualified to teach all students in the section. The menace of fines for trustees for neglect of duty was implicit, but present nonetheless.[87]

Teachers, especially those trained in the Normal School, also actively opposed attempts by school supporters and trustees to curtail the official course of studies, or to allow exemptions from it. John Porter, a trustee in section 6 of Darlington Township claimed that the poor parents in his section could only afford to send their children to school in the winter, and were particularly concerned that they learn to read and write. Despite the efforts of the trustees to accommodate this concern, the teacher insisted that the students study geography, and buy geography books. When they refused, he expelled a large group of them.[88] David Forbes was concerned that his 'slow' daughter be taught to read and write, but the school teacher insisted she study grammar and geography.[89] Where teachers did attempt to vary the official programme to accommodate local interests, they might also be disciplined by the local superintendent. The education office instructed H. Cameron, local superintendent for Ross & Westmeath Townships, to threaten to withhold the school grant from a teacher who 'openly refuses or wilfully neglects to follow' the order of studies prescribed by the Council of Public Instruction.[90] A teacher in Townsend, who had so many students that he attempted to exclude those in advanced subjects, was instructed to teach all subjects but to give less time to each, and to 'vary his programme & time table accordingly'.[91]

The trustees in section 4 of Usborne Township were disgusted with the Normal School teacher they hired in 1858. This teacher asserted his authority under regulations from the Council of Public Instruction to demand uniformity in the use of textbooks and the provision of supplies. The trustees complained that he refused to admit children who didn't know the alphabet into the school, and attempted to exclude all those over eighteen as well. Students without slates were not admitted, and the trustees protested that 'if they should want a Peace of Pencil they are Sent on Some occasions two Miles home for it.' The trustees offered to pay the teacher to resign, but he refused.[92] When Alexander Henderson suspended students for not having books, one parent tried to have him charged before the local magistrate.[93] A teacher in section 10 of Eps Township refused to use the officially approved Morse's *Geography*, insisting that students acquire Lovell's. A teacher in Townsend also refused to teach Morse's text, and when people refused to supply Lovell's geography text, he stopped teaching geography.[94] A. Brown of South Mountain Township sought official instructions about a situation in which three arithmetic texts were used in her school, and in which school supporters also attempted to make her teach algebra.[95]

While some school supporters were undoubtedly opposed to supplying books to their local school out of parsimony, a simple economic analysis does not exhaust conflicts over school supplies. In addition to objecting to the expense of supplying the school, ratepayers protested against being taxed without being consulted. In some instances as well, opposition to demands from teachers that students be equipped with books was opposition to collective modes of instruction, classification, and the coincident loss of control over schooling by those subjected to it. For instance, J.H. Forde, a teacher in North Gower wrote to the education office in 1868 asking

> whether I am justified in sending home pupils who are not furnished with books etc. for the class to which they belong. The parents assert I have a right to teach them in what books they see fit to give them, and if they require other books in addition to

> those which they already have, I have no right to place them in a lower class, or send them home.

Forde remarked that if he was to classify students, 'it is imperative for each pupil (if able) to have authorized books, as is generally used in that class.' But parents opposed this, and Forde had been 'assailed by a few who rebel against those new books etc...'[96] Again, Francis Malcolm complained to the education office in 1870 that his children had been excluded from the local school because he attempted to interpret some of the passages in the Canadian Readers for them. He wrote,

> In the new series of school books there is certain lessons containing theological ideas which I am conscientiously opposed to my children learning. Opposite some of these ideas I made a few marginal notes in order to save them from contamination with what I believe to be error. The trustees with speaking about it refuse my children further admittance except I purchase new books, or excise the pencilling. The books belong to me.[97]

Neither of these cases were simply concerned with questions of the cost of schoolbooks, but rather with their connection to practices or doctrines considered offensive by school supporters.

## The Education Office and Local Control

In the early 1850s, the education office responded to queries about the rights of different parties in the determination of the course of studies by affirming its acceptance of the powers of school supporters. For instance, when the village trustees in Prescott fired a teacher in 1853 for refusing to teach Goldsmith's *History of England* on the grounds that it was offensive to the parents of Catholic children, the chief superintendent supported the trustees. He wrote that teachers could not refuse to teach what they were instructed to teach by trustees. The right of refusal rather rested *with parents of school children.*[98] This was probably an extension of the 'delicate treatment' urged by the Board of Education in disputes over texts.

However, by the late 1850s the traditional rights of school supporters in these matters were sharply curtailed in official policy, and by the 1860s, had largely been abolished.

For example, local conflicts surrounded the manner of teaching writing. As reading in the Normal School method was about meaning, rather than intonation, writing instruction meant to convey an easily verifiable method of expressing meaning. Students were to be taught a 'plain round hand' which was simple and easily legible. Writing instruction was no longer to involve the transmission of decorative styles. As the Council of Public Instruction wrote to the Normal School writing master in response to his co-authored writing text, sound method was concerned with

> teaching a plain round hand that can be easily read—
> the very object for which writing, as well as printing, was intended.[99]

In one of these disputes over writing in 1855, the chief superintendent replied to a Normal School graduate that

> although it is the teacher's right to teach each subject in his school in the manner he thinks best, yet I think it is the right of a parent or guardian to say whether his child shall be taught to write in a round or running hand. But the manner of teaching the Child to write either hand is with the teacher.

Ryerson went further, adding that it was 'the right of the parent to say whether his child shall or shall not be taught certain subjects or skill[s] of [a] particular kind.'[100]

The question was put again by a school trustee in section 1 of Moulton Township in 1857. Here a school supporter had refused to allow his son to study grammar and refused to send any grammar books to school. The teacher refused to admit the boy without them, and the trustees did not know how to act. Disputes over grammar teaching were common, but here one of the trustees posed the question explicitly:

> Question.
> Has the Teacher or the Parent the right to decide what Study the Pupil Shall follow and the manner time and place in the school.

The chief superintendent replied that 'the parent has a right to say what branches his child shall study.' However, the parent had no right to determine 'what book the child shall use in studying any branch or subject, nor in what classes he shall study, nor in what manner he shall be taught.' Not only this, but Ryerson added, 'a teacher is not required to take a child's word for discontinuing the study of any branch, or commencing a new one, but only the request of the parent personally or in writing.'[101]

This initial position of official toleration (and at the same time, organization) of school supporters' determination of areas of study did not apply to students themselves. Teachers, with the approval of trustees, specified what students would learn, in keeping with the official programme of studies. In section 3 of Kitley Township, for instance, a recently hired Normal School teacher told his students to write a composition. This was a novel phenomenon, and a 16 year old boy refused. When the teacher asked him for an explanation, he said 'he would not write such trash'. The teacher suspended him, and his father sought a ruling on the question from the chief superintendent. Ryerson was quite explicit. 'There would be an end to all discipline,' he wrote, 'if each pupil could decide what should & should not be taught in a School....the Dept. approves of the conduct of the Teacher.'[102] The interests of students and the interests of the public were incompatible in principle in this view.

Control over the course of studies in many areas continued to be exercised by students themselves, by parents, and by ratepayers. The head master of Kincardine Union School complained that parents did not send books for some subjects which they did not wish taught.[103] School supporters in Preston objected to the teaching of physiology,[104] in Cornwall Township to English history,[105] in Londesborough and elsewhere to grammar,[106] and in other places to geography.[107] A.J. Fotheringham, a teacher from Thorold, found it difficult to teach effectively if he acceded to the demands of students--- who he said were supported by ratepayers--- for exemptions from some subjects.[108]

By the mid-1860s, the education office was insisting that parents and students had no right to demand exclusions or exemptions in relation to the official programme of studies. The chief superintendent wrote to the trustees of the Union School in Belmont in 1864,

> Nor can a ratepayer require particular subjects to his children & others ommitted. If such were allowed there could be no classification of the pupils; no

proper competition among the pupils, & some of them might be half the time unemployed.... The School is established to teach certain subjects & in regular order; it is not for any one person to interfere with the system thus provided for & prescribed.[109]

In a later communication to the trustees in Woodhouse, Ryerson argued that teachers were completely independent of parents in the area of the course of studies, and could also enforce the official subjects.

The teacher alone can decide what studies pupils shall pursue in the School. He may confer with the parents in particular cases but he is not bound to follow their counsel... the teacher is the judge as to what the pupil shall or shall not learn & can award punishment in all cases of neglect or omission to follow his instructions.[110]

The distance traversed in the formal organization of school knowledge from the 1840s to the 1860s was remarkable: from a free market in schooling, on which students studied such books as 'subscribers might care to send,' to the uniform, graded and 'useful' course of studies enforced by the Council of Public Instruction—over the opposition of school supporters and students if necessary. This was a major transformation indeed. School knowledge became official knowledge, rationally administered to a population, certified through examination, enforced in many cases by direct violence in the schoolroom.

## Limitations

Of course, policy statements from the centre did not automatically transform existing educational relations. Policy had to be disposed in the locality, made effective, put in place and enforced. Local school managers could oppose aspects of official policy, and in the area of the course of study could do so fairly effectively. With the support of local proprietors, they could hire teachers who would not insist on all aspects of the official course of studies, or who might not be capable of teaching the entire course. They hired and fired teachers, and this gave them considerable influence.

Again, as the necessity of the 'school disturbers' clause in the School Act of 1853 indicates, teachers who taught in ways uncongenial to rate-payers frequently needed protection against those rate-payers. David Linn, the secretary of the trustees in section 4 of Storrington Township complained in 1866, for instance, that

> there are parties who go to the School, dictate to the Teacher what branches & books their children shall study, how they shall study what amount of tasks they shall get and forbid the punishment of their children at school...[111]

A teacher in Springford wondered in 1869,

> Have parents or guardians any right to meddle with a Teacher's mode of conducting a school by telling him he must do so & so; and must not do so & so? must or must not punish in certain ways &c? Have they any right to come into the school room and dictate to the Teacher how he must govern the school and threaten to beat him if he don't do as he commands?... is there nothing I can do to prevent the parents from coming to the school and abusing me...?[112]

Direct intervention of local school supporters into pedagogical space and process was very common during this period, and undoubtedly limited the capacity of local educational managers to administer official knowledge in official ways. As we shall see at more length in the following chapter, popular opposition to the enforcement of the official curriculum at times spilled out of the school itself, and connected with other local authority structures, to render the administration of state knowledge difficult. William Plunkett, for instance, a teacher in section 25 of North Dumfries, beat a student for 'not bringing his books to school, bad lessons, & not trying to perform his exercises after being repeatedly told.' Plunkett was arrested in the school house by the Baliff, after the student's father lodged a complaint with the local justice, and was fined $12 and costs.[113] These forms of local opposition were under constant pressure from the normalizing power of educational practice, but they were very common in this formative period. Control over school knowledge was wrested away from students and school supporters only through a process of struggle.

## Collective Instruction

The curricular reforms of the period 1846-50 assumed that schools would be graded and that students would exposed to a common curriculum in groups. The modes of individual instruction, in which small numbers of students or even individual students learned particular subjects in a face-to-face relation with the teacher, were to be abandoned. An official body of knowledge was specified, and as we have seen in chapter six, it was held that 'the teacher makes the school'.

The discourse of public educational reform in Canada West embodied an explicit critique of the forms of collective instruction current in many parts of Europe and America known as 'monitorial' schooling. In these methods, which were first generalized by Andrew Bell and Joseph Lancaster,[114] groups of as large as six hundred students were instructed by one teacher with the aid of student assistants or 'monitors'. Only very rudimentary instruction was offered, and that by rote. The system failed miserably, on the whole, and was consistently criticized by a variety of educational writers for its inability to form the selves of students. As we have seen in chapter three, Egerton Ryerson in Canada West participated in this criticism, and urged expanded instructional activity.

In the 1860s, Ryerson maintained the same position. For example, John Paton wrote in 1862 that the Kingston schools were overcrowded, and the children of the rich were taking places designed for those of the poor. He suggested the employment of monitors, but Ryerson replied, 'the employment of monitors is the Lancasterian plan,-- has never been satisfactory to *the parents of children taught by monitors* & has never been successful. It has long since been abandoned in countries where it was once introduced.'[115]
However, the official plan for expanded instructional activity by highly trained teachers quickly encountered insurmountable limits. Enrollments were so large and teachers so few that the possibilities

of enriched instructional activity were very restricted. By the middle 1850s, the education office was receiving a considerable correspondence from teachers seeking ways to cope with huge classes. 'This Dunnville School is too large for one teacher,' wrote N.L. Holmes in 1856. 'The males and females are about equal in number, there being about 150 of each. The girls have two teachers while I have sole charge of the boys. Were the boys any thing like equal, in point of qualifications, I could manage them; but they are not....'[116] At best, the qualified Normal School teacher was supposed to be able to teach a homogeneous class of 50-60. By 1865, average enrollments were 81+ per teacher, and country schools usually had five classes. In this situation, educational administrators sought to use monitors.

J. Gray, the superintendent for Oro Township, proposed a monitorial school plan in 1855. 'The Free School System,' he wrote in July, 'has so increased the attendance, that many of the Teachers find themselves unable to undertake their duties.' Gray suggested the enactment of a pupil-teacher training system for Canada, like that in operation in England. One monitor would be appointed for a school with 45 pupils and two for 70 pupils. Monitors would be paid five pounds, supervised by the local superintendent, and admitted to the Normal School. The deputy superintendent replied that monitors were allowed, as local school administrators wished, and Gray's plans deserved 'public attention.'[117] 'Is it possible for two teachers to impart efficient instruction to an average of 135 pupils without the aid of monitors?' wondered W.A. Gordon and Anne Ward of Wardsville.[118] 'I am teacher of a Common School and have under my charge 126 pupils,' wrote Alfred Letercheux of Portsmouth. 'Having no assistant I am compelled to have recourse to monitors.'[119] The Principal of the Brantford Central School advocated the employment of monitors to aid 'Miss Turnbull' and 'Miss Muklejohn' in 1862, and a teacher in section 9 of Usborne Township earned $700 a year by teaching an entire school with the aid of two monitors.[120]

However, school supporters frequently opposed the use of monitors, and students themselves at times refused to serve. W.A. Gordon and Anne Ward attempted to compel students to act as monitors, with little success.[121] J.P. Hollway from London appointed a female student as a monitor, but she refused to serve, on her father's insistence. When she refused to hear the younger students read, Hollway attempted to suspend her.[122] John Muir returned to his seat and insisted, '*I am not going to be teached by Scholars,*' when L.F. Hardie attempted to turn over his arithmetic class to a monitor. '*My father told me I was not to be teached by Scholars.*' Hardie suspended Muir, but the trustees forced him to re-admit the boy.[123] By 1864, the Court of Queen's Bench had ruled that no part of the school tax could be paid to any but legally qualified teachers. The education office counseled local school administrators that they should pay monitors by private subscription.[124]

## Conclusion

The transformation in the structure and organization of school knowledge effected by the education office in Canada West over the course of the two and a half decades from 1846 to 1871 was remarkably extensive. Books, blackboards, slates, individual desks, inkwells, and much of the other apparatus of collective public instruction, became general throughout the province. Instructional methods changed. Collective instruction tended to replace individual instruction. School knowledge and skills were oriented towards practice and meaningfulness, and away from decoration and religious doctrine. The control exerted by school consumers and teachers over school knowledge and school methods was removed in principle, and increasingly in practice, and was vested in a centralized public authority. The free market in school knowledge largely disappeared. School knowledge became state knowledge, uniform, specified from the centre, administered to students in homogeneous classes, and enforced at times by the application of physical violence.

The promise of these reforms was democracy, culture and pleasure. They announced themselves in these terms. Yet the material and political conditions of schooling in Canada West nullified this promise. Many people experienced official knowledge as unpleasant and official methods as ineffective. Enriched instructional activity was undercut by collective instructional methods and by the press of numbers under conditions of material deprivation. Tax supported schools, in conjunction with wider political economic transformations, increased school enrollments, at the same time as the imposition of political 'qualifications' reduced the supply of potential teachers.

Local school supporters frequently acted to seize the democratic and pleasurable dimension of educational discourse, and at times to direct this against the reality of bureaucratic educational authority. The central education office just as frequently asserted the priority of its authority structures against local participatory democracy and student pleasure. The contradiction of pleasure and external authority could not be resolved within the confines of the educational system. It generated conflicts which dominated educational institutions and relations throughout the formative period. School rooms were frequently the sites of violent struggles, in which teachers attempted to 'govern' by physical, as well as moral force. School supporters frequently insisted upon the 'gentle' teaching promised by educational reformers, but as the next chapter shows, educational administrators were not prepared to dispense with the use of physical violence in instruction.

## Notes

1. Curtis, 'Schoolbooks and the Myth of Curricular Republicanism: The State and the Curriculum in Canada West, 1820-1850,' *Histoire Sociale/Social History* 16(32), 1983:305-29.
2. See for example, V.E. Parvin, *The Authorization of Textbooks for the Schools of Ontario, 1846-1950*. (Toronto: University of Toronto Press, 1965).
3. My own copy is *Fifth Book of Lessons, for the Use of Schools*. (Toronto: Robert McPhail, 1861). It is the *Fourth Book of Lessons* which is full of political economic doctrine. The *Fifth* is much more natural-theologic. For age-grading of the readers, PAO RG2 C6C, A Martin, local superintendent, Napanee, 6 March 1860.
4. I cover this question at length in 'The Speller Expelled: Disciplining the Common Reader in Canada West,' *Canadian Review of Sociology and Anthropology*. 22(3) 1985:346-68. See also, Elizabeth Mayo, *Lessons on Objects*. (London: Seeley's, 1851).
5. PAO RG2 C6C, Dexter D'Everardo, Fonthill, 19 October 1846.

6. PAO RG2 B2, Minutes of the (Second) General Board of Education, 30 October 1846.

7. PAO RG2 C1C, Ryerson to D'Everardo, 30 October 1846. Also, Ryerson to R. Waugh, District Superintendent, Johnstown District, 3 September 1847. 'I think the Gentler method will be found more successful in accomplishing the object we have in view.'

8. See Curtis, 'Schoolbooks,' and Parvin, *Authorization of Textbooks*.

9. PAO MU972 General Manuscripts Collection, Robert McKee Moore's Register and Day Book, W. Gwillimbury Twp; Ardagh's remarks are in the entry for 21 August 1846.

10. J.G. Hodgins, *Documentary History of Education in Upper Canada*. (Toronto: L.K. Cameron, 1894-1910)VI:67.

11. PAO RG2 C6C, Benjamin Hayter, District Superintendent, Cobourg, 18 March 1850; Thomas Marshall, Teacher, section 6, Ellice & Logan, 12 February 1870.

12. Curtis, 'Schoolbooks'.

13. PAO MU972, Dally replaces Moore in 1846.

14. PAO RG2 C6C, T.J. Grove, Mosa, 18 February 1852.

15. PAO RG2 C6C, J.L. Hughes, Teacher, Brantford, 7 April 1851.

16. PAO RG2 C6C, 'A normal school teacher' 18 November 1856; Trustees, section 5 West Flamboro, 17 February 1860; Teacher, section 11 Haldemand, 26 June 1862.

17. These are to be found in PAO RG2, F2, 'Miscellaneous School Reports'.

18. PAO RG2 C6C, John Langworth, Trustee, Goderich, 16 December 1856; C1T, Ryerson to Langworth, 29 December 1856.

19. PAO RG2 C6C, T. Cross, Chatham, 20 July 1852.

20. PAO RG2 C6C, 'Resolution', Board of School Trustees, Preston, 4 April 1853.

21. PAO RG2 C6C, John Holmes, Section 7 Wolfe Island, 8 March 1853.

22. PAO RG2 C6C, for instance, H. Goring, Wolfe Island, 8 March 1853.

23. PAO RG2 C6C, W.D. Donaldson, section 4 West Flamboro, 19 January 1856; C1Q, Hodgins to Donaldson, 29 January 1856.

24. PAO RG2 C6C, E. O'Neill, section 3 North Norwich, 24 March 1864; C2, Ryerson to O'Neill, 29 March 1864.

25. PAO RG2 C6C, J.M. Mechum, Berlin, 11 February 1862.

26. PAO RG2 C6C, W.M. Wilson, Simcoe, 27 January 1852.

27. PAO RG2 C6C, Thomas Sloan, superintendent, Morris & Grey, 11 June 1858.
28. PAO RG2 C6C, Rev. R. Stevenson, local superintendent, East Williams, 24 April 1862.
29. PAO RG2 C6C, H. Doyle, Trustee, section 3 Usborne, 13 April 1863.
30. PAO RG2 C6C, David Williams, Teacher, section 3 Hallowell, 2 February 1857.
31. See R.D. McDowell, *The Irish Administration, 1801-1914.* (Toronto: University of Toronto Press, 1964).
32. For one salvo in the battle, PAO RG2 C1F, Ryerson to Catholic Bishop of Toronto, 13 March 1852.
33. PAO RG2 C1N, Ryerson to Trustees, section 3 Lancaster, 24 January 1855; Ryerson to A.S. Bain, section 3 Lancaster, 20 January 1855.
34. PAO RG2 C6C, Geo. Cox, London, 13 January 1859.
35. PAO RG2 C6C, A. Sinclair, Teacher, section 10 Beckwith, 26 January 1857; C1T, Ryerson to Sinclair, 31 January 1857.
36. PAO RG2 C6C, James Gibson, section 13 Markham, 23 June 1859.
37. PAO RG2 C6C, Robert Brown, Cornwall, 22 February 1858; C1X, Ryerson to Brown, 25 February 1858; see earlier C1O, Ryerson to Superintendent of Common Schools, Cornwall, 20 June 1855.
38. PAO RG2 C6C, Edward Clegg, Trustee, section 9 Wellesley, 24 July 1856.
39. PAO RG2 C6C, T.J. Hodgskin, superintendent, Etobicoke, January ? 1851.
40. PAO RG2 C1N, Ryerson to Rev. William Fraser, superintendent, W. Gwillimbury, 7 February 1855.
41. PAO RG2 C6C, David Baptie, Teacher, section 8 S. Dumfries, 21 February 1859; C2, Ryerson to Baptie, 24 February 1859; also, C6C, D. Muirhead, Trustee, section 4 Otonabee, 28 April 1862.
42. See Curtis, 'Speller Expelled'.
43. The quotation is from William Hutton's annual report for 1849:'I have done as much as I possibly could to consign to disuse the unmeaning, and unintelligible, and enslaving columns of the spelling book.' in *Annual Report of the Chief Superintendent of Education....1849.*
44. In this regard see Richard Altick, *The English Common Reader.* (Chicago: University of Chicago Press, 1963); R.K. Webb, *The British*

*Working Class Reader*. (New York: A.M. Kelley, 1971). Much work remains to be done in this area, particularly in connecting the spread of particular elements of educational technology to new political objectives for education. See Keith Hoskin, 'Examinations and the Schooling of Science,' in R. Macleod (ed) *Days of Judgement*. (London: Nafferton, 1982):213-35.

45. PAO RG2 C6C, J. Stewart, superintendent, Stratford, 12 January 1855.
46. PAO RG2 C6C, John Nairn, superintendent, Huron County, 18 May 1855.
47. PAO RG2 C6C, John Carson, Teacher section 2 Tecumseh, 11 January 1862.
48. PAO RG2 C6C, W.A. McCullough, Greenwood, 31 December 1856; C1T, Ryerson to McCullough, 5 January 1857.
49. PAO RG2 C6C, T.W. Lillie, Teacher, South Crosbie, 15 November 1854.
50. PAO RG2 C6C, Superintendent, Ingersoll, 13 February 1854. But one must be careful with this kind of denunciation. I don't wish to argue that Ingersoll was full of organic proletarian intellectuals. 'Know-nothingism' was common in Canada West, and I see no virtue in defending it against the progressive edge of pedagogical reform. At the same time, we must not lose sight of the fact that education was about the formation of sound bourgeois character in the lower orders. This was a class initiative, and the rejection of 'interventionist' pedagogy should not be equated to a rejection of all pedagogy.
51. PAO RG2 C6C, Trustees, section 12 Vaughan, 15 February 1853.
52. PAO RG2 C6C, John Richardson, Trustee, section 10 Caledon, 5 December 1862.
53. PAO RG2 C6C, William Galt, Scarborough, 14 March 1856. These people were also *right!* The education office was forced to reintroduce spelling books in 1867.
54. PAO RG2 C6C, John Barker, Warwich, 17 May 1851; C1E, Ryerson to Barker, 7 June 1851.
55. PAO RG2 C6C, H. Armstrong, Teacher, Matilda, 9 May 1861.
56. PAO RG2 C6C, T.N. Robertson, Teacher, Fenelon Falls, 20 July 1858; Daniel Wright, superintendent, Fenelon Falls, 27 July 1858.
57. PAO 'Schoolbooks Collection', Lindley Murray, *The English Reader,* an edition from 1816 has the flyleaf inscription.
58. PAO RG2 C6C, George Grafftley, Teacher, Claremont, 24 January

1859.
59.PAO RG2 C6C, Edward Scarlett, 'Report on the State of Education, Co. of Northumberland, 1855-6' March 1856.
60.PAO RG2 C6C, R Monteath, superintendent Reach & Scugog, 9 March 1857.
61.PAO RG2 C6C, H. McRae, superintendent, Charlottenburgh, 12 March 1857; G.H. Grierson, Trustee, Central School, Oshawa, 4 March 1858.
62.PAO RG2 C1E, Ryerson to T.W. Lillie, South Crosby, 25 November 1854.
63.PAO RG2 C6C, John C. Butts, Teacher, Ontario, 29 April 1857.
64.PAO RG2 C1U, Ryerson to Butts, 11 May 1857.
65.PAO RG2 C6C, J. Cooper, superintendent, Woodstock, 6 February 1856.
66.PAO RG2 C6C, Wm. Gunn, superintendent, Division 1 Bruce County, 11 November 1856.
67.PAO RG2 C1T, Ryerson to Gunn, 3 January 1857.
68.PAO RG2 C6C, H. McColl, Teacher, section 4 Lobo, 24 April 1863.
69.PAO RG2 C6C, 'Minutes', County School Convention, County of York, 20 February 1860.
70.PAO RG2 C6C, A. Macallum, Hamilton Central School, 8 June 1861.
71.PAO RG2 C6C, for instance, Trustee, section 1 Wilmot, 30 June 1866.
72.PAO RG2 C6C, A.A. Munro, Mallorytown, 10 May 1864; C2, Ryerson to Munro, 14 May 1864.
73.For example, Richard Whately, *Introductory Lectures on Political Economy [1833]*. (London:J.W. Parker, 1855):133-4.
74.PAO RG2 C6C, Otto Klotz, Preston, 4 March 1865; for the plan of the Preston free school, see Otto Klotz, Preston, 2 August 1852.
75.PAO RG2 C2, Ryerson to Rev. Robert Torrance, Guelph, 15 April 1869. There were other similar threats which had worked.
76.PAO RG2 C2, Ryerson to Klotz, 13 March 1865.
77.PAO RG2 C6C, Otto Klotz, Preston, 12 April 1865; *Memorial to the Council of Public Instruction of Upper Canada, From the Board of Public Instruction of the County of Waterloo*. (Galt: Reporter Office, 1865).
78.*Annual Report of the Chief Superintendent of Education, 1865:10-11*.

79. PAO RG2 C2, Ryerson to J.W. Dawson, President of McGill College, 8 November 1859.
80. Parvin, *Authorization of Textbooks:38-9*.
81. Brian Simon, *The Two Nations and the Educational Structure, 1780-1870*. (London: Lawrence & Wishart, 1974) I have expanded these arguments in 'Curricular change and the Red Readers: history and theory,' forthcoming in G. Milburn ed. *Quality in the Curriculum*.
82. Parvin, *Authorization of Textbooks,:37*; PAO RG2 C6C, J. Lowes and others, North Oxford, 24 April 1851.
83. PAO RG2 C6C, Trustees, section 11 Mountain, 2 November 1856; C1T, Ryerson to Trustees, 8 November 1856.
84. PAO RG2 C6C, H.M. Switzer, Palermo, 27 November 1852; Ryerson to Switzer, 30 November 1852.
85. For another example, PAO RG2 C6C, James Carey, section 2 Loughborough, 23 January 1865; C2, Ryerson to Carey 26 January 1865.
86. PAO RG2 C6C, Local superintendent, Haldimand, 11 December 1854; C1M, Ryerson to superintendent, 16 December 1854.
87. For example, PAO RG2 C2, Ryerson to W. Price, Trustee, section 11 Toronto, 21 June 1864.
88. PAO RG2 C6C, John Porter, Trustee, section 6 Darlington, 16 March 1863.
89. PAO RG2 C6C, David Forbes, section 3 Roxborough, 27 April; 20 May 1863.
90. PAO RG2 C6C, H. Cameron, superintendent, Ross & Westmeath, 12 April 1866; C2 Ryerson to Cameron, 21 April 1866.
91. PAO RG2 C2, Ryerson to J.B. Goodspeed, Townsend, 13 September 1865.
92. PAO RG2 C6C, Trustees, section 4 Usborne, 21 July 1858.
93. PAO RG2 C6C, Alexander Henderson, section 9 Carrick, 5 March 1870.
94. PAO RG2 C6C, John Mather, Trustee, section 10 Eps, 8 May 1863; Allen M. Crook, Townsend, 2 January 1863.
95. PAO RG2 C6C, A. Brown, South Mountain, 4 March 1861.
96. PAO RG2 C6C, J.H. Forde, North Gower, 9 March 1869.
97. PAO RG2 C6C, Francis Malcolm, Innerkip, 31 March 1870.
98. PAO RG2 C6C, County School Convention, Brockville, 25 February 1853; C1H, Ryerson to Board of Trustees, Prescott, 4 March 1853.

99. PAO RG2 C2, Ryerson to H.G. Strachan, Writing Master, Normal and Model Schools, 12 April 1864.
100. PAO RG2 C1M, Ryerson to D.Y. Hoyte [Hoit?], Teacher, London Township, 17 January 1855.
101. PAO RG2 C6C, A. Brownson, Trustee, section 1 Moulton, 22 January 1857; C1T, Ryerson to Brownson, 26 January 1857.
102. PAO RG2 C6C, J.G. Scovil, Trustee, section 3 Kitley, 6 March 1862; Francis Wright, Kitley, 6 March 1862; C2, Ryerson to Wright, 17 March 1862; Ryerson to Scovil, 17 March 1862.
103. PAO RG2 C6C, Albert Andrews, Head Master, Kincardine, 26 December 1862.
104. PAO RG2 C6C, Otto Klotz, Preston, 1 April 1870.
105. PAO RG2 C6C, Emma Bartley, Teacher, section 11 Cornwall, 27 September 1865.
106. PAO RG2 C6C, David R. Gordon, Teacher. Londesborough, 1 October 1866.
107. PAO RG2 C6C, Trustees, section 4 Brant, 15 June 1867.
108. PAO RG2 C6C, A.J. Fotheringham, Thorold, 5 March 1867.
109. PAO RG2 C2, Ryerson to Trustees, Union School Section 1 Belmont, 11 January 1864.
110. PAO RG2 C2, Ryerson to A.J. Pegg, Secretary, Woodhouse, 12 February 1866.
111. PAO RG2 C6C, David Linn, Trustee, section 4 Storrington, 6 February 1866.
112. PAO RG2 C6C, W.R. Latimer, Teacher, Springford, no.4112 May 1869.
113. PAO RG2 C6C, William Plunkett, section 25 N. Dumfries, 8 November 1859.
114. Joseph Lancaster, *Improvements in Education, as it respects the industrious classes of the community.* (London: Darton and Harvey, 1805); D. Salmon (ed) *The Practical Parts of Lancaster's Improvements and Bell's Experiment.* (Cambridge: Cambridge University Press, 1932).
115. PAO RG2 C6C, John Paton, Kingston, 15 January 1862; C2, Ryerson to Paton, 20 January 1862, *my italics.*
116. PAO RG2 C6C, N.L. Holmes, Dunnville, 10 November 1856.
117. PAO RG2 C6C, J. Gray, superintendent, Oro Township, Orillia, 9 July 1855.
118. PAO RG2 C6C, W.A. Gordon and Anne Ward, Teachers,

Wardsville, 1 September 1865.
119. PAO RG2 C6C, Alfred Letercheux, Teacher, Portsmouth, 10 April 1865.
120. PAO RG2 C6C, Trustees, section 9 Usborne, 2 January 1869; 'School Trustees Meeting' Brantford, 7 February 1862.
121. see note 118.
122. PAO RG2 C6C, J.P. Hollway, Teacher, London, 25 August 1860.
123. PAO RG2 C6C, L.F. Hardie, Teacher, section 23 Burford, 18 January 1866.
124. PAO RG2 C2, Ryerson to Chas. Rathburn, Trustee, Drumbo, 14 January 1865, contains the notification of the CQB decision; also,C1CC, Ryerson to Andrew Fraser, Trustee, Martintown, 24 December 1859.

# Chapter Eight: Pedagogy, Punishment and Popular Resistance

By the late 1840s, middle class educational theory as a whole had come to imagine the possibility of a gentle, pleasurable and effective education for the working class.[1] Many writers and several managers of well-known schools had come to argue for the complete abolition of corporal punishment in school government. Scottish writers and pedagogues were particularly influential in this regard. In several Scottish schools corporal punishment had been completely eliminated and this fact was widely publicized in the educational literature. The works of James Pillans and David Stow attracted an international audience.

Pillans' *Principles of Elementary Teaching,* first published in 1828, mounted a systematic attack on the use of corporal punishment in schools. Pillans noted that the 'trend of the age' was 'to substitute mental activity and agreeable excitement' in school teaching, 'in place of the languour, weariness, and aversion to all things scholastic' which had hitherto prevailed.[2] He stressed that in keeping school, *'corporal punishment is not to be resorted to till every other method of correction has failed,'* and claimed that 'if the child is properly trained from the commencement, I deny the necessity of the lash in any instance.'[3] Pillans' denunciation of corporal punishment became standard fare in later works. He wrote that the lash,

> is bad, because it humbles, degrades, and lays prostrate the understanding of the sufferer,--- because it establishes disagreeable and disgusting associations with the business of mental cultivation, --- because, however equitably the stripes may be doled out in number and severity, they affect very differently different tempers, and are felt most acutely by those least deserving of punishment,--- because they make a hero, in the eyes of his school-fellows, of the most hardened offender, --- because the infliction of them, with its usual accompaniments, consumes time unprofitably, --- and because, however administered, they have a tendency to estrange the pupil, not from

his books only, but also from his teacher.[4]

In the school run by David Stow in Glasgow, corporal punishment was also largely abolished. Stow argued that 'we ought never to associate the idea of punishment with what we should love. A child ought to love school, and his teacher, and his exercises.' Students should be led to obey 'from a fear of offending, rather than from a fear of the rod.'[5] Stow published a list of rules for effective and gentle school management which included, *'Never push a child or pull him out by the arm.* To speak ought to be sufficient......' and,

> When a pupil disobeys or breaks a rule, *do not scold* --- picture out his fault...if a second or repeated offence... punish him by depriving him of something he enjoys. Take care, however, that the deprivation be short, and not such as will tempt his companions to feel more for his punishment than sympathize with you in your displeasure and condemnation of the offence committed.[6]

In both the High School of Edinburgh, where Pillans taught, and Stow's Glasgow school, carefully planned and continuous pedagogical activity, rich instructional materials, and a bond of 'sympathy' between teacher and students removed the occasion for corporal punishment. These institutions were very influential in shaping the views of contemporary educators in many countries.

In the summer of 1837, for example, Dr. James Kay, then an Assistant Poor Law Commissioner, but later (as Sir J.P. Kay-Shuttleworth) Secretary to the English Privy Council Committee of Education, had a disturbing experience. He was sent to investigate a case of cruelty alleged against a Mr. Drouet who ran a contractor's establishment for boys. As a punishment, two boys in this establishment had been chained to a log for periods of up to a week. The log weighed between ten and twelve pounds and the chains were a yard and a half long. The schoolmaster 'had been a captain in the artillery, and it was clear that he kept his 120 boys in order by the liberal use of a cane across the shoulders.'[7] Shortly thereafter, Kay visited the schools of Edinburgh and Glasgow. He was enormously impressed, and recruited trained Scottish teachers for the workhouse schools in his district and for the training school at Battersea which he opened soon after.[8] In his widely-read second report on the Battersea school, Kay claimed that skillful teaching could eliminate the necessity of the rod in the schoolroom.[9] In an unpublished paper entitled 'On the Punishment of Pauper Children in Workhouses' (1841), Kay urged the publication of an order by Poor Law Commissions banning all corporal punishment of workhouse children. He explicitly connected a reform of this practice to more general political reform.

> One great step in the reformation of judicial procedure was the disuse of torture, which led to more rational and just methods of investigation. In the same way, the prohibition of Corporal chastisement in Schools may be regarded as a means of rendering all the processes of instruction rational.[10]

For Kay, proper school punishments aimed at the conscience and not at the flesh of the child. They were to be rare, corrective rather than exemplary, and delivered only after due reflection by the master. He urged teacher training and the creation of an affectionate bond with students as means of eliminating physical punishment.[11]

Virtually identical views were published in 1840 by the Secretary of the Massachusetts Board of Education, Horace Mann. Mann argued that some corporal punishment would always be necessary, given that children came to school with 'inadequate upbringing', but progressive educational practices could minimize physical violence. Mann also emphasized the necessity of reaching the conscience of the student, and pointed to the limitations of corporal punishment in this regard. 'A child may surrender to fear, without surrendering to principle. But it is the surrender to principle only which has any permanent value....Punishment excites fear.... and fear is a most debasing, demoralizing passage.'[12] The teacher, in Mann's view, should strive progressively to move from physical to moral means of school discipline.

> ... the teacher's physical power is superior to the pupil's physical power (for the teacher has a legal right to summon all necessary assistance to his aid); and, with this superiority, he must begin the work of reform. Order must be maintained; this is the primal law.... As soon as possible, however, the teacher must ascend from the low superiority of muscular force to the higher and spiritual ones; and he must forever cultivate the higher, that they may the sooner

supersede the lower.[13]

Mann's writings influenced a broad spectrum of contemporary opinion, including a section of the artisanal population. He was particularly important in acquainting an English-speaking public with the methods of schooling prevalent in Prussia where, he claimed, 'inductive' pedagogy had displaced corporal punishment. In a passage on the Prussian schools which was widely reproduced, Mann wrote that during the entire time of his visit to Prussian schools,

> I never saw a blow struck, I never heard a sharp rebuke given, I never saw a child in tears, nor arraigned at the Teacher's bar for any alleged misconduct.... I heard no child ridiculed, sneered at, or scolded for making a mistake.... No child was disconcerted, disabled, or bereft of his senses, through fear.... I enquired whether corporeal punishment [was] allowed or used, and I was uniformly answered in the affirmative. But it was further said, that, though all Teachers had liberty to use it, yet cases of its occurrence were very rare, and these cases were confined almost wholly to young scholars.[14]

Lyman J. Cobb, the author of the popular *Cobb's Spelling Book*, published *The Evil Tendencies of Corporal Punishment as a Means of Moral Discipline in Families and Schools, Examined and Discussed* in 1847, and this work circulated in Canada West. Cobb presented thirty more or less detailed arguments against the use of corporal punishment, and listed forty alternatives to or 'preventives of the rod'. Corporal punishment was said to debase those who administered it and to degrade those who received it. It could not address the 'heart' of the student, and in no way could improve the offender. It encouraged lying by students, created sympathy for the offender on the part of witnesses, and thus undercut the authority of the teacher. Parents opposed the whipping of their children at school, and hence would also question the teacher's authority.

Those most likely to be punished by physical violence, according to Cobb, were the least shrewd and artful. The beating of students thus created that individual so feared by middle class educators: the intelligent rogue, the sly deceiver; a person trained at school to dissemble; a liar equipped with the intelligence and ability derived from the course of study.

Punishment destroyed all pleasure that students might take in their education. It created a spirit of antagonism at school which discouraged attendance and made students hate to learn. Punishers habitually lost control of themselves, particularly in face of the refusal of students to yield, which Cobb regarded as itself almost inevitable. Punishers resorted to violence rather than attempting to reason with miscreants, and the student never reasoned with at school could not grow up to be a reasonable being. Cobb concluded,

> It also HARDENS the feelings of all pupils to see the teacher walking the school-room with a whip constantly in his hand.... It is neither *just, republican,* nor *democratic* to occupy the time of the school, hour after hour, in whipping a *portion* of the boys, when the *majority* are NOT disobedient.[15]

The alternative to physical violence in the schoolroom, for Cobb as for middle class writers generally, was the creation of constant and interesting activity. Such activity would at once practically develop the capacities of students and create bonds of affection between teacher and student. Cobb argued,

> The parent or teacher, should, *first of all,* secure the LOVE and AFFECTION of his children or pupils. He will then have an *unlimited* control over their minds and conduct.... The great advantage of government by LOVE instead of by FEAR, or by the ROD, is, that, in the former case the *bad feelings* of the child or pupil can not, by any possibility, be excited....[16]

More important still, 'the child or pupil, who obeys his parent or teacher from LOVE *purely,* can be relied on, when *absent,* as well as when *present.*'[17] The student's freely experienced emotions would be the basis for effective self-regulation, and educators could rest secure in the knowledge that they were not educating a generation of enemies of civilization. Educational practices which could transform political rule into 'free obedience,' by making students embrace and internalize definite habits of mind and body, were of central importance to middle class educators concerned with the moral and political discipline of increasingly independent working class populations.

But while middle class educators in Europe and America tended to regard the regular use of physical violence in the schoolroom as an educational failure, they still viewed schoolroom activity as hedged about by the teacher's and the state's monopoly over the means of violence. Schoolroom governance, most of these educators argued explicitly, was like any form of civil rule: gentle means were possible because authorities could have recourse to violent means if they so chose.[18] The Secretary of the British and Foreign School Society likened the rod in the school to the American Federal Arsenal at Harper's Ferry. There the American government had at its disposal an enormous accumulation of the means of violence, but these arms (in 1847!) lay entirely idle. In civil society as in school, the commands of those in authority were obeyed because they were known to be backed ultimately by force. As this observer remarked,

> ...you know, that if compliance with the just demands of your government is refused, and resistance is sustained, force after force will be brought to bear upon you.... Such ought to be the character of all government.[19]

He also remarked,

> ...no good will be done unless the child knows that *authority is at hand* if reason should fail.... I account that moral discipline little worth, which does not teach a child to submit to authority *simply as authority.*[20]

The Master of the Albany Normal School wrote, in a teacher's manual distributed to school libraries in Canada West,

> The true way and the safe way...is to rely mainly on moral means for the government of the school, — to use the rod without much threatening, if driven to it by force of circumstances, and as soon as authority is established, to allow it again to slumber with the tacit understanding that it can be awakened from its repose if found necessary. The knowledge in the school that there *is* an arm of power, may prevent any necessity of an appeal to it.[21]

The successful creation of schooled subjectivities was seen to be possible only where the school was hedged about by a monopoly of violence.

The study of the theory and practice of school punishment is particularly interesting for the insight it offers into the politics of school government. Schooling is a form of ruling, and while school management manuals attempted to specify and limit corporal punishment, they also elaborated in great detail techniques for 'governing' the schoolroom without its use. Teachers were given practical instruction in quelling dissent, in identifying and co-opting potential student resistance, in forming and managing the 'public opinion' of the school, and in the substitution of productive educational labour for the 'idleness' which was held to encourage dissent and disorder. The parallels between more general political theories of governance in the liberal state, and techniques of school government are simple and direct.[22] The political state is an educational state; the educational state is a political state. The two are moments in a unity.

In Canada West during the period 1850-1871, the public discourse of educational reform gave rise to a troublesome contradiction for the education office. The official *Journal of Education* and the public speeches of some school administrators, Ryerson's *Report* of 1846 and lectures in the Normal School, and other official statements, contributed to the growth of a popular belief in the 1860s that corporal punishment in any form had been prohibited in common schools. The progressive thrust of educational reform--- that education could indeed tap the well-springs of human nature and for that reason would be experienced by the student as a form of pleasure--- was assumed by many school supporters to be both official policy and the measure of the schools. However, in reality, the education office's preoccupation with education as moral discipline and political subordination frequently *necessitated* the application of physical violence to the student population. Popular struggle surrounded attempts by teachers, backed by the education office, to beat resistant students.

The local magistracy played an important role in struggles between teachers and students. Violent teachers, over the protests of the education office, frequently found themselves arrested at school or summoned to appear before the local magistracy. Many teachers were fined for beating students, and some were threatened with imprisonment as well. Local justices were frequently jealous of the power structures established by the School Acts, from whose exercise they were formally excluded, and frequently acted as counterweights to these structures. However, in a further instance of the increasing density of local political rule, from the late 1850s magistrates began to seek direction from the Education Office itself with respect to the exercise of the powers to which these same magistrates laid claim in school matters. The education office, from 1862, increasingly left the definition and regulation of *excessive* school violence to the magistracy, while consistently defending the right of the teacher to apply what it defined as *normal* violence. The normalization of the power to punish remained partial, however, for this power was contested locally.

## Precedents

As we saw in chapter two, early in the 1840s many elected school Commissions acted to regulate and limit the application of physical violence in the schools. School Commissions specified procedures for the application of punishment, in some cases detailed the offences for which it was to be applied, the attitude to be adopted by the teacher, the nature of the instruments of punishment, and the bodily targets of blows. Before systematic interventions by the education office limited local educational autonomy and bolstered the authority of the teacher in the school, violence by teachers was regulated in a simple and direct manner by local consumers of education. The bureaucratic limitation of punishment was the obverse of a process which aimed at breaking direct community control of the conduct of education. The formal limitation of the power to punish was at the same time an explicit recognition of the state's right to punish the population at school, through the agency of the teacher, and in pursuit of the (imperfectly-) legitimated objective of political socialization. State educational reform did not abolish violence at school. It aimed rather to achieve a monopoly over the use of violence for teachers. This meant the practical removal of access to the use of violence from students and school supporters. It would be facile and erroneous to read the campaign against corporal punishment simply as a 'movement towards greater humanism.'

In his autobiographical description of schooling in the 1830s,

Canniff Haight recalled sitting 'under the rod of an Irish pedagogue--- an old man who evidently believed the only way to get anything into a boy's head was to pound it in with a stick through his back.'[23] When Haight was six or seven years old, he was severely beaten by another teacher for some trivial error in his lessons. The beating was interrupted by the older scholars.

> Two strong young men attending the school remonstrated with the master, who was an irascible Englishman, during the progress of my punishment, and they were given to understand that if they did not hold their peace they would get a taste of the same, whereupon they immediately collared the teacher. After a brief tussle around the room during which some of the benches were overturned, the pedagogue was thrown on the floor, and then one of them took him by the nape of the neck, and the other by the heels, and he was thrown out of doors into the snow. There were no more lessons heard that day.

The following day, after an investigation by local school supporters, 'the teacher was dismissed, and those guilty of the act of insubordination were admonished.'[24] J. Carmichan recalled a Niagara District schoolmaster of the 1820s who,

> struck a boy in the head with a round rule an inch in diameter, he fell to the floor insensible and was carried out to the snow to revive. It is satisfactory to know that the big boys 'bate the schoolmaster.'[25]

Not only did students have access to the means of physical violence, but physical violence was often an approved pedagogical device. In Norfolk County in a similar period there was a teacher named 'Mr John Corkins,' who, although 'not a bad teacher,... had a curious habit of rolling his silk handkerchief into a ball and shying it at any one whom he saw violating any of his rules.' Any person struck was obliged 'to return the handkerchief and receive a castigation on the hands for misdemeanor.' Another of Corkins' favorite punishments for the offense of fighting was to make the students 'cut jackets'.

> The boys who had been breaking the rule in this respect were each required to take a beech rod about

four feet long, as tough and limber as a whalebone whip, and standing about three feet apart, were made to flog each other well, while the teacher stood by with a similar rod in his hand, and if he saw that either boy was inclined to favour the other by lessening the force of his strokes, he would say, 'Lay on harder, boys,' and apply his own rod to the back of the delinquent. The cure was harsh, but generally effectual.[26]

Physical violence was certainly present— and perhaps even routinely present— in the common schools before the reforms of the 1840s. Yet it is important to notice that it was regulated directly by students and school supporters at the local community level. If teachers used violence defined locally as excessive, students were capable of responding directly and in kind. The collective physical power of the students in most cases undoubtedly exceeded that of the teacher.

I do not wish to argue that state schooling can be evaluated simply in terms of the frequency with which direct physical violence was used by teachers against students. State schooling may well have produced teachers who beat students less frequently than did teachers under the market or community regulation of schooling. Physical violence at school was a means to an end. It is not in principle any more brutal than emotional violence at school. Indeed the Education Office at least officially urged physical violence as useful in school government for the humiliation which might surround its application. Still, the promise of educational reform was pleasure in schooling, pleasure which stemmed from a basic coherence between educational practice and the social interests and capacities of students. In this light, the application of physical violence by teachers to students is an index of the ideological character of the project of state schooling. To the extent that the practices of state schooling could be sustained only through the application of violence to a population deprived of the means of responding in kind, the 'gentle' promise of education in state schools is shown to have been a false promise.

Again, the 'gentle' pedagogical reforms instituted by the education office in Canada West were not about removing from teachers the power to use physical violence. Quite the contrary. This right was preserved explicitly, and the School Acts and Regulations attempted to bolster it. Pedagogical reform was rather about dispossessing students and local school supporters of their power to direct physical violence at the teacher, and of their conventional powers to intervene in school room practice. Just as the construction of the national state involved the development of a governmental monopoly over the means of violence, so the development of the educational state involved a bureaucratic monopoly over the means of school violence. Teachers were quite explicitly empowered to use the degree of force which might be employed by a 'judicious parent' in governing a child. The precise content and nature of this force were left intentionally indefinite, and in the design of the School Acts, disputes over this matter were to be resolved through school arbitrations which were to involve neither the magistracy, nor students nor school supporters directly.

Parents, school supporters and students were subject to fines or imprisonment on conviction based on the evidence of one 'credible witness' (practically, the teacher) for disturbing a school. 'Disturbing' was defined in regulations and in legislation in a manner sufficiently broad to include everything from making noise outside the school to challenging the authority of the teacher in the school.

'Gentleness' and 'humanity' in pedagogical practice, then, were situated in a transformed structure of power relations. Only where the subjects of education were deprived of access to the means of educational violence, and where a monopoly over the application of physical violence was accorded to teachers, could 'non-violent' (=emotional) means predominate in school government. And however 'pleasant' or 'humane' educational reformers may have seen such means to be, these same reformers regarded 'gentle' means as more *effective* ways of producing reliable political subjects.

## Published Views of Corporal Punishment

The education office discussed the question of corporal punishment and school government in a variety of forums. In addition to his support for gentle pedagogy in the *Report on a*

*System of Public Elementary Instruction,* Egerton Ryerson toured the country in 1847 and delivered a lecture entitled 'On the Importance of Education to an Agricultural, and a Manufacturing People' in most county towns. In this lecture he argued that 'moral and religious culture is even more important than a knowledge of letters.' Moral discipline and a love of learning, however, were mutually compatible, and the teacher who provided moral training on a regular basis would find that intellectual training would be easily secured. This teacher would also be able to govern easily in the schoolroom.

> Though punishment is sometimes necessary, where moral influence has done its utmost, the conscience is, in all ordinary cases, an infinitely better disciplinarian than the rod. When you can get children in a School to obey and study, because it is right, and from a conviction of accountability to God, you have gained a victory, which is worth more than all the penal statutes in the world....[27]

Once again, 'free and cheerful obedience' was the ultimate aim of education as political socialization. It was to be secured through moral discipline, and where moral discipline worked, corporal punishment was minimized and repressive criminal law unnecessary.

The *Journal of Education for Upper Canada* did not explicitly consider the question of corporal punishment until 1853, but earlier discussions of school governance and authority were presented, most often as propaganda for teachers. An early number of the *Journal* reprinted the section *Duties of Teachers of Common Schools* from the Act of 1850, and here teachers were enjoined to treat students 'with kindness combined with firmness; and to aim at governing them by their affections and reason, rather than by harshness and severity.'[28] In September of 1849, the *Journal* reprinted an address entitled 'Hints on School Government' which had been read before the Essex County Teachers' Association. Here the duty of teachers was said to be to 'prepare boys and girls to become men and women; to educate boys who are to become governors of the nation, and girls who are to become mothers of future statesmen and rulers; and in order that these may, each in their own turn rule wisely, *they must learn to obey.*' It was comparatively easy to 'maintain an unlimited despotism in the school room,' or to bribe students into obedience by rewards and punishments, but this writer argued that the only true foundation for obedience at school was mutual respect and love between teacher and student.[29]

In 'Laying the Foundations--- The Teacher,' which appeared in July 1851, an account of the best form of school government was again presented. 'The reign of the school-room should not be a "reign" of terror, or trickish cunning, or imbecile softness. It should be a kind, but inflexible reign of righteousness.' Teachers were warned against striking students and urged to rely on moral discipline. 'If you strike a blow,' teachers were counselled, 'it may secure a sullen submission for a moment; but if you implant a principle, it will be a guardian angel for a lifetime.' This article stressed as well that 'there must be obedience in the school-room,' but this obedience 'should not be mere brute submission to superior power.' Those made to obey at school through physical force rather than moral discipline could not be trusted politically in later life. 'What can we expect but rash and disorderly action in mature life from those whose early years have felt no influence but the tight rein and curb bit?'[30]

Much of the material in the *Journal of Education* was intended for the public education of parents. Official communications in the *Journal* and elsewhere aimed at the production of 'good' or 'proper' parents, who would willingly support the moral and political discipline of schooling. An important discussion of the proper position of parents in the politics of schooling was presented in 'Mutual Relations of Parties Interested in a School,' which appeared in May 1852. This article actually began by stating that parents and *'they alone'* exercised the power of 'reward and punishment' over children. Teachers were merely 'auxiliary' in the lives of children, and should be directed by the wishes of parents. However, it soon became clear that 'parents *as they are,* and parents *as they should be,* are very different classes' of people. Where parents would not treat their children *properly*---- as this was defined by the state school---- then teachers had to act in their place.

> Reward and punishment ought to be in the parent's hand even when their ground is school conduct; for thus the scholar learns that teacher and parent are but continuations each of the other...... but if parents will not assume this duty thankfully, then it of course devolves upon the teacher.[31]

'Rules for Home Instruction' presented the kind of pre-school discipline the education office sought from parents. 'From your children's earliest infancy, inculcate the necessity of instant obedience,' this article began. Children were to be punished for wilful disobedience, and parents were to 'remember that a little *present* punishment, when the occasion arises, is much more effectual than the threatening of a greater punishment, should the fault be renewed.'[32] In 'Schools at Home,' parents were urged to take all occasions for the education of their children.[33] In 'Co-operate with the Teacher,' parents were instructed to do everything necessary for the successful operation of the process of schooling, and to support disciplinary practices, including corporal punishment. A key paragraph read,

> every parent should understand that it is expected of him that, in sending his children to school, he tacitly delegates to the teacher power to govern them while in school, unless he expressly reserves it, and requests the teacher to send the children home to be corrected when disobedient. And when this power is delegated, it is reasonably supposed on the part of the teacher that he may use such means to restrain or constrain the children under his charge as are employed by parents. The teacher must establish his authority by bringing all to line in obedience to his will. Unless this be done, the first requisite of a good school will be wanting. When the teacher finds it necessary, as he sometimes will, to use force, in order to secure submission and obedience, the parent should not interfere.... the parent should no more meddle here than he would with the neighbourhood government of parents over their children.[34]

The possibility that parents might reserve the right to punish to themselves, or that alternatives to corporal punishment might be successfully employed, was explicitly discounted in 'School Discipline' which appeared in the January 1853 number of the *Journal*. 'Many have taken strong ground against' corporal punishment, this article noted, and 'public sentiment has always been averse to the infliction' of it. Yet, the 'most ardent supporters of *moral suasion*' were commonly those with the least experience of practical schoolroom government. In Boston, where parents declared that corporal punishment should be abandoned and replaced by expulsion, 'truant-players increased to an alarming multitude.' Lawlessness prevailed on the streets, and the opponents of corporal punishment at school were soon silenced by a general cry for its restoration.[35]

Many other discussions of corporal punishment in school government were reprinted in the *Journal of Education* during the 1850s and 1860s. Dr. Arnold was quoted in support of 'liberal principles' which necessitated 'restraint' in society as in school, and which called for the practical demonstration of the natural subordination of boys at school.[36] A system of graded punishments was described in 'School Discipline', with corporal punishment as a last resort.[37] 'The Use of the Rod' argued that the failure of parents to curb their children created the necessity for punishment at school, and was at the root of general social unrest. 'What are those scenes of domestic strife that destroy the peace of families,' the article demanded, 'those disgraceful riots that result in the loss of life and destruction of property, and those filibustering expeditions fitted out in defiance of government and threatening national safety, but the natural consequences of unbridled passion?'[38] The moral regulation of children at home was seen as a means to general social peace and political order.

The Principal of Cheltenham Training College argued that teachers should govern by sympathy in the schoolroom, and resort to corporal punishment only as a last resort.[39] There were many other examples of the same arguments,[40] including one presented in *The School House; Its Architecture, External and Internal Arrangements*, which first appeared in 1857. Written by John George Hodgins, the Deputy Superintendent of Education, this work presented the official view of 'School Discipline' in detail. 'There must be punishment' in school, Hodgins wrote, 'but it should consist in the moral sense of disgrace, and not in the animal sense of pain.' If teachers were to punish effectively, they must take care to have 'public opinion, or what is called 'sympathy of numbers' ' on their side in the schoolroom. Hodgins then reprinted a lengthy article by Charles Schackle who opposed corporal punishment on the grounds of its danger to health. Schackle wrote that 'moral affections of the brain are produced by painful, cruel, disgraceful, and unjust arts, such as Corporal Punishment, especially blows on the head.' Such blows awakened 'hatred, horror, and disgust,' in the student, made the student regard the teacher as 'nothing but a gaoler' and made the school something 'he abhors as a prison.' Schackle admitted that 'good order can only be maintained by a certain severity in schools,' but argued that this severity should be closely regulated.[41] Hodgins also presented a list of rules for teachers conducting corporal punishment, and these closely resembled the lessons taught on the subject in the Normal School.[42]

## School management in the Normal School

Both instruction and practice with respect to punishment in the Normal and Model schools were frequently matters of dispute in the 1850s and 1860s. Some of the model school teachers had themselves been instructed in schools where corporal punishment was abolished. For instance, G.R.R. Cockburn, the Rector of the short-lived Model Grammar School, had been a student of Professor Pillans in the High School of Edinburgh.[43] The Normal School teachers consistently urged student teachers to govern their schools by force of character and moral suasion. The chief superintendent frequently claimed in official correspondence that no corporal punishment was countenanced in the Normal School course. The publication of these claims at the local level may well have contributed to the popular belief that corporal punishment was forbidden at school.

But the notebooks of Maria Payne, an 18-year-old graduate of the 41st Session of the Normal School, show that student teachers were in fact instructed in the use of corporal punishment. Payne's first notebook begins with the proposition that 'there must be perfect order in School. This is the one prime requisite to teaching. There must be student order in moving on the floor &c.' Payne learned such tactics for maintaining order as seating arrangements and methods of classification. She also learned, 'a pupil who is mischievious--- make him a monitor and the whole of his influence will be in the scale of order. This is a splendid mode of getting order.' Payne was instructed not to 'draw out a code to hang up because some offence may be committed that is not in your code.'

The teachers were to have 'One rule Do right Every act can be brought under this.'

Still, the Normal School master taught that 'you require some punishment to make them keep rules, as little punishment as is possible. Avoid flogging.' The teachers-in-training were to avoid some punishments, 'those that show petty revenge and carelessness as to feelings of the pupils. Do not strike knuckles or do anything of the kind. Do not use them even occasionally. Do not pull their hair or tweat their nose.' Corporal punishment was explicitly *permitted*, so far as one can judge from Payne's notes, but its use was to be carefully regulated. 'Corporal punishment can be given only by long deliberation. It must not be given on the spur of the moment— never strike a pupil while you are angry.' Again, student teachers were counselled 'Do not Strike the head.' This was said to kill students with a tendency to 'Hydrocepolis' and 'consumption.' 'Improper' punishments included 'tieing a pupil up by the thumbs, or putting a stick between the teeth— or holding a nail, or holding out a book.' Payne learned that 'some children never think of obeying their parents till they are flogged,' and 'if you cannot manage without it you may flog.' But good teaching was held to minimize the need for punishment, and the master claimed that corporal punishment had been employed only thirteen times in the Hamilton schools in five years. Payne also transcribed a considerably detailed body of material with respect to alternatives to corporal punishment and with respect to administering corporal punishment effectively where it was necessary.[44] In the later 1860s, the Deputy Superintendent began offering a regular course of lectures to Normal School students in School Law, and this may well have been in response to growing concerns with the teacher's power to punish.[45]

## Henry Wright and David Fotheringham

Early in 1858, David Fotheringham became master of the Boys' Model School at Toronto. In July, the Chief Superintendent received a letter from W.R. Wright, who claimed that his son Henry had received a 'severe' and 'brutal' punishment from Fotheringham,

> the Master having taken down his trowsers and trashed him on the bare bottom, leaving ten or twelve blood marks of from eight to ten inches in length.... I will here remark that in the whole of my school career I never remember an instance of such punishment as now described, it being inflicted with a cane; for if a boy was birched the disgrace was considered so great as to be remembered by his schoolmates for life.

Wright claimed this was not the first such punishment administered by Fotheringham, and urged Ryerson to stop the practice.[46]

Fotheringham, however, insisted that he had followed approved procedure in administering punishment.

> ...the boy and another... struck each other in the face, & fought before the class until both bled from the nose. They were both sent to me and remained with me for some time. I then deferred the case till I could have time to enquire into the matter.... I made inquiries before the Division [i.e.class] and ascertained their undoubted guilt. (I may here mention that among the 1st Div. a disposition had been manifested for quarrels of the kind, and its criminality pointed out.) I then without any cause of irritation, & I think with a consciousness of duty took them apart from the class (so that they did not know how the boys were punished) and corrected them with a piece of cane (bamboo) about 20 or 24 inches in length. The boys were placed across my knees & I have no recollection of raising my hand above my shoulder. The skin must have been reddened otherwise the punishment could not have been so severe as the case deserved....[47]

This case was discussed in the Council of Public Instruction, and on 25 August Ryerson wrote to Fotheringham to inform him that henceforth all students deserving corporal punishment in the Model Schools were to be referred to the Normal School Master. Fotheringham responded indignantly to this order. He claimed it changed his conditions of employment, for his engagement had promised him disciplinary autonomy. He offered to resign if his autonomy were limited. Ryerson attempted to conciliate Fotheringham, offering him his protection in relations with the Council, if Fotheringham would appreciate the necessity of the subordination of the Model to the Normal School. But while Fotheringham was prepared to accept this in principle, he protested against any practical interference with his punishment practices. The Model School master, he remarked, was best situated to understand the necessity of punishment in his school, where the students could not be governed like the adults in the Normal School. In any case, Fotheringham claimed that he punished less frequently than his predecessor, having had recourse to the rod only once in four and a half months. He added,

> You also state that I use the rod in a way at variance with what has been inculcated in the Normal School. I am not aware of ever having done so. The case... was done calmly, after about twenty four hours' deliberation... and precisely as I have seen boys punished in the School before I got charge of it... several years ago, a person... still in the employ of the Council, dealt so harshly with a pupil that he and his brothers were withdrawn; and that was at a time when corporeal punishment was professedly discarded....

Fotheringham concluded that his resignation was in Ryerson's hands, and while he was anxious to remain master of the Model School, he wished the entire matter to be considered by the Council. In the interim, Fotheringham sought direction— quite self-consciously— from Ryerson himself in cases of discipline in the School. Soon after, however, Fotheringham's resignation was accepted.[48]

The documents in this case are incomplete, but Fotheringham's claim that corporal punishment by caning was common in the Model Schools was never contested by Ryerson. There is some hint that a job outside of Toronto was arranged for him, and Fotheringham reappeared as a Provincial School Inspector in the 1870s— the crowning of a successful educational career. This was a difficult period in internal relations in the official schools, with the unsatisfactory performance of Watts in the Model Grammar School, with dissatisfaction rife around the performance of the music teachers, and other events. Fotheringham's leaving the school was probably more a product of his lack of respect for bureaucratic lines of authority, than for his use of the cane. In any case, there is strong evidence to suggest that the Normal School taught teachers to use, and Model School teachers did use, corporal punishment.

This is an important matter for understanding educational administration in Canada West. If even under the best technical conditions of state schooling corporal punishment was indispensable, it must have been routine where 'rich instructional activity' was less developed. Ryerson's consistent denial (detailed below) that teachers at the Normal School were ever trained in the techniques of corporal punishment exposed those who followed their training to local opposition. In practice, teachers were left to apply whatever degree of force would be tolerated at the local level, and if they exceeded this degree of force, they could expect at best only the most general expression of support from the education office. Violence against students--- which was in fact inherent to the system of public education--- was thus made to appear a personal failing on the part of teachers who could not match the reputedly gentle governmental practices in the Model Schools. This was an administrative tactic for containing opposition to public education, and a tactic which used local opposition to police the occupation of teaching. In the later 1860s, individual teachers were commonly sacrificed by the education office to local opposition, while the authority of the *office* of teacher was defended vigorously. Particular acts of violence were deplored, while the right of teachers to use violence was upheld.

## Urban Schools

Official reports from large urban schools in the 1850s and 1860s point to a reduction of corporal punishment in school government. The *First Annual Report of the Superintendent of Public Schools of the City of Hamilton* --- the city where the the 'Normal School system' was first adopted, claimed that

> the severer forms of discipline formerly thought indispensable to school government have been gradually superseded by the moral influence of the Teach-

> er.... It is gratifying to know that corporal punishment has been inflicted on but six or eight cases during the entire year.

In cases where corporal punishment was necessary, parents were held to be at fault, although the character of the teacher was also partly in question. 'With different Teachers the necessity of using brute force as a punishment exists just in proportion to the amount of moral power and energy of character possessed by each.'[49]

Still, in the Hamilton school report for 1861, the role of corporal punishment in the schools was described, and conditions for its administration were specified. Punishment must have been sufficiently common for its regulation to be necessary.

> On no account should passion, whatever the provocation, intermingle in the discipline of the school. The head must never be touched, and the more grief the teacher evinces, the more effectual is the correction likely to be. The only rule is, do right, to which we would add love your pupils.... The monthly reports, and the other notes sent to parents, are found almost omnipotent in their controlling influence with the higher divisions....[50]

Similar information came from the Goderich Common School. Here 'corporal punishment is wisely permitted by our rules, but it is seldom resorted to.' Where punishment was necessary, it was because parents produced disobedient children. Parents 'encourage in the child, rebellion against the teacher, and the child diffuses the same spirit among his fellows, and so the evil goes on increasing, until the teacher has no alternative left, but to use the ferule....' Happier schools and children would result, the Goderich school reports claimed, if parents would listen less to their children about school matters.[51] Here, as in much of the official discourse of education, 'responsible' and good parents were those who implicitly counselled obedience to the school and did not believe accounts of school discipline.

The 'Rules and Regulations of the Union School' in Paris for 1859 made no mention of corporal punishment. Disrespectful pupils were to be suspended.[52] The Board of Education for the City of Kingston ruled that teachers were,

> ...required to practice such discipline in the Schools as

would be exercised by a kind and judicious parent, and shall avoid corporal punishment in all cases where good order can be preserved by milder measures. When special corporal punishment is inflicted, it shall take place only in the presence of the school; and every case shall be recorded in the diary, the teacher being held responsible for the due exercise of this discretionary power.[53]

## Violence at School

William Fraser, the Superintendent for the 1st District of Bruce County, delivered an address 'To the Common School Teachers' in May of 1862. 'On the subject of punishment,' he insisted, ' avoid every species of cruelty. In training animals this is to be carefully avoided how much more with moral and rational beings.' He asked, 'is it not cruel for a Teacher to take the skull of a horse or cow, full of vermin & dirt; tie the same to the neck of a child, & make it stand at the door, & all the scholars laughing at the cruel and foolish scene? If this does not break the spirit of that child it will be sure to make any high spirited creature, from that moment, hate both the School and the Teacher.' Fraser continued,

> Others make the poor children stand at the door on one leg, as if they were geese & thrashed when they cannot support the centre of gravity.... Others open a board or trap-door in the floor, & drive them down there; telling them it is full of rattle snakes or ghosts; enough to drive them into fits.... Some Teachers punish them in wrath & rage which is always evil, striking them in the head, by the fist, the ruler or anything that comes to hand, and especially hurtful to hit them in the ear.... If the rod should be used, it ought to be used only sparingly ....

Fraser urged teachers to govern firmly, but by affection,[54] and repeated this message often. 'We have to improve on the past,' he informed teachers in 1863, 'railing and sarcasm, the wearing out of the switch and the tase, with the punishment of wrath and passion, ought and must be done away with.'[55]

However, the correspondence of the education office reveals that this kind of propaganda had little effect on many teachers. The information available about the conduct of education in many schools in the 1850s and 1860s reveals that state schooling involved the regular application of severe physical violence to the student population by teachers.

Where educational administrators opposed 'excessive violence' at school, however defined, they could often not do so effectively or efficiently. Even William Fraser was relatively powerless in the face of recalcitrant teachers. In May of 1864, Fraser consulted Ryerson about a teacher who had been 'beating the children with a stick till their hands are blistered stiff & swollen & that for nothing deserving the name of offences.' Local school supporters had taken the teacher before a magistrate who claimed he had no authority in school matters. This was the response which the education office sought from the magistracy, but this teacher refused to stop beating the students. Fraser himself warned the teacher a second time. 'I plainly told him at last the stick you shall not use you may take a switch or strap & for real crime if nothing else will do take their back side but lay aside your stick.' But the teacher continued to beat the students' hands, and parents refused to send them to school. Fraser sought Ryerson's permission to suspend the teacher's certificate, but this correspondence took at least another ten days, during which time the teacher continued in the school.[56]

Teachers were frequently in a rage when they punished children, and schoolroom battles were common and often publicized in the local press. The range of afflictions practiced upon students was broad. A Trustee from Windham Centre wondered if his school corporation could fire a teacher convicted of assault on Ann Pettis, a ten year old girl, who

> did write on a slate very unbecoming langue for any person to write the words is as follows Henry Dunbar focked Synthey Walters in Dunbars barn Walters girl saw the slate took to the master he called her up and did not com he went to her and whipe her on the [illegible] with a leather strape then stepped back on the floor and told her the

> second time to come out on the floor which time he took her by the hand and led her out on the flore and whipe her most cruelly left the mark in four different places two stripes on the left cheak one on her hand or reast one on her back and another on her side which remained for several days....[57]

R.F. White complained in 1852 that the teacher in his section would 'turn up the little girls' petticoats and ... turn down the boys pantaloons'.[58] R.J. Morrison taught in section 8 of Raleigh Township, and protested attempts by the Township Superintendent to suspend his certificate for violence in the schoolroom. Morrison claimed that his punishments were mild: for fighting, 'I took hold of each & threw him on the floor & kept him there, till he promised before the school, that he would not do the like again,' and for inattention, 'I took him by the arm & turned him round, in doing so he stumbled and fell on the edge of one of the seats and cut his forehead a little, but was well in a few days.' However, Phillip Andrew, the Superintendent, wrote that Morrison's 'usual manner' of punishing 'consists in pulling a boy violently forward by the collar & tripping his legs from under him so as to call him to fall on the ground.' When Morrison did this 'to a boy about 10 years old the boys head came in contact with a form or desk and the child was severly cut over the eye....' Morrison contested this account, claiming the boy was actually 18, and that of his 63 scholars only 12 'boyes' had been corrected in that way in 15 months.[59]

'My Daughter Agnes has an impediment in her speech,' wrote John Evans from East Gwillimbury, 'and is very bashful.'

> she was unable to pronounce the letter A and the teacher Mr McPherson put her in the lobby a little before 12 and kept her there without any Dinner, and whipped her about 3 O'Clock so severe, that her back was Black and Blue, the marks that were left on her being so as to correspond with the Ruler with which they were inflicted, the Teacher actually said he wished he had given her more....The same Teacher also attempted to commit a rape on a young Girl attending his school in Whitchurch....

Evans took the teacher before the local magistrate.[60]

In section 2 of Mono Township a teacher 'made a number of

children on account of not having the morning task... stand up against the wall from morning till 6PM and would not allow them one bite of victuals....'[61] In Hampton, George White's child was beaten 'unmercifully' for fighting at noon, punished 'with a Ruler I should say an unlawful wheapon to be used in Schools it denotes rashness & brutality of a Man.... is there not a law to punish such rough shod riding as this....'?[62] John Hudson of section 3 in London Township was reported by his trustees in 1860 to be 'using some of the children attending harshly he has been in the habit of using a rod and sometimes a ruler to correct them on Tuesday last he struck one little boy eight years old with a switch on the side of the head the end of the switch came round and cut under the right eye cut the nose and went into the left eye....' A doctor said the child would lose the eye, and although the teacher paid for medical care and claimed the injury was accidental, the boy's father was demanding his dismissal.[63]

'I took the liberty of tapping a girl on the shoulder so that I might draw her attention to the lesson on the Black Board,' wrote a teacher named W.J. Black in 1862, 'and by my doing so, she goes to her seat pouting and sulking, giving the example to the school,--- such an example I don't allow.' Black continued, in a common description of the escalation of violence once begun, 'I then ordered her to her work 2 or 3 times, but I got no reply and she did not go to her work when told in the presence of the school, so I came up with a small rod and struck her just twice on the back as she was lying between two seats sulking, which I understand...have left marks across the back....' Black wondered if he could legally do this.[64]

Charles Clarke deafened a student in his Wardsville school.[65] In section 1 of Georgina Township the teacher was said to beat boys, many of them close to his own age of 16, with 'a bow, which is used in the juvenile sports of a back country.'[66] The trustees of Concord claimed their teacher cruelly beat the pupils, 'he would put a pupil down and break his neck if he did not submit' and the teacher claimed to carry a loaded revolver in the school.[67] A school supporter in Petrolia protested the refusal of the trustees to remove a violent teacher. John Morrison claimed the teacher 'whipped my little girl ten years old over the Shoulders with a rawhide until he left her all black. Second he whipped my Grandchild of six years old with a raw hide until his back was black and blue.' Morrison claimed the teacher beat another boy 'over the head with a stick until he left lumps on his head.'[68] C.E. Abraham complained that her certificate was suspended by the local superintendent just because she 'had to be a little severe on the first start, so that they would not get the upper hands.' But the superintendent, John Lees, claimed that 'one little girl about five years of age had been handled so roughly by her that she was sick and unable to go to school for a week'. Later, in 'quite a fit of passion,' Abraham hung two of the scholars. 'A rope was produced, and she took two of them, put the rope across their breast and under their arms, and tied it behind, she then made them walk along one of the benches, fastened the rope to a hook in [the] wall, drew the bench from under their feet, and left them hanging there.'[69] James Lawson punished lying by making a student 'stand in the floor with a paper tied on his forehead on which is written the word 'LIAR'.'[70] As we have seen in chapter five, this and many other similar forms of punishment contributed to low rates of attendance at school.

## Community Justice and Punishment

The School Acts of 1850 and 1853, and the regulations published by the Council of Public Instruction attempted to contain educational conflicts within largely educational structures of administration. Arbitrations involving representatives of teachers and trustees, supervised by the local superintendent, were to decide all matters of conflict within the school, with the exception of 'school disturbances'. The latter were held to originate only from within the community or the student body, not from among the teachers; beatings of students by teachers were not covered. These structures of administration were meant to empower central government locally through the office of teacher. They removed key powers of local educational self-management. However, in the case of a brutal teacher, educational administrative structures were themselves relatively impotent. Trustees could not legally break an agreement with a teacher before its expiry; parents and other school supporters were barred from the schoolroom; collective resistance from students could be prosecuted under the Act as a 'disturbance'. The local superintendent, upon investigation, or the chief superintendent acting through this local officer, could suspend teachers' certificates and remove teachers from contact with students, but in the nature of the case, such a proceeding was slow and uncertain.

Practically, school supporters continued to oppose brutal teachers directly, by intervening in the schoolroom. They also sought the support of the local magistracy. The education office received a steady stream of correspondence from teachers taken to court and fined for punishing students. Some of these instances received very wide publicity, with direct appeals to community sentiment and with the active involvement of the press. One such was the 'Brockville School Difficulty'.[71]

There is a certain irony in this case. In 1859, the editor of the Brockville *Recorder* published an article entitled 'The Government of Children in Public Schools', which was reprinted in the *Journal of Education*. This article noticed that new rules for the town common school made 'no recognition of corporal punishment and appeal at once to the moral sense of the pupils.' 'The rod,' the editor was happy to note, 'has ceased to reign universally in our public schools,' and he urged 'that a feeling of self respect should be instilled into the minds of pupils attending our public schools. Teachers should frequently reason with them, address them in their collective capacity as a community who have a character to maintain before the public.' The editor went so far as to argue that students would 'naturally' resist physical force, no matter how much their parents might tell them to obey, and hence kindness was the only effective mechanism in school government.[72]

In April 1860, the teacher in Brockville's Victoria Central School attempted to punish a boy named Kincaid for playing at school. Kincaid was called up and instructed to hold out his hand to be strapped, but refused. The teacher then struck him with a leather strap, and asked him again if he would hold out his hand. Kincaid again refused and then was hit several times with the strap. When he tried to return to his seat, the teacher 'caught him by the coat collar and struck him about the legs, and again asked him to hold out his hand.' Kincaid refused, complained he was being choked, and when the teacher released him, ran out of the school and home to his father.

Kincaid senior went to one of the town magistrates and got a warrant for the teacher's arrest, which was executed immediately. Kincaid then paraded his son through the streets of the town, showing the marks of his beating to public view, and demanding the conviction of the teacher. The teacher put up bail, but soon thereafter was convicted of assault by a majority of one of thirteen assembled magistrates. The editor of the *Recorder* was aghast at this proceeding. The magistrates had 'done their best to tie up the hands of the teacher.' Several boys in the town had already boasted that 'they had driven the last teacher away, and that they would drive this one away too.' The fining of the teacher thus threatened the maintenance of all order in the town schools. One of the magistrates who voted against conviction had been asked what he would do in Kincaid's position and replied, 'however grieved I might be at such an event, I would, to support the discipline of the school, have said nothing about it.' According to the editor of the *Recorder*, this was the position which all 'the magistrates out to have taken also.' The town superintendent of schools wrote to the education office that the case 'renders it necessary for us to know how discipline can be enforced with safety.'[73]

The editor of the *Recorder* was not inconsistent in celebrating the abandonment of the rod in 1859 and then insisting upon its necessity in 1860. Gentle means at school were preferable, but violent means would be employed where necessary. Indeed, again, gentle means were possible because they were known to be sustained ultimately by violent means. While the editor found it pleasant to see the moral discipline of the youth of Brockville taking place without the use of the rod, what was important to him was the end of moral discipline; the use of the rod was merely a relatively unattractive means to this end.

Many teachers had an experience similar to that of the master of the Victoria Central School in the decades after the Act of 1850. A teacher in Whitby was fined in court for whipping a boy and cutting his cheek.[74] David Johnston was taken to court for beating two children, one of them for insolence and the second for chewing gum and denying it. 'Having my pointer in my hand,' he wrote in the second case, 'a pointer about the eighth part of an inch in diameter at the butt and two feet long I struck him on the back four times not raising my elbow from my side after which he went to his seat laughing.'[75] A teacher in Murray Township was fined for striking with his fist a student who refused to sweep the school.[76] A teacher in St. Mary's was taken to court for punishing boys for fighting after school hours,[77] and A.J. Campbell of Carlisle was fined $16.85 for striking a girl with his pointer who had been 'slandering' him out of school. 'The Magistrates considered the children to be free from my authority as soon as they leave the School,' Campbell complained.[78] B.F. Pearson was fined $4 for leaving 'three or four marks' on the back and for discolouring the arm of a student who had called him 'a d-d old b-r'.[79] Hugh McDiarmid was fined for punishing a girl for 'stubbornness'.[80] One of Jacob E. Summers' students hated school. One morning this person announced to the other students that school was cancelled. Summers beat the student severely but was fined $10 for doing so.[81] Walter Meacham was fined 50 cents and costs for beating a little girl on the hands, face and head for swearing.[82] Robert Irvine was fired by his trustees for using the rod 'pretty freely on 2 or 3 occasions, so as to obtain proper submission' and when he protested he was taken to court and fined.[83] Other teachers were fined for beating students for a variety of 'offences:' refusing to sweep the school, lieing, refusing to study, not learning lessons, being truant, disobedience and swearing.[84]

In many of these instances, the level of violence escalated rapidly as students resisted or refused to accept physical punishment, and as students at times joined together to oppose the teacher. Slates, inkwells, books, lengths of stove wood, leather straps and wooden whips became weapons, blows fell on hands, heads, arms, wrists, backs and legs, desks were overturned, and apparatus was broken as teachers attempted to beat students into submission.[85]

## Demands for Policy

Faced with the possibility of fines for punishing students, many teachers attempted to obtain some exact and defensible specification of the limitations and legitimate grounds of the teacher's exercise of the power to punish from the education office. 'If whipping is necessary--- are there any parts of the culprit on which we are not allowed to inflict punishment,' asked G.W. Cook.[86] J.M. Westover wondered, 'have I a right to punish pupils (in order to maintain proper order and discipline) by whipping, until there are marks left upon them?'[87] And H.J. Brine asked 'whether any particular weapon is considered a lawful weapon for inflicting corporal punishment or is it left to the discretion of the Teacher'?[88] John Agnew wanted to know if it was 'legal to chastise a pupil with a rawhide or ruler'[89] and for Alexander McDonald the question was 'to what extent a Teacher can whip, how old must the pupil be before whipping is illegal, and the best method of treating hard cases without expelling them.'[90] 'I like teaching very much,' wrote Thomas Mackie of Euphrasia Township, 'except when it is necessary to use correction. I don't like whipping; but many of them are under little restraint at home, and cannot always be brought to a state of order in School without it.' The problem was, he continued, 'I cannot, however, find in the... [Educational] Manual any definite rules, either in regard to the extent of my authority; or how it may be lawfully exercised.'[91]

As with the question of the limits of the teacher's authority over students who were between school and household, attempts by teachers and others to gain a clear view of the power to punish continued throughout the two decades after 1850, and were continually frustrated. In early 1869, John Le Boutilier, a trustee in section 6 of Sidney Township reiterated the concerns of local adminstrators.

> When a scholar (under school age) attending a Common School, violates a rule of the School and will not submit to Corporal punishment as the penalty, but desires to leave the School or go home, would the Teacher be justified in forcing him to submit to punishment? What limit is there to a Teacher's punishing? Can he use any Whip or Rod he chooses? It seems to me it would save a great deal of trouble & litigation did Teachers know how far they are justified in proceeding with punishment, & some modes of inflicting punishment should be prescribed by law.

No official reply to these queries has survived. However, the *Educational Manual* stated quite clearly that while school attendance was not compulsory, once students entered the school room, they became subject to the school regulations and could not leave without the permission of the teacher.[92]

## Purposive Vagueness

The education office most commonly replied to such queries simply by citing the general provisions of the School Acts or of the school regulations. Comment on the merits of particular cases was usually avoided. When Lewis Allen asked what whip to use in punishing children, and if he was justified in marking their skin, the deputy superintendent merely quoted the official regulations.[93] Ryerson did the same in a letter to H.M. Day, who was threatened with dismissal for hitting a six year old girl 'about half a dozen blows between the elbow and the shoulder' with a ruler.[94] Thomas Heritage sought direction in a case where a teacher had corrected two boys for disturbing the school, and where 'one boy receives it quietly, the other boy turns saucy on him, and gets more of it, when he gets worse calls the Teacher names and threatens to throw his book in his face.' The boy's father sought the teacher's dismissal. Ryerson cited the regulations in reply.[95]

The school regulations were vague. With respect to corporal punishment they simply stated:

> A teacher as well as a parent should endeavour to govern children by their affections; but a teacher as well as a parent ought to exercise firmness, no less than tenderness in the government of children; and should, as well as the parents, use the rod if he thinks it necessary to ensure obedience. The first requisite in school discipline is obedience on the part of pupils; and a teacher must use all the means necessary to maintain it--- mild means if sufficient, but severe means if he thinks it necessary. Should it be known or supposed by pupils, or children, that the teacher or parent had no right to chastise them for disobedience, school or family government could not be maintained....[96]

Teachers were required to maintain 'proper order and discipline.'[97]

While teachers were bound by law and administrative regulation to enforce order at school--- and parents were enjoined to secure subordination in children at home---- and while the latitude offered to teachers to determine the amount of force they might apply was great, the practical questions which concerned teachers were not answered here. These questions, as we have seen, were whom could a teacher hit? with what instrument? on what part of the body? how many times? and with how much force? But the vagueness of the regulations was not accidental. The force to be disposed in the educational state was meant to be a *practical* power for the making of selves---- 'force after force' until submission was secured, until selves were in fact made. This force could not be contained bureaucratically nor specified in detailed rules: the political objectives of schooling and the particular circumstances of their realization would determine the nature of the force to be applied--- 'mild means if sufficient, but severe means' if necessary. This force could only operate effectively if it became a normal force, a force whose legitimacy was established empirically through the submission of students and others to it, and whose normality resided in the taken-for-granted character of state educational persons and relations. Only if 'parents' consented to act in concert with the school in the subordination of 'children', only if scholars consented to become 'schoolchildren' and accepted the process of training, would schooling entirely succeed.

Educational administrators had at least some conscious awareness of this. They argued that no bureaucratic limits to punishment in the schoolroom could be specified, nor at the same time, could the teachers be given a completely unlimited power. Teachers needed room to manouevre in the school room, and for this reason their power to punish should not be confined within specific limits. At the same time, teachers could not be left to feel that no limits of any sort existed to their power to punish, for they might abuse this power. The education office promoted the contradictory notion of a vaguely specific power.

When Johnston Neilson found himself forced out of the Johnstown District Model School for his punishment practices, he wrote to the chief superintendent for advice. Ryerson emphasized that teachers must rule to teach in the schoolroom, and stated his belief that 'the rod cannot be altogether dispensed with as an instrument of government and discipline.' Ryerson insisted that no specific rules could be laid down for the administration of punishment. A teacher must be free to punish. But by the same token, if the rules gave an unlimited power then a brutish teacher 'could hack and bruise the children of the neighbourhood at his pleasure.'[98] On the other hand, when John Wanless was fined $1 in court after he 'had occasion to chastise, for contumacy in the class, a boy, the son of one of the Trustees, Mr. Springer, who is also a J.P.,' and was then fired as well, the local superintendent wrote the Education Office to demand if the law had any business intervening in cases of school punishment. J.G. Hodgins, the deputy superintendent, replied that the law clearly gave teachers the power to punish, 'the extent and mode of that punishment is however very properly left indefinite.'[99] And in 1868, when (as we shall see) the education office had reluctantly conceded the right of the magistracy to intervene in cases of school punishment, Ryerson wrote to Anthony Horner of Wilton that 'the regulations in regard to discipline are designedly vague--- nor would it be wise to limit the power of the magistrate in such cases.... No corporal punishment is permitted to be used in our model schools & yet it does not affect the continuing of our teachers in their profession.'[100]

## The Education Office and Punishment

Despite the refusal of the education office to specify clear and definite limits to the power to punish, the chief and deputy superintendents did intervene on a number of occasions in local disputes over punishment. In these cases, the teacher's right to punish was consistently upheld, although individual teachers were at times disciplined. The authority of the office of teacher was bolstered, even where particular occupants of it were not supported in their activities.

Ryerson wrote to George Hendry, the Brock District Superintendent, in April of 1847 with his opinion of a case in which a teacher, a graduate of Cambridge University, had been fined for beating a ten year old girl in school. Ryerson wrote that it was unnecessary for Hendry to suspend the teacher's certificate, unless he knew of 'something disqualifying in his moral character.' Ryerson could imagine cases in which corporal punishment was called for and added 'you know, as well as I, that there are in the Schools both boys and girls who should either be removed from the School, or severely corrected in it, and without doing the one or the other, the authority of the Master or the discipline of the School could not be maintained for a week.' Ryerson hoped to see the day when corporal punishment would not prevail in school, but he 'would not recommend the disqualifying of a Teacher because he has been trained up under the rod.'[101]

A debate over the powers of teachers to exclude pupils from the schools in Brantford attracted a good deal of attention in the summer of 1859. Ryerson intervened in this debate, offering a lengthy statement for publication in the local press, and outlining the proper attitude of parents to the school and of the public to schoolmasters involved in cases of discipline. When Charlie Ryerson was sent home from the Toronto Model School for being three minutes late, Ryerson claimed that he 'admonished' the boy, even though he thought the punishment rather severe. In all cases of school discipline, he continued, 'teachers should be sustained in the exercise of their authority, and admonished privately if necessary.'

> Masters responsible to me have employed language and feeling in cases of discipline that I regretted; by the evident tendency and object of the proceeding being to maintain order and submission in the School, I have felt it my duty to sustain them against complainants, when I have afterwards conversed with them on the propriety and advantage of exercising discipline in a somewhat different manner.

Teachers 'must not only have large powers but a large discretion to maintain proper discipline,' and under no circumstances should parents be allowed to come into a school and demand explanations of teachers, certainly 'not before the pupils of the school, where the teacher must be supreme.'[102]

'The Teacher's authority should be sustained,' wrote Ryerson to a local superintendent named Angus Bell, 'even if exercised too strictly.' In such cases, the teacher should be 'privately conversed with & counselled.' Ryerson continued, 'there is no greater want in the country than that of proper respect for lawful authority,' and 'children who are thoroughly raised into the spirit of obedience to their parents & teachers, are likely to make the best Christians, parents & citizens in their course in life.'[103]

The teachers of London, who wrote collectively for advice with respect to punishment practices, were told that corporal punishment was not used in the Model Schools, but 'we maintain the right to employ it if necessary.' Ryerson urged the abandonment of physical punishment, but noted that this required 'good government of the pupils by the parents at home, and also their cordial co-operation with the authorities of the School.' The use of systems of merit and demerit was suggested, with the suspension of difficult students.[104]

In many instances, the education office left the resolution of local disputes over punishment to local officers. R.N. Grant, superintendent for Flamborough East Township, wondered if he should suspend the certificate of a teacher fined $2 and costs after 'one of his pupils, about ten years of age, was beaten by him with a ruler on the hands until the fingers were quite disfigured.' Ryerson replied that no corporal punishment was allowed in the official Model Schools, and that Grant should use his discretion in the case.[105]

Archibald Sinclair, taken to court for injuring a child who refused to be punished, asked for advice from the education office, but was told by the chief superintendent 'it is no part of the duty of this Dept. to counsel you in regard to the system of discipline which you have adopted in your School, especially as it has become a subject of investigation before a magistrate.'[106] A group of parents in section 8 of Fredericksburgh Township complained at length of the brutality of the local school teacher. This teacher had been hired for six months, but beat the students so viciously that most were withdrawn from the school. At the end of six months, two trustees held a private meeting with six ratepayers and hired the same teacher again. The parents of some students in the section complained to the District Superintendent and to the Township Council, but neither would intervene. Depositions made before a local magistrate claimed the teacher had beaten Wm. Douglass' son 'over the head so that he carried the mark and suffered distress for upwards of one week.' Charles Mullett had been 'taken hold of...by his--- privates and his shoulder and thrown' over a desk, and Ross Millar testified that Pheby Delilah, his daughter, had been kept repeatedly in after school, and objected to returning. Millar claimed that the next time the teacher kept her in, he went to the school house and 'saw Irvine Diamand [the teacher] lift the child Pheby Delilah who was at that moment lying on her back on one of the benches up and... rubbed or brushed down her clothes & turned partly round and buttoned up his trousers.' Ryerson also refused to intervene, claiming

> ...the law does not authorise me to interfere with Trustees in this respect; for they, as the elected representatives of the inhabitants of their School Section, have a right to employ whom they please as Teacher.... Furthermore, if the Trustees will not take up the complaint to which you refer, I have no right to interfere in the matter.[107]

A Normal School graduate named Archibald Andrews was fined $11.75 for 'unmercifully beating a child aged six years, a feeble and emaciated thing.' The local superintendent declared, 'I wonder any man could treat a child so vilely'. The superintendent wondered if he should suspend the teacher's certificate, and Andrews himself wrote a detailed account of the events. The girl had hit two others with a stick during recess.

> I knew she did it and I told her I would flog her and flog her till she would tell the truth. I had her by the left hand and the rod I had which I sometimes used for a pointer.... I gave her about twenty slaps stoping every four or five and asking her did she do it and she still persisted in denying it till she got all I gave her.... I hit her with said rod on the side of the left shoulder she is marked but no blood is drawn.

Andrews added that 'when you were lecturing to the Normal school students you said the less flogging the better but that it often had to be done.'

Ryerson denied any such statement about flogging in a letter to Andrews, but also wrote to the local superintendent declining to intervene and expressing his doubt that the Board of Public Instruction would suspend the teacher's certificate.[108]

In many other instances, however, the education office was quite prepared to offer advice, counsel and assistance to teachers involved in punishment disputes, and quite prepared to sustain the authority of teachers who punished violently. A case of corporal punishment was publicly debated in Smith's Falls in the winter of 1860. Alexander Wood complained to the Education Office that his son had been beaten by the teacher at school. Wood had told the boy to leave the school, rather than accept punishment, but the teacher prevented the boy from doing so, and then the trustees refused him readmission until he would apologize to the teacher. The local superintendent wrote to Ryerson that the Board of Trustees was having trouble with insubordinate boys at school, and was using strict measures to deal with them. Wood's son, he claimed, was not beaten, except perhaps during a struggle, and after the boy left the school, Alexander Wood himself assaulted the teacher. The teacher in question, Stewart Moug, wrote a detailed description of events.

> I punished Wood and another boy for the tearing of a book by beating them on the hands with a strap. After Wood being punished I heard him use some incoherent language while sitting in his seat which a boy who was convenient to him at the time has since informed me was to the effect that I had better not repeat such chastisement. I then directed him in an authoritative manner to cease talking and upon his continuing to utter indistinct sounds I went over to his seat and beat him a second time with the strap, when he snatched up his cap and ran to the door to which place I followed him arriving there as soon as he. He then caught hold of me by my necktie and upon his doing so I beat him pretty severely upon the hands legs and arms with the strap untill I compelled him to take his place in the school...

Moug stressed, however, that he did not hit the boy on the head at any time.

Ryerson supported Moug in this matter, writing to Alexander Wood that 'the boy doubtless met with severe punishment' but this was 'after attempting to leave the School and offering violent resistance to the Master.' And while the boy was punished by the master, 'that punishment furnishes no justification for the boy's offence.'[109]

John Mackenzie, a graduate of the 18th session of the Normal

School, sought advice from the education office after he was fined $2 and costs for 'whipping a girl, about 10 years of age, on the palms of the hands, & somewhat further up on the arms'. Ryerson suggested that while Mackenzie had the legal power to punish, 'a judicious parent would not deem it necessary to strike a little girl on the arms with a strap' for the offence of turning around in her seat. Ryerson urged 'the adoption of a System better calculated to appeal to the moral sense of your pupils.'[110]

James Farington was a Normal School graduate teaching in his first school in Eastwood in 1865 when he was fined $1 and costs for hitting a boy 'four or five strokes over the back of his hand.' The boy had been making his fellow students laugh during a spelling match, and Farington claimed his 'character is such a nature as to render him ungovernable if he were not dealt with very stringently and what is far worse he is greatly encouraged by his parents.' He knew that Ryerson was 'well aware that a teacher trained at the Normal School was never trained to corporal punishment---and it has and ever will be my greatest object to crush it if I can and only to practise it when it is unavoidable.' Ryerson replied at length.

> I have been able to govern my own children without the rod; nor do I advocate its use in a school; but there are cases in which, I believe, a Teacher cannot govern a school without using the rod sometimes, & that with a good deal of severity. A Teacher cannot be expected to dispense with the use of the rod in a school, unless the government of all the pupils by their own parents at home is perfect.... Children that are lawless at home, cannot be expected to obey law at school without some chastisement....'[111]

At times as well, the education office argued that the objective of subordinating students at school justified the application of all the means necessary to achieve it. J. McCainon of Bridgewater complained of the teacher's treatment of his son.

> ...he whiped a boy of mine about six years old with a stick of rock elm that is three four inches long the size of the Stick is at the one end Seven eigts of an inch in Diameter and at the little end about half an inch in diameter he used that hard wood Stick over the little fellows head in such a manner as to cause a

> red lump on his tempe and leave his eye black and
> once before he whiped him with the ruler on the
> head so that the child complained of his head aching
> for three or four Day....

Ryerson refused to comment on the merits of McCainon's complaint, but he did reply at length.

> It is common to use a ruler, — applying it to the
> culprit's hand — as an instrument of correction; but
> sometimes a boy obstinately refuses to hold out his
> hands, for the correction, when it may be necessary to
> apply to apply [sic] the ruler to some other part of
> his body. I do not myself approve of using a ruler,
> much less a large stick, as an instrument of
> correction in a school; I think a <u>strap</u> or <u>elastic whip</u>
> should be used; but any <u>disorderly</u> pupil <u>must be</u>
> corrected until he submits, however severe the
> correction, as no order could be kept in any school in
> which the Master is not supreme.[112]

In this matter, as in many others, the response of the Education Office was contradictory. In some cases, the Office intervened to recommend that brutal teachers be fined or suspended, although such cases are comparatively rare. When Robert Wallace was beaten for fighting out of school to such an extent that 'the lad's back and arms were black and blue and in one spot on the shoulder the skin was off about the size of a quarter of a dollar,' Ryerson commented that it was 'quite clear that the Teacher exceeded the bounds of reasonable punishment & he therefore deserves to have a slight fine inflicted upon him.'[113] A Normal School graduate named Charles Clarke was fired after a school arbitration for beating an eleven year old girl on the head and shoulders, a beating which left her deaf. This teacher held a Provincial Certificate. The complaint of the local superintendent against Clarke was forwarded to the headmaster of the Normal School, who ordered the suspension of Clarke's certificate. Clarke's defense that 'Mr. Robertson did not tell us that we should never use a rod; on the contrary he said that on some occasions it would be imperative to use it' was of no avail.[114] A. Harvey, the local superintendent for Houghton, wrote for advice in the case of W.W. Hutchins, a teacher fined for schoolroom punishment. Harvey said that 'one of the justices that tried the case told me that the skin was cut on the side of the childs neck so that it bled from his ear to his chin.' He stated that 'the day has gone by when School teachers were allowed to govern a school with whips composed of elastic wood—— children are reasonable beings, and can be governed by moral swasion and love.' Hodgins instructed Harvey to suspend Hutchins' certificate until the next meeting of the County Board of Public Instruction, and when the local trustees complained that Hutchins was a popular teacher and that magistrates had no business interfering with schools unless trustees complained, Hodgins replied that justices and the County Board were competent to decide the questions at issue.[115]

## Popular Belief and Punishment

As we have seen, the education office had a contradictory and confused attitude towards corporal punishment. On the one hand, educational administrators looked forward to the day when corporal punishment at school would not be necessary. The elimination of corporal punishment was possible, given an educational psychology which had unlocked the secrets of the 'child mind', given energetic and competent teachers, given the subordination of children by parents at home, and given rich and continual instructional activity. Education officers urged the minimization or abandonment of corporal punishment wherever possible. At the same time, the authority of the teacher in the schoolroom was to be sustained, if necessary with physical force. This justified the application of violence to recalcitrant or disobedient students. Education in state schools would be intrinsically pleasurable to students, and this pleasantness would eliminate the need for physical violence. But pleasure as defined by the education office did not include any serious principle of student autonomy. Things which students might have found pleasurable, such as learning at an individual pace, studying what interested them, learning collectively or in groups, and expressing their pleasure through laughing, joking, playing and so forth, were defined as illicit in principle. Pleasure in the official view was contained in the routines and rituals of regulated schooling; any forms of pleasure not so contained were to be eliminated.

But the official campaign for 'gentle' schooling contributed to the growth of a belief in many parts of the province that corporal punishment was illegal under the School Acts. Local school supporters read the contradictory public discourse of school government in terms of their own interests in schooling. These frequently conflicted with those of the education office. Magistrates often enforced the popular belief in the illegality of school violence.

As early as 1854, William Rath, a superintendent of schools in Perth County, complained of popular opposition to corporal punishment. In his annual report he wrote,

> Another great defect in the Schools is a want of proper discipline--- this evil is almost universal--- I think it arises partly from the prevalence of a somewhat fashionable doctrine--- an importation from the United States--- that teachers should never on any occasion use a rod in School....[116]

James Sim, the local superintendent from Hawksville, wrote in 1862 with alarm about 'a growing practice among parents in some School Sections to try to limit the power of the teacher in the government of the school.' This practice, 'every sensible man must know,' would certainly 'put an end to School order. It is indeed reprehensible on the part of a teacher,' Sims continued, 'to inflict corporal punishment for every trifling offence,' and every teacher ought 'to govern with kindness and reason, remembering that the child under his care is the germ of an intelligent being.' But in cases where 'parents not only do not co-operate with the teacher but speak disparagingly of him in the presence of their children' the results would 'soon be obvious in the behaviour of the whole school.'

> When a child hears the father or mother say 'I will not allow the teacher to whip my children;'--- the child if a little inclined to be vicious goes to school not so much to learn as to put himself in an attitude of defence [*sic* defiance]. The teacher sees the defiant spirit manifested by such; and that, like a plague it is spreading in his School, and, he sets about checking it. He reasons, he expostulates, but it is all in vain. He next resorts to the rod, and in punishing some rebellious culprit he inflicts strips which slightly discolour the skin and what is the result? He is

> summoned before a Justice of the Peace and condemned, and then returns to his school dispirited because deprived of the power to enforce his authority at all hazards.

'In sections where this is done,' Sim concluded, 'it is nearly impossible for a Master to teach or command respect.'[117]

W.A. Gordon was arrested for beating a student on the back with a rawhide strap. 'There seems to be a strong feeling against the practice amongst parents generally,' Gordon complained, after the student's father assaulted him in the school room. But how, he wondered, was he to teach? 'With a School averaging 130, in charge of but two teachers, it is no easy matter to dispense with corporal punishment.' And worse still, 'there is a Magistrate who has been boasting for a long time that if a Teacher were brought before him for inflicting any corporal punishment he would make an example of him.' The chief superintendent merely referred Gordon to the *Educational Manual*.[118]

J. Lawson, a teacher from Battersea, was summoned for striking a student 'six or eight times' and 'on the back and shoulders only'. 'When the J.P. found that the charges could not be proven,' Lawson complained, 'he said it was contrary to law to strike a child at school at all --- a late Act had been passed to that effect--- he was very sorry but he was under the necessity of fining me.'[119]

Other teachers complained that it was technically difficult to govern in the schoolroom without the use of corporal punishment. 'Respecting corporal punishment in schools,' wrote John Sharpe, a teacher from section 1 of Hinchinbrooke Township, 'my local superintendent and a majority of the trustees of this section are under the impression that it has been abolished, and I have therefore dispensed with it for about a month but do not believe it works well---- and I lose much time leaving a class up to go round watching and coaxing and reasoning to induce quietness.'[120]

George Bell, the local superintendent for Stamford, claimed that 'the want of any provision for settling difficulties arising between a Teacher and parents respecting the discipline of the school' was 'a great defect in the School law.' In one township school, the teacher attempted to punish a girl named Ida Spencer for 'insubordination'. When Spencer was told to hold out her hands for punishment, 'she folded her arms and began to kick the Teacher.' The teacher then beat her across the arms and back with a ruler, was summoned and fined $4 and costs for assault. George Bell complained that events such as this were 'seriously affecting the rights of Teachers, and the discipline of the Common School.' He called for legislation to prevent the intervention of magistrates in all but extreme cases of school punishment.[121]

## The Education Office and the Magistracy

Egerton Ryerson had constructed the School Acts in an effort to contain educational conflicts within directly educational administrative structures. Arbitrations were intended to deal with all matters of dispute between teachers (who embodied the authority of the state) and trustees (who represented local educational interests). The School Regulations attempted to bolster this administrative containment of conflict in the domain of punishment by requiring teachers to keep punishment registers. All acts of physical punishment in a school were to be recorded and explained in the register, which was to be inspected by the local superintendent and then destroyed after the annual public examination of the school.[122] The magistracy was to have no active role in educational administration, and especially in the late 1840s and early 1850s, the education office had been particularly active in its insistence that trustees were empowered by the School Acts to take various administrative initiatives without any involvement by the magistracy. The power of trustees to order and execute the distraint of property in school tax disputes without the warrant of a magistrate, for instance, had been successfully defended in the late 1840s and early 1850s.

As we have seen, however, magistrates in many parts of the province intervened in cases of school punishment to fine teachers. The magistracy operated, to a certain extent, as a counterweight to the attempts by the education office to constitute the office of teacher as one from which to exert moral force upon the population. This intervention was regarded as problematic by many educational adminstrators, and was initially opposed by the education office itself.

When William Plunkett was arrested in the schoolroom of section 25 North Dumfries Township by the Bailiff, taken to court and fined $12 and costs for beating a student in a way sanctioned by his trustees, he sought advice about an appeal from the education office. Ryerson wrote to him in reply that the magistrate in question could not legally fine him. 'The Teacher is the Parent ruler of the School for the time being, and is accountable to his Trustees and Local Superintendent for the manner in which he exercises his authority.'[123] 'When attending the Normal School in 1856,' W.E. Gorshine of Walkerton wrote, 'I was advised to get along in school' without corporal punishment 'if possible; but never was forbidden to inflict corporal punishment.' But when he beat a student lightly in the summer of 1859, he was taken to court and fined $1 and costs. Ryerson deplored this intervention of the magistracy in school matters. The teacher was legally empowered to employ corporal punishment, he insisted, and if he punished too severely, the local superintendent could suspend his certificate. 'If such interference by a Magistrate in school matters be sanctioned,' Ryerson concluded, 'there must soon be an end to all order and discipline in schools.'[124] 'Teachers ought to be sustained in the just exercise of their authority,' complained a local superintendent named William Clelland, after the teacher in section 8 of Scott Township was fined for slapping a fifteen year old girl across the face. They 'should not be lightly interfered with, more especially when the interference comes from parental partiality too ready to listen to filial complaints.'[125]

By the early 1860s, however, the education office had been forced to accept that the magistracy would act in cases of excessive punishment at school. But on the other hand, already by the late 1850s, some magistrates had begun to seek explicit instructions from the education office in cases of school punishment. The normalization of the authority of the education office was extended in the 1860s.

The Grammar School teacher in Caledonia had a morbid fear of insects. A thirteen year old boy put a dead bee wrapped in a paper on the teacher's desk, and after finding it, the teacher made the boy take off his coat and whipped him on the back with a cowhide strap until he bled. A school supporter called this punishment a 'degradation'. Ryerson conceded that while teachers had a legal power to punish, they might nonetheless exceed this power. 'A magistrate,' he concluded, 'can of course investigate & decide the point.'[126] John Abbott of Mariposa gave a student 'about fourteen lashes more or less' with a beech rod 'for bad behaviour in school which is too degrading to mention.' 'It marked him some,' Abbott noted, and he was sentenced in court to a fine of $4 with $3 in costs or 14 days in gaol. After directing Abbott to the sections on punishment in the *Educational Manual*, Ryerson remarked that 'suspension for gross misconduct is preferable to severe corporal punishment— (which is not practiced in our Model Schools) and cases may occur when the interference of the magistrate would be necessary.' He also pointed out that he had no power over magistrates.[127] Similar comments were made to other teachers.[128]

A. Campbell and Daniel Gilbert, both magistrates, sent Ryerson transcriptions of the entire testimony in cases which they heard concerning school punishment.[129] Niel Eastman, a magistrate in Arkana, wondered if teachers could forcibly eject students from the schoolroom, and if the students resisted, he wondered if he should convict them of assault and battery.[130] A justice of the peace named J.H. Thompson from Vroomaster wrote to the Education Office for guidance in a case where a teacher beat a female student for disobedience and suspended her. When she refused to leave, 'he then whipped her with the taws again.' Could the teacher, Thompson wondered, legally punish the student after having suspended her?[131] A justice of the peace from Wardsville in Middlesex County wrote to Ryerson in 1868 wondering,

> as several complaints have been made to me of late against School Teachers for cruelty or beating pupils some of them twenty one years of age, you will please let me know if there is any law for a Teacher to beat pupils either old or young or if there has been any decision on the Subject before the Judges of the Superior Courts.
> NB. I fined one Teacher $10 for cutting a boy on the Head fearfully another had thrashed a lad with a raw-hide in a cruel manner another was beat on a lame hand.
> I would be sorry to be too severe but residing quite near Several Schools I would like to be posted in the

matter.[132]

This increasing willingness of magistrates to seek instruction in educational matters points to the alignment of local elites on the side of educational administration. It also points to an increasing density in educational authority relations, and foreshadows the normalization of educational administration. That the Education Office should come to appear to the local magistracy as the 'normal' or 'natural' source for information about the justice and acceptability of violence at school mirrors a practical disempowering of school supporters and students. In such situations the education office both found itself connected to local schooling through an additional knowledge/power circuit, and was able to use this connection to extend a conception of legitimate educational violence at the local level.

## Conclusion

By 1871 the normalization of relations of authority in the educational state remained partial. Community regulation of the schools was markedly weakened by the increasing solidity of administration and by the increasing density of administrative relations. But community intervention remained common. The 'good parent' sought by the education office,---- a parent prepared to bolster the authority relations of the school, to ignore student complaints, to beat again at home the student beaten at school,---- this parent was more an ideal than a real character. Only in the early twentieth century did such 'good parents' become sufficiently common that 'Home and School Associations' were formed to 'interest' parents in the education of their children.

The monopoly over the means of violence at school which the Education Office sought through the office of teacher was frequently contested. Many teachers were made vividly aware of the limits to their power to punish. G.M. Sheldon, the teacher at Dawn Mills in 1866, certainly was. 'A few days ago,' he wrote,

> I slightly chastised a little girl in my school for an act of wilful disobedience and in the evening her father came to me in a fearful rage, was with

> difficulty induced to refrain from violently
> assaulting me, and after much abusive language said
> if his child 'did not behave herself in school, turn her
> out' but 'if I ever touched her again he would stamp
> the guts out of me.'[133]

Maggie Graham of Florence had an argument with a boy about lighting the school fires. He became 'saucy', and she tried to punish him before the class, but

> he screamed very much before ever I hit him. I then
> got my gad (a small one) and he broke it he then
> screamed as if he was being killed, I told him if he
> would scream that way again I would slap his ears
> (at this time I never yet had hit me[*sic* him]) he then
> screamed again and I slapped his ears, one slap on
> each ear with my open hand, I sent a boy after
> another gad and before I whiped him with it his
> father came in; caught me by the shoulder and said; I
> was not going to whip his boy (you d--d dirty
> huzza)....[134]

This boy undoubtedly knew that his father was within earshot.

In the formative period of the educational state, students at school often had recourse to the protection of parents or other community members in their relations with teachers. Yet the direction of official policy in the 1850s and 1860s was increasingly clear. It sought, and increasingly secured, a realignment of educational structures such that effective force could be directed at the population with the objective of making political selves. The campaign for 'gentle' pedagogy involved a practical disempowering of students and school supporters, and the normalization of violence directed by teachers at students. 'Excessive' violence could be treated as the failure of individual teachers, while the right of teachers to beat students was strengthened in principle. Only in the 1970s was this right successfully challenged.

## Notes

1. I outline the more distant history of the marginalization of corporal punishment in educational theory in ' 'My ladie birchely must needes rule': corporal punishment from Mulcaster to Lancaster', paper presented to the Canadian History of Education Association, Halifax, 1986.
2. James Pillans, *Principles of Elementary Teaching.* (Ediburgh: Adam Black, 1828.):14-15. Compare also *The Rationale of Discipline. as exemplified in the High School of Edinburgh.* (Edinburgh: Maclachlan & Stewart, 1852.)
3. Pillans, *Principles:* 25-6.
4. Pillans, *Principles:* 30-1.
5. David Stow, *The Training System.* 6th ed. (Glasgow: Blackie and Son.):122.
6. Stow, *Training System:* 423-4.
7. A.M. Ross, 'Kay-Shuttleworth and the Training of Teachers for Pauper Schools,' *British Journal of Educational Studies,* 15, 1967:275-83.
8. Ross, 'Kay-Shuttleworth':276-9; Sir J.P. Kay-Shuttleworth, *Four Periods of Public Education [1862].* (Brighton: Harvester, 1973.):287.
9. Kay-Shuttleworth, *Four Periods:* 287.
10. James Kay, 'On the Punishment of Pauper Children in Workhouses [1841],' (Battersea: College of S. Mark and S. John, 1961.) *Occasional Papers,* 1:14.
11. Kay, 'Punishment of Pauper Children:' 15-24.
12. Horace Mann, *Life and Works. Volume II: Lectures and Annual Reports on Education.* (Cambridge: 1867.) 1840:342; 361.
13. Horace Mann, *The Life and Works of Horace Mann. Volume III: Annual Reports on Education.* (Boston: H.B. Fuller, 1862.) 1839:448.
14. Horace Mann, *Report of an Educational Tour.* (London: Simpkin, Marshall & Co., 1846.):169-70. This edition of Mann's report of his tour of 1844 contains notes by W.B. Hodgson of the Liverpool Mechanics' Institute. The quotation is reproduced in Egerton Ryerson, *Report on a System of Public Elementary Instruction for Upper*

*Canada.* (Montreal: Lovell and Gibson, 1847.): 168-9.
15. Lyman Cobb, *The Evil Tendencies of Corporal Punishment as a Means of Moral Discipline in Families and Schools. Examined and Discussed.* (New York: M.H. Newman & Co., 1847.):84.
16. Cobb, *Corporal Punishment:* 104-8.
17. Cobb, *Corporal Punishment:* 104.
18. This point is made in more detail elsewhere. See P. Corrigan, B. Curtis and R. Lanning, 'The Political Space of Schooling,' in T. Wotherspoon, ed., *The Sociology of Education.* Toronto: Methuen, 1987.) Curtis, 'My ladie birchely.'
19. Henry Dunn, *Principles of Teaching.* 10th ed., (London: Sunday School Union, c.1847):26-7.
20. Dunn, *Teaching:* 25-6.
21. D.P. Page, *Theory and Practice of Teaching.* (New York: A.S. Barnes, 1852.):203.
22. see note 18.
23. Canniff Haight, *Country Life in Canada Fifty Years Ago: Personal Recollections and Reminiscences of a Sexagenarian.* (Toronto: Hunter, Rose and Co., 1885.):18.
24. Haight, *Country Life:* 159-60.
25. PAO RG2 E2 (Documentary History Manuscripts), J. Carmichan, Niagara, 4 March 1894.
26. J.A. Bannister, *Early Educational History of Norfolk County.* (Toronto: University of Toronto Press, 1926):131.
27. J.G. Hodgins, ed., *Documentary History of Education in Upper Canada.* (Toronto: L.K. Cameron, 1894-1910.) VII:148.
28. *Journal of Education for Upper Canada (JEUC),* 1848:350.
29. *JEUC,* 1849: 142. Original emphasis.
30. *JEUC,* 1851: 102-3.
31. *JEUC,* 1852: 72. Original emphases. Also in this regard see chapter four above, and J. Donzelot, *The Policing of Families.* (New York:Vintage Books, 1979), and Fiona Paterson, 'Schooling the Family,' paper presented to the British Sociological Association, 1986.
32. *JEUC,* 1852: 123-4.
33. *JEUC,* 1852: 169.
34. *JEUC,* 1852: 173-4.
35. *JEUC,* 1853: 7.
36. *JEUC,* 1853: 17-18.
37. *JEUC,* 1854: 174-5.

38. *JEUC*, 1855: 3.
39. *JEUC*, 1855: 66-8.
40. For example, *JEUC*, 1856: 104; 1869:54; 86; 121; 1870: 87; 124.
41. J.G. Hodgins, *The School House; Its Architecture, External and Internal Arrangements.* (Toronto: Department of Public Instruction, 1857.):128-41.
42. Hodgins, *Schoolhouse:* 137-9.
43. PAO RG2 C6C, 22 June 1861; a packet of correspondence concerning the Rector of the Model Grammar School.
44. PAO MU975, Education Papers Collection, 1860-69. Maria Payne Notebooks, Toronto Normal School, 1869.
45. PAO RG2 C6C, E.S. Smith, 26 June 1869, no.1008.
46. PAO RG2 C6C, Wm. Wright, Toronto, 9 July 1858.
47. PAO RG2 C6C, David Fotheringham, Model School, 12 July 1858.
48. PAO RG2 C6C, D. Fotheringham, Model School, 2 October 1858; 21 September 1858; 31 August 1858; C1Y, Ryerson to Fotheringham, 16 September 1858; 25 August 1858.
49. PAO RG2 G4 (Forms and Circulars), *First Annual Report of the Superintendent of Public Schools for the City of Hamilton for 1855.*
50. PAO RG2 G4, *Report of the Public Schools for the City of Hamilton for the year 1861.*
51. PAO RG2 G4, *Report of the Common School, Town of Goderich, for 1857.*
52. PAO RG2 G4, *Rules and Regulations of the Union School, Paris, C.W. 1859.*
53. PAO RG2 G4, *Rules for the Government of the Public Schools in the City of Kingston. May 1863.* This 'spectacular' power was disapproved of in the Normal School method. See note 47 above.
54. PAO RG2 C6C, William Fraser, District 1, Bruce County, 7 May 1862. 'To the Common School Teachers of District No.1, Co. of Bruce.'
55. PAO RG2 C6C, William Fraser, District 1, Bruce County, 15 January 1863. 'To the Trustees and Ratepayers of School District No 1 County of Bruce.'
56. PAO RG2 C6C, William Fraser, Kincardine, 11 March 1864; C2, Ryerson to Fraser, 18 March 1864.
57. PAO RG2 C6C, Charles Robertson, Trustee, no. 10, Windham Centre, 9 June 1859.
58. PAO RG2 C6C, R.F. White, Trustee, no place, 29 March 1852.

59. PAO RG2 C6C, R.J. Morrison, Raleigh, 31 March 1855; Philip Andrew, Raleigh Plains, Chatham, 31 March 1855; R.J. Morrison, No. 8 Raleigh, 6 April 1855; Trustees, No.8 Raleigh, 6 April 1855.
60. PAO RG2 C6C, John Evans, East Gwillimbury, 27 June 1859.
61. PAO RG2 C6C, David Dick, Trustee, No.2 Mono, 30 June 1860.
62. PAO RG2 C6C, Geo. White, Hampton, 29 May 1861.
63. PAO RG2 C6C, John Hudson, Teacher, No. 3 London Township, 5 May 1860; Trustees, No. 3, 5 May 1860.
64. PAO RG2 C6C, W.J. Black, Teacher, Colborne, 10 November 1862.
65. PAO RG2 C6C, J.S. McColl, Superintendent Aldborough, 9 May 1863.
66. PAO RG2 C6C, Moses Hill, U.S.S. 1, Georgina Township, 28 February 1865.
67. PAO RG2 C6C, Trustees, Concord, 15 February 1868.
68. PAO RG2 C6C, John Morrison, Petrolia, 1 March 1869.
69. PAO RG2 C6C, C.E. Abraham, Ancaster, 13 March 1867; John Lees, Superintendent, Ancaster, 29 March 1867.
70. PAO RG2 C6C, Jas. Lawson, section 4 Loughboro, 19 February 1870.
71. After the 'Brantford School Difficulty' in A. Prentice and S. Houston eds., *Family, School & Society in nineteenth century Canada.* (Toronto: Oxford University Press, 1975.):107-14.
72. 'The Government of Children in Public Schools', *JEUC*, 12, 1859:123-4.
73. 'School Punishments' from the Brockville *Recorder*, 12 April 1860, in PAO RG2 C6C, J.H. Johnson, Superintendent, Brockville, 10 April 1860.
74. PAO RG2 C6C, H. Eliot, Whitby, 7 March 1854.
75. PAO RG2 C6C, David Johnston, Teacher, Melville, 14 March 1854.
76. PAO RG2 C6C, Henry Fieldhouse, Murray, 28 March 1855.
77. PAO RG2 C6C, Trustees, St. Mary's, 9 May 1855.
78. PAO RG2 C6C, A.J. Campbell, Teacher, Carlisle, 25 May 1860. See the discussion of 'The Limits of the Pedagogical Sphere' in chapter four above.
79. PAO RG2 C6C, B.F. Pearson, Teacher, Hawksville, 14 June 1862.
80. PAO RG2 C6C, Hugh McDiarmid, Chatham, 10 December 1862; C2, Ryerson to McDiarmid, 17 December 1862.
81. PAO RG2 C6C, Jacob E. Summers, Teacher, East Williamsburgh,

18 August 1862.
82. PAO RG2 C6C, Walter Meacham, Teacher, Rednersville, 9 February 1867.
83. PAO RG2 C6C, Robert Irvine, Teacher, section 2 Gloucester, 8 August 1865.
84. PAO RG2 C6C, James Smith, Trustee, Enniskillen, 30 May 1867; John Garland, Teacher, Mitchell, 22 April 1868; J.P. Flanagan, Teacher, section 11 Brant, 29 September 1868; Stephen Pashley, Teacher, Belleville, 25 November 1868; F. Sellers, Teacher, section 17 Walpole, 20 June 1870; H. Cruickshank, Teacher, Ancaster, 2 September 1870; William Henry, Teacher, Enniskillen, 12 October 1870.
85. For example, PAO RG2 C6C, George Leighton, Teacher, section 19 Chinguacousy, 31 May 1865; William Russell Jn., Teacher, section 13 Ramsay, 21 April 1863; D. Morrison, Superintendent, Beckwith, 2 July 1856.
86. PAO RG2 C6C, G.W. Cook, Teacher, Merrittville, 2 June 1855.
87. PAO RG2 C6C, J.M. Westover, Teacher, Staffordville, 11 March 1865.
88. PAO RG2 C6C, H.J. Brine, Teacher, Oakland, 22 May 1866.
89. PAO RG2 C6C, John Agnew, Teacher, Sydenham, 27 January 1867.
90. PAO RG2 C6C, Alexander Mc Donald, Teacher, Wardsville, 12 October 1867.
91. PAO RG2 C6C, Thomas Mackie, Euphrasia, 19 April 1870.
92. PAO RG2 C6C, John Le Boutilier, Trustee, section 6 Sidney, 12 March 1869; *The Educational Manual for Upper Canada.* (Toronto: 1861.):128. *Pupils.* 'No pupil shall be allowed to depart before the hour appointed for closing school, except in case of sickness, or some pressing emergency; and then the master's consent must first be obtained.' These regulations had the force of statute law.
93. PAO RG2 C6C, Lewis Allen, Teacher section 17 Ernesttown, 20 May 1856; C1R, Hodgins to Allen, 7 June 1856.
94. PAO RG2 C6C, H.M. Day, Teacher, section 13 Brock, 17 February 1859; C2, Ryerson to Day, 23 February 1859.
95. PAO RG2 C6C, Thomas Heritage, Trustee, section 5 Peel, 25 January 1859; C2, Ryerson to Heritage, 31 January 1859.
96. *The Educational Manual for Upper Canada.* (Toronto: 1856.): 140-1.

97. *Educational Manual:* 82.
98 PAO RG2 C1C, Ryerson to Johnston Neilson, Kitley, 4 March 1847.
99. PAO RG2 C6C, Robert Brydon, Superintendent, Waterloo, 9 June 1856; C1R, Hodgins to Brydon, 18 June 1856
100. PAO RG2 C2, Ryerson to Anthony Horner, Wilton, 15 February 1868; C6C, Anthony Horner, Wilton, 15 February 1868.
101. PAO RG2 C1C, Ryerson to George Hendry, Woodstock, 3 April 1847; also C1E, Ryerson to Elias Burnham, Peterborough, 20 September 1849; C6C, Burnham to Ryerson, 14 September 1849. Burnham wrote about a brutal teacher: 'George Preston says the teacher beat a little girl of his--- aged five years--- so much that she was all black on several parts of her body & legs--- & that he could not get her to go to school again, except now & then with great difficulty that she would go & hide in the fields--- during school hours--- that previously she was glad to go to school.' Ryerson replied that he could not judge this case without information about the 'conduct and character' of the children. Some children would resist correction, 'which induces the necessity of greater severity.'
102. PAO RG2 C1BB, Ryerson to P.A. Muir, Headmaster, Brantford Common School, 6 September 1859; C6C, Muir to Ryerson, 26 August 1859. This is 'the Brantford School Difficulty' reproduced in Prentice and Houston, *Family, School and Society.*
103. PAO RG2 C6C, Angus Bell, Singhampton, 8 September 1862; Thomas Kiernan, Teacher, Singhampton, 9 September 1862; C2, Ryerson to Bell 12 September 1862 for the quotation; Ryerson to Kiernan, 12 September 1862, '...sternness is as essential as kindness.'
104. PAO RG2 C1BB, Ryerson to James C. Brown, London, 8 October 1859.
105.PAO RG2 C6C, R.N. Grant, Flamboro East, 5 March 1867; C2, Ryerson to Grant, 10 March 1867.
106. PAO RG2 C6C, Archibald Sinclair, Teacher, Mayborough, 9 March 1867; C2, Ryerson to Sinclair, 21 March 1867.
107. PAO RG2 C6C, Silvanus Mullett (and 15 others), section 8 Fredericksburgh, 8 January 1850, w. deposition of Ross Millar; C1E, Ryerson to Mullett, 9 March 1850.
108. PAO RG2 C6C, Archibald Andrews, Teacher, Osgoode, 10 June 1870; J.R. Cousins, Superintendent, Osgoode, 11 June 1870; C2, Ryerson to Andrews, 25 June 1870; Ryerson to Cousins, 25 June

1870.

109. PAO RG2 C6C, Alexander Wood, Smith's Falls, 8 February 1860; W. Aitken, Superintedent, Smith's Falls, 21 February 1860 (includes Stewart Moug to Trustees, 20 February 1860); C1CC, Ryerson to Wood, 29 February 1860.

110. PAO RG2 C1CC, Ryerson to John Mackenzie, Teacher, Westminster, 20 March 1860; C6C, John Mackenzie, Westminster, 10 March 1860.

111. PAO RG2 C2, Ryerson to James Farrington, Teacher, Eastwood, 22 February 1865; parts of Ryerson's remarks cited here are scored out in the draft; the final version has not survived.

112. PAO RG2 C6C, J. McCainon, Bridgewater, 19 May 1864; C2, Ryerson to McCainon, 23 May 1864.

113. PAO RG2 C6C, George Bull, J.P., Stirling, 21 April 1866; C2, Ryerson to Bull, 28 April 1866.

114. PAO RG2 C6C, Charles Clarke, Wardsville, 22 April 1863; 1 May 1863; J.S. McColl, Superintendent, Aldborough, 1 May 1863; Clarke to education office, 14 May 1863. Ryerson's reply is missing.

115. PAO RG2 C6C, A. Harvey, Superintendent, Houghton, 15 July 1855; Trustees to education office, 29 August 1855, w. W.W. Hutchins to trustees attached, w. J.P. to trustees attached; C1T(?), Hodgins to Harvey, 25 July 1855; Hodgins to trustees, 11 September 1855.

116 PAO RG2 C6C, Wm. Rath, Superintendent, Co. of Perth, 12 April 1854.

117. PAO RG2 C6C, James Sim, Superintendent, Hawksville, 12 February 1862; C2 Ryerson to Sim, 21 February 1862.

118. PAO RG2 C6C, W.A. Gordon, Teacher, section 4 Mosa, 26 February, 6 March 1867; C2, Ryerson to Gordon, 11 March 1867.

119. PAO RG2 C6C, J. Lawson, Teacher, Battersea, 16 November 1869.

120. PAO RG2 C6C, John Sharpe, Teacher, section 1 Hinchinbrooke, 22 March 1869.

121. PAO RG2 C6C, George Bell, Superintendent, Stamford, 14 September 1870. (no.6571)

122. *Educational Manual.* 1861:126.

123. PAO RG2 C6C, William Plunkett, Teacher, section 25 N. Dumfries, 8 November 1859; C1BB, Ryerson to Plunkett, 12 November 1859.

124. PAO RG2 C6C, W.E. Gorshine, Teacher, Walkerton, 23 August, 7 September 1859; C1BB, Ryerson to Gorshine, 27 August 1859.
125. PAO RG2 C6C, William Cleland, Superintendent, Scott, 7 April 1869; Trustees, section 8 Scott, 8 April 1869; notice Joseph Gaulets, J.P., Uxbridge, 20 April 1869, asks for Hodgins' comments on the case.
126. PAO RG2 C6C, W. Thomson, Caledonia, 19 June 1862; C2, Ryerson to Thomson, 25 June 1862.
127. PAO RG2 C6C, John T. Abbott, Teacher, Mariposa, 21 April 1862; C2, Ryerson to Abbott, 29 April 1862.
128. PAO RG2 C6C, William Roche, section 18 Charlotteville, 13 March 1868; C2, Ryerson to Roche, 21 March 1868; C6C, William Tytler, Head master, St. Mary's Union School, 31 May 1870; C2, Ryerson to Tytler, 7 June 1870.
129. PAO RG2 C6C, Alexander Campbell, J.P., Acton, 9 February 1859; Daniel Gilbert, J.P., Gilbert's Mills, 5 March 1868.
130. PAO RG2 C6C, Niel Eastman, J.P., Arkana, 17 December 1861.
131. PAO RG2 C6C, J.H. Vroomaster, ?May 1866.
132. PAO RG2 C6C, J.P. Grove, J.P., Wardsville, 27 February 1868.
133. PAO RG2 C6C, G.M. Sheldon, Dawn Mills, 21 May 1866.
134. PAO RG2 C6C, Maggie Graham, Florence, 10 February 1868.

# Conclusion

Speaking of the period between 1780 and 1830 in England, Corrigan and Sayer have argued that 'abstract forms of property [came] to be ...normalized as a new moral code of individualized character.'[1] The practical struggle for the construction of bourgeois hegemony in this period involved the creation of institutions which would structure the conditions of rule into the selves of the ruled. Practice in a range of institutions---- schools, prisons, asylums, Mechanics' Institutes, libraries and others--- aimed at the moral discipline of the working class. These were all educational institutions in a broad sense.

'What a moral revolution would be produced among the masses,' proclaimed the Scottish educator David Stow, if popular schooling were well organized.[2] Like all of his contemporaries in Europe and America, Stow insisted that this 'moral revolution' would be the result of a systematic *habituation* of the working class. 'We cannot lecture a child into good manners,' he insisted, 'or change habits of any kind by the longest speech. The physical, intellectual, or moral habit, is only changed by a succession, or rather by a repetition of *doings.* ' And he added that 'obedience---- instant obedience, ought to be the daily and hourly practical lesson in every department.'[3]

The process of educating the population in Canada West after the reforms of 1846-50 involved the construction of routines and rituals of obedience. The creation in the population of new habits, attitudes, orientations, desires; the channeling of popular energy into particular regulatory forms supportive of a bourgeois social order--- these were the objectives of education. Over time, these objectives have been absorbed into the *texture* of state schooling.[4] They have become implicit, taken for granted, normal. State schooling can only present itself as the path to a literate, enlightened, advantaged population--- as it now often does--- where the means it employs to this end have ceased to be visible. This invisibility is two-sided.

Looking back in 1885 upon his education in the schools of the 1830s, Canniff Haight wrote,

> The school houses then were generally small and uncomfortable, and the teachers were often of a very inferior order. The school system of Canada, which has since been moulded by the skillful hand of Dr.

> Ryerson into one of the best in the world...was in my day very imperfect indeed...when the advantages which the youth of this country now possess are compared with the small facilities we had of picking up a little knowledge, it seems almost a marvel that we learned anything.$_5$

It is not startling to see a respectable middle class author writing of the schools of 1885 as if they were better than those of 1835. What is *startling* here— precisely because it is so ordinary— is Haight's estimation of schools in the 1830s and schools in the 1880s as simply different versions of the same phenomenon.

This perception— by someone who straddled the two periods of state and community schooling— points to the increasingly successful normalization of the educational state. By the 1880s in Ontario, education had come to be so completely identified with state schooling that even those who had lived an alternative reality came to relive their experience in new social categories. As a social process and social condition aimed at the remaking of moral character, state schooling changed the terms in which those subject to it understood themselves and the world they inhabited. And, it must be stressed, for most of these the vision of an alternative educational state vanished.

Canniff Haight's satisfaction with the reformed schools of the 1880s was not mirrored in the self-reflection of all of those schooled to obedience. There are few letters from students in the official correspondence of the education office. Students were frequently written about, but 'official' writing was not the channel through which they usually expressed their reactions to state schooling. The exceptions, however, are remarkable.

In 1870, shortly before the School Act of 1871 which made school attendance for a limited period compulsory in Ontario came into effect, a person from Bracebridge named E. Travers wrote to the chief superintendent,

> I am one of those boys that played truant, and I wish you would permit me to defend myself and show those Teachers that are so eager to get the law of compulsion in force that there is no necessity for such a law, if they would do their par[t] well, instead of murmuring against us. I will now show

why we played truant. at the age of six I began to go to school and in a few months I could read in the second Book then the teacher gave us a task in the multiplication table; well I was one of those thick skull Blockheaded fellows as he called me; well nothing but to stand on the floore during recess day after day until I became disgusted.... My mental calibre was not sufficiently developed to study Geometry and Algebra, therefore I think if my teacher had used me as a child and let me had a map that I might have drawn some of the Islands, read and write, I would have loved to go to school....[6]

The clerk in the education office scrawled across the face of this letter, 'No reply.'

This letter should be read as a cry of anguish, but we must also attend to the way in which this student's ability to understand his condition has been confused. While the school's representation of him to himself as inferior ('thick skull Blockheaded' and lacking 'mental calibre') clearly hurts, he has accepted--- or nearly accepted it. And what he can conceive as the means to recover his initial pleasure in education is to be 'used...as a child,' to go backwards to that period before the process of his schooling began in earnest. But this 'use' of him by the state school was the glaze for its mirroring of his inferiority. The normalization of 'good moral character' by the state school was, and continues to be, a process of confusing and disorganizing the abilities of much of the schooled population to make sense of the political structure of the world. As Fred Inglis points out, it is the construction and management of popular 'ignorance.'[7]

Capitalist societies are hedged about by relations of force; antagonistic class relations are kept from disintegration by a constant boundarisation and compression exerted by state forms. Force and the potential for violence permeate all social relations in such societies. The basis of political order in the general right to property presumes the existence of 'the state', a general force capable of defending right. Right itself, as Kay and Mott demonstrate is force, and general rights assume general forces. But it is misleading to conceive of these forces simply as institutions, as what Engels called 'armed men' and their 'material appendages, prisons, and coercive institutions of all kinds.'[8]

## Conclusion 369

The achievement of 'security of property' has involved a process of the saturation of society with relations of force. For the 'modern citizen', these relations work as a (social) 'grammar' of the natural, neutral, universal, and— above all— Obvious.[9]

Political power is based ultimately on a monopoly of violence, as many people have remarked. But in capitalist societies where commodity production and exchange assume the 'free' worker and equality in the marketplace, the regular and quotidian application of violence is ineffective and inefficient. With the decline of feudal regimes and with the increasingly solidity of the social monopoly of the means of violence, political power increasingly comes to be based upon rational administration and moral regulation. Elias[10] has charted the coincident development of a monopoly over the means of violence in the period of absolutism and the appearance of systematic pressure on members of the ruling classes for the 'refinement of manners.' In the liberal democratic or representative state, the monopoly of the means of violence itself becomes the object of rational administration. Here the interest of ruling classes in political governance as self-formation intensifies, as the 'irresistible progress of civil liberty' advances.

The individual subject of right is both a necessary postulate and a practical accomplishment of bourgeois society. The purchase and sale of commodities presupposes the encounter in the marketplace of buyer and seller enjoying an undisputed claim as proprietors. Law embodies this subjectivity as a fundamental principle, and philosophical theory takes it as a point of departure from the early seventeenth century.[11] But capitalist societies exist on the basis of a range of social contradictions whose maintenance is continuously problematic. General rights to property, formal equality before the law, citizenship, are the practical bases for substantive propertylessness, inequality, political exclusion and subordination.

By 1871 social relations in the new province of Ontario had been situated in an educational state, and 'every system of public education,' as Egerton Ryerson remarked in passing in *A Special Report on the State of Popular Education on the Continent of Europe,* 'is a system of compulsion.'[12] Educational administrative structures and practices affected most of the population directly. The schools had become a force in the land, and this quite literally; sites for the application of moral forces specified by the respectable classes to the population as a whole.

As sites from which to 'diffuse useful knowledge' and 'sound habits' throughout society, public schools can be understood as at once elements in attempts by respectable classes to solidify their rule, to mediate class conflict and to colonize civil society. Public schools were seen by their proponents as outposts in the moral wilderness of popular culture, and as institutions whose social role would be to civilize and humanize a barbarous population. Public schools would perform these functions through the application of moral force. The energies of the population would be laid hold of, selectively developed and strengthened, channeled and directed. Such schools, so the fiction runs, were 'provided' into a vacuum. In fact, as I (and others) have shown, this 'provision' was a reworking of the 'popular clamour for learning' into a form of silence and subordination.

This was an effort at the mediation of class conflict, and mediation is not in any simple sense repression. The mediation of class conflict involved an attempt to change it into something else, to transform it. Public schooling was at once public construction, the creation of that sphere of universality— the public— without which the private sphere cannot itself exist. The education office attempted to make the sphere of public instruction a neutral sphere, a sphere above politics, where the rich man and the poor man (and women) would be on conditions of equality. This meant the elaboration of a set of common conditions to which all students in the educational sphere would be subject. A common curriculum, a common pedagogy and a common christianity would form the substance of educational treatment, and this formally equal treatment would create conditions of social harmony.

Of course, the 'public' realm of schooling was contradictory. The conditions of universality in the public were the conditions of bourgeois hegemony. Access to this realm of harmony and equality, and treatment in it, depended upon the student's adoption of behavioural traits with a *specific* content, and also upon the visible adoption of signs of a particular orientation to this sphere. This, of course, is precisely mediation; respect for private property became respect for the teacher in the educational domain. 'Respect for others' came in practice to be seen as personal cleanliness, punctuality, orderliness. In other words, educational practice mediated class relations both by substituting abstract authority figures for particular priests and proprietors, and by inflecting authority relations, in such a way that they became personal and psychological relations. Educational practice contributed to the construction of bourgeois hegemony by normalizing particular forms of character and comportment.

The explicit content of lessons aimed to bolster the authority and property relations congenial to the bourgeoisie and to enlist popular energy in the support of capitalist accumulation. 'A rich man, even though he may care for no one but himself, can hardly avoid benefiting his neighbours.' 'Can it be supposed that the poor would be better off if all the property of the rich were taken away and divided among them......? The poor would then be much worse off than they are now....' 'God has appointed to each his own trials, and his own duties...'[13] Official knowledge presented the patriarchal, linguistic, ethnic, political economic and religious interests of the ruling class as the general interest of society.

The image of the public school as an internal colonial outpost is useful. It is also a sensible image in terms of the architecture of the public. The ideal school--- only approximated in towns and villages--- separated from the local community by a stout fence and whose playgrounds were accessible only through the school house, was a sort of pure state space. Here relations would obtain which would themselves be educative and 'like heat in the atmosphere,' these relations would 'be diffusive'.[14] The separation of the sexes, the architectural enforcement of 'discretion,' the safe development of the forces of the body, the cultivation of the 'delicate' senses through exposure to flowers, the lessons in economy transmitted by the school garden, and in morality through selfless care for this public good, would create ideal citizens. The force exerted in this moral crucible would radiate outwards into the local community, and in part this radiation was visible. The sight of the school house, the knowledge that the fortress was near, would influence the behaviour of the colonized population.

Complementing this image was the massive and fortress like collection of buildings which housed the Education Department, the Normal and Model schools. These buildings themselves dominated the north-eastern centre of Toronto, with the tower of the Normal School rising above an imposing portico and surrounded by decorative gardens open to the population of Toronto on limited terms.

The education office was connected to the local conduct of schooling through administrative circuits of knowledge/power which allowed central officers to intervene at least in situations which might have involved principles of the system as a whole. When the central educational authority became impatient for local intelligence it sent its superintendents to collect information in the local school.

Powers of educational management pertained to local representatives of property. While these powers were closely specified and hedged about with legal restrictions, the public school was publicly controlled. But 'public' management must be closely contrasted with direct communal management. The development of local public educational administration was a process of empowering the *representatives* of property in certain areas, while disempowering most of the local community. Between 1836 and 1871 control over educational organization and management moved radically away from students and the financial supporters of schools. In principle, and increasingly in practice, what was studied at school, by whom, under what conditions and on what occasions was determined by a central educational authority. As we have seen repeatedly in this study, school supporters and students opposed this process practically in school room and local community. But this opposition took the form of persistent and localized skirmishes. Movements of provincial opposition to public education as such, or to centralized educational management did not arise. Public education came to monopolize the terrain of educational provision, to the point that the possibility of alternative forms was largely lost.

But I do not suggest that we be content to contemplate popular resistance to the state school as an object of romance. Resistance was not itself inherently progressive. Students and local school supporters were frequently unable to counterpose to the school any consistent vision of an alternative educational reality. What is instructive about resistance in part is the fact that the logic and practices of educational administration contained local opposition largely within themselves. By defining educational matters as the exclusive preserve of a select group of public officials and by enforcing this definition at law, the central authority appropriated the powers of educational self-management commonly exerted by school supporters. This appropriation was legitimated by the interposition of barriers of expertise and 'sound moral character' between public officers and school supporters. At the same time, the administrative encapsulation of educational opposition turned the latter at times into a force of police for the public educational system. Tax payers disgruntled by high rates might report local deviations from official policy to the central authority. School supporters angered by pedagogical practices might report 'moral' failings of the teacher to the local superintendent. Not only did such practices allow the system of educational administration to expose its own officers to a public scrutiny which facilitated the central monitoring of local practices, but they also tended to normalize the *fact* of central authority.[15]

Indeed, once set in motion, the administrative organization of public education produced its own developmental logic, in which local opposition contributed to the growth of administrative structure. Educational interventions generated local opposition which in turn generated new educational interventions and new forms of opposition. At key points during the period between 1850 and 1871, the accumulation of educational opposition resulted in major system alterations. The reform of the curriculum in 1866 is an instance of persistent opposition being ultimately beyond the powers of containment of administrative practice.

On the whole, however, local opposition to central policy initiatives tended to extend and solidify administrative structures. Attempts by local school supporters to continue various forms of educational self-management against the interests of the education office were quashed and in several instances, the chief superintendent sought and publicized the judgement of the Court of Queen's Bench. The practice of boarding the teacher, for instance, was declared illegal, as was the practice of direct voting on substantive questions in school meetings, and the calling of special meetings by school supporters. The exposure of attempts at the counter-organization of educational space increasingly narrowed the field of effective opposition, while containing educational practice in state forms. A political consequence of the practical installation of bourgeois hegemony is the limitation for members of other classes of the capacity to envision an alternative social order. The logic of administration is the inflection and deflection of struggle based ultimately on class exploitation into individual character and onto derivative objects.

In the schoolroom itself, the reality of opposition to coercive pedagogy led the education office to elaborate and publicize an array of practices and administrative devices designed to counter or circumvent opposition. 'Irregular attendance', which as we have seen, was often a counter-definition of the social role of education, was combated by an array of tactics: barring late-comers, locking the school door, awarding demerit points, demanding notes from parents, demotions of students and so forth. Out of these attempts to discipline a resistant population emerged many of the now commonplace educational administrative categories (the 'truant,' the 'school phobic') and devices (the report card, for instance, as a sort of moral balancesheet, meant to evaluate and announce the behaviour of the student). These devices and techniques fashion and work schooled subjectivities.

The dynamic of educational administration was itself a process of state-building, insofar as it produced a 'technology of power,' and an arsenal of instruments of educational governance. At the same time, the administrative category system became increasingly self-referencing. Established initially to work a series of moral and political transformations upon the body politic through the creation of particular educational identities, as people came to live these educational identities, specifically educational criteria came to be experienced as the true measure of self-worth. Educational improvement, in part, came to be lived as self-improvement, and specifically 'educational' criteria were intensified in the measure of self identity. Educational failure became individual social failure, and in this way class differentiation has come to be defended as an individual characteristic rather than opposed as a form of social violence.

Consider the separation of the teacher from the local community. As we have seen, initially access to this occupation was easy. No clear barriers of knowledge/power existed between teachers and students where the teacher did not possess a monopoly over official knowledge, nor superiority based on age, physical or moral force. The practical separation of teachers from students and the more general population in need of instruction was effected by the imposition of 'educational' qualifications to the office, and the ongoing inflation of these qualifications. The ritual of the teacher's examination, that 'bureaucratic baptism of knowledge,'[16] in which teachers were publicly certified as 'knowledgeable' and 'moral',

## Conclusion 375

separated teachers from students and others. This was a political separation, initially, a separation whose formal dimension was more real than its substance: examined teachers did not know any more than their students in principle. However, the mobilization and administration of this population under the School Acts allowed for the increasingly selective application of criteria of 'respectability' and competence to candidates for admission to the office of teacher. A certificate of good character from a clergyman, the intention to teach, having reached a certain age, a respectable appearance, a plain round hand, a knowledge of techniques of school management, and other things could be demanded from candidates for teaching certificates. Administration effected a real separation of the teacher from the local population. The provisional character of all certificates for teaching— a character itself enforced over the opposition of teachers— subjected them in principle to regular scrutiny.

Educational administration as state formation superimposed an administrative grid upon civil society, elaborated and disposed practices and devices aimed at the regulation and transformation of popular character and culture. Administration set in motion a dynamic of development in which administrative controls over education became increasingly dense.

Yet a central aspect of educational administration was precisely the significant vagueness of educational relations. While administrative relations became more clearly specified, and while the political space of schooling was solidified, the limits of educational powers and behaviours were imprecise. We have seen this repeatedly in local conflicts over the precise meaning of 'strictly temperate habits,' over the limits of the teacher's authority, and over the power to punish. This persistent vagueness points to two dimensions of educational power.

First, educational power could not be contained within bureaucratic structures. The 'educational' did not simply reside in a definite set of practices which could be localized in time and space. Power was indefinite; both in practice and in the intentions of educational officials it spilled out of the schoolroom and its vicinity. Educational reform was intended as a process of subordinating and remaking the 'lower orders.' The governing classes and central educational administrators sought the creation of an education which would not simply cease at the schoolroom door and which would not exist simply between nine in the morning and four in the afternoon. Educational practice sought to create selves, and to anchor political relations congenial to private property and established authority in the characters of those educated. Representative educational administration in the locality was itself seen as educational in this sense. The formal universality of bureaucratic administration could not contain what was substantively a class politics.

Second, the indefiniteness of educational power points to the existence of the educational state-as-condition. The creation of the educational state was the construction of a general condition of discipline for the population as a whole. This condition was based on a created sense of nearly complete vulnerability to a potential educational force, and in the educational condition all actors were so susceptible.

The efficacy of this condition is based precisely upon the socially constructed 'ignorance' of those subjected to it, an 'ignorance' predicated on the absence of knowable limits. The teacher who might punish 'too much', who might be 'intemperate,' whose certificate was subject to recall at the discretion of anonymous officials, the trustees who might become personally liable for unknown corporate misdemeanours, the local resident who might be charged as a school disturber, the student who might be punished for 'insufficient attention,' for 'being saucy,' for laughing or making others laugh, all of these educational persons were potentially subject to a coercive force of an indefinite nature. And devices and practices structured into the administration of public education attempted to assure the visibility of all educational activities. Tours of inspection, annual reports, report cards, public examinations, and so forth, made visible the activities of those involved in schooling.

The vagueness of educational power created an important tactical space, room to manoeuvre, for educational authority. For local school supporters, of course, it also created space in which to counter-organise and contravene official policy. But educational space was a space illuminated by the techniques of scrutiny and examination which joined the central authority and local schools in relations of knowlege/power. This was not a dark space in whose corners educational opposition could hide; or at least, the level of lighting here was continually increasing, and relations were becoming more visible to the eye of power.

As well, the power at work in the educational realm is not adequately expressed in a model of bureaucratic administration. This was what Foucault calls a 'normalizing' power, a power whose efficacy resided in its transformation of the alien into the quotidien, the other into common sense. It is most obviously visible in the centrality of 'habituation' in pedagogical practice. Students habituated to certain kinds of behaviour at school would exhibit that behaviour outside of schools. The efficacy of 'respect for authority', for instance, lay not in students' mental appreciation of its moral correctness, but in their *practical* behaviour towards authority. *Habituation,* it should be remembered, was to precede intellectual instruction and to form its basis. A normalizing power operated by turning social and political relations into character structures. It made power real by embodying power relations in students. These power relations would ideally disappear; they would be lived as a sense of self, as an identity.

Such relations of power call into question the entire model of economic base/ institutional superstructure through which an earlier, partial Marxism has attempted to make sense of bourgeois society. Their analysis should also make one question a notion of bourgeois 'hegemony' which does not move beyond ideology. To the extent that educational development succeeded, it embraced all relations in civil society. The state should not be thought of as something 'above' or 'apart from' economic, domestic, religious or any other kind of social activity. To the extent that pedagogical practice colonized individual character, and to the extent that it became a general condition of discipline, all members of Canadian society have come to *embody* a particular capitalist state, as voice, gender, desire, age, situation.

This was no accident. It is precisely what state educational reformers struggled for. As Egerton Ryerson himself observed in a lecture called 'The Nature and Importance of the Education of Mechanics,' 'Education, properly speaking is, or rather should be, Practical Life in principle; Practical Life is Education in action.'[17] Education was meant to inculcate forms of self which would then be lived as natural; social life would simply become education in action.

Again, education cannot be understood simply as ideology. While one may understand the origins of educational practices in a class ideology mediated through educational forms of universality, educational hegemony did not work mainly through ideology. *Habituation* was at the core of educational practice. Pedagogy sought to lay hold of the selves of the population, to selectively develop individual forces, to regularize this development, to transform certain principles of social existence into dimensions of individual psychology. Thus, while students at school in Canada West read lessons in schoolbooks which clearly expressed the interests of the bourgeoisie as the interests of society as a whole, the success or failure of pedagogy did not depend upon their belief in or disbelief of these lessons. The success or failure of pedagogy depended rather upon the presence of students for such lessons, upon the inculcation in students of a particular attitude towards themselves and others in the process of being exposed to such lessons. The practices of instruction---- the silencing of students, the enforcement of 'cleanliness' and 'respect for authority', attendance norms, and at the same time, the practical monopolization of 'real' knowlege by the school--- were the measures of pedagogical practice. Bourgeois society is not held together only by the glue of ideology; a materialist analysis must attend to the practical organization of human energy. Bourgeois hegemony depends upon the inculcation, registration and implantation of the conditions of rule in individual character structure. Where this hegemony is established, rule disappears in a fundamental sense. Rule colonizes the self and is lived as a set of internal imperatives, desires, appetites, fears, tastes, habits, horizons.....

It is important to stress the presence in bourgeois educational reform of a discourse of pleasure. There was a progressive dimension to state educational reform. The vision of rich development for all members of society, the promise of a heightened and empowered individuality and the conception of universal social peace and prosperity were all progressive elements in the movement for state education. They reappear periodically as the terms in which the Educational State is defended. As I have shown repeatedly, educational reform announced itself to the population of Canada West as something which would be both democratic and intrinsically pleasing to students. The educational sphere was to be a sphere of harmony and equality, placed above the struggles of civil society. In this realm rich instructional activity would create joyful educational relations. The enrichment of the learner who learned to draw, to sing, to do 'gymnastics', to read wonderful stories of natural beauty, who learned about the fascinating habits and customs of animals, plants, and foreigners, who learned how society worked and who discovered the principles of historical development, was one of the main promises of public education. Indeed most histories of education in Canada West have accepted this promise of educational reform as the reality of educational practice. Educational reformers believed that they had understood once and for all the secrets of human psychological development and had mastered the means of shaping that development. The educational press was incessantly celebratory in its descriptions of real schools in Canada West.

Yet this notion of educational pleasure was class- and gender-specific. It's vision of utopia was one in which the working class freely embraced its subordination and took select modes of intellectual pleasure as compensation for material and political subordination; where women enjoyed male dominance in a sphere of 'private life' which mirrored the authority relations of the public; where young people were content to be 'children.' While many, if not most people in Canada West were prepared to support and sustain *some* conception of educational pleasure, concrete educational practices commonly did not produce pleasure. People at school did not enjoy many dimensions of real schooling; they opposed real educational practices, and they counterposed to these some alternative conception of educational pleasure. Faced, however, with a choice between popular pleasure and the principles of bourgeois political authority, educational administrators consistently chose authority. The progressive dimension of reform was continually limited by the maintenance of relations of subordination and domination in the Educational State.

Finally, while this Educational State in Canada West had its peculiar features, it was certainly not unique. Educational state-building in Canada West both drew upon and influenced an international experience. Educational reformers in Canada West were connected to their counterparts in other countries, and actively participated in a vibrant international ruling class political culture. The Canadian public schools embodied the pedagogical practices of Prussia and France, the inspectoral experience of Holland, France, Prussia, Scotland, England and Ireland, a curriculum derived from a religiously-glossed political economy applied to Ireland, and administrative devices developed in the United States. The Educational State as it existed in Canada West was publicized internationally through various media: an international educational literature, the reports of educational commissions from various countries, and International Expositions, like that held in Philadelphia in 1876. Leading school administrators in Canada West and later Ontario regularly met with their counterparts in other countries. The accomplishments of the Ryersonian educational administration were and continue to be trumpeted by later generations, from the work of George Ross in the 1890s to that of educational planners in the 1980s.[18] The educational condition and the educational project remain central constituents of political rule in the bourgeois order.

## Notes

1. Philip Corrigan and Derek Sayer, *The Great Arch: English State Formation as Cultural Revolution*. (Oxford: Blackwell, 1985):116.
2. David Stow, *The Training System*. (Glasgow: Blackie, 1840):102.
3. Stow, *Training System:* 12.
4. Philip Corrigan, 'In/forming Schooling,' in D. Livingstone ed. *Critical Pedagogy and Cultural Power*. 1986.
5. Canniff Haight, *Country Life in Canada Fifty Years Ago*. (Toronto: Hunter Rose, 1885.):19.
6. PAO RG2 C6C, E. Travers, Bracebridge, September 1870, no.6744.
7. Fred Inglis, *The Management of Ignorance*. (Oxford:Basil Blackwell, 1985).
8. Geoff Kay and James Mott, *Political Order and the Law of Labour*. (London: Macmillan, 1982); Frederick Engels, *The Origins of the Family, Private Property and the State*. New York: International, 1969:154-8.
9. Philip Corrigan makes this point forcefully at various points in his extensive contributions to the literature. In addition to the material cited above, see also the unpublished paper 'Together we are Ontario,' and 'Re/membering Modernity' in *Border/lines,* 6, 1986.
10. Norbert Elias, *The History of Manners* and *Power and Civility*. (New York: Pantheon, 1978; 1980)
11. E.B. Pashukanis, *Law and Marxism: A General Theory*. (London:

Ink Links, 1978.) C.B. Macpherson, *The Political Theory of Possessive Individualism*. (Oxford: Oxford University Press, 1962)
12. Egerton Ryerson, *A Special Report on the State of Popular Education on the Continent of Europe*. (Toronto, 1868):164. Ryerson is making specific reference to property taxation.
13. Series of National School Books, *Fourth Book of Lessons* (Toronto: Brewer & McPhail, 1857):224-231. Remove the religious overgloss and these statements could be from any of the classic political economy texts.
14. Egerton Ryerson, 'Circular to the Teacher of Each Common School in Upper Canada on His Duty Under the New Common School Act of 1850,' reprinted in J.G Hodgins, ed. *Historical and Other Papers and Documents Illustrative of the Educational System of Ontario*. (Toronto: L.K. Cameron, 1911-12.) III:238.
15. PAO RG2 C6C, Archibald Gillies, Teacher, Cold Water, 27 August 1858; Ryerson to Gillies, 30 August 1858. The extent to which the education office and the Chief Superintendent came to be perceived, at least by teachers and 'respectable' local residents, as authorities on all matters of educational import, on questions of 'real' knowledge and on matters of self-expression, cannot be overemphasized. For the committee of five from St. Thomas (?) who wrote to know how to pronounce the word 'Messrs.' and for Archibald Gillies, a Teacher from Cold Water, who wondered 'which of its sounds do Speakers, in general, give to the letter 'a' when used as an article,' the education office was the final arbiter of all such questions. 'Speakers in general give to the letter 'a' when used as an article its first sound according to Webster, as in Fate,' responded Ryerson to Gillies in three days. The reference for the teachers asking about how to pronounce 'Messrs.' I thought too quaint at the time to document, but it sticks in my mind.
16. Karl Marx, *Critique of Hegel's Philosophy of Right*. (Cambridge: Cambridge University Press, 1970.):51.
17. Egerton Ryerson, 'The nature and importance of the education of mechanics,' reprinted in J.G. Hodgins, ed. *Documentary History of Education in Upper Canada*. (Toronto: L.K. Cameron, 1894-1910.) XI:40.
18. In this regard, see John Millar, *The School System of the Province of Ontario*. (Toronto, 1898); George Ross, *The Schools of England and Germany*. (Toronto, 1898). These two--- DeputyMinister

and Minister of Education respectively in the 1890s cheer the Ryersonian legacy and see their own efforts as a direct continuation of it. So do the authors of *Towards 2000.* (Toronto: McClelland and Stewart, 1971.)

# Bibliography

### Archival Sources

The main sources upon which this study is based are contained in the Education Records Group of the Public Archives of Ontario. The Education Office preserved the major part of its enormous correspondence with field officers, trustees, parents, school supporters and others. A huge body of incoming general correspondence has been preserved, and a substantially smaller body of general outgoing correspondence has also survived. The main sections of Record Group 2 (Education) examined for this study are as follows:

### RG2 A

Minutes of the General Board of Education, 1823-1833.

### RG2 B

Minutes and Correspondence of the (Second) General Board of Education and the Council of Public Instruction, 1846-1871.

### RG2 C1

Outgoing General Correspondence, 1842-1860.

### RG2 C2

Draft Outgoing General Correspondence, 1860-1871.

### RG2 C6C

Incoming General Correspondence, 1842-1871.

### RG2 E1

Documentary History Manuscripts.

### RG2 F2

Local Regulations, Reports and Population Returns, 1842-1848.

### RG2 F3A

Annual Reports of District Superintendents and District Councils, 1842-1849.

### RG2 G4

Miscellaneous School Reports.

### RG2 H1

Normai and Model School Records.

### RG2 L5

Personnel Records.

## RG2 Q

Printed Forms, Circulars, and Pamphlets.

In addition, the following manuscript sources were consulted:

## MU972

Robert McKee Moore's Register & Day Book, West Gwillimbury Township.

## MU973

Proceedings of the Carleton County Board of Public Instruction, 1852-1865; John and Catherine McGibbon Copybooks.

## MU975

Maria Payne, Notebooks, Toronto Normal School, 1869.

## MU1375

Hodgins Papers.

## MU1765

John Macdonald (Cornwall) Papers.

## MU2109

Memoirs of Eliza Blair Keyes; Manuscript of *The Canadian*

*Arithmetic.* 1845.

**MU2323**

Hamnett Pinhey Papers.

**MU2883**

Steele (John) Papers.

**MU3274**

Ker Family Papers.

**School Books Collection.**

**Printed Material**

Abella, I.M. 'The Sydenham Election of 1841', *Canadian Historical Review,* XLVII, 4, 1966:326-343.

Acton, J. et al eds., *Women at Work: Ontario, 1850-1950.* Toronto: Women's Educational Press, 1974.

Adams, Howard *The Education of Canadians, 1800-1867.* Montreal: Harvest House, 1968.

Aitchison, J.H. 'The Municipal Corporations Act of 1849,' *Canadian Historical Review,* XXX, 1949:107-22.

Akenson, D.H. *The Irish Educational Experiment.* Toronto:

University of Toronto Press, 1970.

_____ *The Irish in Ontario.* Toronto: University of Toronto Press, 1985.

Althouse, J.G. *The Ontario Teacher, 1800-1910.* Toronto: Ontario Teachers' Federation, 1967.

Althusser, Louis 'Ideology and Ideological State Apparatuses,' *Lenin and Philosophy.* New York: Monthly Review Press, 1971: 127-186.

Altick, R.D. *The English Common Reader: A Social History of the Mass Reading Public, 1800-1900.* Chicago: University of Chicago Press, 1963.

Angus, Margaret 'Health, Emigration and Welfare in Kingston, 1820-1840,' in D. Swainson ed. *Oliver Mowat's Ontario.* Toronto: Macmillan, 1972:120-35.

Apple, Michael *Ideology and Curriculum.* London: Routledge and Kegan Paul, 1979.

Bailyn, Bernard *Education in the Forming of American Society.* New York: W.W. Norton and Company, 1960.

Bannister, J.A. *Early Educational History of Norfolk County.* Toronto: University of Toronto Press, 1926.

Barnard, Henry *School Architecture.* [1847] New York: Teachers' College Columbia, 1970.

Barton, Len et al eds., *Schooling, Ideology and the Curriculum.* Lewes: The Falmer Press, 1980.

Bellomo, J.J. 'Upper Canadian Attitudes towards Crime and Punishment,' *Ontario History,* 64, 1972:10-26.

Belok, M.V. *Forming the American Minds: Early School Books & Their Compilers, 1783-1837.* Agra, India: Satish Books, 1973.

Bendix, Reinhard *Nation-Building and Citizenship.* New York: Wiley, 1964.

Bidwell, Charles 'The Moral Significance of the Common School,' *History of Education Quarterly,* 6, 1966:50-91.

Binder, F.M. *The Age of the Common School.* Toronto: Wiley, 1974.

Bleasdale, Ruth 'Class Conflict on the Canals of Upper Canada in the 1840s,' *Labour/le Travailleur,* 7, 1981:9-39.

Bourinot, Sir J.G. *Lord Elgin.* Toronto: Morang, 1903.

Bowles, S. and H. Gintis, *Schooling in Capitalist America.* New York: Basic Books, 1976.

Boyce, G.E. *Hutton of Hastings: The Life and Letters of William Hutton, 1801-1861.* Belleville: Hastings County Council, 1972.

Brougham, Henry Lord *Speeches, Volume II.* Philadelphia, Lea and Blanchard, 1841.

Brown, G. 'The Grit Party and the Great Reform Convention of 1859,' *Canadian Historical Review,* XVI, 1935:245-65.

Brunschwig, Henri *Enlightenment and Romanticism in Eighteenth Century Prussia.* Chicago: University of Chicago Press, 1974.

Buller, Charles *Responsible Government for Colonies.* London: James Ridgeway, 1840.

Burroughs, Peter *The Canadian Crisis and British Colonial Policy, 1828-1841.* Toronto:Macmillan, 1972.

Burwash, Nathanael *Egerton Ryerson.* Toronto: Morang, 1903.

Butterfield, P.H. 'The Educational Researches of the Manchester Statistical Society, 1830-1840,' *British Journal of Educational Studies,*

22, 1974:340-59.

Campbell, H. et al *A History of Oro Schools, 1836-1966.* Oro Township, Ontario: Oro Township School Board,1967.

Clarke, W.K.L. *A History of the S.P.C.K.* London: S.P.C.K., 1959.

Canniff, William *History of the Province of Ontario.* Toronto: A.H. Hovey, 1872.

Careless, J.M.S. ed. *The Pre-Confederation Premiers: Ontario Government Leaders, 1841-1867.* Toronto: University of Toronto Press, 1980.

-*The Union of the Canadas.* Toronto: McClelland and Stewart, 1967.

-*Brown of the Globe. Volume I: The Voice of Upper Canada.* Toronto: Macmillan, 1959.

Catermole, William *Emigration.* Toronto: Coles Canadiana, c.1970.

Carrothers, W.A. *Emigration from the British Isles.* London: P.S. King, 1929.

Chalmers, Thomas *The Christian and Civic Economy of Large Towns.* Glasgow: Chalmers & Collins, 1821.

Cobb, Lyman J. *The Evil Tendencies of Corporal Punishment as a Means of Moral Discipline in Families and Schools, Examined and Discussed.* New York: M.H. Newman, 1847.

Coleman, H.T.J. *Education in Upper Canada.* New York: Teacher's College, Columbia, 1907.

Collins, Randall *The Credential Society.* New York: Academic Press, 1979.

-'Some Comparative Principles of Educational Stratification.' *Harvard Educational Review.* February 1977:1-27.

Colqhuon, J.C. *The System of National Education in Ireland: its Principle and Practice.* Cheltenham: Wm. Wright, 1838.

Corbin, Alain *Les Filles de Noce.* Paris: Aubier, 1982.

Corrigan, Paul *Schooling the Smash Street Kids.* London:Macmillan, 1979.

Corrigan, Philip ed., *Capitalism, State Formation and Marxist Theory.* London: Quartet Books, 1980.

-Re/membering Modernity,' *Border/lines,* 6, 1986.

-'In/forming Schooling,' in David Livingstone ed., *Critical Pedagogy and Cultural Power.* 1986.

-'On Moral Regulation: Some Preliminary Remarks,' *Sociological Review.* 29(1) 1981:313-37.

-'Curiouser and Curiouser: a largely bibliographical comment on Hall's 'English intelligentsia',' *British Journal of Sociology,* 31(2) 1980:292-7.

-and Bruce Curtis 'Education Inspection and State Formation: A Preliminary Statement,' Canadian Historical Association *Papers* 1985:156-71.

-Bruce Curtis and Robert Lanning, 'The Political Space of Schooling,' in T. Wotherspoon, ed. *The Sociology of Education.* Toronto:Methuen, 1987.

-and Val Gillespie, *Class struggle, social literacy and idle time.* Labour History Monographs, Brighton: John Noyce, 1978.

-------- and Derek Sayer, *The Great Arch: English State Formation as Cultural Revolution.* Oxford: Basil Blackwell, 1985.

Cornell, P.G. *The Alignment of Political Groups in Canada,*

*1841-1867.* Toronto: University of Toronto Press, 1962.

Craig, A.R. *The Philosophy of Training.* London:Simpkin and Marshall, 1847.

Craig, G.M. *Upper Canada: The Formative Years, 1784-1841.* Toronto: McClelland and Stewart, 1963.

Creighton, D.G. *The Empire of the St. Lawrence.* Toronto: Macmillan, 1970.

-'The Economic Background of the Rebellions of 1837,' in W.T. Easterbrook and M.H. Watkins, eds., *Approaches to Canadian Economic History.* Toronto: McClelland and Stewart, 1967: 222-236.

Cross, M.S. 'The Lumber Community of Upper Canada, 1815-1867,' in J.M. Bumsted ed., *Canadian History Before Confederation.* Georgetown: Irwin-Dorsey, 1972:307-29.

Cruickshank, Marjorie 'David Stow, Scottish Pioneer of Teacher Training in Britain,' *British Journal of Educational Studies,* 14, 1966:205-15.

Curtis, Bruce 'Curricular change and the Red Readers: history and theory,' forthcoming in G. Milburn ed. *Quality in the Curriculum.*

-' 'Littery Merritt,' 'Useful Knowledge,' and the Organization of Township Libraries in Canada West, 1840-1860,' *Ontario History,* LXVIII, December, 1986:284-312.

-'The playground in nineteenth century Ontario: theory and practice,' *Material History Bulletin,* Fall, 1985:21-30.

------- 'The Speller Expelled: Disciplining the Common Reader in Canada West,' *Canadian Review of Sociology and Anthropology,* August, 1985:346-68.

-'Capitalist Development and Educational Reform: Comparative Material from England, Ireland and Upper Canada to 1850,' *Theory and Society,* 13, 1984:41-68.

-'Schoolbooks and the Myth of Curricular Republicanism: the State and the Curriculum in Canada West, 1820-1850,' *Histoire Sociale/ Social History,* 16, 32, 1983:305-29.

-'Some recent Marxist contributions to Education: A Review Essay,' *Insurgent Sociologist,* IX, 1983:103-9.

-'Preconditions of the Canadian State: Educational Reform and the Construction of a Public in Upper Canada, 1837-1846,' *Studies in Political Economy,* 10, 1983:99-121.

-'Capital, the state and the origins of the working class household,' in B. Fox ed. *Hidden in the Household: Women's Domestic Labour Under Capitalism.* Toronto: Women's Press, 1980:101-34.

-and Barry Edginton 'Uneven Institutional Development and the 'Staple' Approach: a Problem of Method,' *Canadian Journal of Sociology,* 4, 1979:257-73.

Danylewicz, Marta, Beth Light and Alison Prentice, 'The Evolution of the Sexual Division of Labour in Teaching: A Nineteenth- Century Ontario and Quebec Case Study,' *Histoire Sociale/Social History,* 16, 31, 1983:81-109.

Darling, W.S. *Sketches of Canadian Life: Lay and Ecclesiatical.* London: David Bogue, 1849.

Davey, Ian 'The Rhythm of Work and the Rhythm of School,' in Neil Macdonald and Alf Chaiton eds. *Egerton Ryerson and His Times.* Toronto: Macmillan, 1978:221-253.

-'School Reform and School Attendance: The Hamilton Central School, 1853-1861,' in M.B. Katz and P.H. Mattingly, eds. *Education and Social Change.* New York: New York University Press, 1975:294-314.

Davidoff, Leonore 'Class and Gender in Victorian England,' in J.L.

Newton et al eds. *Sex and Class in Women's History*. London: Routledge Kegan Paul, 1983:17-71.

Davin, Anna 'Child Labour, the Working-Class Family and Domestic Ideology in 19th Century Britain,' *Development and Education*, 13, 1982:633-52.

-'Mind that you do as you are told: reading books for Board School girls, 1870-1902,' *Feminist Review*, 3, 1979.

De Carlo, Giancarlo 'Why/How to Build School Buildings,' *Harvard Education Review*, 39, 4, 1969:12-35.

Dehli, Kari 'Women and Class: Home and School Relations in the Toronto Board of Education, 1900-1970,' Phd in progress, OISE.

Dent, J.C. *The Last Forty Years: Canada Since the Union of 1841*. Toronto: George Virtue, 1881.

Denton, F.T. and George, P.J. 'Socio-Economic Influences on School Attendance: A Study of a Canadian County in 1871,' *History of Education Quarterly*, 14, 1974:222-32.

Dick, Thomas *On the Improvement of Society by the Diffusion of Useful Knowledge. [1833]* in *Collected Works*. Volume II. Hartford: Sumner & Goodman, 1847.

*Dictionary of Canadian Biography*. Toronto: University of Toronto Press.

*Dictionary of National Biography*. London: Smith Elder & Co.

Donzelot, J. *The Policing of Families*. New York: Vintage, 1979.

Doughty, Sir A.G. ed. *The Elgin-Grey Papers, 1846-1852*. Ottawa, 1937.

Dowling, P.J. *A History of Irish Education*. Cork: Mercier Press, 1971.

Duke, Francis 'The Poor Law Commissioners and Education,' *Journal of Educational Administration and History.* III, 1, 1970: 7-23.

Duncan, Kenneth 'The Irish Famine Immigration and the Social Structure of Canada West,' in M. Horn and R. Sabourin eds., *Studies in Canadian Social History.* Toronto: McClelland and Stewart, 1974:140-63.

Dunham, Eileen *Political Unrest in Upper Canada, 1815-1836.* Toronto: McClelland and Stewart, 1963.

Dunn, Henry *Principles of Teaching.* 10th edition. London: Sunday School Union, c.1847.

Durkheim, Emile *Moral Education.* New York: Free Press, 1961.

-*Textes.* Paris: les editions de minuit, nd.

Edgeworth, R.L. and Maria *Essays on Practical Education.* London: Hunter, Baldwin, Cradock and Joy, 1815.

-*Memoirs of Richard Lovell Edgeworth.* Shannon: Irish University Press, 1969.

Education, Ontario Department of *A Brief History of Public and High School Text-Books Authorized for the Province of Ontario, 1846-1889.* Toronto: Warwick and Sons, 1890.

Elias, Norbert *The History of Manners.* New York: Pantheon, 1978.

-*Power and Civility.* New York: Pantheon, 1982.

Ellis, Alec *Books in Victorian Elementary Schools.* London: The Library Association, 1971.

Ely, Richard 'The Origins of the Debate over 'Secular' Instruction,' *History of Education, 9, 1980:143-57.*

Engels, Frederick *The Condition of the Working Class in England.* Moscow: Progress Publishers, 1973.

Ermatinger, C.O. *The Talbot Regime.* St. Thomas: Municipal World Ltd., 1904.

Ewart, A. and J. Jarvis, 'The Personnel of the Family Compact,' *Canadian Historical Review,* VII, 1926:209-21.

Finkelstein, Barbara 'Pedagogy as Intrusion,' *History of Education Quarterly,* 2, 1975.

-ed. *Regulated Children, Liberated Children.* New York: 1975.

Flint, David *William Lyon Mackenzie: Rebel Against Authority.* Toronto: Oxford University Press, 1971.

Foster, John *An Essay on the Evils of Popular Ignorance.* London: J. Holdsworth, 1821.

Foucault, Michel 'The Subject and Power,' in H.L. Dreyfus and Paul Rabinow, *Michel Foucault: Beyond Structuralism and Hermeneutics.* Chicago: University of Chicago Press, 1983.

-*Power/Knowledge.* New York: Pantheon, 1980.

------- *Discipline and Punish.* New York: Vintage, 1979.

-*The History of Sexuality. Volume I.* New York: Pantheon, 1978.

-*The Archaeology of Knowledge.* New York: Harper and Row, 1972.

Fowke, V.C. *Canadian Agricultural Policy.* Toronto: University of Toronto Press, 1978.

Fox, W.S. 'School Readers as an Educational Force,' in J.M Bumsted, ed., *Canadian History Before Confederation.* Georgetown, Ontario: Irwin-Dorsey, 1972:362-73.

Fraser, Joshua *Shanty, Forest and River Life in the Backwoods of Canada.* Toronto: Lovell & Son, 1883.

Fregier, H.-A. *Des Classes Dangereuses de la Population dans les grandes villes....* Paris: J.-B. Balliere, 1840.

Gaffield, Chad 'Demography, Social Structure and the History of Schooling,' in *Approaches to Educational History,* Winnipeg: Monographs in Education, V, Spring 1981:85-111.

Gardiner, L.R. *Durham and Canada: crisis of self-government.* London: Edward Arnold, 1975.

Gardner, Phil *Lost Elementary Schools of Victorian England.* Kent: Croom Helm, 1984.

Garner, John *The Franchise and Politics in British North America, 1755-1867.* Toronto: University of Toronto Press, 1969.

Gidney, R.D. and D.A. Lawr, 'Who Ran the Schools? Local Influence on Education Policy in Nineteenth Century Ontario,' *Ontario History,* LXXII, 3, 1980:131-43.

-'Bureaucracy vs Community? The Origins of Bureaucratic Procedure in the Upper Canadian School System,' *Journal of Social History,* 13, 1980:438-57.

-'Egerton Ryerson and the Origins of the Ontario Secondary School,' *Canadian Historical Review,* 60, 1979:442- 65.

-'The Development of an Administrative System for the Public Schools: The First Stage, 1841-50,' in N. McDonald and A. Chaiton, eds., *Egerton Ryerson and His Times.* Toronto: Macmillan, 1978:160-84.

Gidney, R.D. and Millar, W.P.J. 'From Voluntaryism to State Schooling: The Creation of the Public School System in Ontario,' *Canadian Historical Review,* LXVI, 1985:443-473.

------ 'Rural Schools and the Decline of Community Control in Late Nineteenth Century Ontario,' *Proceedings of the 4th Annual Agricultural History of Ontario Seminar.* 1979.

Gidney, R.D. 'Elementary Education in Upper Canada: A Reassessment,' in M.B. Katz and P.H. Mattingly, eds., *Education and Social Change: Themes from Ontario's Past.* New York: New York University Press, 1975:3-26.

-'Centralization and education: the origins of an Ontario Tradition,' *Journal of Canadian Studies,* VII, 4, 1972:33-48.

------ 'Upper Canadian Public Opinion and Common School Improvement in the 1830s,' *Histoire Sociale/Social History,* V, 9, 1972:48-60.

------ 'The Rev. Robert Murray: Ontario's First Superintendent of Schools,' *Ontario History,* LXIII, 4, 1971:191-204.

Gilmour, Robin 'The Gradgrind School: Political Economy in the Classroom,' *Victorian Studies,* December 1967.

Glazebrook, G.P. de T. *Life in Ontario: A Social History.* Toronto: University of Toronto Press, 1968.

------ *A History of Transportation in Canada. Volume I: Continental Strategy to 1867.* Toronto: McClelland and Stewart, 1964.

-*Sir Charles Bagot in Canada: A Study in British Colonial Government.* Toronto: University of Toronto Press, 1929.

Goffman, Erving *Asylums: Essays on the social situation of mental patients and other inmates.* Garden City: Anchor Press, 1961.

Goldstrom, J.M. *The Social Content of Education.* Shannon: Irish University Press, 1972.

------ 'Richard Whately and political economy in schoolbooks,

1833-80,' *Irish Historical Studies,* XV, 1966:131-45.

Graff, H.J. *The Literacy Myth: Literacy and social structure in the nineteenth century city.* New York: Academic Press, 1979.

-'Towards a Meaning of Literacy: Literacy and Social Structure in Hamilton, Ontario, 1861,' in M.B. Katz and P.H. Mattingly, eds., *Education and Social Change.* New York: New York University Press, 1975:246-70.

-'Literacy and Social Structure in Elgin County, 1861,' *Histoire Sociale/Social History,* 6, 1973:25-48.

Greer, Allan 'The Pattern of Literacy in Quebec, 1745-1899,' *Histoire Sociale/Social History,* 11, 1978:296-335.

Guillet, E.C. *Pioneer Arts and Crafts.* Toronto: University of Toronto Press, 1973.

-*Early Life in Upper Canada.* Toronto: Ontario Publishing Company, 1933.

Guizot, Mme. *Lettres de Famille sur l'Education.* Paris: Pichon et Didier, 1828.

Gunn, W.M. *Religion in Connexion with a National System of Instruction.* Edinburgh: Oliver and Boyd, 1846.

Haight, Canniff *Country Life in Canada Fifty Years Ago.* Toronto: Hunter Rose, 1885.

Hamil, F.C. *The Valley of the Lower Thames, 1640-1850.* Toronto: University of Toronto Press, 1973.

Hamilton, David 'Adam Smith and the moral economy of the classroom system,' *Journal of Curriculum Studies,* 12, 1981:281- 91.

Hamilton, Elizabeth *Letters on the Elementary Principles of Education.* London, 1810.

Hamilton, Rev. R.W. *The Institutions of Popular Education.* London:Hamilton, Adams, 1845.

Harrison, J.F.C. ed. *Utopianism and Education: Robert Owen and the Owenites.* New York: Teachers' College Columbia, 1968.

Henderson, J.L.H. ed. *John Strachan: Documents and Opinions.* Toronto: McClelland and Stewart, 1969.

Hincks, Sir Francis *Reminiscences of His Public Life.* Montreal: William Drysdale, 1884.

Hodgins, John George ed. *Historical Documents and Papers Illustrative of the Educational System....* Toronto: L.K. Cameron, 1911-12.

-ed. *The Establishment of the Schools and Colleges in Ontario, 1792-1910.* Toronto: L.K. Cameron, 1910.

-ed. *The Documentary History of Education in Upper Canada....* Toronto: L.K. Cameron, 1894-1910.

-*The Legislation and History of Separate Schooling in Upper Canada.* Toronto: W. Briggs, 1897.

-*A History of Canada and of the other British Provinces in North America.* Montreal: John Lovell, 1866.

-*The School House; Its Architecture, External and Internal Arrangements.* Toronto: Department of Public Instruction, 1857.

Hopkins, J.C. ed. *Canada: An Encyclopedia.* Toronto: Linscott, 1898.

Hoskin, Keith 'Cobwebs to Catch Flies,' Unpublished paper, Joint School of Classics, University of Warwick, 1984.

-'Examinations and the Schooling of Science,' in R. Macleod, ed. *Days of Judgement.* London: Nafferton, 1982:213-35.

Houston, S.E. 'Politics, Schools and Social Change in Upper Canada,' in M.B.Katz and P.H. Mattingly, *Education and Social Change*. New York: New York University Press, 1975:28-56.

-'Victorian Origins of Juvenile Delinquency: A Canadian Experience,' in Katz and Mattingly, 1975:83-109.

Humes, W.M. and Paterson, H.M eds., *Scottish Culture and Scottish Education, 1800-1980*. Edinburgh: John Donald, 1983.

Humphries, Stephen *Hooligans or Rebels? An Oral History of Working Class Childhood and Youth, 1889-1939*. Oxford: Basil Blackwell, 1981.

Inglis, Fred *The Management of Ignorance: A Political Theory of Curriculum*. Oxford: Blackwell, 1985.

Jackson, Eric 'The Organization of Upper Canadian Reformers, 1818-1867,' in J.K. Johnson ed., *Historical Essays on Upper Canada*. Toronto: McClelland and Stewart, 1975:96-121.

Johnson, L.A. *History of the County of Ontario, 1615-1875*. Whitby: County of Ontario, 1973.

Johnson, Richard ' 'Really useful knowledge': radical working-class culture, 1790-1848,' in J. Clarke et al eds., *Working Class Culture: Studies in History and Theory*. London: Hutchinson, 1979.

-'Elementary Education: The Education of the Poorer Classes,' in *Government and Society in Nineteenth Century Britain. Commentaries on British Parliamentary Papers*. Shannon: Irish University Press, 1977:5-67.

-'Educational Policy and Social Control in Early Victorian England,' *Past and Present*, 49, 1970:96-119.

Johnson, S.C. *A History of Emigration from the United Kingdom to North America, 1763-1912*. London: Routledge, 1913.

Jones, G.M. 'The Peter Perry Election and the Rise of the Clear Grit Party,' *Ontario History,* XII, 1914:164-75.

Jones, Karen and Kevin Williamson 'The Birth of the Schoolroom,' *Ideology and Consciousness,* Autumn, 1979:59-110.

Jones, R.L. *History of Agriculture in Ontario, 1613-1880.* Toronto: University of Toronto Press, 1977.

Kaestle, Carl *Pillars of the Republic: Common Schools and American Society, 1780-1860.* New York: Hill and Wang, 1983.

-*The Evolution of an Urban School System: New York, 1750-1850.* Cambridge: Harvard University Press, 1973.

-and Maris Vinovskis *Education and Social Change in nineteenth-century Massachusetts.* Cambridge: Cambridge University Pres, 1980.

Katz, M.B. 'The Origins of Public Education: a Reassessment,' *History of Education Quarterly,* Winter, 1976:381-407.

-*The People of Hamilton, Canada West.* Cambridge: Harvard University Press, 1975.

-*The Irony of Early School Reform.* Boston: Beacon Press, 1968.

-------and P.H. Mattingly, eds., *Education and Social Change: Themes from Ontario's Past.* New York: New York University Press, 1975.

Kay, Geoff and James Mott *Political Order and the Law of Labour.* London: Macmillan, 1982.

Kay, Joseph *The Social Condition and Education of the People in England and Europe.* London: Longman, 1850.

-*The Education of the Poor in England and Europe.* London: J. Hatchard, 1846.

Kay-Shuttleworth, Sir J.P. *The School, in its Relations to the State, the Church, and the Congregation.* London: J. Murray, 1847.

—*Four Periods of Public Education, as Reviewed in 1832, 1839, 1846 and 1862.* Brighton: Harvester, 1973.

Kay, Dr. J.P. 'On the Punishment of Pauper Children in Workhouses,' *Occasional Papers,* 1, 1961, Battersea: College of S. Mark & S. John.

Kaye, J.W. *The Life and Correspondence of Charles, Lord Metcalfe.* London: Bentley, 1854.

Keilty, Greg ed. *1837: Revolution in the Canadas.* Toronto: New Canadian Press, 1974.

Knox, Vicesimus *Liberal Education: or, a Practical Treatise on the Methods of Acquiring Useful and Polite Learning.* London: Charles Dilly, 1795.

Lady, A *The Young Lady's Friend: A Manual of Practical Advice and Instruction to Young Females on their entering upon the duties of life after quitting school.* London: Parker, 1853.

Lancaster, Joseph *Improvements in Education, as it respects the industrious classes of the community....* London: Darton & Harvey, 1805.

Landes, W.M. and L.C. Solomon 'Compulsory Schooling Legislation: An Economic Analysis of Law and Social Change in the Nineteenth Century,' *Journal of Economic History,* 32(1), 1972:54-91.

Landon, Fred *Western Ontario and the American Frontier.* Toronto: McClelland and Stewart, 1967.

Langdon, Stephen 'The Emergence of a Canadian Working Class Movement, 1845-1875,' *Journal of Canadian Studies,* May, August 1973:3-13; 8-25.

Langton, H.H. ed., *A Gentlewoman in Upper Canada: The Journals of Anne Langton.* Toronto: Clarke Irwin, 1964.

Lapp, D.A. *The Schools of Kingston: Their First Hundred and Fifty Years.* Unpublished M.A. dissertation, Department of History, Queen's University, 1937.

Lazonick, W. 'The Subjection of Labour to Capital: The Rise of the Capitalist System,' *Review of Radical Political Economics,* 10, 1, 1978:1-31.

Legget, Robert *Rideau Waterway.* Toronto: University of Toronto Press, 1972.

Lehmann, W.C. *John Millar of Glasgow, 1735-1801.* Cambridge: Cambridge University Press, 1960.

Locke, John *Some Thoughts Concerning Education.* Merston: Scholar Press, 1970.

Longley, R.S. *Sir Francis Hincks: A Study of Canadian Politics, Railways and Finance in the Nineteenth Century.* Toronto: University of Toronto Press, 1943.

Love, J.H. 'Cultural Survival and Local Control: The Development of a Curriculum for Upper Canada's Common Schools in 1846,' *Histoire Sociale/Social History,* 15, 1982:357-82.

-*Anti-Americanism, Local Concerns and the Response to Social Issues in Mid-19th Century Upper Canadian School Reform.* Unpublished Ph.D. dissertation, Department of History, University of Toronto, 1978.

Lower, A.R.M. *The North American Assault on the Canadian Forest.* Toronto: Ryerson Press, 1936.

Lucas, Sir C.P. *Lord Durham's Report on the Affairs of British North America.* Oxford: Clarendon Press, 1912.

McCaffrey, J.F. 'Thomas Chalmers and Social Change,' *Scottish*

*Historical Review,* LX, 1, 1981:32-60.

McCann, Phillip, ed. *Popular Education and socialization in the nineteenth century.* London: Methuen, 1977.

-'Samuel Wilderspin and the Early Infant Schools,' *British Journal of Educational Studies,* XIV,2, 1966:188-204.

McCutcheon, J.M. *Public Education in Ontario.* Toronto: T.H. Best, 1941.

McDonald, Neil 'Political Socialization Research, the School and the Educational Historian,' in *Approaches to Educational History,* Winnipeg: Monographs in Education, V, Spring 1981:65-84.

-'Egerton Ryerson and the School as an Agent of Political Socialization,' in N. McDonald and A. Chaiton, eds., *Egerton Ryerson and His Times.* Toronto: Macmillan, 1978.

McDowell, R.B. *The Irish Administration, 1801-1914.* Toronto: University of Toronto Press, 1964.

Macpherson, C.B. *The Political Theory of Possessive Individualism.* Oxford: Oxford University Press, 1962.

Maddock, F.L. ed. *Pioneer Days in School Section No. 12, Puslinch Township.* Guelph: Guelph Publishing Co., 1935.

Magill, M.L. 'John Henry Dunn and the Bankers,' in J.K. Johnson, ed. *Historical Essays on Upper Canada.* Toronto: McClelland and Stewart, 1975:194-215.

Mann, Horace *Life and Works. Volume III.* Boston: Fuller, 1968.

-*Life and Works, Volume II.* Cambridge, 1867.

-*Report of an Educational Tour.* London: Simpkin and Marshall, 1846.

Martin, Ged *The Durham Report and British Policy.* Cambridge: Cambridge University Press, 1972.

Marx, Karl 'On the Jewish Question,' *Karl Marx, Frederich Engels, Collected Works.* Volume 3. New York: International Publishers, 1975:146-74.

—*Critique of the Gotha Programme.* Peking: Foreign Languages Press, 1972.

Mathews, Mitford M. *Teaching to Read, Historically Considered.* Chicago: University of Chicago Press, 1968.

Mayo, Charles and Elizabeth Mayo *Practical Remarks on Infant Education.* London, 1841.

Mayo, Elizabeth *Lessons on Objects.* London: Seeleys, 1851.

Metcalfe, George 'Draper Conservatism and Responsible Government in the Canadas, 1836-1847,' *Canadian Historical Review,* XLII, 4, 1961:300-24.

Meyer, J.W. et al 'Public Education as Nation-Building in America: Enrollments and Bureaucratization in the American States, 1870-1930,' *American Journal of Sociology,* 85, 3, 1979:591-613.

Meyer, Phillipe *L'Enfant et la raison d'etat.* Paris, 1980.

Millar, John *An Historical View of the English Government.* London: Mawman, 1803.

Millar, J.A. 'Factories, Monitorial Schools and Jeremy Bentham: The Origins of the Management Syndrome in Popular Education,' *Journal of Educational Administration and History,* V, 1, 1973:10-20.

Miller, J.C. *Rural Schools in Canada: Their Organization, Administration and Supervision.* New York: Teachers' College, Columbia, 1913.

Miller, P.J. 'Women's Education, 'Self-Improvement,' and Social Mobility--- a late eighteenth century debate,' *British Journal of Educational Studies,* 20, 1972:302-14.

Moir, J.S. ed. *Church and State in Canada, 1627-1867.* Toronto: McClelland and Stewart, 1967.

Monboddo, Lord *Of the Origin and Progress of Language.* Edinburgh: Kincaid & Creech, 1773-4.

Moodie, Susannah *Roughing it in the Bush.* Toronto: McClelland and Stewart, 1923.

Morehouse, Frances 'Canadian Migration in the Forties,' *Canadian Historical Review,* December, 1928:309-29.

-'The Irish Famine Migration of the Forties,' *American Historical Review,* 33, 1927-8:579-92.

Morgan, Alexander *Rise and Progress of Scottish Education.* Edinburgh: Oliver and Boyd, 1927.

Myers, Gustavus *A History of Canadian Wealth.* Toronto: James Lewis & Samuel, 1972.

Necker, Albertine Adrienne de Saussure *Progressive Education, Commencing with the Infant.* Boston: W.D. Ticknor, 1835.

Newnham, W. *The Principles of Physical, Intellectual, Moral and Religious Education.* London: J. Hatchard, 1827.

Norman, E.R. *The Conscience of the State in North America.* Cambridge: Cambridge University Press, 1968.

O'Driscoll, D.C. *Ontario Attitudes Toward American and British Education, 1792-1950: A Comparative Study of International Images.* Unpublished Ph.D. dissertation, University of Michigan, 1974.

Onn, David 'Egerton Ryerson's Philosophy of Education: Something

Borrowed or Something New?' *Ontario History,* 61, 1969:77-86.

Osborne, B.S. 'Kingston in the Nineteenth Century: a Study in Urban Decline.' in D.J. Wood, ed., *Perspectives on Landscape and Settlement in Nineteenth Century Ontario.* Toronto: McClelland and Stewart, 1975:159-81.

Owen, Robert *A New View of Society and other writings.* London: Dent, 1972.

Page, D.P. *Theory and Practice of Teaching.* New York: A.S. Barnes, 1852.

Parsons, Talcott 'The School Class as a Social System: Some of its *Functions in American Society,*' in *Social Structure and Personality.* New York: Free Press, 1964.

Parvin, V.E. *Authorization of Textbooks for the Schools of Ontario, 1846-1950.* Toronto: University of Toronto Press, 1965.

Paterson, Fiona 'Schooling the Family,' Paper Presented to the British Sociological Association, Manchester, 1986.

Pentland, H.C. 'The Role of Capital in Canadian Economic Development before 1875,' *Canadian Journal of Economics and Political Science,* November, 1950:457-474.

-'The Development of a Capitalistic Labour Market in Canada,' *Canadian Journal of Economics and Political Science,* 1959:450-61.

Pestalozzi, J. H. *How Gertrude Teaches her Children.* London: Allen & Unwin, 1915.

Pillans, James *Educational Papers.* Edinburgh: Gordon, 1862.

-*The Rationale of Discipline.* Edinburgh: Maclachlan and Stewart, 1852.

-*Principles of Elementary Teaching.* Edinburgh: Adam Black, 1828.

Pim, Jonathan *The Condition and Prospects of Ireland.* Dublin: Hodges and Smith, 1848.

Pollard, Sidney 'Factory Discipline in the Industrial Revolution,' *Economic History Review,* Second Series, 16, 1963-4:254-71.

Pratt, David 'The Social Role of School Textbooks in Canada,' in R.M. Pike and Elia Zureik, *Socialization and Values in Canadian Society. Volume II: Political Socialization.* Toronto: McClelland and Stewart, 1975:100-126.

Prentice, Alison and Marta Danylewycz 'Themes in the History of the Women Teachers' Association of Toronto, 1892-1914,' in Paula Bourne, ed. *Women's Paid and Unpaid Work.* Toronto: forthcoming.

-'Teachers' Work: Changing Patterns and Perceptions in the Emerging School Systems of Nineteenth and Early Twentieth Century Canada,' *Labour/le Travailleur,* 17, 1986.

-'Teachers, Gender and Bureaucratizing School Systems in Nineteenth Century Montreal and Toronto,' *History of Education Quarterly,* 24, 1984.

Prentice, Alison 'From Household to School House: The Emergence of the Teacher as a Servant of the State,' *Material History Bulletin,* 20, 1984:19-29.

-'Men and Women at Toronto Normal School,' paper presented to the Canadian History of Education Association, Vancouver, 1983.

-'Towards a Feminist History of Women and Education,' in *Approaches to Educational History,* Winnipeg: Monographs in Education, V, Spring 1981:39-64.

-'The Public Instructor,' in N. McDonald and A. Chaiton eds. *Egerton Ryerson and His Times.* Toronto: Macmillan, 1978.

-*The School Promoters.* Toronto: McClelland and Stewart, 1977.

-'The Feminization of Teaching in British North America, 1845-1875,' *Histoire Sociale/Social History,* May 1975: 5-20.

-'Education and the Metaphor of the Family: An Upper Canadian Example,' in M.B. Katz and P.H. Mattingly eds. *Education and Social Change: Themes from Ontario's Past.* New York: New York University Press, 1975.

-and Susan Houston eds. *Family School and Society in nineteenth century Canada.* Toronto: Oxford University Press, 1975.

Robin, Martin 'The Working Class and the Transition to Capitalist Democracy in Canada,' *Dalhousie Review,* 47, Autumn, 1967:326-342.

Robson, A.H. *The Education of Children Engaged in Industry in England, 1833-1876.* London: Kegan Paul, 1931.

Rose, George ed. *A Cyclopedia of Canadian Biography.* Toronto: Rose, 1888.

Ross, A.H. *Reminiscences of North Sydenham.* Owen Sound: Richardson, Bond & Wright, 1924.

Ross, A.M. 'Kay-Shuttleworth and the Training of Teachers for Pauper Schools,' *British Journal of Educational Studies,* 15, 1967:275-83.

Ross, G.W. *The School System of Ontario: Its History and Distinctive Features.* New York: Appleton, 1896.

Ross, P.N. 'The Free School Controversy in Toronto, 1848- 1852,' in M.B.Katz and P.H. Mattingly, eds. *Education and Social Change.* New York: New York University Press, 1975:57-80.

Royle, E. 'Mechanics' Institutes and the Working Classes, 1840-1860,' *The Historical Journal,* 14, 1971:305-21.

Ruddick, J.A. 'The dairy industry in Canada,' in H.A. Innis, ed. *The*

*Dairy Industry in Canada.* Toronto: Ryerson Press, 1937.

Rusche, G. and Kirchheimer, O. *Punishment and Social Structure.* New York: Russell and Russell, 1968.

Ryerson, Egerton *The Story of My Life.* edited by J.G. Hodgins. Toronto: William Briggs, 1883.

-*A Special Report on the State of Popular Education on the Continent of Europe....* Toronto, 1868.

-*The New Canadian Dominion: Dangers and Duties of the People in Regard to their Government.* Toronto: Lovell and Gibson, 1867.

-*The School Book Question: Letters in Reply to the Brown-Campbell Crusade Against the Educational Department for Upper Canada.* Montreal: John Lovell, 1866.

-*Report on a System of Public Elementary Instruction for Upper Canada.* and *Special Report of the Measures which have been Adopted for the Establishment of a Normal School.* Montreal: Lovell and Gibson, 1847.

-*Sir Charles Metcalfe Defended Against the Attacks of his Late Counsellors.* Toronto: British Colonist, 1844.

-('A Canadian') *The Affairs of the Canadas.* London: J. King, 1837.

Ryerson, Stanley *Unequal Union.* New York: International, 1968.

Salmon, D. ed. *The Practical Parts of Lancaster's Improvements and Bell's Experiment.* Cambridge: Cambridge University Press, 1932.

Sanderson, C.R. ed. *The Arthur Papers.* Toronto: University of Toronto Press and Toronto Public Libraries, 1943.

Saunders, R.E. 'What Was the Family Compact?' in J.K. Johnson, ed. *Historical Essays on Upper Canada.* Toronto: McClelland and Stewart, 1975:122-139.

Schecter, Stephen 'Capitalism, class, and educational reform in Canada,' in Leo Panitch, ed. *The Canadian State*. Toronto: University of Toronto Press, 1978:373-416.

Scherck, M.G. *Pen Pictures of Early Pioneer Life in Upper Canada*. Toronto: William Briggs, 1905.

*School Manual for Upper Canada, The* Toronto: Thompson and Company, 1856; 1861.

Scott, A. F. 'The Ever Widening Circle: The Diffusion of Feminist Values from the Troy Female Seminary, 1822-1872,' *History of Education Quarterly*, Spring, 1979:3-25.

Silber, Kate *Pestalozzi: The Man and His Work*. London: Routledge & Kegan Paul, 1973.

Simon, Brian *The Two Nations and the Educational Structure, 1780-1870*. London: Lawrence and Wishart, 1974.

-ed. *The Radical Tradition in Education in Britain*. London: Lawrence and Wishart, 1972.

Sissons, C.B. ed. *My Dearest Sophie: letters from Egerton Ryerson to his daughter*. Toronto: Ryerson Press, 1955.

Sissons, C.B. *Egerton Ryerson: His Life and Letters*. Toronto: Clarke, Irwin, 1947.

-'Ryerson and the Elections of 1844.' *Canadian Historical Review*, XXIII, 1942:157-176.

Skelton, O.D. *The Life and Times of Sir Alexander Tilloch Galt*. Toronto: Oxford University Press, 1920.

Smaller, Harry 'Early Teachers' Associations in Ontario, 1840- 1900,' Ph.D., OISE, 1987.

Smith, Adam *An Inquiry into the Nature and Causes of the Wealth of Nations.* London: Methuen, 1930.

*-The Theory of Moral Sentiments.* Indianapolis: Liberty Classics, 1976.

*-Lectures on Jurisprudence* Indianapolis: Liberty Classics, 1976.

Smith, J.V. 'Manners, Morals and Mentalities: Reflections on the Popular Enlightenment of Early Nineteenth-Century Scotland,' in W.M. Humes and H.M. Paterson, eds. *Scottish Culture and Scottish Education, 1800-1980.* Edinburgh: John Donald, 1983:25-54.

Smith, T.L. 'Protestant Schooling and American Nationality, 1800-1850,' *Journal of American History,* 53, 4, 1967:679-95.

Smith, William *Political Leaders of Upper Canada.* Freeport, New York: Books for Libraries Press, 1968.

Society for the Diffusion of Useful Knowledge *The Schoolmaster: Essays on Practical Education.* London: Knight, 1836.

Soltow, Lee and Edward Stevens, *The Rise of Literacy and the Common School in the United States.* Chicago: University of Chicago Press, 1981.

Speisman, S.A. 'Munificent Parsons and Municipal Parsimony: Voluntary vs Public Poor Relief in Nineteenth Century Toronto,' *Ontario History,* LXV, 1973.

Spelt, Jacob *Urban Development in South-Central Ontario.* Toronto: McClelland and Stewart, 1972.

Splane, R.B. *Social Welfare in Ontario, 1791-1893.* Toronto: University of Toronto Press, 1965.

Spragge, G.W. 'John Strachan's Contribution to Education, 1800-1823,' in J.K. Johnson ed. *Historical Essays on Upper Canada.* Toronto: McClelland and Stewart, 1975:74-85.

-'Elementary Education in Upper Canada, 1820-1840,' *Ontario History*, XLIII, 3, 1951:107-22.

-'The Upper Canada Central School,' *Ontario History*, XXXII, 1937:171-91.

Steedman, Carolyn *Policing the Victorian Community*. London: Routledge & Kegan Paul, 1984.

Stelter, G. and A.F.J. Artibise, *The Canadian City*. Toronto: McClelland and Stewart, 1977.

Stow, David *The Training System*. Glasgow: Blackie, 1845.

Sullivan, Robert *Lectures and Letters on Popular Education*. Dublin: William Curry & Co., 1842.

-*The Spelling Book Superseded*. New York: McFeeters, n.d.

Talbot, E.A. *Five Years' Residence in the Canadas*. London: Longman et al, 1824.

Talman, J.J. 'The Position of the Church of England in Upper Canada, 1791-1840,' in J.J. Johnson ed. *Historical Essays on Upper Canada*. Toronto: McClelland and Stewart, 1975:58-73.

-'The Newspaper Press of Canada West, 1850-1860,' *Transactions of the Royal Society of Canada*, XXXIII, 1939: 149-72.

Teeple, Gary 'Land, labour and capital in pre-Confederation Canada,' in Gary Teeple ed. *Capitalism and the National Question in Canada*. Toronto: University of Toronto Press, 1972: 43-66.

Thompson, E.P. 'Time, work-discipline, and industrial capitalism,' *Past and Present*, 38, 1967:56-97.

-*The Making of the English Working Class*. Harmondsworth: Penguin Books, 1968.

*Toronto Normal School Jubilee Celebration.* Toronto: Warwick, 1898.

Traill, Catherine Parr *The Backwoods of Canada.* Toronto: McClelland and Stewart, 1966.

Tucker, G.N. *The Canadian Commercial Revolution.* Toronto: McClelland and Stewart, 1970.

-'The Famine Immigration to Canada, 1847,' *American Historical Review,* 36, 1930-1:533-49.

Tyack, David and Michael Berkowitz 'The Man Nobody Liked: Toward a Social History of the Truant Officer, 1840-1940,' *American Quarterly,* 29, 1, 1977:31-54.

Tyack, David 'Ways of Seeing: An Essay on the History of Compulsory Schooling,' *Harvard Educational Review,* 46,3, 1976:355-89.

Tyrrell, A. 'Political economy, whiggism and the education of working class adults in Scotland, 1817-40,' *Scottish Historical Review,* 48, 1969:151-65.

Wallace, W.S. *The Family Compact: A Chronicle of the Rebellion in Upper Canada.* Toronto: Glasgow Brook, 1915.

Walker, A.N.B. *History of Education in Ontario, 1791-1841.* Unpublished M.A. dissertation, Bishop's University, 1946.

Walker, F.A. *Catholic Education and Politics in Upper Canada.* Toronto: Dent, 1955.

Ward, J.M. *Colonial Self Government: The British Experience, 1759-1856.* Toronto: University of Toronto Press, 1974.

Waterloo County, *Memorial to the Council of Public Instruction of Upper Canada from the Board of Public Instruction of the County of Waterloo.* Galt: Reporter Office, 1865.

Webb, R.K. *The British Working Class Reader, 1790-1848.* New York: A.M. Kelley, 1971.

Weber, Max *Essays in Sociology.* edited by C.W. Mills and H.H. Gerth, New York: Oxford, 1958.

West, E.G. 'The Role of Education in Nineteenth-Century Doctrines of Political Economy,' *British Journal of Educational Studies,* XII, 1964:161-72.

Whately, Richard *Introductory Lectures on Political Economy.* London: Parker, 1855.

Wilderspin, Samuel *The Infant System.* London: Hodson, 1852.

Willis, Paul *Learning to Labour.* Westmead: Gower, 1977.

Wilson, Allan *The Clergy Reserves of Upper Canada.* Ottawa: Canadian Historical Association, 1969.

Wilson, G.E. *The Life of Robert Baldwin: A Study in the Struggle for Responsible Government.* Toronto: The Ryerson Press, 1933.

Wilson, J.D. 'The Teacher in Early Ontario,' in F.H. Armstrong et al eds. *Aspects of Nineteenth Century Ontario.* Toronto: University of Toronto Press, 1974:218-36.

-'Adult Education in Upper Canada before 1850,' *The Journal of Education,* 19, 1973:43-54.

-'Common School Texts in Use in Upper Canada prior to 1845,' Bibliographical Society of Canada, *Papers,* IX, 1970:36-53.

Woods, John *Account of the Edinburgh Sessional School.* Edinburgh: Wardlaw, 1829.

Wright, A.W. ed. *Pioneer Days in Nichol.* Mount Forest, 1932.

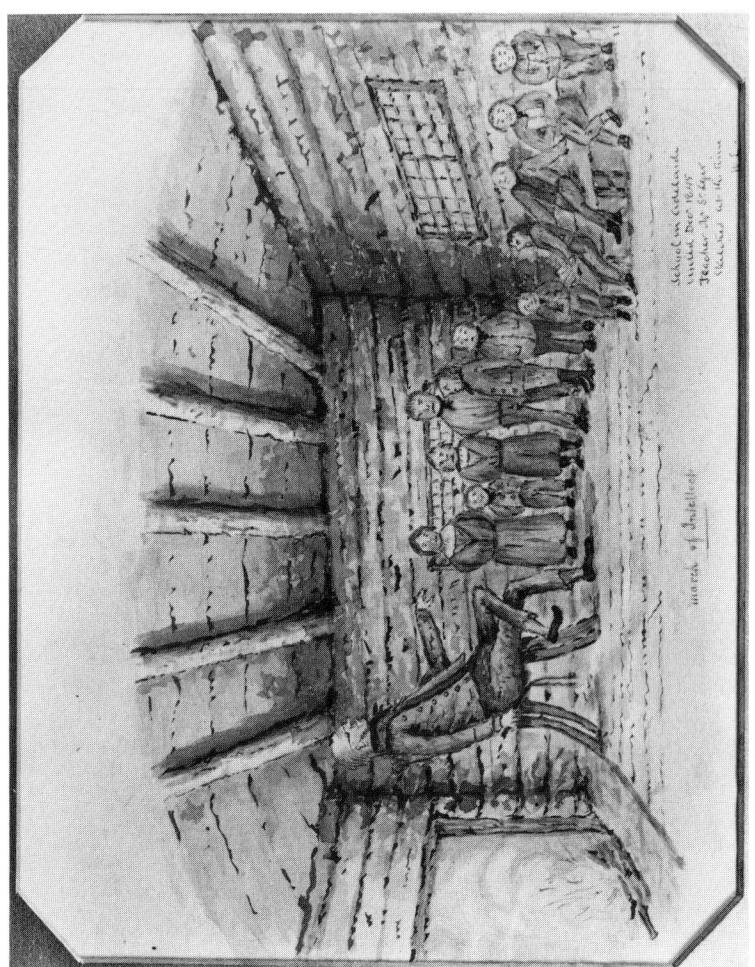

1 'The March of Intellect'
Charles Elliot, one of the first District School Superintendents, drew this sketch and added the 'School in Adelaide, Visited Decr. 1845, Teacher Mr. St. Leger, Sketched at the time'. This presents the typical common school before centralized state control from the perspective of the respectable school visitor. Notice the 'tawse' or whip in the teacher's hand, the few books, the absence of classes and the lack of school 'furniture'. Such views were not shared by most school supporters.

2 Pine Grove School, Denham County, 1870s (?)
By the 1870s more 'bush' schools were being constructed from plank with shingled roofs. Notice the exposed woodpile.
(*Courtesy Public Archives of Ontario*)

3 The Elementary School, Actinolite Ontario
This school probably dates from 1850–1860.
(Courtesy Public Archives of Ontario)

4 Schoolhouse, Blenheim Township School Section 10
Constructed in 1860, photographed 1905. *(Courtesy Public Archives of Ontario)*

5 The Old Schoolhouse, Picton Ontario
This school dates from the 1860s or earlier. Notice the chimney.

(*Courtesy Public Archives of Ontario*)

6 The Schoolhouse, Glenwood Ontario

This school dates from about 1860, and approaches the ideal rural school as conceived by the Education Office. It is separated from 'interference by the public' by a stout stone fence. The low building attached at the rear is likely the woodshed. The roof of the privies is visible in the left center of the picture, and one can also distinguish the top of the fence which separated boys' and girls' playgrounds.

(*Courtesy Public Archives of Ontario*)

7 First Known School, Williamston Ontario
School reformers frequently campaigned against the school held in a rented house. *(Courtesy Public Archives of Ontario)*

8  The Schoolhouse, School Section 6, Whitchurch, York County
This school was completed in 1872 and is photographed here *circa* 1900. In addition to the trim 'board and batten' construction, notice the separate entrances for boys and girls and the woodshed in the left of the photograph. (*Courtesy Public Archives of Ontario*)

9 Schoolhouse, York County
This unidentified school house was constructed in 1874 and photographed *circa* 1885. Separate entrances are visible in the front of the school, which probably also contained cloakrooms or 'lobbies'. The school proper is to the rear.
(*Courtesy Public Archives of Ontario*)

425

10 and 11 (overleaf) 'Improved' Schools of the late 1860s and 1870s
One of the large elementary schools in Hamilton Ontario as it appeared in 1868, and Toronto's Dufferin School, constructed in 1873. Both of these schools dominated the neighbourhoods in which they were situated. (*Courtesy Public Archives of Ontario*)

12 Egerton Ryerson, Assistant Superintendent of Education, 1844–1846; Chief Superintendent of Education, 1847–1876, *circa* 1860

(*Courtesy Public Archives of Ontario*)

13 John George Hodgins, *circa* 1890
Hodgins served as Deputy Superintendent of Education under Ryerson from 1844, and after Ryerson's retirement was Deputy Minister of Education and Historiographer.

(*Courtesy Public Archives of Ontario*)

14  Archibald Macallum
First Master of the Toronto Boys' Model School, 1848–1858.

(*Courtesy Public Archives of Ontario*)

15 The Toronto Normal School, circa 1860 (Courtesy Public Archives of Ontario)

**16 A Lesson at Uno Park School**

Although it probably dates from the 1880s or later, this picture speaks volumes about approved instructional practice. Notice the silent students as the teacher reads; the separation of the genders; the raised platform which affords the teacher a better view of the schoolroom; the severe dress of the female teacher; the blackboard and flowers.

(*Courtesy Public Archives of Ontario*)

17 'The Burning of the Parliament Buildings, Montreal 1849'

The social violence surrounding the burning of the colonial parliament by a Tory-inspired mob in April 1849 pushed moderate Reformers in the Canadas to support centralized public education. A view from the *London Illustrated News*.

(*Courtesy Public Archives of Canada*)

# INDEX

Abbott, J. 355
Abraham, C.E. 336
Acheson, E. 245
Adam, J. 192
age
  and school attendance
    205-6
Agnew, J. 201, 340
agriculture
  and student non-attendance
    at school 185-6
Allen, L. 170, 341
Amendment Act (1853) 132
American books
  in Canadian schools 267,
    269, 288-9
Amnesty Bill (1840s) 125
Anderson, Rev. J. 234
Anderson, W. 169
Anderson, W.C. 239
Andrew, P. 334
Andrews, A. 346
Annexation Manifesto (1849)
  126
Annual Report for 1865
  [Ryerson] 289-90
Ardagh, S.B. 86
Ardagh, S.D. 270
Arithmetic 63
Armstrong, H. 284
Armstrong, J.G. 163
Arnold, Dr 325
Arthur, Sir George 39, 45
Assistant Superintendent of
  Common Schools 81, 82-3
Assistant Superintendent of
  Education 55, 56-7, 68-9,
  76-9
Austin, J. 167
authority
  see also education, and
    authority legitimization
    of 140

Bagot, Sir Charles 80-1
Baldwin, R. 51, 80
Baldwin-Lafontaine ministry
  81, 97, 122, 125-6
Barker, J. 284
Barker, M. 242
Barr, J.E. 255
Battersea
  training school at 312-13
Beattie, W. 169
Bell, A. 300, 344-5
Bell, G. 352-3
Bell, M.E. 202
Bell, W. 201-2
Bible
  excluded from schools 273,
    274-6
  used in schools 78-9, 273-6
Bicknell, N. 240
Bidwell, M.S. 97
Black, W.J. 335
Blacksbury, J. 225
Blake, A.H. 64, 66-7
Blake, V.E. 206
Boag, J. 193-4
books
  see also Irish texts
  American used in Canadian

schools 267, 269, 288-9
choice for use in schools of 78-9, 86, 113, 115, 123, 124, 267-73, 288-9
Boston School Committee 26, 106-7
Bosworth, N. 86
bourgeois hegemony
and education 366-80 [and passim]
Bowes, E. 161, 256
Bradford, E. 64
Bradshaw, G. 209
Brenan, J. 158
Brine, H.J. 340
Brockbill, J. 234
Brockville Victoria Central School 337-8
Brokovski, E. 161
Brougham, Lord 26, 111
Brown, A. 294
Brown, J. 67
Brown, R. 277, 278
Bruce, J. 152
Bruce, W. 25
Buchannan, J. 195
Buller, A. 42-5
Burwell, M. 36-7
Butts, J.C. 287
Byrns, J. 197

Cambell, K.A. 234-5
Cameron, A. 197
Cameron, H. 293
Cameron, J. 193
Cameron, M. 123-5
Cameron School Act (1849) 123-5, 130
Campbell, A. 355
Campbell, A.J. 339
Campbell, D. 241
Canada East 81
Canada West
see also Ontario; Upper Canada elementary

schooling in, passim
secondary education in 9-10
Canadas
Union of the 48, 51
Canadian Readers 291, 295
capitalist society
social contradictions in 369
Carlyle, W. 251
Carmichan, J. 319
Carrick, W. 238
Carroll, Mr 87
Carroll, J. 153
Carroll, W.B. 221
Carson, J. 282
Carswell, J. 240
Carter, T.S. 256
Cartwright, J.S. 80
Catholic church
and non-sectarian schooling 274-6
opposition to public education from 150
Central National School 38
centralization 12, 45, 53-4, 55, 56-64, 78, 82, 82, 84, 87, 114-19, 126, 129, 131, 140-82, 222, 225-6, 236, 242-3, 258, 267, 269, 275, 281-3, 291-303, 336, 372-3, 381n17
Chalmers, T. 37, 148
Charbonnel, Bishop de [Toronto] 150
Charlottesville
'Rules and Regulations' for schools in (1840s) 57-8
chief superintendent [School Act, 1846] 115, 117, 118, 119
chief superintendent [School Act, 1850] 131
Christianity
see also Catholic church and educational reform 1846-50 273-6
in Ryerson Report 109-12

church
 and education 38-9, 43, 44, 109-12, 150, 273-6
Clarke, G. 335, 349
classics
 in curriculum 276-8
'Clear Grit' party 127
Clegg, E. 277
Clelland, W. 354
Clergy Reserves 110
Close, E. 239
Close, J. 238-9
Cobb, L.J. 314-15
Cobb's Spelling Book 314
Cockburn, G.R.R. 217, 218, 326
Coleman, G. 242
collective instruction 268-9, 281, 292, 294, 300-2
Collins, J. 285
Colonial Office 80-1
Colonist [newspaper] 98-9
Commission of Government Departments (1839) 45
Commissioners of Common Schools 70, 71, 74-5, 157-9
Common School Act (1838) 36-7
compulsory attendance
 see school attendance
Connecticut
 school revenue in 1840s in 53
'continuation' schools 209
Cook, G.W. 340
Cooper, Mr 250
'Co-operate with the Teacher' 324
Corkins, J. 319-20
Corn Laws 123, 125
corporal punishment 58-60, 105, 167, 168, 169, 200, 303, 311-57
 see also punishment; violence

alternatives to 105, 167, 168, 169, 326-7
belief in illegality of 351-3
in 1840s 58-60
in Model Schools 327-30
in Normal School 200, 346, 348
popular opposition to 350-3
published views on 321-6
Corrigan, P. and Sayer, D. 366
Council of Public Instruction 60, 132, 244, 269-70, 290, 298, 328-9, 336
County Boards of Public Instruction 222, 237-45, 270
County Clerks
 central instructions to 143
county superintendents 82
Court of Queen's Bench 189, 224, 302, 373
Craigie, Dr 46, 47, 75-6, 79
Crossley, H.T. 204
curriculum
 central control over 269, 291-303; see also centralization
 content in 1840s 62-3
 contraction of 278-9
 and increased specification of school knowledge 278-9
 local control and the 83
 reforms of 1846-50 in 268-9

Dally, L.M. 185, 272-3
Daly, D. 97
Daniels, S. 204
Davey, I. 184-5
Davie, R.H. 244
Day, C. [Solicitor-General] 52-4
Day, H.M. 341
decentralization 35-6
 see also centralization
detention
 in school 167-8, 169

D'Everardo, D. 269
Dickson, A. 60
District Boards of Education 22-3
District Councils Act (1841) 53, 55-6
District Model Schools 83, see also Model Schools
district superintendents 85-7
Donaldson, W.D. 274,5
Donoghue, Mr 153
Donovan, P. 244
Douglass, W. 345
Draper, W.H. 51, 52, 97
Draper-Harrison ministry 80
Drouet, Mr 312
Duncombe, C. 9, 25-36, 255
  biographical details on 26
Duncombe Report (1836) 25-36
Dundas
  'graded system' of instruction in 207-8
Dunn, M. 256
Dunn, R. 202
Durham, Lord 41-5
Durham Report (1839) 41-5
Durkheim, E. 183
Durnion, Mr 205
Duties of Teachers of Common Schools 322

Eastman, N. 355
Edgeworths 26
Edinburgh
  High School 312
  Normal School 101
education
  see also school knowledge; schooling
  and administrative practice 113-14, 373
  and administrative vagueness 162-6, 375-6
  aims of 14-15, 28
  and authority 286-91, 302-3, 316, 376, 379
  and bourgeois hegemony 366-80
  and centralization, see centralization
  and changing politico-economic conditions 27-8
  and 'children' [1850s] 145-50
  and Christianity 109-12, 273-6
  and civil society 141-3, 157, 165-6, 370, 377-8
  and class relations, see social class
  and colonization of the self 378
  as compulsion 369-70
  and corporal punishment, see corporal punishment
  and decentralization 35-6
  and discipline 376
  English Radical views of Canadian (1830s) 41-5
  and extension of administrative structures 373
  and gender relations, see gender
  as governance 114-18
  and government 111-12
  and 'habituation' 377, 378
  as 'humanistic' 104, 105-7
  and 'ideal citizens' 371
  and limits on central policy 156-61
  and moral discipline 26-8, 29-30, 108, 183, 223, 229-30, 232, 234-5, 245-52, 312-18, 322-6, 330-1, 338, 366-7, 370, 371, 374, 377
  nature of 26-7
  and parents [1850s] 145-50
  and pedagogical space 140-82
  and physical violence, see corporal punishment;

437

physical violence;
punishment
as pleasurable 17-18, 32-3,
104-7, 286-91, 302-3,
311-12, 317, 320, 350,
378-9
as political socialization 78,
318, 322
and polotical stability 98
and popular culture 375
popular opposition to
12-14, 16-18, 149-73,
183-210, 267-303, 311-
65, 372-3
and power relations 13,
140-82, 291-5, 311-57,
375-7
as practical 102-3
and procedure 100, 111
and property 38-9, 48, 76,
87, 132, 366-72, 376
proposed management of
[1830s] 33-6
and punishment, see
corporal punishment;
punishment
purposes of 12
Reform party views on
(1830s) 33-6
and regularity of behavior
183
and religion 38-9, 43, 44,
58, 109-12, 150, 273-6,
302
and responsible government 113
and rote learning 103
and school attendance, see
school attendance
and self-government 33,
102, 106, 127-8, 141-2
and social class, see
social class
and social discipline 143
and social equality 13

and social 'ignorance' 376
social possibilities of 32-3
and the state, passim
and subjectification 102, 106,
110, 111-12
and subordination 379; see
also education, and sub-
jectification
and technology if instruction
135n22
and 'technology of power' 374
Tory party views on (1830s)
36-9
and universal 110-11, 157,
370
for women in 1830s 30-1
Education Acts [mid-nineteenth
century] 143, 144, 199, 245-6
see also School Acts
Education Commission (1839)
45-8, 76
Report on the 45-8
education office
and magistracy 353-6
power of the 353-6, 372
and punishment 343-50
educational administration
and authority 147-50
in 1850s 140-82
1850-71 140ff
and opposition 18
Educational Depository 270
Educational Manual 145, 189,
224, 233, 340-1, 352, 355
educational organization,
passim
context of in mid-nineteenth
century Canada 12-14
Education Commission (1839)
proposals for 45-8
in 1830s 33-6
in 1840s 53, 56-64, 70-9, 81-
7, 112-25
in 1850 127-31
English Radical proposals

for in 1830s 43-5
  and School Act (1841) 54-5, 70-9
  and School Act (1843) 81-7
  Tory party proposals in 1830s for 37
educational reform, passim
  and authority 148-50
  as conscious human activity 14
  criticisms of 70-6
  in 1830s 22-50
    English Radical views on 41-5
    Radical party views on 25-36
    Tory party views on 36-9, 45-8
  in 1840s 51-96, 97-138
  in 1850s 140ff
  international influences on 379-80
  opposition to, see education, popular opposition to
  and public construction 91-138
  and social organization 148-50
educational state
  normalization of 367-71
Edward, W.M. 62
elementary schooling
  in Canada West, passim
Elgin, Lord 122, 125-6, 127
Elias, N. 369
Eliot, C. 85-6
Elmslie, G. 62-3, 221
Engels, F. 368
English Readers 63, 267-8, 279, 285
English Spelling Book 63
enrollments 279, 302-3
Essay on the Parochial Schools of Scotland 37

ethnicity
  and school attendance 206-7
Evans, J. 334
Evil Tendencies of Corporal Punishment, The 314

family
  educational administration and the 145-8
'Family Compact' 23
Farington, J. 348
female teachers
  see also teachers
  advantages of 30-1, 255-6
  as assistants 254
  and authority 257
  and career hierarchy 255-7
  and correspondence with education office 67, 182n120
  in 1830s 30-1
  in 1840s 56, 61, 64-9
  and equal pay 72, 73
  income of 64-9, 72, 73, 254-5
  moral regulation of 196-7, 256
  qualifications of 252-4
  and school fund 64-9
  and summer employment 69, 205, 252
  supervision of 257
  wages of 254-5
Ferguson, W. 235
First Annual Report of the Superintendent of Public Schools of the City of Hamilton 330-1
Five Years' Residence in the Canadas 146-7
Flanagan, Rev. J. 68
Flanagan, J.P. 161
Fletcher, Mr 196
Fletcher, J. 187
Flood, J. 67-8, 187, 192
force
  in society 368-9

Forde, J.H. 294-5
Fotheringham, A.J. 297
Fotheringham, D. 327-30
Foucault 165, 377
Fowler, J. 59
Fox, C. 239
France
  pedagogical practices in 379
Fraser, W. 332-3
Futhey, R. 238

Galt, W. 283
Gamble, J.W. 71
gender
  see also female teachers
  and correspondence with education office 182n120
  and educational reform 49n3, 379
  in Normal School 246-7
  and schooling 12, 13
  and separation in schools 157-8
  and teaching careers 252-7
General Board of Education 22-3, 270
Geography 267, 294
German, G. 254
Gibson, J. 276-7
Gilbert, D. 355
Gilbert, R.H. 167
Girardin, M. 102
Glasgow
  schools in 312
Glyne, J.S. 195
Goldsmith 295
Gordon, W.A. 301, 352
Gore District 119-20
Gorshine, W.E. 354
Goshe, S. 65
'Government of Children in Public Schools, The' 337
Graffe, T. 65
Grafftley, G. 285

Graham, Mr 248
Graham, M. 357
Grammar School Act (1839) 38
Grammar School Acts (1807/8) 38
grammar schools 38, 188, 207-8
Grant, R.N. 345
Grasset, H.J. 45-6
Gray, J. 301
Green, J. 194-5
Grey, D.R. 172
Gunn, H. 153-4
Gunn, W. 200, 287

Hagerman, J.D. 256
Haight, C. 318-19, 366-7
Hamilton, G. 195
Hamilton Central Schools
  rules of (1853) 148-9
Hardie, L.F. 302
Harper's Ferry 316
Harris, M. 251
Harrison, S.B. 46, 51
Harrison Resolutions 52
Hart, S. 85
Harvey, A. 349-50
Head, Sir Francis Bond 45
Henderson, A. 294
Hendry, G. 343-4
Henry, T. 171-2
hidden curriculum 9
Hincks, F. 53, 80, 81, 84, 118
'Hints on School Government' 322
History of England [Goldsmith] 295
Hodgins, J.D. 20
Hodgins, J.G. 247, 275, 325-6, 343, 350
Hodgson, J. 250
Hoit, D.Y. 246
Holloway, J.P. 301
Holmes, N.L. 301
Home District Council
  Education Committee of 71

Horner, A. 343
House, J.G. 227
House Education Committee 43
Howee, J. 234
Hudson, J. 335
Hughes, J. 273
Hume, J. 26
Hutchins, W.W. 349-50
Hutton, W. 86, 188, 270

'infantilization' 146
Ingersoll, L. 64
Inglis, F. 368
International Expositions 380
Ireland
  curriculum in 108, 379
  education in 101, 108, 110, 379
  schools books used in, see Irish texts
  school burning in 151
Ireland, J. 221
Irish Commissioners of National Education 229
Irish Readers
  see Irish texts
Irish texts 86, 237-8, 267-76, 280-4, 286-91
  and absence of Canadian content 272, 289
  and bourgeois social politics 291
  and 'common Christianity' 273-6
  generalization of 269-73
  opposition to 286-91
  as outdated 272, 289
  poor quality of copies of 273
  reading in 280-4
  and reading as pleasurable 286-91
  statistics on adoption of 270
  and teachers' reading

instruction methods 284-6
Irvine, R. 339

Jackson, A.E. 161
Jameson, R.S. 75
Johnston, D. 338-9
Johnstown District Model School 87
Jones, Mother 251
Journal of Education 120, 226, 233, 270, 317, 322, 323, 324-5, 337

Kay, G. and Mott, J. 368
Kay, Dr J. 312-13
  see also Kay-Shuttleworth
Kay-Shuttleworth, Dr J. 111, 312-13
Keating, J. 235
Keefer, J. 86-7
Keillor, A.J. 153
Kincaid 337-8
King's College 38, 45, 46
Kirkham, S. 267
Kirland, A. 68
Klotz, O. 288-90

Lafontaine, L.H. 80
Lamont, J. 192-3
Lancaster, J. 300
Lane, E. 64-5
Latin
  in common schools 276-8
Lauder, A.W. 239
Lawson, J. 336, 352
Lawson, P. 240
'Laying the Foundations' 323
Le Boutilier, J. 340
Lees, J. 336
Letercheux, A. 301
Lillie, T.W. 282, 286-7
Linn, D. 151, 152, 299
Lively, H. 71-2
local community
  see also education, popular

resistance to
and control over teachers 222-5
and education 83-5, 87-8, 124, 132, 142-3
Lovell [geography textbook] 294
Lower Canada
educational reform in 42-4
Lyons, J. 243

McCamon, J. 348-9
McCaul, J. 46
Mcullough, J. 255
McCullough, W. 282
McCurdy, W.H. 169
Mac Dermid, D. 61-2
McDiarmid, H. 339
McDonald, A. 340
McDonald, J. 75
McDonald, P. 168
MacFarland, Mr 173
McGill, Rev. Robert 47
MacGregor, A. 242
McGuire, W.H. 65-6, 67
M'Kee, A. 153
Mackenzie, J. 347-8
Mackenzie, W.L. 26
Mackie, R.R. 67
Mackie, T. 340
McKilligan, J. 194
Mackintosh, W. 163
McLachlin, Mr 172
McLauchlin, Rev. A.A. 242
Macleod, D.R. 74
McNab, Rev. Alexander 101
magistrates
and school punishment 353-6
Malcolm, F. 295
Maloy, H. 156
Mann, Horace 101, 103, 105, 111, 313-14
Marshall, T. 271-2
Mavor 63, 284

Meacham, W. 339
Mechum, J.M. 275
Meilleur, Dr 43
Metcalfe, Sir Charles 97, 98-9, 100
Midland District School Society 22
Migoleton, A. 221
Millar, P.D. 346
Millar, R. 345-6
Misener, J.C. 160
Mitchell, S. 64
Model Grammar School 329
Model Schools 85, 86, 87, 191-2, 217, 326-30, 345, 371
attendance at 191-2, 199-200
buildings for 371
class sizes in 191-2
and corporal punishment 327-30, 345
establishment of 85, 86, 87
'monitorial' schooling 300
monitors 300-2
Montgomery, J. 193
Moore, R.McK. 185
moral discipline
see education, and moral discipline
Moral Education 183
Morris, J.F. 221
Morrison, J. 335-6
Morrison, R.J. 334
Morrison, T. 25
Morse 267, 294
Mott, J.
see Kay and Mott
Moug, S. 347
Mowbray, R. 74
Muir, J. 301-2
Mullett, C. 345
Murray [and English Reader] 63, 268, 279, 285
Murray, R. 46, 47-8, 55, 68-9, 70, 71-2, 75, 76-9, 81, 82, 98, 220, 267, 273-4

appointment of 46, 55, 98
and Bible in schools 78-9, 273-4
and female teachers 68-9
and status of teachers 70, 220
and teachers' self-regulation 77-8
views on School Act (1841) of 76-9
music
  teaching of vocal 106-7
'Mutual Relations of Parties Interested in a School' 323

Nairn, J. 240
'Nature and Importance of the Education of Mechanics, The' 377
Navigation Acts 123, 125
Naylor, F. 152-3
needlework
  in schools 278
Neelands, J. 200
Neilson, J. 74, 87, 342-3
Nesbitt, N.K. 204
Newman, J.B. 200
Normal School 115, 116, 132, 148-9, 199-200, 219, 222, 241, 243, 245-52, 277, 281, 283, 284-5, 293, 294, 296, 301, 317, 326-7, 328-30, 346, 348, 371
  atmosphere of 246-7
  boarding houses for 247-9
  building for 371
  and corporal punishment 326-7, 328-30, 346, 348
  establishment of 116, 219
  method taught at 148-9, 245-52, 277, 281, 283 284-5, 293, 294, 296
  moral regulation at 246-52
  and school attendance 199-200
  school management in 326-7
  statistics on 246
  student workload at 251
  'underlife' of 249-50, 251
North American 247

Oakwood County Board 242
O'Donnele, J. 64
'On the Importance of Education ...' 322
'On the Punishment of Pauper Children in Workhouses' 313
Ontario
  see Canada West; Upper Canada
Ontario School Act (1871) 184
O'Shanahan, J. 190

'panopticism' 165
parents
  and authority 145-9, 201
  and corporal punishment 323-5, 351-3, 356-7
  and curriculum 295-9
  expectations of 145-6
  and 'indifference' to schooling 187, 198, 210
  opposition to central educational policy 151-6
  public education of 323-4
  and rights regarding the curriculum 295-8
  and school discipline 331
Parrinton, A. 233
Parrish, W. 194
Paton, J. 300
Payne, M. 251, 326-7
Pearson, B.F. 339
pedagogical space
  and administrative vagueness 162-6
  limits of 156-61
  opposition to 150-6
  and the schoolday 166-73
Peers, Rev.Mr 32

Pepper, M. 161
Perry, P. 127
Pestalozzi, J. 101
Pettis, A. 333-4
physical violence
  see also corporal punishment; punishment; violence
  forms of 332-6
  and local community 318, 320
Pillans, J. 103, 311-12, 326
Pillar, Mr 206
Pinkey, H. 86
Plunkett, W. 299, 354
political power
  and violence 368-9
political socialization
  and education 78, 318, 322
  in 1830s 39-41
'Politics as a vocation' 140
Poole, W. 70
Poor Law Commissioners 312-13
populism
  and School Act (1843) 83-4
Porter, J. 293
Potter, Dr 106
Powley, J. 239
prayers
  in schools 275-6
Prentice, A. 146
Preston 288-9
Price, J. 52-3
Priest, G.M. 170
Principles of Elementary Teaching 311
Privy Council [England]
  Committee of Education 312
procedures
  in educational administration 100-1
Pronouncing Dictionary 63
property

and education 38-9, 48, 151
and popular culture 175-6n18
Prussia
  pedagogical practices in 379
  schooling in 101, 104-6, 314, 379
public schooling, passim
  see also education
  popular opposition to 12-14, 16-18, 149-73, 183-210, 267-303, 311-65, 372-3
punishment
  see also corporal punishment; physical violence; violence
  administrative vagueness regarding 341-3
  and arbitration 353-6
  and community justice 336-9
  demands for policy on 339-41
  education office and 343-50
  and Fotheringham-Wright case 327-30
  and magistracy 353-6
  in Model Schools 327-30, 345
  and Normal Schools 326-7, 328-30, 346, 348
  and opposition to teachers 336-9
  popular belief and 350-3
  precedents for 318-21
  published views on 321-6
  in schools 311-57
  in urban schools 330-2
punishment registers 353

radical liberalism
  see also Reform party
  and education 26
  and women's education 31
Radicals [English]
  and educational organization in Upper Canada 24
  and social regulation 25
  views of Canadian education of 41-5

Ramine, W. 167
Rath, W. 351
reading
  as 'decorative' art 268, 280
  and examinations 281
  and interrogation 280, 281, 284-5
  methods of instruction in 279-84
  objectives of 279-84
  as oral activity 280
  as pleasurable 286-91
  and subjectification 108-9
  as 'useful' 268, 279-84, 286
Reading Book for Girls' Schools 271
Rebellion Losses Bill 125
Rebellions (1837-8) 12, 24, 36-7, 38, 41, 125
Recorder 337-8
Reform alliance (1840s)
  disintegration of 125-7
Reform party
  see also Baldwin-Lafontaine ministry
  educational policy of 23, 25-36, 52-3, 84
  and educational reform in 1830s 23, 25-36
  and educational reform in 1840s 52-3
  foundation of 79-80
  and local government 88
  and nature of the state 23-4
  and pedagogical method 32-3
  and political crisis of 1843 100
  and political reform 122-3
  after Rebellion of 1837 51
  and Rebellion Losses Bill 125-6
  and responsible government 84
  and School Act (1846) 118
  and school finance 121-2
  and social regulation 24-5
  and women's education 30-1
Reid, Rev.W. 68
religious instruction
  see education, and religion
Report on the Affairs of British North America
  see Durham Report
'Report on the State of the Province'
  see Sullivan Report
Report on a System of Public Elementary Instruction for Upper Canada A (1846) [Ryerson Report] 99, 101-7, 109-12, 219-20, 317, 321-2
responsible government
  definition of 51-2
  and educational reform in 1840s 51-96
  Ryerson and 98
  and School Act (1843) 79-84
Roberts, E. 144
Robertson, A. 256
Robertson, T.J. 217, 246, 248, 259, 251-2
Robinson, J.B. [Chief Justice, Upper Canada] 220
Rogers, J.B. 160-1
Roman Catholicism
  and non-sectarian schooling 274-6
  opposition to public education from 150
Root, V. 170-1
Ross, G. 380
Rossell, Mr 208
'Rules for Home Instruction' 324
Ryerson, C. 344
Ryerson, E. 33, 51, 77, 88, 97-9, 100-25, 127-31, 154,

163, 164, 169, 170, 172, 191, 198, 219-21, 228, 231-3, 236, 242, 243, 247, 267, 269, 270-1, 275, 276, 278, 286-9, 293, 296, 297, 298, 300, 317, 321-2, 328-30, 333, 341, 342-5, 346, 347, 348, 349, 354-6, 367, 369, 377, 380
see also Ryerson Report
biographical details on 97-8
and Cameron School Act 124-5, 127
and Christianity 100, 109-12
and corporal punishment 317, 321-2, 328-30, 333, 341, 342-5, 346, 347, 348, 349, 354-6
and curriculum 107-12, 278
and defence of the Crown 98-9, 100
and educational crisis of 1848-9 120-5
and educational organization 88, 112-18, 127-31
and educational reform 77, 101-20, 127-31, 367, 380
European tour by (1844-5) 101-7
and gender 109, 247
and music teaching 106-7
and pedagogical method 102-8, 300
and procedure 100-1
and progressive education 101-7
and religion 109, 275, 276
and responsible government 98
and School Act (1846) 112-20
and School Act (1850) 33, 127-31
and school books 267, 269, 270-1, 286-9
and social class 109
and subjects in elementary education 107-9, 278
and teacher training 219-21, 242, 243, 293
and teachers' authority 163, 164, 169, 170, 172, 231-3, 296, 297, 298, 317, 321-2, 328-30, 333, 341, 342-5, 346, 347, 348, 349, 354-6
Ryerson Report
see Report on a System of Public Elementary Instruction for Upper Canada, A

Sanders' Series [schoolbooks] 288-9
Sangster, J.S. 246, 248, 249
Sayer, D
see Corrigan and Sayer
Scarlett, E. 224, 235, 285
Schackle, C. 325-6
School Act (1816) 22
School Act (1824) 22
School Act (1835) 26
School Act (1841) 52, 54-5, 56-64, 70-9, 81, 83, 152, 157, 170-6
School Act (1843) 53, 79-87, 112-13, 205
School Act (1846) 112-20, 205, 218, 229, 269
School Act (1847) 117-18
School Act (1849) 229
School Act (1850) 12, 33, 60, 127-31, 145, 153, 157, 159-60, 190, 222, 226, 229, 231, 292, 322, 336
School Act (1853) 152, 175n10, 202-3, 299, 336
School Act (1871) 367

School Acts 150, 151, 267, 273, 276, 317, 321, 341, 351, 353, 375
  see also preceding entries for particular Acts
School Amendment Act (1853) 207, 231, 233
School Architecture 226
school attendance 168-91, 183-216, 374
  see also school non-attendance
  methods of securing 198-210
  statistics on 189
  structural causes of non- 184-90
school building 190-2, 226-8, 371-2
School Commissioners 72, 73, 79
'School Discipline' 324, 325
School House, The 325
schoolhouses
  used by religious groups 227-8
school knowledge
  see also education; schooling
  and bourgeois hegemony 291
  and centralization 267-303; see also centralization
  and classics 276-8
  and collective instruction, see collective instruction
  and control over curriculum 291-303; see also centralization
  definition of 267-310
  and educational apparatus 280-1, 302
  and 'interrogation' practices 268, 280, 281, 284-5
  and Irish textbooks, see Irish texts
  and local control 295-8
  and 'natural theology' movement 268
  nature of 78-9
  as pleasurable, see education as pleasurable
  and reading, see reading
  and religion, see education, and religion
  as 'scientific' 268
  specification of 278-9
  as 'useful' 268
'School Lands' 22, 53
school non-attendance
  see also school attendance
  overcrowding and 190-2
  structural causes of 184-90
  and unpopular teachers 192-8
School Regulations 353
school revenue
  and gender of teachers 65-9
school trustees
  see trustees
schoolday
  hours of the 166-8
  limits of the 166-73
schooling
  see also education; school knowledge
  age of access to 205-6
  and 'childhood' 16
  differing conceptions of 198-
  and moral character 14-15
  as moral force 29-30; see also education, and moral discipline
  and nature of knowledge, see school knowledge
  as non-sectarian 273-6
  as pleasurable, see education as pleasurable

popular opposition to 12-14, 16-18, 149-73, 183-210, 267-303, 311-65, 372-3
  techniques of 12, 15-16
  as universalistic, see education, and universality
schools
  access to 204-5, 226-8
  attendance at, see school attendance
  authority in, see teachers, and authority
  Bible used in 78-9, 273-6
  blackboards in 280-1
  burning of 150-6
  and 'civilizing' mission 193, 223, 224, 370
  class sizes in 300-1
  classics in 276-8
  damage to 150-6
  distribution of 70
  financing of 70-1, 83, 120-1, 123, 129-30
  overcrowding in 190-2
  physical punishment in 311-57; see also corporal punishment
  prayers in 275
  punishment in 311-57; see also corporal punishment
  reasons for non-attendance at 184-98
  recesses in 171-3
  violence in 332-6; see also corporal punishment
'Schools at Home' 324
Scotland
  elimination of corporal punishment in schools in 311-12
Secret Societies Bill 97
sectarian education 110, 150, 276
  see also education, and religion
separate schools 110, 150, 276
Sharpe, J. 352
self-government
  and education 102
  and social subordination 102
Self-Help 291
Sheldon, G.M. 356-7
Sherwood-Daly ministry 122
Slee, T. 154-6
Smiles 291
Sim, J. 351
Sinclair, A. 345
Sir Charles Metcalfe Defended ... 98-9, 100
Smyth, T. 64
social class 12, 13-14, 90n31, 111, 116-17, 140, 146-8, 187-8, 291, 206n50, 366-71, 374, 376-80
social relations
  in mid-nineteenth century Canada 146-8
'Special Report on the State of Popular Education ..., A 369
Spelling Book 284
Spelling Book Superseded 280
Spence, R. 72-3, 118-19
Spencer, I. 352-3
Spurzheim, Dr 26
state
  and administration 140
  and authority 149-50
  and educational policy, passim
  nature of the 12-13, 23-4
  and power, passim
  and subjectification 17, 149-50
Steinson, H. 200-1
Stow, D. 103, 106, 247-8, 311, 312, 366,

Strachan, J. 267
Strachan, John (Bishop of York, Toronto) 22, 36, 38
Strathan, Mr 208
Street, G. 228
students
  and agricultural work 185-6
  and attendance at school 183-216
  behaviour outside school of 157-61, 162-6
  and cleanliness 203-4
  and curriculum 297-8
  and detention 2-4
  freedom of movement of 168-71
  and illness 191-2
  and non-attendance at school, see school non-attendance
  opposition to central education policy by 154, 156
  reactions to state schooling of 367-8
  resistance to physical punishment by 336-9; see also corporal punishment
  and seasonal agricultural demands 185-6
Sullivan 280
Sullivan, R. 20n2
Sullivan, R.B. 39-41
Sullivan Report (1838) 39-41
Summers, J.E. 339
Superintendent of Education 54, 99
superintendents
  power of 234-6
suspensions 169-70
Sydenham, Lord 51, 52, 80, 98

Talbot, E.A. 146-8, 257

Taylor, J. Orville 26
teacher training 61-2, 217-66
  see also Normal School
teachers
  see also female teachers
  accommodation arrangements for 77, 189-90, 223-5, 373
  and administrative vagueness regarding physical punishment 342-3
  as agents 220-222
  associations of male 66-7
  and authority 157-61, 162-6, 166-73, 222-3, 238, 258, 324, 330, 339-41, 343-50, 353-6
  behaviour of 192-8
  and 'boarding around', see teachers, accommodation arrangements for
  and brutality 193-4; see also corporal punishment
  and bureaucratic administration 217-66
  and certification 222, 237-45, 374-5; see also teacher training
  characteristics of 217-18
  'civilizing' mission of 193, 223, 224, 370
  and class sizes 300-1
  and community control 77-8, 222-5
  competence of 209, 221
  and complaints about Irish texts 286-7
  and curriculum 293-4, 295-9
  and demands for policy on physical punishment 339-41
  and detention 204
  and drunkenness 195-6, 235-6
  duties of 229-30
  and examinations 237-45, 270, 272, 374-5
  and exclusion of pupils 344-5

and fines for use of
  physical violence 337-9,
  343-9, 353-4
incomes of 64-5
and lack of school books
  272-3
and measures against
  lateness 199-202
and monopoly over
  violence 316, 318-21,
  330, 350, 356-7; see
  also corporal punish-
  ment
and moral discipline, see
  education, and moral
  discipline
moral regulation of 245-52
organizations of 72-3
payment of 83
and physical punishment
  311-65; see also
  corporal punishment
and power 160, 165, 218;
  see also teachers, and
  authority
qualifications of 225-8,
  374-5
quality of 85-6
and reading instruction
  284-6
and regular school
  attendance 188-9; see
  also school attendance
and regulations 234-6
and religious non-
  conformity 196
salaries of 70, 72, 73
and school attendance,
  see school attendance
and seasonal agriculture
  190
and self-organization
  76-7, 93n65
separation from local
  community of 374-5

and sexual misconduct 197-8
social status of 190
statistics on sex of 252-4
status of 70
and student cleanliness 203-4
tenure of 70
training of 61-2, 217-66
and uniform textbooks 271-3
as unpopular 192-8
and violence 311-65; see also
  corporal punishment
teaching
  feminization of 252-5; see
    also female teachers
  policing of 230-6
teaching methods 268-9, 277-8,
  280-1, 302-3
  see also collective instruction
Testaments
  used in schools 78-9, 273-6
textbooks
  see also Irish texts
  revisions of 286-91
Thompson, E.P. 185
Thompson, J.H. 355
Thomson, G. 240
Thomson, W. 63
Thornton, P. 78, 85
Thornton, R.H. 239
'Time, Work-discipline and
  Industrial Capitalism' 185
'To the Common School
  Teachers' 332
Toronto
  educational crisis in (1848-9)
    120-2
Toronto Reform Association 97,
  99
Tory party
  and Draper-Harrison
    ministry 80
  educational policy 23, 36-9,
    45-8
  and nature of the state 23
  and Sherwood Daly

ministry 122
and social regulation 24
Township Commissioners 55, 57-7, 81, 157-9
Travers, E. 367-8
Treffey, J. 78-9
Trotsky, L. 140
truancy 160
trustees
　and curriculum 293, 295-6
　powers of 86, 144, 175n10, 292-3, 295-6, 353
　in School Act (1850) 128-9
　and tax for school finance 84, 144, 175n10, 292-3, 353
Tuthill, J.T. 156

union schools 209
Unsworth, E. 254
Upper Canada
　see also Canada West; Ontario
　educational reform in 1840s in 51-96, 97-138
　elementary education in 1830s in 22-50
　literacy in 15
Upper Canada College 38
urban schools
　corporal punishment in 330-2
'Use of the Rod, The' 325

Vancock, J.M. 192
Vanflooring, L 255
Viger, D.B. 97
violence
　see also corporal punishment; physical violence; punishment
　monopoly over means of 316, 318-21, 330, 356-7, 369
　normalization of 357

and political power 368-9
teachers and, see teachers

Walker 63
Walkingame 63
Wallace, R. 349
Wallis, L. 63-4
Wanless, J. 343
Ward, A. 301
Warder 72, 118, 121
Waterloo County
　Board of Public Instruction 289, 290
Watts 217-18, 329
Weber, M. 140, 141
Westover, J.M. 340
Whately, Archbishop of Dublin 102, 110
White, G. 335
White, R.F. 334
Willard, E. 26
Williams, D. 276
Williams, R.J. 234
Williams, W.B. 243
Wilson, G. 221
Wilson, N. 158
Wiltse, J. 118
Wolfe Island
　sectarian conflict on 274
women
　see also female teachers
　education in 1830s of 30-1
　and rural economy 255-6
　and teaching in Upper Canada, see female teachers
Wood, A. 347
Wood, P. 74
Wright, H. 327-30
Wright, T.N. 284
Wright, W.R. 327-30
writing
　methods of teaching 296

York Central School 22, 23
Young, T.C. 247
Young, W. 154